Creativity

Creativity: Theory, History, Practice offers important new perspectives on creativity in the light of contemporary critical theory and cultural history. Innovative in approach as well as argument, the book crosses disciplinary boundaries and builds new bridges between the critical and the creative. It is organised in four parts:

- *Why creativity now?* offers much-needed alternatives to both the Romantic stereotype of the creator as individual genius and the tendency of the modern creative industries to treat everything as a commodity.
- *Defining creativity, creating definitions* traces the changing meaning of 'create' from religious ideas of divine *creation from nothing* to advertising notions of *concept creation*. It also examines the complex history and extraordinary versatility of terms such as *imagination, invention, inspiration* and *originality*.
- *Creation as myth, story, metaphor* begins with modern re-tellings of early African, American and Australian creation myths and – picking up Biblical and evolutionary accounts along the way – works round to scientific visions of the Big Bang, bubble universes and cosmic soup.
- *Creative practices, cultural processes* is a critical anthology of materials, chosen to promote fresh thinking about everything from changing constructions of 'literature' and 'design' to artificial intelligence and genetic engineering.

Rob Pope takes significant steps forward in the process of rethinking a vexed yet vital concept, all the while encouraging and equipping readers to continue the process in their own creative or 're-creative' ways. *Creativity: Theory, History, Practice* is invaluable for anyone with a live interest in exploring what creativity has been, is currently, and yet may be.

Rob Pope is Professor of English at Oxford Brookes University and a National Teaching Fellow. His previous books include *Textual Intervention: Critical and Creative Strategies for Literary Studies* (Routledge, 1995) and *The English Studies Book* (Routledge, 2nd edition 2002).

In praise of this book

'*Creativity* has filled a vital gap on my bookshelf where it was meant to be all along. There is no other approach to creative thought quite like this: fresh, lively, wide-ranging in its scholarship, often left field and always disconcertingly spot on.'

Jo Shapcott, poet and Royal Literary Fund Fellow

'With its strikingly fresh arguments, its scintillating constellation of critical voices, and its provocative mappings of the topography of thought, *Creativity* is less an academic study than a highly imaginative theoretical fiction that offers the open-minded student countless possibilities to 'create' in unexpected and fascinating ways. Rob Pope's *Creativity* is that rare thing—an *event* in critical discourse.'

Julian Wolfreys, Professor of English, University of Florida

'The most thorough, creatively-devised and exciting book on this subject that I have read to date. *Creativity* is an essential resource for anyone in the worlds of creative writing and literary studies.'

Robyn Bolam, Chair, National Association of Writers in Education and Professor of Literature, St Mary's College, University of Surrey

'Rob Pope plumbs (sounds, explores) the paradoxes and powers of creativity with verve, wit and urgency. This is a creative work in its own right, deftly conceived and masterfully crafted.'

Richard Kearney, The Charles Seelig Professor in Philosophy, Boston College

'The only book in the field with such a rich inclusiveness. A genuinely interdisciplinary project, profound and profoundly imaginative in range and critical scope. The syntheses of theory and practice are genuinely ground-breaking in this field.'

Ronald Carter, Professor of Modern English Language, University of Nottingham

'There is never a dull moment as Pope explores an important topic which has seen no conclusive explanations but very many partial and thought-provoking ones.'

Derek Attridge, Professor of English and Related Literature, University of York

'I've been waiting for a book exactly like this one. Rob Pope combines historical and critical insights into the term 'creativity' with a very practical sense of how these insights might be used. As a writer on campus, I can't rate this book highly enough. Superb!'

Graeme Harper, Chair, UK Centre for Creative Writing Research Through Practice, University of Portsmouth

'Breath-taking; an important and energetic book. For an author to achieve the rigour and practical applicability of a textbook as well as the academic and depth-informed qualities of a monograph, whilst creating at the same time ample room for discursive and associative play, is no mean feat – but this is Pope's ongoing signature and paraph.'

Mario Petrucci, BBC Radio 3 Poet in Residence

'An outstanding book. It is well read, well written, innovative and intellectually stimulating.'

Robert Eaglestone, Royal Holloway, University of London, and Series Editor of
Routledge Critical Thinkers

'Displays enormous cultural, philosophical and scientific range; not to mention wit and, indeed, creativity. Pope's lucid, directive prose will allow students and arts practitioners as well as academics to apply his insights and methodologies in their own work.'

Fiona Sampson, Editor, Poetry Review

'This is a many-faceted enquiry, original and challenging in its inclusiveness and range, its bold, ambitious scope served by a gentle, open approach. Mr Pope proves himself a spirited and empowering champion of creativity.'

Nicole Ward Jouve, Department of English and Related Literature,
University of York

Creativity
Theory, History, Practice

Rob Pope

Routledge
Taylor & Francis Group

LONDON AND NEW YORK

First published 2005
by Routledge
2 Park Square, Milton Park, Abingdon, Oxon, OX14 4RN

Simultaneously published in the USA and Canada
by Routledge
270 Madison Ave, New York, NY 10016

Routledge is an imprint of the Taylor & Francis Group

© 2005 Rob Pope

Typeset in Baskerville by The Running Head Limited, Cambridge
Printed and bound in Great Britain by MPG Books Ltd, Bodmin

British Library Cataloguing in Publication Data
A catalogue record for this book is available from the British Library

Library of Congress Cataloging in Publication Data
Pope, Rob.
Creativity : theory, history, practice / Rob Pope.
  p.   cm.
  Includes bibliographical references and index.
1. Creation (Literary, artistic, etc.) I. Title.
BH301.C84P67 2005
153.3'5–dc22   2004018251

ISBN 0–415–34915–X (hbk)
ISBN 0–415–34916–8 (pbk)

In memory and celebration of Paul O'Flinn

I am the daughter of Earth and Water,
    And the nursling of the Sky;
I pass through the pores of the ocean and shores;
    I change but I cannot die.
For after the rain when with never a stain
    The pavilion of Heaven is bare,
And the winds and sunbeams with their convex gleams
    Build up the blue dome of air,
I silently laugh at my own cenotaph,
    And out of the caverns of rain,
Like a child from the womb, like a ghost from the tomb,
    I arise and unbuild it again.

(from Percy Shelley, *The Cloud*, 1820)

Contents

Acknowledgements

It is no accident that acknowledgement contains the word knowledge. Much of what we know comes to us through other people, and most things only make sense if we bear other people in mind. It is therefore with a deep sense of obligation as well as pleasure that I thank the following for their inspiration, encouragement and support. They cannot be held responsible for anything that has gone wrong; but they can take much of the credit for anything that goes right.

Nathalie Blondel, Ron Carter, Bob Eaglestone, Graeme Harper, Mario Petrucci and two anonymous reviewers gave invaluable advice when the manuscript was in its early 'baggy monster' stage. Talia Rodgers handled the book-to-be with great tact while it was rapidly metamorphosing, and Liz Thompson magicked it into shape and up to speed. (Thanks, too, to John Drakakis for letting it spread its wings and fly out of his series.) Derek Attridge, Joy Hendry, Richard Kearney, Simon Kövesi, Nicholas Royle, Fiona Sampson, Jo Shapcott, Nicole Ward Jouve and Julian Wolfreys all gave much-appreciated encouragement and last-minute advice while the book was finally coming together; and Annie Jackson made it happen with a keen eye for detail and rare flair for layout. Thanks to all these people, and to everyone else at Routledge and The Running Head. Most of the words may in some sense be mine; but the book in your hands is very much theirs.

Also teeming between its covers – though I'd now be hard pressed to put a time and place to each – are countless traces of conversations, workshops and seminars with friends and colleagues over the years. Especially influential (and always great fun) have been work and play with: Robyn Bolam, Hilary Jenkins, Sean Matthews, John McRae and Mario Petrucci for the British Council; Claire Woods and David Homer at the University of South Australia; David Stacey at Humboldt State University; and Yoshiaki Shirai at Yokohama City University. Similarly pervasive is the influence of immediate colleagues in English at Oxford Brookes, including the sheer joy of teaching kinds of critical-creative writing with Helen Kidd and Jane Spiro. Colleagues from other disciplines and departments – Dai Griffiths in Music, Shelley Sacks and Ray Lee in Art, Bob Hughes and Claire Squires in Publishing, and Phil Whitehead in Performance – have constantly reminded me of creativities between and beyond words; while Gary Browning, Roger Griffin, Joy Hendry and John Geake continue to reaffirm my faith in that most vital and vulnerable of academic institutions: the passing conversation that becomes a long one – on corridors, in doorways, and halfway up the stairs.

Some of the ideas and materials in this book have been developed with students at Oxford Brookes University: on my undergraduate courses 'Comedy, Creativity, Critique' and 'Changing Stories' and my postgraduate course 'Changing Literature'; also with those doing research degrees with me. Though they are too numerous to mention here, I have particular faces and names in mind, and I hope they will excuse the relative anonymity of these collective gestures.

For providing institutional support and some of the time to research, reflect and write, I am grateful to the Arts and Humanities Research Board, the National Teaching Fellowship Scheme, and the School of Arts and Humanities, Oxford Brookes; with particular thanks to Bernard O'Donoghue and Robyn Bolam for writing references and to Alan Jenkins for helping work up a crucial application. Finally, for their tolerance and good humour when the rest of the time came out of what was properly theirs/ours (at week-ends and in holidays), I am more than grateful to my wife Tanya and our children Ivan and Sasha.

Rob Pope
February 2005

The author and publishers would like to thank the following for permission to use copyrighted material.

Chapter 5

Billy Marshall-Stoneking, 'Passage', from *Made in Australia: The OZlit Collection, Vol. 3*, 1974, ed. Gisela Triesch and Rudi Krausman. By kind permission of Gangan Books, <http://www.gangan.com>.

Jo Shapcott, 'Thetis', from *Her Book: Poems 1988–98*, 2000. By kind permission of Faber and Faber.

Chapter 7

'Design' by Robert Frost from *The Poetry of Robert Frost*, ed. Edward Connery Lathem. © 1936 Robert Frost, © 1964 Lesley Frost Ballantine, © 1969 Henry Holt and Company. Reprinted by permission of Henry Holt and Company, LLC. Also published by Jonathan Cape. Used by permission of the Estate of Robert Frost and the Random House Group Limited.

'Final Notations' by Adrienne Rich from *The Fact of a Doorframe: Selected Poems 1950–2001*. © 2002, 1991 Adrienne Rich. Used by permission of the author and W. W. Norton and Company Inc.

Excerpts from 'The Disease Collector' (fourteen lines) by Jason Schneiderman from *The Penguin Book of the Sonnet: 500 Years of a Classic Tradition in English*, ed. Phillis Levin. © 2001 Phillis Levin. Reproduced by permission of Penguin Books Ltd and Viking Penguin, a division of Penguin Group (USA) Inc.

Excerpts from *A Number* by Caryl Churchill. © 2002 Caryl Churchill Ltd. Reprinted by permission of Nick Hern Books Ltd, <http://www.nickhernbooks.co.uk>.

Excerpts from pp. 6–9 and 102–9 of *Language and Creativity* by Ronald Carter, published by Routledge, 2004. Reprinted by kind permission of the publisher.

Excerpts from *Japanese Jokes* by kind permission of Peter Porter.

Nine lines from 'Howl' by Allen Ginsberg from *Collected Poems 1947–1980*.

© 1955 Allen Ginsberg, reprinted by permission of HarperCollins Publishers Inc. Also from Allen Ginsberg, *Selected Poems 1947–1995* (first published in *Howl*, 1956, Penguin Books, 1997). © Allen Ginsberg 1956, 1997.

Excerpts from 'Chain of Decay' by Mario Petrucci from *Heavy Water*, 2004. Reproduced by kind permission of Enitharmon Press, <http://www.enitharmon.co.uk>.
Excerpts from *Certain Fragments* by Tim Etchells, published by Routledge, 2004. Reprinted by kind permission of the publisher.

'I Live in Music' by Ntozake Shange from *Nappy Edges*. © 1978, 1991 Ntozake Shange. Reprinted by permission of St Martin's Press, LLC and Russell and Volkening as agents for the author.

Chapter 8

Excerpts from *Chaosmos* by Magda Cârneci, translated from Romanian, in *Orient Express: The Best Contemporary Writing from Enlargement Europe*, ed. Fiona Sampson, Volumes I and II. Reprinted by kind permission of Magda Cârneci and Fiona Sampson.

Every effort has been made to trace and contact copyright holders. The publishers would be pleased to hear from any copyright holders not acknowledged here so that this section may be amended at the earliest opportunity.

. . . before the beginning

It's not beginnings and endings that count, but middles. Things and thoughts advance or grow out from the middle, and that's where you have to get to work, that's where everything unfolds.

(Deleuze 1995: 161)

Practically speaking, there is no 'creation from nothing' (*ex nihilo*). There is always something 'before the beginning', just as there is always something 'after the end'. Put another way, everything is 'all middle'. The present book is no exception. This preface is itself prefaced by acknowledgements; and a bibliography and index follow the apparent conclusion 'after the end . . .'. All this surrounding apparatus is significant. It is a reminder that there are many more hands and minds in the making of a book than one. The bibliography, for example, points to ways out of as well as back into the book and confirms that it exists in relation to other texts as well as being a text in its own right. All this apparatus also intimates that the present book could have been different: however apparently finished, it is always a 'work in process'. Beginning and ending 'in the middle of things' (*in medias res*), it moves in many directions and dimensions and constantly promises or threatens to turn into something else. Being one thing, it offers to become many others.

In this way, *Creativity* as a material object poses plenty of questions about 'creativity' as a theoretical project. Is creativity best conceived as initiating things, continuing them or completing them? Or is it something we always come at from the middle? Is 'being creative' something we can ever be or do entirely on our own, or must it always be done with or with respect to others? Further, are we to think of 'creation' in terms of achieved objects and finished products, what was supposedly creat*ed* by some one-off act (by a god or artist or author, for instance) and now exists only as past fact? Or are we to grasp creation in terms of networks of relations and continuing processes: creat*ing*, with the emphasis upon ongoing activity in the present (by us, here and now, for instance)? Is creativity something that happens 'over there', what we observe others doing? Or is it rather something that happens to us immediately 'in here', as participating subjects? In short, is creativity an 'it' or a 'we' – then or now? Or is it sometimes, under different cultural and historical conditions, something else entirely? These are handy questions to begin with, not least because they persist in various forms throughout the book and are still being asked at the end.

Preliminary definitions, overall aims

Because we need starting points, 'creativity' will be provisionally defined as the capacity to make, do or become something fresh and valuable with respect to others as well as ourselves. Each of the key terms needs to be weighed in turn:

> *provisionally* because there are many other definitions in this book, some of which are sometimes preferred to this one
>
> *capacity* because it is a 'potentiality' or 'possibility' and may or may not be realised in fact, as an act or an achieved state (though preferably it is)
>
> *make, do or become* because creativity can be realised through an object (made), an action (done) or an ongoing process (of becoming); it is therefore not strictly an 'it' or 'thing' at all
>
> *fresh* because this means more than just 'new' or 'novel' and because 'refreshing' may involve making strange things familiar as well as familiar things strange
>
> *valuable* according to the exchange rate of some changing system of values – personal and social, aesthetic and ethical. (We might therefore talk more complexly of 'ex/change rates', because processes of exchange/transaction nearly always entail processes of change/transformation)
>
> *with respect to others* because we never create anything fresh or valuable in utter isolation; we always create in relation to other people and other things (present or absent, remembered or projected), and ideally we do this in every sense with 'respect' to others
>
> *ourselves* of which there is not just one per person but many, some of which need to be created too.

While the overall project of this book is to explore 'creativity', as provisionally defined above, it has several more specific aims:

* to encourage an understanding of creativity that gets beyond stereotypical notions of the inspired individual genius, the extraordinary mind, and the artist as outsider, even while acknowledging the historical force and continuing appeal of such notions;
* to recognise that 'being creative' is, at least potentially, the natural and normal state of anyone healthy in a sane and stimulating community, and that realising that potential is as much a matter of collaboration and 'co-creation' as of splendid or miserable isolation;
* to help develop a vocabulary for talking about creativity that blends ancient, modern and contemporary theoretical perspectives and depends for much of its dynamism upon a tension between them (drawing attention, for instance, to the fact that 'original' used to mean 'going back to the origin, ancient' but now tends to mean 'novel, modern', and that 'genius' has often been identified with places and peoples rather more than with individuals);
* to draw on ways of understanding creativity current not only in literature and the arts but also in the sciences and technology, in the East as well as the West, and in popular as well as elite cultures (examples include the many and various ways of conceiving 'chaos' and 'order' or 'play' and 'game'); and equipped with that

understanding to take a fresh look at areas such as 'aesthetics' and concepts such as 'imagination' that until recently have been theoretically unfashionable;

- to insist upon a vision of creativity that embraces radical forms of *re*-creation and includes actively engaged kinds of re-vision, re-membering and re-familiarisation (as distinct from the relatively passive notion of 'recreation'), and thus resists casual notions of divine creation 'from nothing' or of purely spontaneous expression welling up from nowhere;
- to explore the intimate and shifting relations between 'the creative' and 'the critical', and to grasp the fact that, historically as well as theoretically, the one often turns out to be the other: most obviously in such activities as critique, adaptation, parody and translation, but in principle every time some existing material (language, images, sounds, bodies) is transformed into something judged to be fresh and valuable;
- to nurture an understanding of creativity that furthers practice as well as theory, helping build bridges between, for example, the practices of creative writing and literary and cultural theory, and encouraging 'original' syntheses of all of them in the context of contemporary social structures and technologies.

If this relatively small book is to fulfil such ambitious (and strictly impossible) aims it must rely on its readers to fill out – and challenge – the necessarily brief gestures made here. In other words, the present piece of writing invites readers to be creative as well as critical. It offers questions as much as answers, and encourages problem-posing rather more than problem-solving. It also, finally, opts for clusters of provocative quotation from many sources rather than insisting on the authority of a nominally single-voiced author (me). That said, the book has an agenda, albeit a relatively open one, and it has its own designs, on the materials as well as the reader.

The book in brief

> Look before you leap is criticism's motto. Leap before you look is creativity's.
> (E. M. Forster, *Two Cheers for Democracy*, 1951)

The book is organised in four main parts. Though it has a cumulative argument and can be read from cover to cover, the parts and chapters can also be approached in any order. Cross-referencing enables easy movement around the book; detailed Contents and an Index lead straight to particular topics or terms. For a fuller grasp of the book's agenda, it makes sense to read Part 1 early on. Otherwise leap in and jump around as you see fit. The substance of each part and chapter is as follows.

Part 1 argues the need for a refreshed and re-valued conception of creativity. Chapter 1 challenges the residual model of the creative person as individual 'genius' and the currently dominant model of the 'creative industries' concentrated in advertising, marketing and 'image' manipulation. It identifies alternative modes of creative practice and various models of radical aesthetics.

Part 2 is chiefly concerned with abstract definitions and arguments, and in that sense is more 'theoretical'. Chapter 2 attempts to define creativity historically, showing that while the overall trajectory seems to be from divinity to humanity, from religious notions of creation to secular notions of creativity, the actual paths taken are far more complex and vexed. Chapter 3 attempts to define creativity in more overtly theoretical terms. It is built around a single, multipart sentence beginning 'Creativity is . . .', and with every word added it is suggested that we begin again from different premises. Although by the end of the sentence creativity, or creativi*ties*, may not have been absolutely defined, by a kind of cumulatively progressive logic, it/they may have been demonstrated. Chapter 4 explores intersecting and reciprocally defining cultures of creativity by drawing together key terms that operate across the arts and sciences, signalling issues picked up in Part 3.

Part 3 takes a deeply historical and broadly cross-cultural view of ancient myths of creation and modern versions of creativity. Chapter 5 looks at retellings of ancient creation myths, while Chapter 6 reviews scientific accounts of the beginning of the universe and of life. In both cases the resources of story and metaphor are seen as absolutely fundamental to the processes of making sense and establishing 'truth'. These chapters seek to reformulate the relations between 'artistic' creation and 'scientific' creativity, gesturing beyond the 'two cultures' as currently conceived.

Part 4 is a critical anthology of creative practices. The selection of texts, organised chronologically by medium and genre, represents a wide range of cultural processes and is meant to be suggestive, not comprehensive. Chapter 7 offers a 'case study' of creative practice in one mode: writing. It provides a history and a critique of what has been understood by 'creativity' and 'writing' broadly conceived, including 'creative writing' as currently understood, with an emphasis on literatures in English. Chapter 8 gathers instances of creative practice drawn from many modes and media: from the performing arts to computer games. Though the texts are verbal, they engage with the creative dynamics of sight, sound, movement and touch, severally and together. This is an invitation to celebrate the creative potential of many 'worlds' and the processes engaged which reach across the arts, sciences, technology and culture at large. Creativity is the prerogative of all, not the preserve of the few.

The overall aim, then, is to enrich the sense of what 'being creative' has been, is currently and may yet be. Conversely, every attempt has been made to avoid a dutiful plod through great works and famous names. This applies to 'great theorists and critics' no less than 'great artists' and 'great scientists'. An orthodox critical canon, like an orthodox creative canon, is soon stultifying if observed slavishly. In any case, as the book is designed to demonstrate, the relation between 'criticism' and 'creativity', like that between 'theory' and 'practice', is better conceived as a *connection* rather than a *distinction*, reciprocally defining rather than mutually exclusive. As the epigraph that heads this section reminds us, 'Look before you leap is criticism's motto. Leap before you look is creativity's'. Leap into or across this book as you feel moved. There are many lines of enquiry that cross and re-cross within it; but few start or finish in one place. The way you use it will establish the shape it has for you.

Part 1

Why creativity now?

Creativity is of immediate interest to just about everyone: Am I creative? How creative am I? Can I become more creative? But no one can think or talk about it for long without getting into highly involved issues: about whether only certain special people are creative or everyone is potentially creative in some way; and whether some activities – or cultures or periods – are more creative than others. What is creativity anyway? Is it the same as genius or talent or originality? Or had we better use other terms entirely – such as invention and discovery and innovation? Arguments around creativity are hardly surprising. The concept has an ancient and continuing past rooted in notions of divine creators and mythic moments of creation; a more recent, specifically human history framed chiefly in terms of creative arts and artists; and current applications that range from advertising and public relations ('creating the right image') to business studies and education ('creative management', 'creative problem-solving'). Computer programmes ask us to 'Create File', and 'creative accounting' has become the regular euphemism for what used to be called 'cooking the books'.

It tends to amaze people, therefore, that the first recorded use in English of the abstract noun 'creativity' is as recent as 1875 (see *OED* 'creativity'). Certainly, cognate forms such as 'creation', 'creator' and 'create' were around much earlier, first with religious and then with artistic senses. But what do we actually mean by 'creating' and 'being creative' nowadays? How much has the more or less human and secular notion of 'creativity' taken over from the earlier divine and sublime senses of 'creation'? What are we to make of all the various claims on 'creativity' staked by artists and advertisers, educationists and entrepreneurs? Does it really matter whether we talk of 'producing' or 'generating' – rather than of 'creating' – everything from ideas and images to wealth and health? And how is contemporary critical theory at last coming to terms with a concept that it studiously suppressed for so long? Part 1 sets about framing these issues at length, and points to some fresh and perhaps surprising possibilities.

1 Creativities old, new and otherwise

'Renault – Créateur d'automobiles' *versus* 'Citroën Picasso'
(Rival car advertising campaigns 2002–)

These days, information technology, communications, and advertising are taking over the words 'concept' and 'creative,' and these 'conceptualists' constitute an arrogant breed that reveals the activity of selling to be capitalism's supreme thought.
(Deleuze 1995: 137)

The above epigraphs help set the contemporary scene. The first is from rival car campaigns waged on UK television and throughout Western Europe at the beginning of this century. The second is from an interview with the philosopher Gilles Deleuze towards the end of the last century. Both prompt fundamental questions about what may or may not be meant by 'creativity' nowadays. And both, in context, gesture backwards and forwards to images of creativity that have existed or may yet exist. Neither presents a complete picture, but taken together they help establish some initial terms of reference.

The Citroën 'Picasso' advert is the kind of playful, parodic and highly finished media product we have come to expect from the contemporary 'creative industries'. It offers an amusing narrative of a fully automated car assembly-line in which 'naughty' robots indulge themselves by spray-painting the cars in wavy patterns and wild colours. Eventually they are brought to order and paint the cars as they should – but not before they have signed each with a multicoloured flourish: **Picasso** (the logo of this particular model). Meanwhile, Citroën's competitor, Renault, continues to present itself corporately as *Créateur d'automobiles*. At least three things are worth noting. One is that both the advertising agencies and their employers, the car companies, clearly reckon it worthwhile to trade on the arty image of being 'creative': whether the quasi-divine image of being a 'creator of automobiles' or the genius of the wayward artist. This is in preference, presumably, to presenting themselves as, say, 'car manufacturers' or 'producers'. Another key feature, especially important in a UK English-speaking context, is the appeal to the comparative exoticism and cosmopolitanism of the French slogan and the 'bad-boy' reputation of the Spanish artist. Both are sufficiently recognisable and stereotypical to have an immediate impact. The third significant aspect relates specifically to the mini-narrative developed in the Citroën Picasso advertisement. The opposition and transition between a kind of carnivalesque chaos at the beginning (the robots being wildly expressive) and the sober order that is *almost* imposed at the end (they settle to painting the cars properly, retaining just a flash of free expression in the signed logo) give a clear overall message: these cars offer machine-like dependability but with a human touch, automated technology spiced with artistic technique. In short, like Renault, Citroën does not just produce cars – it *creates* them. In claiming to do so, both these multimillion-dollar international business corporations assume a kind of god-like power and artistic prestige. What's more, they do this with all the resources of the modern multimedia and the ready currency of popular culture at their disposal.

In their witty, knowing ways these campaigns offer potent images of what creativity has come to mean in the postmodern world. Above all this is a matter of 'creating the right image'. To achieve this, all and any of the other readily available images of cre-ativity, notably those of God the Creator and the artist as creator, may be pressed into service. This is also image creation in the service of a fantastically enhanced and largely illusory vision of industrial production. It works by glossing over the human labour and material resources involved in car production and, in their place, offering a humorously humanised vision of playful yet super-serviceable automata. 'Creating the right image' also involves completely cutting out the 'wrong' image: negative aspects of the consumption and use of cars in the modern world, from road accidents to pollution. Other car advertisements do this by showing their product performing in wide-open, car-less spaces such as mountain roads and deserts, or miraculously evading the pressures of urban traffic by some cunning ruse.

Gilles Deleuze (second epigraph) will have nothing to do with this conception of creativity. It is precisely the appropriation of the terms 'concept' and 'creative' by 'information technology, communications, and advertising' that he sees as a pressing contemporary problem and it is to counter such a perverted image of creativity that he urges the claims of his own discipline, philosophy. For Deleuze, 'The function of philosophy, still thoroughly relevant, is to create concepts'; further, 'Philosophy [. . .] is by nature creative or even revolutionary because it is always creating new concepts' (Deleuze 1995: 136). There are several things that need to be said about Deleuze's conception of creativity – and of philosophy. Firstly, he has a very distinct vision of the specifically *creative* function of philosophy, and it is not one to which all philosophers would subscribe or with which all readers will be familiar. (The issues and figures will be revisited later, but, basically, Deleuze writes in the radically politicised tradition of Nietzsche and Foucault where knowledge is a form of power, and, more generally, in the pragmatic tradition of James, Dewey and Bergson where 'truths' are made, not just found.) To get a preliminary idea of Deleuze's 'creative' conception of philosophy we may turn to *What Is Philosophy?* (1991), the last major work he co-authored with the psychotherapist and political activist Felix Guattari. As their English translators put it, this book is a kind of 'manifesto produced under the slogan "Philosophers of the world, create!"' (Deleuze and Guattari [1991] 1994: vii). Crucially, for Deleuze and his co-writer, creation is recognised as taking place in all areas of life, not just art nar-rowly conceived or even philosophy broadly conceived.

Deleuze and Guattari distinguish three main domains or 'intersecting planes' in which creation can occur: (i) *philosophy*, in so far as it is primarily involved in the creation of *concepts* (abstract systems of virtual worlds); (ii) *art* (including *literature*), in so far as it is primarily involved in the creation of *affects* (sensory embodiments of possible worlds); and (iii) *science*, in so far as it is primarily involved in the creation of *percepts* (sensory embodiments of functional worlds) (Deleuze and Guattari [1991] 1994: 163–99). The key words here are 'in so far as' and 'primarily', for in any given instance, especially the most significant and valuable (i.e. the most 'creative'), what we actually encounter is an overlapping of domains: 'the three modes of thought intersect and intertwine' such that 'a rich tissue of correspondences can be established between the planes' (pp. 198–9). Deleuze and Guattari coin the term *heterogenesis* for this multi-directional and multidimensional activity of creation (from the Greek for 'varied' plus 'birth'; cf. 'heterogeneous'). The crucial aspect of such a creatively 'varied-birth' is that it involves kinds of intricately interdependent but strictly unpredictable 'becoming' ('being still to come'). As a result, even if the various inputs are known, the precise outputs cannot be foreknown. Deleuze and Guattari summarise their complex conception of creation thus:

> [N]one of these elements can appear without the other being still to come, still indeterminate or unknown. Each created element on a plane calls on other het-erogeneous elements, which are still to be created on other planes: thought as *heterogenesis*.
>
> (Deleuze and Guattari [1991] 1994: 199)

A more general term they use to describe the process is *chaosmos*. This they take from the novelist James Joyce, who coined it in *Finnegans Wake*, and they define it as 'a composed chaos' (p. 205). Umberto Eco also features the term in his *The Aesthetics of Chaosmos* (1989), observing elsewhere that 'Chaosmos [is] a word invented by James Joyce in which you have this sandwich between *cosmos*, which means ordered struc-ture, and *chaos*' (Eco in Kearney 1995: 78). We shall pick up the term, too, because it neatly catches the paradox of many visions of creation and versions of creativity, both ancient and modern: the ways in which kinds of order (*cosmos*) emerge from kinds of apparent disorder (*chaos*), and, conversely, the tendency of kinds of apparent order to dissipate into disorder, which in turn may dissolve or resolve into yet other forms of chaos and . . . or . . . as . . . cosmos. In short, *chaosmos*. The term also resonates with debates in contemporary theory, most obviously those to do with chaos, complexity and emergence, but also with analogous processes explored in other areas. These debates are treated at length in Chapters 4 and 7 of the present book, but we might here cue by a series of questions their potential significance for a fundamentally reconfigured conception of creativity:

- *Chaos, complexity* and *emergence* theories share a concern with emerging orders and dissipative structures 'on the edge of chaos', and lead to an understanding of complexity in terms of substantially regular but strictly non-predictable trans-formations. Areas of application range from patterns of bird migration to fluctua-tions in international money markets.
  So is creativity in some way peculiarly 'chaotic', 'complex' or 'emergent'?
- *Cosmology* investigates the origins and ends of the universe, even to the point of projecting 'parallel universes' and a 'multiverse'. It involves exploring various kinds of singularity, perhaps beginning with the 'Big Bang' and ending with the

'Big Crunch'; but also recognising that there may be universes between as well as beyond.

To what extent is creativity about absolute beginning and endings, or is it rather about the ongoing construction of parallel or multiple 'universes' in the middle?

- *Evolutionary biology* and *genetics* are filling in and substantially redrawing the Darwinian picture of evolution of species by natural selection, through work on the replication and mutation of genes. Genetically modified foods and the cloning of animals or people are the more publicised aspects of issues that reach even deeper. *Is creativity a natural and necessary aspect of all life, or peculiar to humans? What happens when the 'creature' gets to 'create' itself, too?*

- *Neuro-science, cognitive psychology* and *artificial intelligence* are leading to a radical rethinking of the apparently 'mechanical' aspects of human consciousness and the potentially 'living' aspects of computer 'intelligence', through the crossing of computing and communications with life sciences. *Is creativity the sole prerogative of humans or does it extend to (other) machines?*

- *Quantum mechanics* and *theoretical physics* also continue to work through the implications of fundamental insights into the nature of the physical universe. A beginning list includes: (i) the capacity of mass to transform into energy, and vice versa; (ii) an understanding of matter/energy as both a continuous wave and a stream of distinct particles; (iii) the realisation that the observing subject, the observational apparatus and the observed object all play a part in the observation and that the resulting 'measurement' is a product of the relations among them; (iv) the recognition that time and space are intricately interconnected and ultimately interchangeable, and that the resulting 'space-time' may be best imagined 'curved', 'folded' or full of 'holes'. *With so much potential for change and transformation, what's so special – or common – about creativity anyway?*

Clearly, what is at stake is a much enlarged and enhanced conception of creativity. Equally clearly, such investigations reach far beyond the vistas of our car advertisers, for, as Deleuze observes, 'the activity of selling is capitalism's supreme thought' (Deleuze 1995: 136). As a philosopher, his response is to argue for the kind of radical 'concept creation' represented by such terms as *heterogenesis* and *chaosmos*. But he is also mindful of the crucial part to be played in this joint project by the affects of art and the percepts of science. Some of these last are represented in the sketch of contemporary sciences above. Others, we shall see shortly, come from the arts and aesthetics as traditionally conceived and as radically reconfigured. All provide powerful alternatives and antidotes to the kind of commodity aesthetics that dominate the contemporary cultural scene. To be more precise, all offer ways of viewing and valuing – and constantly re-viewing and re-valuing – *creative processes* in so far as these exceed the commercial value of the *created product* alone.

It will come either as little surprise or a great shock, then, that 'creativity' has *not* been a favoured term in literary and cultural theory of the past twenty or thirty years. In fact, during the closing decades of the twentieth century, almost anything to do with 'creators', 'creation' and 'creating' was roundly attacked, to the extent that the rejection of 'creativity' can be seen in retrospect as one of the founding acts of an array of oppositional critiques (Marxist, feminist, postcolonial, etc.). Now that these approaches are themselves established, we might usefully revisit their founding moments and weigh what may have been lost or misrepresented, as well as asking if critics might since have found ways of accommodating creativity on their own terms. What follows, then, is a kind of 'ground-clearing' to establish the basis upon which an enhanced and extended reformulation of the *concept of creativity* might flourish and to clear up some current misconceptions and misrepresentations. Whether the *term* 'creativity' is revived is another matter and of lesser importance, as we shall see throughout the book.

Creation *v* production

Remarkably, almost none of the current standard dictionaries of literary and cultural theory has an entry dedicated to 'creativity'. (The significant exception is *Keywords* (Williams 1983), to which we shall return.) Where one of its cognates such as 'creative' or 'creation' does make an appearance, it tends to be set up as a 'traditional', rather old-fashioned concept to be demystified and dismissed then replaced by other terms. The Marxist critic Terry Eagleton's entry on 'creation' in *A Dictionary of Modern Critical Terms* is characteristic in these respects (Fowler [1987] 1990: 45 6):

> The metaphor of creation has traditionally dominated discussions of literary authorship, with strong implications of the mysterious, possibly transcendental nature of such activity. [. . .] Viewing such an idea as a fundamental mystification of the process of writing, Marxist criticism (in particular the work of Pierre Macherey) has preferred to substitute the concept of literary production, which suggests the essentially ordinary, accessible nature of fiction-making.

Thus, taking Eagleton's cue and turning to Macherey's *A Theory of Literary Production* ([1966] 1978) what we find in Chapter 11, 'Creation and Production', is precisely a summary dismissal of the former term and its complete replacement with the latter. Macherey begins by assuming that '[t]he proposition that the writer or artist is a creator belongs to a humanist ideology', then proceeds to his central assertion that '[t]he various "theories of creation" all ignore the process of working: they omit any account of production'. He concludes by insisting that 'in this book, the word "creation" is suppressed and systematically replaced by "production"' (Macherey [1966] 1978: 66–8). We can take issue with Macherey on several counts here. One is his contention that 'the writer or artist as creator' belongs to 'humanist ideology' alone: counterparts can be found in the Anglo-Saxon '*scop*' and medieval '*makar*' as well as 'poets' of all kinds (from Greek *poiesis*, 'making'); all these words were used to describe human as well as divine creators/shapers/makers (see below, pp. 198–9). Another problem with Macherey's objection is the fact that many ancient myths of creation pay considerable attention to 'the process of making' (see Chapter 5). Meanwhile, many modern theories of 'creativity' (the secular counterpart of 'creation' that Macherey does not mention) spend far more time on the processes of creativity than on its origins or products. Koestler's *The Act of Creation* (]1964] 1989) is a classic example contemporary with Macherey. Csikszentmihalyi's (1996) work on creativity as 'flow' and Bohm's (1998) on creativity as 'dialogue' and 'participation' are just two of the more recent ones.

More striking and perhaps disturbing, however, is the total conviction with which the term 'creation' is 'suppressed' by Macherey and the equally unyielding certainty with which it is replaced by the term 'production'. This is a critical revolution with a vengeance, and it carries the threat as well as the promise of an utterly new wor(l)d order: 'creation' out; 'production' in. Meanwhile, there seems to be no recognition of the inherently dynamic meanings and variously extendable applications of both terms. 'Creation', as will frequently be observed here (see especially Chapter 2), can refer to a product or a process ('a creation' and the 'activity of creating') and can be attributed to divine and human agents as well as to nature and the universe at large (hence 'a creation' and 'the Creation'). We must also recognise the richly suggestive links with **pro***creation* (i.e. sexual intercourse/reproduction) and with **re***creation* (in the weak sense of 'leisure activity') or **re-***creation* (in the strong sense of 're-making'). Macherey's vigorous championing of 'production' tends to ignore or play down the equally rich and to some extent related complications of that term too. Especially in Marxist terms, are we to imagine, say, pre-industrial, industrial or post-industrial *conditions and modes of production*: hand-made, steam-driven or electronically mediated? These are radically different modes of 'production', not just variations on the same process. As Marx would have been the first to allow, with fundamental changes in material conditions and social relations what is nominally the same word changes its exchange value too.

The question can be put more pointedly. At what point(s) does 'production' as a notionally primary or prior event give way to **re***production* as a notionally secondary or subsequent event? For again, in strict materialist terms, the production of something like a meal or a car is a human *re*production of products that already exist (food stuffs, metal and plastics), and these in turn are a human *re*production of natural materials (plants, animals, ores, oils) that already exist. Plants and animals are also the result of 'reproduction' in that other, expressly sexual sense. One can attempt to get round this problem with the compound phrase 'production and reproduction' (as in 'forces of . . .', 'conditions and modes of . . .'), which may also serve to fuse – or fudge – the tricky and always in part arbitrary distinction between 'human' and 'natural'; but that still leaves the precise relation between 're' and 'production' undeclared and largely unexamined. Perhaps, then, we had better recognise that in reality we are always dealing with a series of variously differentiated and constantly re-integrated processes of *re . . . production*. Here the suspension dots are an explicit signal that the matter is always ambiguously and appealingly open. At any moment, we may feel moved or obliged to fill – or jump – the gap as best we can, but the precise way we do this, paradoxically, will in part depend upon the particular moment and mode of (re)production in which we are operating. The answer depends on when and how we pose the question, not just what the question is. We meet a similar impasse, and negotiate a similarly dialectical and apparently paradoxical way through, with the concept of *re . . . creation* in Chapter 3. But, whether we talk in terms of *re . . . production* or *re . . . creation*, it remains a moot point how far we have really moved the debate on unless we engage in a genuinely dialectical process. That means we must reckon on conclusions that are at least in part unpredictable and always need renegotiating.

A resolution of this problem (that is, a way of constantly re-posing it but not solving it once and for all) will be found, I suggest, neither in 'creation' nor 'production', nor even in their several derivatives (recreation, procreation, reproduction, etc.). Rather, it will be generated between both and beyond all. For this, I would insist, is the genuinely *dialectical* – and as far as shared and exchanged language goes, the fundamentally *dialogic* – way in which oppositions get resolved yet not solved. Indeed, even in terms of classical Hegelian dialectics, there is a confrontation between a *thesis* (the proposition) and an *antithesis* (the counter-proposition) which together result in the creation/production/generation/evolution – or whatever term you prefer – of a *synthesis* that, if it is a genuine fusion of the potentialities of both (a 'co-proposition'), will properly be neither and may even be quite improperly 'other-wise'. (Grasping creativity 'other-wise' is precisely what we attempt – and significantly 'fail' – to do in the course of this book.)

Macherey's mistake is to come down unequivocally in favour of 'production' at the expense of 'creation'. As a subversive tactic at the time it was no doubt necessary, so really it is only a mistake if we persist with it in changed conditions (conditions, incidentally, that Macherey helped to bring about). The obvious problems, in hindsight, are that his terms are resolutely binary and that he wants to resolve the dialectic in his own either/or terms (i.e. thesis or antithesis), rather than find another term and concept between and beyond (a fresh synthesis).

To be fair to Macherey, it should be pointed out that later in the book he does develop an alternative critical creative practice dedicated to reading texts for their 'gaps and silences'. Famously, he urges us to look for the 'not-said' (*non-dit*), what the text cannot or will not say at the time, what it accidentally happens or deliberately strives to cover over. This turned out to be a powerfully productive as well as subversive project in the hands of such critics as Jameson in *The Political Unconscious* (1981) and Belsey in *Critical Practice* (1980). A problem only arises when the activity of what came to be called 'resistant reading' or 'brushing the text against the grain' (after Walter Benjamin and then Eagleton himself) is *not* turned on itself: when the critic's own *non-dit* is not held up for interrogation. This is a common oversight of all writers, but it is especially odd, and at the very least inconsistent, in those who claim to be materialist and to follow a dialectical method. As Marx and others insisted, the greatest challenge is to 'negate the negation' – and thereby posit a positive that could not previously be imagined.

Returning to Eagleton's entry on 'creation' we may detect similar grounds for anxiety as well as assent. Here is how Eagleton marshals poststructuralist and psychoanalytic forces in support of his Marxist attack on the notion of 'the creative author' (Fowler [1987] 1990: 46):

> Post-structuralist criticism, in its concern with the potentially infinite productivity of language, and Psychoanalysis, which sees the dream as itself the product of a 'dream-work' or determinate process of labour, both tend to converge with Marxist criticism in its dethronement – to many still scandalous – of the 'creative author'.

There is some truth here. In fact, many mainstream linguists – not just poststructuralists – would argue that language uses substantially finite materials with 'infinite productivity' (Chomsky and Halliday, for instance; see pp. 55–6). It can also be agreed that dreams depend upon a form of 'dream-work' in that they pose and to some extent resolve problems (though it is unlikely they can be reduced to 'determinate' labour; see pp. 71 ff.). What is far from clear, however, is that any of this amounts to a reason for dispensing with notions of creation. One could just as easily argue, as I do later, that it is precisely the inherent *creativity* of language and of dreams that makes them valuable. But what is perhaps most striking here is Eagleton's rhetorical strategy. He gives us iconoclastic 'dethroners' on the one hand and scandalised traditionalists defending 'the creative author' on the other. The polarisation is polemically persuasive, but also glib and potentially reductive. Those same poststructuralists would remind us that the insistence on extreme opposition is an evasive strategy leading to deferral, rather than resolution, of difference (i.e. Derrida's *différance*). 'Creation' is thus being subjected to what would be called a 'violent hierarchy' and, as a consequence, a potentially invaluable 'supplement' is being delayed and denied. Psychoanalysts, too, would remind us that whatever is so strenuously resisted and rejected will inevitably produce a delayed effect and come back in another form. In fact, in both Freudian and post-Freudian terms, a symptomatic rather than a simple reading of the above passage would anticipate an eventual 'return of the repressed', here 'creation'. Further, as Marx reminds us, if the lessons of history are not learnt first time around they tend to be repeated later. This, I argue, is precisely what is happening now.

Radical aesthetics

A 'return' to freshly charged notions of creativity can be traced in a number of recent studies. But before turning to these it is worth indicating the directions which Eagleton's work, and by extension certain central movements in Marxism, have taken in recent years with respect to creativity. For one thing, Eagleton has engaged more directly and sympathetically with radical notions of materialist aesthetics. That is, while continuing to resist idealist and elitist conceptions of 'the true' and 'the beautiful' as well as the postmodern commodification of pleasure and desire, Eagleton increasingly acknowledges that there are kinds and qualities of experience that exceed not only what has been known but what can be currently imagined. Thus he concludes *The Ideology of the Aesthetic* (1990) with the observation that there is a ceaseless 'conflict . . . between two opposing notions of the aesthetic, one figuring as an image of emancipation, the other ratifying domination'. This tension he characterises as at once 'the condition of creative relationship, and a source of violence and insecurity' (Eagleton 1990: 411).

This strain is maintained in the 'Afterword' to the second edition of Eagleton's influential *Literary Theory: An Introduction* (1996). There he recognises 'much that a male-dominated high theory had austerely excluded: pleasure, experience, bodily life, the unconscious, the affective . . .' (p. 194), and concedes that 'The humanist is thus not wrong to trust to the possibility of universal values; it is just that nobody can yet say exactly what they would be, since the material conditions which might allow them to flourish have not yet come into being' (p. 208). In other words, his earlier outright rejection of so-called 'humanist' terms and concepts, such as 'creation', and their wholesale replacement with others of a supposedly more 'materialist' bent, such as 'production', have become tempered by a greater sensitivity to aesthetic discourses in and of their own historical moments. There is therefore a recognition of terms and concepts that need to be salvaged and reinvested with fresh value, re-constructed as well as de-constructed. By the time of his *After Theory* (2003), Eagleton is openly acknowledging the relative narrowness and inflexibility of much of the previous work in cultural theory: 'it [cultural theory] needs to chance its arm, break out of a rather stifling orthodoxy, and explore new topics, not least those of which it has so far been unreasonably shy' (p. 221). One of these topics, without doubt, is creativity, and I would argue that its contribution to a radically transformed materialist aesthetics is long overdue.

In fact, the ground for an energetic and dynamic, not merely determinist, aesthetics was prepared long ago, even if it has apparently lain fallow. Raymond Williams showed a lively interest in creativity and what it could *potentially* mean as well as what it has meant and currently means. His article on 'Creative' in *Keywords; A Vocabulary of Culture and Society* ([1976] 1983) is an illuminating exception to the chronicle of avoidance and vilification to which the concept has been subjected in theoretical circles, concluding with an injunction to 'realize the necessary magnitude and complexity of the interpretation of human activity which *creative* now so indispensably embodies' (Williams 1983: 82–4). Further confirmation of Williams's commitment to a radically open and ongoing (re)construction of an explicitly *creative* consciousness can be found in the concluding words of his *Marxism and Literature* (1977: 212), a book widely regarded as the most comprehensive statement of his mature theoretical position:

> Creative practice is thus of many kinds. It is already, and actively, our practical consciousness. When it becomes struggle – the active struggle for new consciousness through new relationships that is the ineradicable emphasis of the Marxist sense of self-creation – it can take many forms. It can be the long and difficult remaking of an inherited (determined) practical consciousness: a process often described as development but in practice a struggle at the roots of the mind – not casting off an ideology, or learning phrases about it, but confronting a hegemony in the fibres of the self and in the hard practical substance of effective and continuing relationships.

This is creativity as more than mere 'consciousness-raising'; it is the radical refashioning of consciousness. Nor is it simply a substitution of new, fashionable terms for others that are judged old and outmoded, the trading of one abstract ideology for another. For Williams, 'creative practice' involves a grappling deep within the self and within one's relations with others: an attempt to wrest from the complexities and contradictions we have internalised (he uses Gramsci's term 'hegemony') something that helps us live to better purpose. Moreover, such creative endeavour must be a movement through 'the known' into 'the unknown'. It can be worked at in the present but the results cannot be predicted in advance. Hence the open invitation implied in Williams's parting words (p. 212): 'For creativity and social self-creation are both known and unknown events, and it is still from grasping the known that the unknown – the next step, the next work – is conceived.'

To take 'the next step', we shall turn to more recent work on creativity in literary and cultural theory. Isobel Armstrong, for instance, in *The Radical Aesthetic* (2000) makes a concerted case against what she sees as 'the turn to an anti-aesthetic in theoretical writing over the past twenty years' and 'forges, in response, the components of an alternative aesthetic discourse' grounded in 'creative and cognitive life' (Armstrong 2000: 1–2). However, like Williams, she is careful to insist that 'the components of aesthetic life are those that are already embedded in the processes and practices of consciousness'. The latter include 'playing and dreaming' as well as 'language-making and symbol-making', but these are not optional aspects of living: they are 'experiences that keep us alive'. Also, these aspects of the 'aesthetic life' are 'common to everyone, common to what the early Marx called species being. That is why they can become the basis from which to develop a democratic aesthetic' (pp. 2–3). An even more concertedly open and dynamic argument working 'Towards a Materialist Aesthetics of Becoming' (its subtitle) is developed in Rosi Braidotti's *Metamorphoses* (2002; see below, pp. 157, 265).

This commitment to 'creativity' and 'the aesthetic' as common and inclusive is anticipated in some areas of social science research. For example, Paul Willis and others' *Common Culture* (1990) derives from a collaborative action–research and participant–observer project premised upon what the authors call 'grounded aesthetics'. This is defined as 'symbolic activity and transformation in concrete named situations' (Willis *et al.* 1990: 21–6) and serves to underpin a thesis on 'everyday life and symbolic creativity' (pp. 128–52). The project and thesis are framed in direct opposition to an archaic vision of creativity based upon a few privileged individuals (p. 1):

> In general the arts establishment connives to keep alive the myth of the special, creative, individual artist holding out against passive mass consumerism, so helping to maintain a self-interested view of elite creativity. Against this we insist that there is a vibrant symbolic life and symbolic creativity in everyday life, everyday activity and expression – even if it is sometimes looked down upon and spurned. We don't want to invent it or propose it. We want to recognize it – literally re-cognize it.

Acknowledging that 'most young people's lives are not involved with the arts', the authors none the less maintain that such lives 'are actually full of expressions, signs and symbols through which the individuals and groups seek creatively to establish their presence, identity and meaning' (p. 1). As instances of such 'symbolic creativity' they cite (p. 2):

> the multitude of ways in which young people humanize, decorate and invest with meanings their common and immediate life spaces and social practices – personal styles and choice of clothes; selective and active use of music, TV, magazines; decorations of bedrooms; the rituals of romance and subcultural styles; the style, banter and drama of friendship groups, music-making and dance.

All these activities are instances of what the authors term 'work at play'. Similar arguments, with an emphasis upon creativity as active performance and participation, can be found in Joas's *The Creativity of Action* (1996). They correspond to what I elsewhere call active and participatory 're-creation', as distinct from mere 'recreation' as a more or less passive leisure activity (see pp. 84–9). In this respect, like Eagleton's 'ideology of the aesthetic' as 'an image of emancipation' grounded in 'creative relationship' and Armstrong's 'creative and cognitive life' informed and driven by a 'democratic aesthetic', the project of *Common Culture* is not only braced against elitist idealism and individualism but offers a critique of what its authors call 'postmodern pessimism' (Willis *et al.* 1990: 26–7). So, in its way, does Ron Carter's *Language and Creativity: The*

Art of Common Talk, with its insistence that 'linguistic creativity is not simply a property of exceptional people but an exceptional property of all people' (Carter 2004: 13; see below pp. 56, 216–17).

Willis and colleagues point to more or less 'creative' alternatives, too. While acknowledging that 'the market is the source of a permanent and contradictory revolution in everyday culture which sweeps away old limits and dependencies', they also insist that 'commerce and consumerism have helped to release a profane explosion of everyday symbolic life and activity' (Willis *et al.* 1990: 27). Market forces can certainly excite and seek to exploit desires as commodities, but they cannot completely control the ways in which objects are changed and exchanged, nor can they determine how social relations and cultural values are reconfigured in practice. To recall an earlier example, Renault may portray itself as 'Créateur d'automobiles'; but it is up to particular users how they decorate, 'personalise' and use their cars: whether they cover them in stickers or, say, take turns at driving to work with a neighbour. Admittedly these are not *radically* creative options (like avoiding the use of fossil fuels altogether) but they indicate that there are still spaces within and around commodity culture for the *modestly* creative re-appropriation and re-use, including recycling, of commercial 'goods'. More theoretically, we may say that such practices seek out *surplus* or *supplementary values* in personal and social terms, over and above – or between and beyond – those of *commercial value* narrowly conceived.

This kind of creativity is what Roland Barthes, following the anthropologist Claude Lévi-Strauss, refers to as *bricolage*, the capacity to re-combine existing elements of culture in patterns and with purposes that make sense to users, not just providers (see Hawkes 1977: 51–2, 121–2). Its counterpart in contemporary cultural studies is an approach called 'gratifications and uses', with the emphasis upon resourceful and perhaps subversive 'abuse'. A counter- or sub-cultural example is the early Punk use of zips and safety pins as personal ornaments and badges of group identity. For the cultural critic Dick Hebdige, such aberrant yet resourceful (ab)uses of the objects and practices of the dominant culture are the very acts that constitute the counter- or sub-culture (see his *Subculture* (1979) and *Cut 'n' Mix Culture* (1988)). In the more self-consciously 'high art' spheres of parody and 'metafiction' (in painting, sculpture, film, photo and video as well as the verbal arts), the strategies of collage, montage and pastiche offer a 'poetics' that, as Linda Hutcheon argues, may also be informed by a variety of 'politics': ranging from the reactionary, to the resistant, to the genuinely alternative (see Hutcheon 1988). Again, it all depends how far 'personal' and 'cultural' values are reckoned to operate between and beyond, not just within, 'commercial' values.

The writers featured in the present section share a concern with resourceful resistance and radical alternatives to the dominant ideology of commodity aesthetics. Such responses often call themselves 'creative'. The problem is that capitalism is also richly resourceful and, within the bounds of an ethic of selling and buying and an economics of production and consumption, brazenly 'creative', too. As a result, most notionally resistant or subversive gestures may themselves be quickly reappropriated and reproduced as a saleable 'style' – what George Melly in the 1960s ominously hailed as the transformation of 'revolt into style'. Attempts at difference are fed back into the cycle of selling and buying, production and consumption, then duly regurgitated as the latest range of mass-produced yet 'personalised' car stickers or even 'green' motoring commodities such as lead-free petrol. Punk, too, was quickly commercialised and politically anaesthetised through clip-on accessories, expensively 'distressed' clothing, hair-gels and dyes, all removable when respectability called. At worst – the *best* scenario for the lifestyle merchants – being 'creative' amounts to nothing more than choosing and purchasing the latest design for your new, highly expendable and soon obsolete mobile phone or computer system. At best – the *worst* scenario for the pedlars of an always unobtainable tomorrow – it means making and decorating one yourself out of odds and ends that you find lying around. Further, if you want to be *really* 'creative', you might opt to use another mode of communication entirely: not the next round of audio-visual communications technology, but perhaps such 'retro-' technologies as letters or even face-to-face, real-time conversation!

The continuing problem – and possibility – as Marx reiterated throughout his writings on the materialist conception of history, is that 'people make history, but not in conditions of their own making' (Marx 1963: 67–81). In the present terms, we may say that any aesthetics is *constrained* by the existing materials and conditions in which people work and play. And yet, in so far as it is genuinely radical ('emancipating' is one of Eagleton's words, 'democratic' one of Armstrong's, 'common' one of Willis and colleagues), it also *creates* fresh conditions and relations and values. To be sure, none of this can categorically define what is 'fresh' nor can it resolve the problem of 'value' (notice that the preliminary definition of 'creativity' included 'the capacity to make, do or become something *fresh* and *valuable* . . .', p. xvi), but the above arguments help to refine the definition and re-pose the problem. So may those that follow.

Re-imaging imagination

'Imagination', like 'creativity', is a term associated with an older critical idiom that has not been favoured in theoretical circles over the last couple of decades. Yet, as Raymond Williams observes, a 'difficulty is especially apparent when *creative* is extended' such that a 'specialised sense of imagination is not a necessary term' (Williams 1983: 84). Put more positively, a radically recast notion of creativity entails some fundamental rethinking about what may be meant by imagination. Richard Kearney's *Poetics of Imagining: Modern to Postmodern* (1998) offers one such revaluation, and a transformed concept of creativity is central to his project. Building on his earlier theoretical work on the 'poetics of the possible' and his historical exploration of *The Wake of Imagination* (Kearney [1988] 1994), he proposes that we revisit and extend Romantic and post-Romantic models of imagination in light of recent work in phenomenology, hermeneutics and deconstruction. As two of his reference points, he takes Samuel Taylor Coleridge's definition of the 'primary imagination' as 'the repetition in the finite [human] mind of the eternal act of creation in the infinite I AM' (*Biographia Literaria*, Ch. 13) and Charles Baudelaire's celebration of the poetic imagination as 'the queen of the faculties . . . which decomposes all creation and creates a new world' (Kearney 1998: 4). Suspended thus between notions of the finite and the infinite, the timely and the eternal, the decomposed and the created, Kearney sites his version – and sights his highly metaphorical vision – of a specifically 'creative imagination' in a succession of moments stretching from antiquity to postmodernity: from 'the imaginative powers of making' of the ancient Greeks (*poiesis* as 'making' and *technê demiurgikê* as 'primal craft') to the variously 'ludic' (playful, game-like) and 'performative' (enacted, self-realising) models of contemporary poststructuralism and phenomenology. What these processes have in common, Kearney insists, is 'the human power to convert absence into presence, actuality into possibility, "what-is" into "something-other-than-it-is"' (p. 4).

For Kearney, moreover, it is the *human* aspect of creativity that is at stake in the present highly technologised and pervasively mediated communications culture. He points with foreboding as well as fascination to what he sees as 'a crisis of identity for imagination . . . most graphically expressed in the fact that one can no longer be sure who is actually making our images – a creative human subject or some anonymous system of reproduction' (p. 7). Further, Kearney declares that 'it is precisely in a cyber-culture where the image reigns supreme that the notion of a creative human imagination appears most imperilled' (pp. 7–8). This may come across as eminently sensible or quaintly reactionary; it partly depends how far you equate imagination with a broadly humanist and specifically verbal culture. For instance, it may sound distinctly old-fogeyish to those for whom the push-button, icon-clicking culture of the net and mobile phones is in every sense 'virtually second nature'. Then again, it is precisely the question of how 'unnatural' is that second nature vis-à-vis actual human bodies in time and space that is so vexing.

This leads us to matters of ethics as well as aesthetics. For Kearney such concerns are at the core of his conception of 'creative imagination'. Focusing on narrative in particular, he distinguishes three ways in which both story-telling and history-making, when responsively and responsibly undertaken, engage us in acts of *re*-creation as well as creation (Kearney 1998: 241–57, here 255). These are: '(1) the *testimonial* capacity to bear witness to a forgotten past; (2) the *empathic* capacity to identify with those different to us (victims and exemplars alike); (3) the *critical–utopian* capacity to challenge official stories with unofficial or dissenting ones.' The 'poetics of the possible' thus opens up the way for a 'politics of the possible'. It is precisely in Kearney's refusal to divorce the critical from the creative functions that we can perceive the grounds for an aesthetics informed by ethics, and vice versa, and this dual ethical–aesthetic (or political–poetic) dimension is common to all the above aspects of the creative imagination – not only the 'critical–utopian'. Kearney continues the project with case studies spanning 'story' and 'history', 'fiction' and 'fact' in *On Stories* (2002).

Other aspects of Kearney's work also help develop models of creative imagination that are sensitive to older critical idioms yet responsive to new conditions. In *The Wake of Imagination* he refines an influential model of 'imagination' first articulated by M. H. Abrams in *The Mirror and the Lamp* (1953), taking Abrams's historical two-stage model and adding a third to cover the contemporary scene. Each is built round an enabling metaphor and may be used to model a particular *kind* of imagination as well as a specific historical *stage*. The result is a robust, if somewhat schematic, overview of the main 'images' through which 'imagination' – and by extension the imaginative aspects of creativity – has been and may still be conceived (after Kearney [1988] 1994, esp. pp. 14–18):

1   Classical and early modern images of the ***imagination as a mirror*** that reflects and re-presents some other reality, also called a 'mimetic', 'reflectionist' or 'representational' model.

2   Romantic and post-Romantic images of the ***imagination as a lamp*** that

generates and radiates its own heat and light, also called an 'expressivist', 'generative' or 'affective' model.

3   Modern and postmodern notions of the ***imagination as a labyrinth of
     looking glasses*** that refract potentially infinite variations on an ultimately illu-
     sory object, also called a 'self-referential', 'metatextual' or 'virtual'/'simulacrum'
     model.

Taken together, these metaphorical models of the imagination challenge stereotypically Romantic notions of what it is to create, as though all creative imagination
generated its light and heat from within the self (2). They remind us that a more
subtle model of creativity must include kinds of *re*-creativity and *re*-presentation,
whether the more or less faithful reflection of something that is held to exist already
(1), or the ceaseless refraction of something that never really existed otherwise (3).
This last type corresponds to Baudrillard's notion of 'the simulacrum', a 'self-similar'
phenomenon that has a *virtual reality as image* but does not depend upon an *actual reality
in the world beyond*. Obvious contemporary examples include computerised simulations
or games, but any image tends to become a simulacrum in so far as it acquires its
own readily recognisable and reproducible identity as an icon: conventional images of
the crucified Christ and seated Buddha hardly less than the logos for McDonald's and
Microsoft®. (For more complex images of 'Real Romantic Writers', see pp. 235–41;
for Baudrillard on 'simulacra', see p. 263.)

   Such models are a strong reminder that the very act of 'imagining' or, more narrowly, 'imaging' creativity is a creative and ongoing process. The creative power of
metaphor is explored at length in Part 3. Here we shall simply note some alternatives
to Kearney's image of the Postmodern as a 'labyrinth of looking glasses'. Deleuze and
Guattari, for instance, in their dedication to philosophy as 'the creation of concepts',
offer the image of 'rhizomes' in preference to that of 'the tree' as a potentially liberating 'image of thinking' (Deleuze and Guattari [1980] 1988: 1–26). Rhizomes include
tubers, such as potatoes, and they can root or shoot from anywhere on their surfaces
depending which way is recognised as 'up' or 'down'; they do not have a distinct 'top'
for the shoots or 'bottom' for the roots, as do most seeds and bulbs and all trees. Rhizomes also spread by underground networks, linking one 'node' to another. Deleuze
and Guattari see all this as a powerful image of genuinely creative thinking: resourceful, flexible and unexpected ('springing suddenly from anywhere, everywhere'), and
developing by subtle transverse networks in unseen, subterranean ways. In contradistinction to rhizomatic growth they place 'the tree'. This they see as an image of the
kind of 'arborescence' that tends to dominate mainstream, orthodox and often
authoritarian thought-patterns, as the tree is characterised by a single, central trunk
with primary and secondary branches and roots that spring from a clearly defined top
and bottom. The tree is organised monolithically and hierarchically on a vertical axis;
rhizomes are organised as a multiplicity, horizontally, in lateral networks. Grasped in
this way, the concept of the rhizome might displace that of Kearney's 'labyrinth of
looking glasses' in characterising the postmodern scene. Alternatively, it might be seen
as a fitting image for any kind of 'multiple', 'horizontal', 'non-hierarchical' development in all sorts of cultural and historical conditions.

   The notion of rhizomatic growth is prefigured in the psychology of learning by
Vygotsky's (1934) concept of the 'zone of proximal development'. This, too, entails

development from 'the known' to 'the unknown' by the most readily accessible but not necessarily linear route. It has been used to inform a whole 'postmodern culture of the mind' in the performance-based approaches to psychology and therapy of Fred Newman and his colleagues (see Holzman 1999).

But there are many more 'images of thought' or 'imaginings of thinking' that may be used to develop an enriched historical and theoretical sense of creativity. Shells, with their naturally regular patterns and infinite variety, were a common image of imagination and creation during the eighteenth and nineteenth centuries (almost as common as that of 'the lamp'; see Ward Jouve 1998: 185–226). Like fossils, they could be interpreted either as instances of 'the beautiful handiwork' of 'God the Creator' or, with the advent of systematic geology and paleontology and under increased pressure from Darwinism, as evidence of unfolding design in evolving nature. In modern mathematics and physics a host of organic and inorganic forms are the objects of intense investigation and reflection, so regular are their underlying patterns but so unique the particular realisations. Thus shells – and snowflakes and crystals – not only remain fascinating objects of study in their own right, but also offer themselves as endlessly stimulating candidates for the modelling of mathematical and biological processes of many kinds, virtual as well as actual, especially when informed by theories of chaos and complexity and explored with the aid of computers (see Stewart 1995 and below p. 129). Whole areas of research and development called biomimetics and bioinformatics are dedicated to the theoretical exploration and practical exploitation of 'naturally occurring objects and processes' for the solution of 'human and artificially generated problems' (see Dewulf and Baillie 1999: 22 ff.). A familiar example is Velcro, a fabric-fastener based on the tiny hook-and-eye design that holds together the strands in birds' feathers.

All these objects and processes, whether nominally 'natural' or 'artificial', are what Lévi-Strauss calls 'goods for thinking with' (*bonnes à penser*) (see Hawkes 1977: 32–58). 'Goods for thinking with' are what cultures build themselves from, both symbolically and technologically. (Dawkins's term is 'memes', Stewart and Cohen's is 'extelligence'; see below p. 274.) In the present instance they have been re-dubbed 'images for imagining', but whatever we call them, such ways of saying and seeing tend to become aspects of our ways of thinking and being. In fact, with the emphasis upon creative transformation and metamorphosis, such processes are best conceived as *ways of becoming*. Thus, as we shall see in Chapter 4, the double helix of DNA in genetics and the 'butterfly effects' of chaos and complexity may be conceived as 'goods for thinking with' in the fullest and most flexible senses: as both material facts and imaginative acts; and as both sciences and arts, where both are in their ways 'creative'. Further dimensions of creative imagination and ways of imagining creativity are opened up in Chapter 8, where we trace the current ascendancy of models and metaphors based upon notions of 'web' and 'net'. However, we must also recognise that the current usage is neither the beginning nor the end of the story and the same applies to the concept that we turn to next.

Inspiration by 'an other'

'Inspiration' is another concept that is currently being revisited and is contributing to an enriched understanding of what may be meant by creativity. Timothy Clark has contributed important work in this area in his *The Theory of Inspiration* (1997), which is framed as 'a study of theories of "creativity" in Western literary history since the Enlightenment' (Clark 1997: 1). More particularly, as signalled by its sub-title, *Composition as a Crisis of Subjectivity in Romantic and Post-Romantic Writing*, the book is as much concerned with the processes and products of 'inspiration' (composition, writing) as with the 'subjects' (writers and readers). Clark resists any mystifying notion of 'inspiration' as something that just 'happens', and re-inscribes the concept within critical discourses that require a sense of cause or agency, whether internal or external.

The key concept here is that of dictation by an other: the sense of the individual moved by a force larger than her- or himself. Clark's use of the phrase is prompted by Derrida, especially his 'Psyche: invention of the other' (Derrida 1992: 311–43), but, as he argues throughout the book, the concept resonates in various ways with both archaic notions of 'the Muse' and modern constructions of 'the Unconscious'. The 'other' that is 'dictating' might therefore be attributed to all sorts of agencies and influences: to a divinity or part of the psyche (*Psyche*, Greek for 'spirit', 'soul' and 'mind', is the name of a classical nymph as well as the defining term in psychology); to language and symbolic systems at large ('it is language that writes, not the author', says Barthes in 'The death of the author' (1977: 142–8)); or to a historical moment, a political movement, an inner emotion, or an outer motivation (all four of these 'mo-' words carry a common sense of 'movement', from Latin *movere*, *motum*). The common factor is the partly explicable, not merely ineffable, experience of being 'moved' and 'taken over' by something or someone perceived to be 'other'. Grasped in this way, Clark affirms, 'Inspiration [. . .] as the notion of composition as dictation by an other, is both the oldest and the most contemporary theory of the genesis of the poetic' (Clark 1997: 283).

We consider some of the continuities and differences between ancient and modern views of inspiration in relation to changing notions of influence, tradition and inter-textuality in Chapter 4. Here I shall simply reaffirm Clark's argument that there is in the present, post-Romantic moment, an acute 'crisis of subjectivity', and that our uncertainty about the nature of 'inspiration' is symptomatic of this. This crisis, he argues, is brought on by an increasingly deep-seated anxiety – or, alternatively, poten-tially liberating ambiguity – about who or what is 'inspiring' us, how, why and to what ends. Technology? Mass media? Capitalism? The psyche? Biology? Desire . . . ? In terms of creativity, this can be reformulated as the persistent question 'Who or what created – or continues to create – whom or what?' But now, as Kearney, Willis, Armstrong, Eagleton and others have intimated in their re-valued notions of 'the aes-thetic' and 'imagination', and as Clark observes with his favoured term 'inspiration', 'New controversies . . . are only just underway: of thought as dictation from an other, on effects of something for nothing in the relay of communications, on forms of imag-inary subjectivity and multiple agencies' (Clark 1977: 284). Moreover, just as Clark is careful to talk of '*effects* of something for nothing', so we must take care to distinguish between *effects* of creativity as they relate to actual agencies, conditions and subjects, and be wary of the more mystifying notion of 'creation from nothing' (*ex nihilo*). That said, Clark's summary remark on the perennial appeal and peculiar dangers of talk about 'inspiration' applies equally well to 'creativity' (p. 283):

The term seems always to occupy a crucial, liminal, uncomfortable and often exasperatingly mobile place in conceptions of the process of composition: it names a space in which distinctions of self and other, agency and passivity, inner and outer, the psychic and the technical, become deeply problematic.

This debate has recently been given a decisive twist in the direction of an expressly theorised conception of 'creation and the other'. In *The Singularity of Literature* (2004; all quotations from Chapter 2), Derek Attridge offers a definition of 'creation' that stresses both its 'active' and 'passive' dimensions and its status as both 'process' and 'product': 'Creation, then, is both an act and an event, both something that is done intentionally by an act of the will and something that happens without warning to a passive, though alert, consciousness.' Prompted by Levinas as well as Derrida, Attridge argues that 'creation of the other' is a matter of openness to ethical responsibility as well as aesthetic responsiveness: 'Thinking creatively about creation means thinking of these as two sides of the same coin.'

To open up yet other spaces in which ideas about creativity are currently being explored and applied, we turn to debates in the public domain. For the past fifty years 'creativity' has been a persistent, prominent item on a variety of agendas, educational and governmental as well as commercial and more broadly cultural. It has also, often relatedly, been an object of specialist academic research in psychology, education and, increasingly, business studies. These developments make a huge difference to what we may mean by and do with the term.

Twentieth-century problems

Remarkably, 'creativity' only surfaced as an object of public concern in the mid-twentieth century, shortly after its appearance as a named subject of academic enquiry, chiefly in educational and psychological circles, during the 1920s. As already indicated, people had long been interested in notions of imagination and inspiration, and, as will be seen in Chapter 3, in such matters as genius and talent, originality and invention. There had also been interest among early twentieth-century intellectuals in what Bergson influentially termed 'creative evolution' (see below p. 43). But it is an arresting fact that the abstract noun 'creativity' was not widely current until the 1940s and 1950s (it did not appear at all in the 1933 edition of *The Oxford English Dictionary*), and when it was used it was invoked in contexts and with applications that were highly specific to that time.

In this respect, 'creativity' (narrowly conceived) is a product of the mid-twentieth century and of the modern West. It is a specifically 'modern' response to problems associated with rapid social and technological change. Creativity is needed, it is insisted, to meet the challenge of accelerating changes of an unprecedented magnitude; and the key areas of both change and challenge are those of scientific discovery, technical invention, commercial competition and military rivalry. The keynote, in every sense, was sounded by J. P. Guilford, a founder of modern creativity research, when in the late 1950s he opened one of the first conferences in the United States expressly devoted to the topic of 'Creativity' (only lately graced with a capital 'C'). Guilford begins by observing that 'an unusually strong interest in the subject [Creativity] is an aspect of our *Zeitgeist*' and that 'the present symposium is one expression of it'. He then lists the reasons why it has 'spirit of the times' status (Guilford [1959] in Vernon 1970: 167):

> The most urgent reason is that we are in a mortal struggle for the survival of our way of life in the world. The military aspect of this struggle, with its race to develop new weapons and new strategies, has called for a stepped-up rate of invention. Having reached a state of stalemate with respect to military prepared-ness, we encounter challenges on all intellectual fronts, scientific and cultural as well as economic and political.

There is clearly more than a whiff of cold-war politics and expansionist capitalism in such statements, along with a more general airing of the appeals and perils of 'progress'. The distinctly modern dilemmas that Guilford sees as contributing to 'the upsurge in interest in creativity' include space travel, global communications and the population explosion. He notes 'The coming of the age of space is a force contribut-ing to the upsurge in interest in creativity. It stirs the imagination and it calls for readjustment at an accelerated rate' (p. 168) – though it is not clear whether creativity is the force driving the space age or what is needed to 'readjust' to it. Meanwhile, in what have now become familiar tropes of a shrinking world and a rapidly expanding global population, he observes:

> In a world grown small so far as travel and communications are concerned and a world in which the exploding population competes ever more strongly for its resources, adjustments in the political and personal-relations areas call increas-ingly for imaginative solutions.

The framing of this recalls Malthusian and Darwinian explanations of competition for resources as one of the checks on population growth.

For Guilford, the collective name for all the 'imaginative solutions' required by the modern world is '*creativity*': 'From any aspect from which we may view the scene, the needs for creativity are enormous' (p. 168). This inaugural hymn to 'creativity' in the public domain prompts three further observations. Firstly, Guilford sees creativity as a cure-all for the ills of a changing society. This is creativity as problem-solver and instrument of social engineering, not as, for instance, problem-*poser* and medium of *self*-expression. Secondly, it is unclear how far Guilford sees creativity as symptom or cure and, indeed, whether creativity is part of the problem. As already mentioned, the space age is seen as 'another force contributing to the upsurge in interest in creativ-ity', but it also 'calls for readjustment at an accelerated rate'. This is creativity as a paradoxical and, one might argue, potentially paralysing response to the challenges of the future. It has everything to do with adaptation *to* the environment but nothing to say about radical adaptation *of* or *with* the environment; it is as though the future is already there in some form, to be responded to creatively, rather than itself in the process of being created. The third observation is of a more general kind: that public pronouncements about and grand claims for creativity (like Guilford's) always have to be read in historical context and in terms of the politics they underwrite.

To illustrate the point, we turn to the pronouncements on creativity of Guilford's contemporary, the American psychologist Carl Rogers. Rogers pioneered 'client-centred' psychotherapy and helped found the 'human growth' movement of the mid-twentieth century. He insisted that 'there is a desperate social need for the creative behavior of creative individuals' on the grounds that 'many of the serious criticisms of our culture and its trends may be formulated in terms of a dearth of creativity' (Vernon 1970: 137). Here he is speaking in the late 1940s, before Guilford's address, in a paper initially presented to a small group of psychotherapists. Notice the similar social agenda for creativity but different emphasis (pp. 137–8):

> *In education*, we tend to turn out conformists, stereotypes, individuals whose education is 'completed', rather than freely creative and original thinkers. [. . .] *In the sciences*, there is an ample supply of technicians, but the number who can creatively formulate fruitful hypotheses and theories is small indeed. *In industry*, creation is reserved for the few – the manager, the designer, the head of the research department – whereas for the many life is devoid of original or creative endeavour.

Rogers's claim for creativity shows a stronger commitment than does Guilford's to individual empowerment and personal satisfaction. It is, broadly speaking, a liberal democratic rather than right-wing republican vision of creativity. It also reveals an anxiety about the sanity and sustainability of the human race as a whole when faced with widespread technological change – not, as in Guilford, the maintenance of the military or commercial edge of just one part of it (p. 138):

> In a time when knowledge, constructive and destructive, is advancing by the most incredible leaps and bounds into a fantastic atomic age, genuinely creative adaptation seems to represent the only possibility that man can keep abreast of the kaleidoscopic change in his world. [. . .] Unless man can make new and original adaptations to his environment as rapidly as his science can change the environment, our culture will perish. Not only individual maladjustment and group tensions but international annihilation will be the price we pay for a lack of creativity.

Rogers's plea for creativity is impassioned and compassionate, but it is still made within a given framework of seemingly inevitable scientific and technological change; and again the aim is to promote compensatory adaptation *to* rather than radically adaptive transformation *of* and *with* the environment. This is a creative but constrained response and it has an admirably liberal but still, in a strict sense, 'reactionary' politics to match. The modern reader may also have picked up the insistent, albeit historically incidental, references to 'man' and 'his' world and 'his science'. With the benefit of feminised hindsight, the question arises that these may be specifically 'man-made' problems, and that creativity as constructed here may be an equally 'man-made' solution. Do women have other problems to pose and solutions to offer? Gendered aspects of creativity will recur throughout the present book; see particularly 'fe<>male' in Chapter 3 and discussion of the male-dominated concept of 'genius' in Chapter 4. Clearly, the voices of these spokesmen for creativity from mid-twentieth-century America are just two among many, but drawing attention to what they said then at least helps us to pose the problem historically and politically, even if there are no final, quick-fix solutions. The same applies, despite its title, to the next section of this chapter.

Twenty-first-century solutions

If the proponents of creativity in the middle of the last century looked to the future to solve its problems, then we now are part of that future. And if we are not part of the solution, we must still be part of the problem. To bring the debate up to date, we turn to some pronouncements on creativity from the end of the twentieth century and the beginning of the twenty-first. Together they help establish the ideological and institutional ranges within which discussions of creativity are currently framed. What they abundantly confirm is that the theory and practice of creativity can only be fully grasped by reaching beyond distinctions between the arts, sciences and technology as conventionally conceived. They also prompt us to revise the history of creativity and recognise that it is only relatively recently – and even then only partially – that these various ways of saying and seeing, knowing and becoming, have been separated out and *dis*integrated. The next chapter charts this process, and Chapters 6 and 8 seek a new level of integration, but first we need to get our bearings in current debates. We shall do this by examining a handful of contemporary texts: Roger Scruton's conservative, polemical 'What is Creativity?' (2001); an overview of a multidisciplinary conference called *Creativity in Question* (2002); a book and web-site dedicated to *The Creative Age: Knowledge and Skills for the New Economy* (Seltzer and Bentley 1999); George Steiner's eloquent and elegiac *Grammars of Creation* (2001); the agenda for a conference called *Transgressing Culture: Rethinking Creativity in Arts, Science and Politics* (2002); and a UK National Advisory Committee's report entitled *All Our Futures: Creativity, Culture and Education* (1999).

Old reactionary creativity?

Roger Scruton is a well-known advocate of idealist aesthetics, back-to-basics education and right-wing politics. His preview of the lecture 'What is Creativity?' that he gave at *The Sunday Times* Hay-on-Wye Book Festival, 30 May 2001, gives a clear idea of what he likes, what he loathes, and why (see *The Sunday Times*, News Review, 20 May 2001). Scruton's piece is an unashamedly opinionated and polemical view of *part* of the subject of this book. It may therefore conveniently stand as an extreme representative of a host of remarkably persistent ideas as to what creativity nowadays not only is and is not, but should and should not be. Scruton, a professor of aesthetics, *can* write in more circumspect and scholarly modes, as in his books on Kant's aesthetics, for instance, but the premises and aims of his scholarship are much the same as those of his (frequent) journalistic polemics and the latter have the advantage here of being unadorned and brief.

The title of Scruton's piece, 'What Mozart had and Tracey hasn't', left contemporary readers in no doubt of his position. Mozart, the famous composer and child prodigy, is a classic instance of the 'genius' and the object of many historical studies in that area (e.g. in Gardner 1998 and Howe 1999). 'Tracey' refers to Tracey Emin, a young photographer and installation artist whose work, often including images of herself, had been recently exhibited to critical acclaim at the Saatchi Gallery in

London. The contrast between the two is reinforced visually. There is an image of the child Mozart in formal dress seated at the harpsichord with his father looking over his shoulder. It carries the caption 'Trained to excel: Mozart did not just let it all hang out. He had a thorough schooling from his father.' Opposite is an image of Emin, crouching semi-naked in a bare room with a rough wooden crate behind her. The caption reads 'Shockingly banal: Emin lacks the skills that make real art'. Meanwhile, in case we had missed the point, the article's sub-heading reads: 'A rigorous education separates the geniuses of the past from today's "creative" artists. Will we never learn, asks Roger Scruton.'

Leaving aside the truth or otherwise of the judgements on Mozart and Emin and the near impossibility of making meaningful comparisons between an eighteenth-century composer-musician and a twenty-first-century photographer-model, there is something deeply revealing and instructive about the way in which Scruton couches his case. His argument basically depends upon a number of systematic oppositions, all of which hinge on his anxiety about applying the term 'creative': hence his inverted commas in 'today's "creative" artists'. The result is a pattern of binary differences and preferences, which might be represented thus:

Past genius	*Today's 'creative' artist*
dead, clothed male	live, unclothed female
'real art'	'shockingly banal'
'rigorous education'	'let it all hang out'
'trained to excel'	'lacks the skills'
'schooling from his father'	

Translating this into the terms of contemporary psychoanalytic criticism (terms Scruton would doubtless resist), we might observe that this model of creativity is fundamentally 'phallologocentric'; that is, it is premised upon 'the word and law of the father' (see Lacan in Leitch 2001: 1302–10). More generally, what Scruton says is both authoritarian and conservative (in his case with a large as well as a small 'c'), and 'reactionary' in the strict sense of reacting to the present by retreating into an illusory past. Conversely, what Scruton evidently abhors is a mix of the contemporary, the live, the spontaneous and the supposedly untutored, all inscribed under the sign of the young and naked female. It is the combined taint of all of these which makes Scruton suspicious of the term 'creative' altogether. For him, 'creativity' largely belongs to a modern, modish and now discredited vocabulary associated with the stereotypical idiom of late 1960s and early 1970s liberalism and hippydom ('let it all hang out').

This essentially unsympathetic version of creativity is announced at the beginning of Scruton's article. Employing paired oppositions very different to those I offer above, he claims that 'A liturgy of opposites has developed in the theory of education: creativity versus routine, spontaneity versus rules, imagination versus rote-learning, innovation versus conformity'. He goes on to insist that 'in the face of all the evidence to the contrary, educationists go on telling us that children learn not by conforming to some external standard, but by "releasing their inner potential" and "expressing themselves"'. Again this is revealing. Scruton is rehearsing stereotypes rather than

quoting any individual and he seems to be woefully (or wilfully) oblivious to what educationists have actually been saying over the past forty years (see Vernon 1970,
Sternberg 1988, 1999) or for that matter what progressive educationists such as
Bruner, let alone politically committed ones such as Freire, were saying in the 1970s
and 1980s (see Abbs 1994). None of these espoused a *merely* subjective notion of self-
expression; indeed, all of them insisted on certain kinds of social awareness and
responsibility, rule-informed behaviour, the staged development of skills, and the
recognition of constraint as a necessary condition for creativity. This is also true of the
founding figures of modern educational philosophy and psychology, for all their manifold differences, from Whitehead and Dewey to Piaget and Vygotsky (see Dewey
[1934] 1954, Vygotsky [1934] 1987, Vernon 1970, Holzman 1999).

   Yet in the event – and to be fairer to Scruton than he is to his imagined adversaries
– the way in which he finally proposes to resolve the 'spontaneity *versus* rules' and
other dilemmas is not that different from some of the classic educationalists. Like
Whitehead and Piaget in particular, he rejects 'the myth that we are all instinctively
creative' along with 'the belief in originality as the sole criterion of artistic merit'. In
the place of such casual celebrations of innate creativity and overweening originality
(both of which Scruton attributes, with a woolliness all his own, to 'the long tradition
of woolly thinking that began with Rousseau'), he offers what is basically a neo-
Classical definition and defence of the creative process:

> Real originality does not defy convention but depends on it. You can only 'make
> it new' [a reference to Ezra Pound's famous modernist dictum] when the
> newness is perceivable, which means departing from conventions while at the
> same time affirming them. Hence originality requires tradition if it is to make
> artistic sense.

This truism (none the less true for all that) had been given its most elegantly poised
expression in the eighteenth century by Alexander Pope in *An Essay in Criticism* and
was reformulated in the early twentieth century for the more conservative among the
modernists by T. S. Eliot in 'Tradition and the individual talent' (see below pp. 232
and 96 respectively). Thus, for better and worse, Roger Scruton's answer to the question 'What is Creativity?' can be placed at the residually 'traditional' end of the
contemporary aesthetic and political spectrum. At best, he reaffirms a model of creativity that is aesthetically neo-Classical and politically gradualist: a vision of the
present firmly rooted in the past, and of originality thoroughly informed by knowledge. (The corollary is that he has little sympathy for Romantic radicals such as
Rousseau and seems to have difficulties coming to terms with modern life in general.)
At worst, he flatly opposes modern 'creative' art as crassly unskilled and unschooled
instances of self-expression, excuses for self-indulgent exhibitionism – and brazenly
'female' to boot. (The corollary is that the best artists are diligent, neatly dressed dead
white European 'geniuses' dutifully subject to the discipline of their fathers.) Scruton
is in every sense a 'classic' representative of defiantly old-fashioned understandings of
the subject of this book, all the more interesting – and irritating – for his systematic
*mis*representation of what has actually been going on in the fields of creative practice
and theory over the past fifty years.

New progressive creativity?

Here are the terms in which the organisers of *Creativity in Question*, an International, Multidisciplinary Conference held at Edinburgh University in March 2002, framed their call for papers in May 2001 (http://arts.qmuc.ac.uk/bacs/creativity):

> What do we *mean* by creativity? Is it an act, a process, a concept, an ideological tactic, or all of these? Why do we affirm and celebrate creativity? Is creativity 'merely cultural' or does it need to be understood in the context of wider social, economic and political processes?

These questions are framed circumspectly and quite openly so as to support further reflection about and research into creativity, though the emphasis throughout is upon 'new' forms of mediation and expression, including new economies. Coming straight from discussion of Scruton's piece, the present reader will be struck by a marked switch of discourse as well as emphasis. We leave behind personal observations exclusively confined to the arts about 'geniuses' and 'creative' individuals (who is or isn't one and why or why not), and pick up issues about the state of knowledge and nature of theory with respect to creativity (what it currently means and how it is understood).

It is also clear that this is 'creativity' as a fully articulated area of academic interest. It has its own theoretical issues and research topics; and, it should be added, the institutional stamp of recognition conferred by dedicated academic journals and associations as well as conferences such as this, burgeoning particularly during the 1990s. At the same time, this is 'creativity' as a matter of public concern and an area of professional expertise. The conference organisers report that 'these questions have been prompted by the increased visibility of talk about creativity in the public domain' and observe, though with evident scepticism, that 'organisations even claim to value the creativity of their workers and that creativity is the solution to any problem'. Such statements recall many of the pioneers of creativity research and organisers of conferences from the mid-twentieth century onwards, especially in America. The main difference now, specialist academic research aside, is the prodigious growth in programmes in 'creative management' (free-standing and in-service) and, more generally, the vague appeal to 'creative management styles' as ways of promoting productive changes in managerial working practice and ethos. 'Creativity' in this area is often used virtually interchangeably with 'innovation' (see Kirton 1994, Rickards 1999 and Sutton 2001). Significantly, the most successful devisers of programmes in these areas often also write popularising self-help books for 'creative thinking' or 'creative living' (De Bono and Csikszentmihalyi are prime examples). This, then, is creativity as it spans the academic and popular spheres as well as education and business.

The crucial trend to note, the organisers of *Creativity in Question* observe, is that 'creativity has become generalised across numerous spheres of activity'. The areas they identify are worth pondering. They include: creativity in organisation and management; creativity, commodification and consumption; creativity, science and technology; creativity and mediation; creativity and sex. Engagements with the arts and education are accommodated under such headings as creativity and the creative industries (evidently including advertising, TV and film); creativity and performance; creativity and critical discourses; creativity and pedagogy. Symptomatic, too, is the fact that there is no section on 'creative writing' or 'creative writers'; though there is one on 'creativity and new forms of authorship'. This expressly draws attention to the kinds of collaborative, serial or syndicated authorship opened up by contemporary media and communications technologies.

Such a confidently, self-consciously 'new' creativity may be greeted in various ways. Certainly, by comparison with Scruton's individualist, elitist and art-based view of 'genius', a conceptualising of creativity in terms of industries, performance and pedagogy amounts to a switch – not just a shift – in paradigm. What is especially urged, or assumed, is an engagement with contemporary modes of production and reproduction of a highly mediated and more or less collective or corporate kind. The emphasis is firmly upon the pervasive roles and functions of technology, rather than those of individual persons, and on 'multidisciplinarity' rather than disciplines as conventionally conceived. Some people will welcome such a radical reformulation of creativity as long overdue, or simply recognise it as an unsurprising fact of life. After all, collaboration is the rule rather than the exception in the modern media (notwithstanding the named 'star' syndrome in film and popular music) and 'creative management', characterised by flatter hierarchies, devolved powers or responsibilities and many-way communication, is sometimes a working reality rather than a rhetorical trick.

For others, however, all this talk of 'new creativity' will smack of a 'brave new world', with all the promisingly utopian and threateningly dystopian connotations of the phrase. The latter are well worth unpacking in the present context. The words 'Oh brave new world that hath such people in it!' are uttered by the inexperienced, impressionable Miranda in Shakespeare's *The Tempest* (1610) as she falls in love with a fine young European nobleman (V.1.186–7). Crucially, this is before she has experienced the darker side of that society: its selfishness, acquisitiveness, greed, indolence and indulgence. The phrase was given a further twist by Aldous Huxley in his science-fiction fantasy *Brave New World* (1932). There the 'civilised' world runs on biological engineering, hi-tech entertainment and psychosomatic drugs. The hero is a lone 'savage' from an American Indian reservation who is in every sense eventually 'taken in' by all of this; finally he kills himself in disgust. The questions for us are similar. Are we, like Miranda, to take the 'new creativity' at face value, as a glamorously and unequivocally 'good thing' – or look beyond the gloss to darker implications and unforeseen consequences? Further, as in Huxley, are we to revel in the superabundant pleasures and supposed powers of the contemporary 'communications revolution' – only to find that its promises are hollow or partial and come at an insupportable cost? It is certainly clear that the brave new world of 'creativity' is far from unproblematic.

To tease out further the problems and the possibilities of 'the new creativity', we shall turn to a fully developed articulation of its relation to technology, business and education. The document in question is *The Creative Age* and its subtitle, *Knowledge and Skills for the New Economy*, gives a clear sense of its aims and emphases. Available as a co-authored booklet published by 'Demos' (Seltzer and Bentley 1999) and through the web-site for the associated policy pressure and lobbying group (www.creativenet.org. uk), it offers a concise and comprehensive statement of the premises underpinning this conception of creativity. Basically, what is involved is a blend of social engineering and skills-based education in the service of a model combining democratic citizenship and competitive commercialism. This is a frankly corporatist model of creativity. In the UK, its political home and primary target, it is precisely the kind of 'new creativity' tailored to both 'new Labour' and late capitalism – with optional attachments for either Conservatives or Liberal Democrats as the occasion arises. The basic premise of the project is that 'creativity can be learned', and its main contention is that 'to realise the creative potential of all citizens and to boost competitiveness in the knowledge economy, we must make radical changes to the education system' (Seltzer and Bentley 1999: 10). Creativity is defined as 'the application of knowledge and skills in new ways to achieve a valued goal'. This is in line with the standard definitions in the specialist literature, where creativity is identified with what is 'new and valuable' or 'original and useful' (see Sternberg 1999: 3 and below p. 57), and so are the 'four key qualities' which, it is insisted, learners must have to be genuinely creative (Seltzer and Bentley 1999: 10–11):

1   the ability to identify new problems, rather than depending on others to define them
2   the ability to transfer knowledge gained in one context to another in order to solve a problem
3   a belief in learning as an incremental process, in which repeated attempts will eventually lead to success
4   the capacity to focus attention in the pursuit of a goal or set of goals.

Significantly, of these four 'qualities' ('abilities', 'capacity', 'belief' – the terminology is slippery here), only the first is concerned with problem-*posing*, the exploration of genuinely new possibilities and radical alternatives. The other three are very much task-driven and goal-oriented, dedicated to problem-*solving* and the achievement of 'success'. The latter may be achieved through 'an incremental process' of learning and 'repeated attempts'; but there is still the overriding sense of this being in 'pursuit of a goal or set of goals'. This is, if you like, *creativity with attitude – problem-solving with a will.* It is also in large measure an employment-oriented and economy-based view of creativity and therefore has something in common with the programmes for training in 'creative management' and the self-help manuals in 'creative thinking' and 'creative living' mentioned earlier.

But there is something more subtle and persuasive – as well as insidious and beguiling – about *The Creative Age* than that. This comes through in the mix of case studies featured in the report (pp. 36–75). One is a support programme for twelve- to twenty-one-year olds in Harlem, New York, designed to help them gain entry to 'good' secondary schools and colleges. Another is Hyper Island, a private university in Karlskrona, Sweden, where new media design is taught across educational and professional sites with the emphasis on collaborative projects developed through commonly owned and run web-sites and extensive use of computer-aided design. All these tend to accentuate the positive in a new technology, new society, virtually New Age fashion ('new' crops up almost as much as 'creative').

There are more than rhetorical grounds for scepticism, however. On further reflection, some of this 'brave new world' turns out to be neither very 'brave' nor all that 'new'. The Harlem programme, for instance, may help individuals, but will it change the underlying system that maintains 'good' schools and colleges at the expense of 'bad'? The Hyper Island programme is 'commonly owned and run' only within the fundamentally inclusive/exclusive premises of a private university. But another example is much nearer home to the present writer. One of the supposed success stories featured in the report is that of the Unipart Group in Oxford, England. This is a car spares manufacturer and supplier less than a mile from where I am writing this. Unipart used to host an in-house university programme and boasted some innovatively co-operative methods of identifying and solving problems (suggestions boxes, focus groups, assembly-line workers on the board, etc.). However, over the past few years it has encountered 'problems', brought on by increased competition in the car industry and general economic recession, and it was found that it could only 'solve' these by such traditional methods as 'efficiency drives', 'stream-lining' and 'down-sizing', including compulsory redundancy. When local push comes to global shove, this kind of slippage from 'new style creative management' to 'old-style managerialism' seems to happen with (un)remarkable ease. United American Airlines was another such case that hit the headlines in 2003.

The point is that in prevailing economic and political conditions there are severe limits to the spheres in which any supposedly 'new creativity' is allowed to function. There are also intrinsic restrictions placed on what is likely to be encouraged as 'new and valuable' within a given institution. For all their insistence on modes of 'new' and 'creative' thinking, the writers of *The Creative Age* choose not to examine or expose this situation. Nor are such global economic conditions confined to odd or purely contemporary examples. They obtain equally for supposed worker-participation and corporate-loyalty schemes in the massive electronics and car industries of South-East Asia. Though home to many of the most vaunted contemporary models of 'creative management', the Sony and Nissan corporations, for example, are confronting similar problems to that of Unipart and dealing with them with similarly 'uncreative', 'old-style' solutions: increases in technology and decreases in work-force. Owenism at the Lanark Mill is a famous example from the (previous) Industrial Revolution. In all these cases it is clear that worker co-operation is at a premium at certain times of growth and change, but that it is eminently expendable at times of recession. Then the 'new creativity' is like any other product, subject to the exchange values of the market. If it is not replaced by one still 'newer', it may still operate as a cover for practices that are at least as old as capitalism and as new as people are prepared to believe. (For relevant critiques of kinds of 'new world order', see Stiglitz 2002, Monbiot 2003 and Pilger 2003. For its technological dimensions, see Brown 1998 and Hughes 2000.)

Nor, emphatically, is the only alternative to the above 'new creativity' a return to long discredited concepts of worker co-operation and state control. (Though I will discuss genuinely dynamic 'co-operation' in Chapter 3.) In any case, Soviet and Chinese models of 'collective ownership' were rarely more than token and always headed by an elite. To attempt to resuscitate them would be deluded. No. Moving beyond merely binary thinking means finding more than a 'third way'. It means opening up fourth, fifth, sixth . . . ways until they become a *multiplicity* (what Deleuze and Guattari call a *heterogeneity*, for example). That is what would be entailed by a genuinely *creative* dialectic that generates a genuinely *fresh* synthesis: not just a muddling, middling, compromise with an inbuilt tendency in times of crisis to tip decisively, and for most people disastrously, in favour of a rich and powerful minority. For 'corporatist' visions of creativity still depend upon who is more or less 'incorporated' as a part of the body politic and economic and what kind of 'body' that is perceived to be (including sexual bodies, procreating and nurturing bodies, for example); just as 'stake-holder' politics still depend upon who is holding the main 'stake', the 'game' they are playing, and whose lives and livelihoods they are prepared to gamble with.

At present, then, pending the development of more fundamentally creative solutions, we can at least identify the nature of the problems, and with them some grounds for hope and action. These may be summarised as follows:

- 'Creativity', as term and concept, is one of the most prized commodities of capitalism, just as (along with 'freedom' with which it is often closely identified) it is one of the most cherished benefits of democracy.
- Creativity, as fully developed thought-in-action, is always both more than and subversive of current market and political values. Indeed, the dynamic of capitalism requires the perpetual abolition of current market values and their replacement with others as yet unknown; just as the present 'democratic' systems are nominally committed to the eventual and hitherto substantially unachieved 'rule of the people' (i.e. *demos* + *kratia*).
- Creatively speaking, therefore, we may reasonably expect (hope, fear) that when all the peoples of the world do get a political voice and power to match, the present systems of values of all kinds will be changed *beyond recognition* − not just *between* the currently available and persistently divisive alternatives.
- In short, creatively speaking/acting/thinking, we need to *become in many ways other-wise*.

Creativity in many ways 'other-wise'

George Steiner's *Grammars of Creation* (2001) articulates positions between and to some extent beyond those outlined in the previous two sections. In some ways it is a deeply 'reactionary' book, in others it is alertly 'progressive' − and in yet others it prompts a critical reading that goes beyond both. A critique of Steiner's book is therefore a useful − though not final − focus for this section. The 'grammars of creation' (what we might otherwise call 'discourses of creativity') that Steiner declares himself to be drawing on come from three overlapping areas: 'the theological or "transrational", the philosophical, and the poetic' (Steiner 2001: 42). These converge in a highly compressed definition of 'creation' as '*that which is enacted freedom and which includes and expresses in its incarnation the presence of what is absent from it or of what could be radically other*' (p. 108, Steiner's emphasis). The book as a whole argues and illustrates this definition. Unpacking it here, however, I shall draw attention to several things. Firstly, the term at issue is 'creation', a concept rich in archaic associations with divinity and art, *not* 'creativity', its more contemporary, secular counterpart. Further, the definition itself has at least three interwoven strands. Steiner understands 'creation':

1 *philosophically and ethically*, as an insistence on absence-in-presence and the accommodation of radical alterity ('what could be radically other');
2 *theologically*, through a preoccupation with 'incarnation' as, in Christian terms, the word made flesh and, more generally, the world as an embodiment or emanation of some ultimately divine principle;
3 *aesthetically − and again ethically and theologically*, in the commitment to creation as

'enacted freedom', whether it be a human expression of liberty as emancipation from constraining forms or the liberality of a deity bringing into being and sustaining as an act of grace.

In short, Steiner's position is complex and multifaceted. On one hand, he invokes a model of creation that some would consider archaically spiritual, mythic, mysterious and even mystifying – in his own terms, 'theological' and 'transcendental'. On another, he draws on philosophical and theological notions of absence, presence and 'the other' that may be aligned with Derrida's (more secular) conception of inspiration as 'dictation by another' as well as Levinas's (more religious) realisation of 'the face of the other' as humanity's immediately felt encounter with what Blake called 'the Human Face Divine'. On yet another, he asserts creation as 'an enacted freedom' that always goes beyond – and never simply derives from – that which already is. His is therefore a specifically performative and act-realised rather than mimetic and object-based model of the creative process.

In many respects Steiner's position bears comparison with that of Derek Attridge in *The Singularity of Literature* (2004). Attridge, too, develops a notion of 'creation of the other' as something that is done *to* as well as *by* the creator (see above p. 19); he also emphasises literature as 'event' and 'performance', in the reading no less than the writing. However, Attridge distances himself from the religious and more mystical aspects of Steiner's 'creation', and finally insists that the latter is an 'everyday impossibility': it embraces both the exceptional creative achievement of Shakespeare and the more routinely creative resource of different forms of greeting (see Attridge 2004, Chapter 10).

Crucial to Steiner's conception of 'creation' is its bracing against the concepts 'invention' and 'discovery'. This is framed as a tension or struggle between competing, but also potentially complementary, world-views: with science dedicated to 'discovery' and technology to 'invention', while religion, mythology and the arts are concerned with 'creation'. Thus: 'To most scientists throughout history the term of reference has been "discovery"; technology has aimed at "invention". The new cosmologies regard "creation" as being ambiguous, mythological and even taboo' (Steiner 2001: 278). Further, Steiner tends to identify technological 'invention' with 'reinvention': the capacity to select and combine already existing materials rather than bring new materials into being, i.e. an 'art of combination': 'An *ars combinatoria* points to invention and reinvention. It does not entail creation as I am trying to define it. Yet it is to creation that literature and poetry above all lay insistent claim' (p. 127). In these respects one might be inclined to characterise Steiner's view of 'creation' as inveterately non- or even anti-scientific and therefore non- or anti-modern. Certainly there is a temptation sometimes to align him with the arts and humanities rather than the sciences side in what is now commonly referred to as 'the Culture Wars' (see below p. 85–90).

But Steiner's position – and interdisciplinary debate – is much more complex than that. Time and again he reveals himself to be grappling with an awareness that 'What we have known of *both* "creation" and "invention" will have to be re-thought' (p. 219, my emphasis). He is also concerned about the technological and political pressure of contemporary mass communications and democratic forms of government, asking 'What will it mean to "create" in the cyberspaces of democracy? Will such creation necessarily become "invention"?' (p. 240). One of Steiner's most vivid answers to his own question takes the form of an extended anecdote illustrating how such 'capital distinctions [between 'creation' and 'invention'] are being eradicated'. Characteristically, this features a conversation between three (male) artists associated with early modernism: Marcel Duchamp, subsequently (in)famous for such 'found objects' (*objets trouvés*) as a urinal duly displayed as a museum exhibit; Constantin Brancusi, primitivist sculptor; and Fernand Léger, cubist and constructivist painter (p. 274, Steiner's emphasis):

> It is in the autumn of 1912 that Duchamp visits the Aeronautics Salon at the Grand Palais in Paris. He is in the company of Fernand Léger and of Brancusi. Turning to the latter, Duchamp challenges: 'Painting is finished [*C'est fini la peinture*]. Who could do better than that propeller? Tell me, could you make that?' In that instant, fundamental permutations occur. The craftsmanship, the formal elegance of the mechanical device is elevated to, and above, that of art. Technology is shown to be the act of *poiesis* (as it will be in Léger's paintings). Art can no longer rival, let alone excel the *technê* of the engineer. *Invention is identified as the primary mode of creation in the modern world.*

Such collisions and coalescences of key terms, and the world-views they represent, are crucial for an understanding of the concept of creativity in the modern world. To underscore the point, I shall stack these 'fundamental permutations' in corresponding pairs. The > is to be read as a 'transforms' symbol: this is a matter of one *becoming* the other, not mere equivalence:

Creation	>	*Invention*
art object	>	artefact, *technê*
poiesis	>	technology
signed painting	>	anonymous propeller
formally symbolic	>	practically functional

These transformations together amount to a fundamental *shift* in paradigm between creativity conceived as 'creation' (an artistic activity carried out by named individuals for more or less formal, symbolic purposes) and creativity conceived as 'invention' (an industrial process carried out by anonymous collectivities for more or less practical, functional purposes). Alternatively, we may see these as *choices* of paradigm that continue to be simultaneously available, depending upon particular contexts. Such a shift/choice had been latent throughout the nineteenth century, fuelled by the convergence of industrial technology and populist visions of applied art for all, alongside the 'art for art's sake' movement for the privileged few. We find the two intertwined, for example, in the 'arts and crafts movements' envisioned by William Morris at the close of that century and inspired by a curious but not uncommon mixture of ideals: retrospective high art in designs, and progressive utopian-socialist in aims. But here, in the early twentieth century, it is significantly underwritten by the marked contrast between a *painted picture* (a static, framed representation of an external, pre-existent world) and an *aeroplane propeller* (a moving part from a modern machine designed to change people's experience of the world of space and time). The shift is therefore from fixed representation to dynamic communication, and from technique narrowly conceived to technology at its broadest.

Steiner's comments run on partly similar lines but finally point in different directions. He acknowledges that Duchamp and other experimental modernists in effect 're-invented creation'. Further, he allows that 'the machine frequently exhibits a conceptual sophistication, a quality of making and even of formal beauty equal to, if not surpassing, those in the arts' (p. 276). But the dominant note of Steiner's conclusion is elegiac. Lamenting 'the ebbing of the theological and the melting-down of transcendentality', he wistfully observes that 'there is no more reinsurance for poetics and the arts in the analogy drawn with divine making'. In a parting gesture that is both celebration and *cri de coeur*, he ventures that 'Creation, in its classic sense and connotations, turns out to have been a magnificently fruitful invention' (pp. 276–7).

One can take issue with many aspects of this view of 'creation' (although to Steiner's credit he acknowledges alternatives even while taking his own line). One such aspect is that Steiner refuses, finally, to make the crucial move from crea*tion* (conceived as a narrowly artistic and ultimately divinely legitimated process) to crea*tivity* (conceived as a broadly human and potentially more-than or other-than human process). Another is that he keeps the creative aspects of collaborative activity, especially those perceived as scientific and technological 'invention', firmly in the background (the propeller above) and reserves the epithet 'creative' for work by individuals operating, however innovatively, in recognisable 'high art' contexts (it is the perceptions of Duchamp and Léger that are foregrounded). Meanwhile, though Steiner never expressly argues against the possibility of radical democracy, the assumptions throughout are strongly hierarchical.

Equally importantly, Steiner fails to engage seriously with – or mentions only to dismiss – contemporary models of the creative process that offer to span the arts and sciences and technology. Signalled above (p. 5), these include models and metaphors drawn from such areas as chaos and complexity, cosmology, evolutionary biology, computing, genetics and artificial intelligence (for a characteristic response from Steiner, see below p. 180). Nor, therefore, does he engage with the revisions to which a host of ancient terms and concepts may be subject when viewed in the light of their contemporary counterparts: 'genius' in the context of current studies of both gender and genetics (Steiner's creative artists are almost all men); 'invention' and 'originality' as terms that already have vexed and complex histories, often with diametrically opposed meaning, and may have similar futures too (this is a deficiency which Attridge also explores in Chapter 3 of his 2004 study). Finally, though Steiner invokes various myths and metaphors of creation to fine effect, he neither theorises nor historicises the terms and is therefore open to the charge of being *casually* mythical or *merely* metaphorical. These are problems I tackle in Chapters 5 and 6.

But the last words here will not be left with Steiner's book nor with my critique of it. They are drawn from very different kinds of text that pose the contemporary 'creativity' question in very different ways. Each has something important but partial to say; but all together – not least by virtue of the fact that they collide as well as overlap – have the potential to say much more. It is up to you to use (and critique and follow up and supplement) these materials as you see fit. Those are the really creative moves 'other-wise'.

Creativity is possible in all areas of human activity, including the arts, sciences, at work, at play, and in all other areas of daily life. All people have creative abilities and we all have them differently. [. . .] Developing creativity involves, amongst other things, deepening young people's cultural knowledge and understanding. This is essential both in itself and to promote forms of education which are inclusive and sensitive to cultural diversity and change.

(from *All Our Futures*, report of the UK National Advisory Committee on Creative and Cultural Education, 1999: 6, 11; available at www.dfes.gov.uk/nacce)

'Creative', 'creation', 'creativity' are some of the most overused and ultimately debased words in the language. Stripped of any special significance by a generation of bureaucrats, civil servants, managers and politicians, lazily used as political margarine to spread approvingly and inclusively over any activity with a non-material element to it, the word 'creative' has become almost unusable. Politics and the ideology of ordinariness, the wish not to put anyone down, the determination not to exalt the exceptional, the culture of over-sensitivity, of avoiding hurt feelings, have seen to that.

(from *On Creativity: Interviews Exploring the Process*, with John Tusa, BBC Radio 3, Tusa 2003: 5–6)

Any act of artistic and scientific creation is an act of symbolic subversion, involving a literal or metaphorical transgression not only of the (unwritten) rules of arts and sciences themselves but often also of the inhibiting confines of culture, gender, and society. Rethinking creativity means challenging established borderlines and conceptual categories while redefining the spaces of artistic, scientific, and political action.

(from *Transgressing Culture: Rethinking Creativity in Arts, Science and Politics*, the agenda of a major international conference held in Sweden in September 2002, www.thirdspaceseminar.org)

Part 2

Defining creativity, creating definitions

> Something relevant may be said about creativity, provided it is realized that whatever we say it is, there is also something more and something different.
>
> (Bohm and Peat 2000: 226)

This part traces the history of the 'create' terms – 'creator', 'creation', 'creature', 'creative' and 'creativity' – to see where complications in their contemporary meanings have come from, and considers what we may mean by these and related terms in the future. This historical perspective is important and interesting in many ways, not least as part of a larger cultural history in which the very concept of 'culture' (including agriculture and horticulture as well as 'Culture') is thoroughly implicated in notions of 'growth' and 'civilisation', and therefore in very different notions of creativity. It also informs the historical overview of a specifically verbal creative practice, 'literature', in Chapter 7.

Any attempt to place the 'create' terms historically always entails some sense of what may be meant by creativity theoretically. That is, we are always involved in what may be called *metacreative* acts: creating definitions even while trying to define creativity. The term is coined by analogy with 'metalanguage', which is an observation *in* language *on* language (the word 'noun' and the phrase 'I say . . .', for example), and with 'metatextuality', which refers to the ways in which texts draw attention to their status *as* texts (a classic example featured in Chapter 7 is *Tristram Shandy* talking about itself as a novel). *Metacreativity*, then, is the apparently paradoxical process of *defining creativity by creating definitions*. This process is carried through in the next chapter. But the issue is signalled here because the only way to resolve the paradox and to get out of the circular logic to which it otherwise consigns us is by appealing to specific, historically grounded meanings. Only then can we fix the play of sense sufficiently to trace trajectories that go in *specific* directions and are realised as instances of *particular* discourse. This is especially necessary with terms as ubiquitous and protean as the 'create' words.

Further, as we shall see time and again, notions of creativity tend to develop in recursive but never identically repeated ways. Certain ideas come round again, but in different forms and to different effect. That is why, in the chapter after this, 'Creativity' is eventually, provisionally, defined as *re . . . creation*. But before tackling that argument we need to get our bearings in the history of creativity. This is a living and evolving history that we are still in the process of creating, and therefore still have the power to de- as well as re-construct. And yet in some ways it's an old, old story . . .

2   Defining creativity historically

Divine creation from nothing

'In the beginning . . .', as far as the Biblical story goes, the act of creation was what God did. In a Judaeo-Christian scheme it was the sole prerogative of the divine agent identified as 'God the Creator'. Thus all medieval uses of 'creatio(u)n' ultimately refer to the Biblical act of creation in Genesis 1.1–3. Moreover, though Genesis is silent or divided on this point (see below pp. 164–5), the medieval orthodoxy was that God created things from the Void or Nothing (*ex nihilo*). Trevisa's translation of Bartholomew the Englishman's *On the Properties of Things* (I, 6; 1398) is typical in these respects: 'The creator . . . fro the begynnynge of tyme creat[ed] . . . the creature . . . of no thynge or of no matere precedent.' The primary identification of Creation as a divine act was to prove persistent; hence the insistence in Davies's treatise *Immortal Soul* (1592; *OED* 'create', sense 1c) that 'To create, to God alone pertains', and even fifty years later the deistical philosopher Thomas Hobbes could declare: 'To say the World was not Created . . . is to deny there is a God' (*Leviathan*, II, xxxi; 1561).

Meanwhile, the notion of 'creation from nothing' also persisted, and was maintained even by a rational empiricist philosopher such as John Locke: 'As when a new Particle of Matter doth begin to exist [. . .] and had before no Being, and this we call Creation' (*Essay on Human Understanding*, II, 26.2; 1690). To be sure, alternative popular and learned traditions existed. Lord Rochester's wittily subversive poem 'Upon Nothing' (1679) sports with the paradoxical possibility of creation out of a 'no-thing' that in its own way was a 'some-thing': 'Nothing! . . . Thou hadst a being ere the world was made, . . . When primitive Nothing Something straight begot. / Then all proceeded from the great united What!' Theologically, this accords with the minority view of creation from chaos, what Aristotle called *Plenum* ('the Fullness') as distinct from 'the Void'. But the dominant official position was still divine creation *ex nihilo* and, as we shall see, this was locked on a collision course with materialist models of evolution in the nineteenth century.

A sense of 'pastness' and 'completeness' is also constitutive in the earliest senses of 'create'. The grammatical reason for this is that the English verb derives from the past participle *creatum* of Latin *creare* 'to produce, to make'. The earliest, thirteenth-century uses of 'create' are therefore all of the past participle 'creat' (was created); and it is only in the late fifteenth century that we begin to find a present tense *create*, and some time after that the present participle *creating*. The sense of 'create' meaning 'what *was* created' (the finished product) rather than 'what *is being* created' (an ongoing process) is therefore constitutive in early usages, and persistent in later ones. Indeed, this emphasis upon what may be called *creation as past fact rather than current act* was to prove of enduring significance. It is maintained in object-centred approaches to aesthetics which stress the overriding importance of the finished work of art as 'the artist's creation', as distinct from practice-based approaches which stress the activity of creating and the more or less artisanal process of making (see below, Chapter 8). Its counterpart in commodity aesthetics – in advertising and marketing, for instance – is an emphasis upon the shiny product for consumption rather than the messy process of production (hence the fanciful glamour of the production process with Renault as '*Créateur d'automobiles*' examined in Chapter 1). An emphasis upon the creat*ed* rather than the creat*ing* aspects of creation is also there in approaches to literature and the arts that stress appreciation of the finished work rather than an understanding of its manner of composition and modes of transmission and reproduction. In all these cases, the model of 'divine creation from nothing' underwrites an aesthetics and a politics of fixed (not fluid) form and absolute (not relative) value.

Humanity begins to create imaginatively

Only gradually and fitfully did a specifically human sense of agency creep into the meaning of 'create'. But even then human powers of creation tended to be tinged – or tainted – with a divine aura. This is the point of the jibe in Shakespeare's *The Comedy of Errors* (III.2.39; *c.* 1594): 'Are you a God? Would you create me new?' In fact, throughout the sixteenth and seventeenth centuries, purely human 'creation' was commonly viewed with suspicion, as something delusive and potentially harmful. Thus Macbeth fears for his sanity at seeing 'A dagger of the mind, a false creation, / Proceeding from the heat-oppressed Brain' (*Macbeth* II.1.38–9; 1606); and Gertrude expresses anxiety about her son Hamlet's apparent madness in similar terms: 'This is the very coinage of your brain: / This bodiless Creation extasie / Is very cunning in' (*Hamlet* III.4.128–30; *c.* 1600). Basically, 'creating' was something that could only properly be done by people with divine support and otherwise had better not be done at all.

By the eighteenth century, however, there was a much more positive link being forged between the power of the human 'Mind' and the capacity to 'create' productive mental images (i.e. Imagination). Thus Mallet (1728, cit. Williams 1983: 83) can speak in the same breath of 'the Muse, Creative Power, Imagination.' And by the close of the eighteenth century there is a growing sense that when humans 'create' this entails the fashioning of something new or novel in contradistinction to the 'imitation' of something old. The distinction between Imitation that is derivative ('a mere copy') and Imagination that is creative and 'original' is central to Edward Young's *Conjectures on Original Composition* (1759; see below p. 57). This is the sense that is carried forward in William Wordsworth's insistence, prompted by Coleridge and through him Kant, that 'every great and original writer [. . .] must himself create the taste by which he is to be relished' (letter to Lady Beaumont, 1804). But even those instances where the verb 'create' seems to have an unambiguously human agent can be more complicated than they first appear. 'I must Create a System, or be enslav'd by another man's; / I will not Reason and Compare: my business is to Create', affirms William Blake with resounding independence. But even here there is more than a tinge of Christianity, albeit a highly idiosyncratic and dynamic version in

Blake's case. The poem from which these lines come is Blake's *Jerusalem* (1804–20: plate 10, 20–1) and its speaker, Los, is a rebelliously resistant life-force or spirit. Politically and poetically charged as this is, it is still partly humanity in the image of divine creator – what Blake elsewhere calls 'the Human Face Divine'. Samuel Coleridge, too, celebrates 'the primary Imagination' as 'the living power and prime agent of all human perception'; but this is still couched in highly metaphysical, quasi-religious terms: 'a repetition in the finite mind of the eternal act of creation in the infinite I AM' (*Biographia Literaria*, 1817, Chapter 13).

A particularly famous instance of a politically radical but still divinely licensed sense of 'created' is to be found in the American Declaration of Independence (4 July 1776): 'We hold these truths to be self-evident, that all men are created equal, that they are endowed by their Creator with certain unalienable Rights . . .'. Thus, notwithstanding the supposedly rational self-evidence of these truths, they are still underwritten by a broadly religious and, in context, specifically Christian view of a 'Creator'. (Interestingly, the latter figure was absent from an early draft, which read 'that all men are created equal and independent, that from that equal creation they derive rights inherent and inalienable'.) Characteristically, too, as with the earlier royal 'creation' of knights and dukes, this appeal to the divine creation/Creator underwrites a programme of privilege as well as rights. For in the event, the 'unalienable Rights' did not extend to women and black slaves, who thus remained substantially alienated from the political process. Evidently, in practice if not in theory, some were 'created' more 'equal' than others.

From creative artists to creative advertising

It is around the middle of the nineteenth century that we have the first firm association of the term 'creative' with an elevated and narrowed view of 'Art' – as in 'Creative Art' and, later, 'the Creative Arts'. 'High is our calling, friend! Creative Art', Wordsworth exhorts his painter-friend, Benjamin Haydon in *Miscellaneous Sonnets* (*c.* 1840). 'The mason makes, the architect creates', declares Robertson in his *Sermons* (1859; see *OED* 'creative' sense 1b); and the hero of George Eliot's *Daniel Deronda* (II.3; 1876) insists on a similar distinction: 'A creative artist is no more a mere musician than a great statesman is a mere politician.' This narrowly artistic, deeply hierarchical view of creation was part and parcel of the late Romantic elevation of the artist/author as genius. It reinforced a distinction between the 'fine' and the 'applied' arts which has persisted to the present: painting pictures as opposed to houses; opera and ballet as opposed to popular ('pop') song and dances; writing poetry as opposed to letters, etc. Thus, notwithstanding the efforts of William Morris and Co. in the late nineteenth-century arts and crafts movement, the association of 'creative' with 'high' art remains primary for many. And it is still going strong, as shown in Chapter 1, in the conflict between, say, Scruton's concept of artistic 'genius' and Willis and others' notion of 'common culture'.

Paradoxically, it was precisely the arty allure and high-class cachet of 'creation' and being a 'creator', often enhanced by a residual sense of divinity, which contributed to the massively extended applications of these terms during the twentieth century. Whether under the banner of democracy or that of consumerism, 'creativity' was something that everybody could aspire to and either claim by right or buy at a price. Thus, as the 1989 edition of the *OED* abundantly attests ('creativity' didn't even have an entry in the 1933 edition), there was a marked multiplication of the spheres of human activity in which all things 'creative' could go on. The 1930s in particular witnessed some of the earliest recorded uses of such phrases as 'creative salesman' (1930), 'creative education' (1936) and even 'courses in creative writing' (1930). This last phrase is worth pausing over. 'Creative writing' is still primarily associated with courses in certain kinds of writing *within* education, as distinct from other educational genres of writing such as 'academic writing' or 'criticism'. Typically, Creative Writing (now often capitalised) refers to courses and even whole programmes devoted to the writing of poetry and prose fiction and latterly script-writing and life-writing. *Outside* education, however, it is interesting to observe that novelists, poets, playwrights, script-writers and biographers tend to refer to themselves by those terms or simply as 'writers' – hardly ever as 'creative writers'. (This applies just as much to writers who have taken courses as those who have not.) 'Creative Writing' as such is very much a creature of the academy.

By the mid-twentieth century, then, it was becoming possible to dub almost any activity 'creative' that the writer had a mind to elevate and celebrate; though the lingering presence of inverted commas round the term was still signalling anxiety about potential inappropriateness. Thus an article in the *Spectator* (14 February 1958) refers somewhat cautiously to '"Creative" commercial jobs such as advertising, designing, modelling, public relations, TV, or on a "glossy" new magazine.' By the later twentieth century, however, those working in the self-styled 'creative industries' of advertising, marketing and public relations – and not just the arts and media more conventionally conceived – show no such diffidence. Indeed, they are often up-front, if not in-your-face, about the 'creativity' of what they do and the 'creative' multimedia resources that they use to do it with. The advertising pitch for *'Renault – Créateur d'automobiles'* was examined at length in the previous chapter. But similar claims are made by all sorts of advertisers seeking to sell a product as a choice of creative lifestyle. *'Whatever the occasion – Create it with Rayware . . . Inspirational Glassware by Rayware'* is just one of the many examples that came to hand while writing this. Deleuze and Guattari characterise this kind of commercial appropriation of creativity as 'an absolute disaster' for genuinely creative thought 'whatever its benefits might be, of course, from the viewpoint of universal capitalism' (Deleuze and Guattari [1991] 1994: 12; and see above p. 4). In this their position agrees with that of Adorno and other members of the Frankfurt School who were developing critiques of commodity aesthetics in the 1930s, at the very time when such forces were first making themselves widely felt. Some postmodernist critics, meanwhile, would take issue with all of them by arguing for a close yet still dynamic relation between art and the market-place, and for creative process as it offers to subvert or exceed the commercial exchange value of the product (see above p. 13). Either way, there are clearly difficulties in extending the term 'creative' so as to include such activities as advertising among the 'creative industries'.

It is precisely the compounding – or confounding – of consumer choice with democratic freedom that makes present constructions of creativity at once so potent and superficially beguiling. The social and historical context of these changes is traced in the previous chapter. Here all that will be added is that nowadays we can apparently 'create' everything from 'the right image' to 'job opportunities' and 'a market'. And it is above all in the public sphere that 'the word *creative*' is most 'lazily used as political margarine' (Tusa 2003: 6). Hence the 'creative' re-presentation of everything from individual policies and personalities by ministerial 'spin-doctors' to whole election campaigns and party images handled by advertising agencies. This is the logical culmination of a commercial-political process first observable in a big way in the US in the 1950s but since widely emulated. ('I Like Ike', the slogan of Eisenhower's presidential campaign, is one of its more designedly memorable products.) It depends upon a construction of democratic freedom *as* consumer choice, and it requires that people be publicly and politically 'creative' within strictly circumscribed limits (by voting for one of a range of substantially similar parties every few years, for example). Smith (1998) offers just such a vision of 'Creative Britain'.

But the story of how the power to 'create' came to be placed at the service of a bland blend – or brand – of commercial democracy is only part of it. To grasp how creativity also became informed by expressly 'scientific' principles, we must pick up another strand in the intertwined history of creation – divine, human *and natural*.

Evolution: natural re-creation from something

By the mid-nineteenth century it was becoming possible to speak of creation in significantly different terms from the orthodox religious notion of creation from nothing (*ex nihilo*). Now, under the pressure of the increasingly empirical 'natural' sciences (especially mechanics), creation could be conceived as the *physical transformation* of something that previously existed. Thus Mansel (1858), along with others reported in *OED* ('creation' sense 1a), declares: 'We can think of creation only as change in the condition of that which already exists.' This is basically creation as *re-creation*. It had always been implicit in earlier materialist science, both classical and enlightenment. Aristotle, for example, unlike the idealist Plato but like the materialist Presocratics and Stoics, had conceived creation as a ceaselessly ongoing process, constantly recycling the materials of the chaotic *Plenum*/'Fullness', not a one-off event coming out of 'the Void' (see below p. 62). The notion of the essential continuity and accountability of physical laws was considerably reinforced in the seventeenth century by the mechanics of Isaac Newton. Thenceforth the emphasis upon strict cause and effect and the observation that every action entails an equal and opposite reaction laid the grounds for a view of something always causing or being caused by something else – not nothing.

However, it was chiefly work in the newer 'natural' sciences (notably geology and biology) that put change and transformation firmly back on the cultural agenda. Crucial in this as in so many other respects were the evolutionary theories of Charles Darwin. His *The Origin of Species* (1859) established the grounds for a dynamic model of species development based upon continuous processes of 'natural selection' and 'adaptation'. Henceforth a literal belief in the Biblical account of creation, especially the view that each species was created once and for all and never changed (the doctrine of 'special creation'), was increasingly difficult to maintain. Reviewing previous and present views of the matter (including his own), Darwin in the introduction to *The Origin of Species* expressly draws attention to the magnitude of the change of attitude involved: 'the view which most naturalists entertain, and which I formerly entertained – namely that each species has been independently created – is erroneous. I am fully convinced that species are not immutable' (Darwin [1859] 1998: 7). And he adds that all the evidence points to 'the conclusion that species had not been independently

created but had descended, like varieties, from other species'. This is a position
Darwin resolutely maintains right through to the formal conclusion of the work
(p. 367): '[S]pecies are produced and exterminated by slowly acting and still existing
causes, and not by miraculous acts of creation.' To be sure, in future editions Darwin
was at pains not to further offend the sensibilities of those (such as the smug Bishop
Wilberforce of Oxford) who were outraged by the radical implications of Darwin's
arguments. Hence the conciliatory, if teasing, tone of Darwin's conclusion in editions
of the 1860s:

> A celebrated author and divine has written to me that 'he has gradually learnt to
> see that it is just as noble a conception of the Deity to believe that He created a
> few original forms capable of self-development into other and needful forms, as to
> believe that He required a fresh act of creation [special creation] to supply the
> voids caused by the actions of His laws.'

This is conciliatory in that it appears to allow for a God who created things at some
point, even though these were 'capable of self-development' and therefore in some
measure independent of subsequent divine intervention. (This recalls the argument
of eighteenth-century deists who accepted God as a kind of grand 'clock-maker'.) At
the same time Darwin is teasing, and highly suggestive, in drawing attention to the
'voids' (gaps, empty niches) in the divine scheme and the fact that 'fresh acts of creation' for each species ('special creation') were a cumbersome, improbable and
finally unnecessary solution. Such gap-filling, Darwin suggests, can be far more easily
and 'naturally' explained by autonomous principles of self-generation: Darwin's key
terms are 'adaptation', 'variation', 'selection' and 'growth with reproduction'
(pp. 368–9). That said, there is nothing merely mechanical or reductively rationalist
about Darwin's vision of evolution. He stresses the 'grandeur' and 'beauty' of 'this
view of life', and the fact that humanity participates in an 'appreciation' of nature
not just its observation. In these respects, Darwin recalls specifically aesthetic arguments to do with 'the sublime' in nature, notably those of Burke and Kant. These,
then, are the words with which he chose to close all editions of *The Origin of Species*
(here Darwin [1859] 1998: 369):

> There is grandeur in this view of life, with its several powers, having been origi-
> nally breathed by the Creator into a few forms or into one: and that, whilst this
> planet has gone cycling on according to the fixed laws of gravity, from so simple a
> being endless forms most beautiful and wonderful have been, and are being
> evolved.

Darwin thus manages to accommodate potentially contradictory discourses and, in his
own way, resolve them. For religious-minded readers, the key concepts here are
'Creator' and the sense of life 'having being originally breathed into a few forms . . .'
which is closely akin to notions of divine 'in-spiration' (see below pp. 91–3). For the
philosophically minded, there is the possibility that these may be 'a few forms' or
'one' (thus holding out the possibility of pluralist as well as monist interpretation); and
for the aestheticians there was both that potential paradox and an enthusiastic celebration of the sheer grandeur and beauty of things. Meanwhile, for the natural

scientists who were Darwin's main initial readership, there is the appeal to 'fixed laws' that none the less go 'cycling on'. And even this, as both modern evolutionary biologists and quantum physicists would be happy to concede, includes the possibility of laws that may themselves be in the process of 'being evolved' (see Chapters 4 and 6 below). Darwin can thus be seen as standing at the crossroads of many intellectual routes, leading from the distant past right up to the present. He also shows himself to be highly skilled in conducting the intellectual 'traffic' that flows in many directions.

But it was the philosopher Henri Bergson who was to give Darwin's concept of evolution a fresh and decisively 'creative' twist. In his hugely influential *Creative Evolution* (*L'Evolution Créatrice*, 1907; trans. 1911), Bergson developed an organicist model of life as itself an intrinsically creative process. Thus in the chapter 'Life as *Creative Change*' (Bergson's emphasis), the 'reality' of life is 'undoubtedly creative' in that it is 'productive of effects in which it expands and transcends its own being' (Bergson [1907] 2002: 192). Such 'reality' is therefore not really composed of 'things' in a static, mechanical sense (the Latin root of 'reality' is *res*, thing), but rather a continuous 'flow'. Similarly, time, for Bergson, is not just a matter of discrete beginnings and endings with mechanically measured units of seconds, minutes, hours, years (i.e. chronological, 'clock' time), but rather a matter of ever-varying and subtly modulating 'duration', which is dependent upon perception of the qualities – not just the quantities – of temporal change as it is actually experienced. 'Flow' and 'duration' are key terms for Bergson. They mark his view of evolution not only as organicist but as phenomenological, too. He is concerned with the perceptual development of phenomena in consciousness and, ultimately, the development of consciousness in – and virtually as – life at large. For 'life' is another of Bergson's key concepts. And it is above all the ceaseless and self-generating development of life from matter – without need of a single originary moment of creation or a single originating creator – that marks his model as *dynamically* and *energetically* materialist: 'Life transcends finality . . . It is essentially a current sent through matter, drawing from it what it can. There has not, therefore, properly speaking, been any project or plan' (Bergson [1911] 1964: 265).

This view of an emphatically *creative* evolution is also sometimes referred to as 'vitalist', in that it represents life as informed by a kind of 'life force' or 'vital impulse' (*élan vital*). However, as with all of Bergson's thinking, it is unwise to reify the latter into an actual and separate 'thing'. Life is not merely *informed* by a force, it *is* life force as it flows and unfolds. Bergson's view of 'life force' is therefore best grasped as a dynamically compound concept. In this respect it can be (and often is) compared with Einstein's contemporary (1905) conception of energy-matter as interchangeable and reciprocally defining aspects of the same process – not separate 'things' at all ($E = mc^2$). More generally, it resembles the 'wave-particle' model of physics in which nuclear processes can be conceived as continuous 'waves' or discrete 'particles', depending how they are measured and for what purposes (see Mullarkey 1999: 71–2, Bergson 2002: 217–18). Einstein was to become the very type of the twentieth-century 'scientist as genius' (see below pp. 104–5). But it was Bergson, too, who appealed to the broader intellectual imagination in the first part of the twentieth century, even to the point of becoming a cult figure. 'Creative Evolution is already a religion and is now unmistakably the religion of the twentieth century', observed George Bernard Shaw in his Preface to *Back to Methuselah* (1921), even adding a personal reference to 'Myself . . .

who believe in the religion of Creative Evolution' to the version prepared for his *Collected Prefaces* (1934).

It would be hard to overestimate (though until recently it has been curiously common to overlook) Bergson's contribution to a profoundly *evolutionary* and itself *creative* encounter with modern notions of creativity (Mullarkey 1999 and Bergson 2002 offer to set this picture right). His influence can be discerned in one of the earliest recorded uses of the abstract noun 'creativity' in English. The philosopher and mathematician A. N. Whitehead speaks in distinctly Bergsonian terms in 1926 of 'the creativity whereby the actual world has its character of temporal passage to novelty'; though he is careful to add that 'Unlimited possibility and abstract creativity can procure nothing' (Whitehead 1926: 90, 152 and see *OED* 'creativity'). And even Whitehead's collaborator, Bertrand Russell, who fundamentally disagreed with Bergson's methods and conclusions – especially his metaphors – was happy to concede that 'Henry Bergson was the leading French philosopher of the present century' (Russell 1946: 819). He dismissed Bergson's philosophy as being 'in the main not capable of either proof or disproof', and therefore in Russell's logical-analytical terms not 'scientific'. But he was still prepared to rank his 'imaginative picture of the world, regarded as a poetic effort' alongside those of Shakespeare and Shelley (p. 838).

Bergson's distinctly 'creative' views of evolution were immensely influential on contemporary and subsequent thinkers. He was also instrumental in helping introduce the work of the American psychologist and philosopher William James to a European readership. Bergson wrote an introduction to the French translation of James's *Pragmatism* ([1907] 1911) in which he endorsed the American's view of 'truth' as a practical 'tool' that enables us to 'fit' changing conceptions of reality, not some fixed idea that stays the same for all time. Bergson summarises the pragmatic project thus: 'We invent the truth to utilize reality, as we create mechanical devices to utilize the forces of nature [. . .] *while for other doctrines a new truth is a discovery, for pragmatism it is an invention*' (Bergson [1911] 2002: 271, Bergson's emphasis). This expressly 'inventive' view of truth is very much in line with Bergson's 'creative' conception of evolution. Both found a sympathetic resonance in the work of John Dewey, another American pragmatic philosopher and an educationist. Dewey seems to have first met Bergson in 1913, and corresponded with him and dedicated a number of his studies to him thereafter. Notable among Dewey's popular and themselves highly influential publications is his *Art as Experience* (1934). This expressly identifies 'the live creature' in Bergsonian terms as the crucial element in 'recovering the continuity of aesthetic experience with normal processes of living' (Dewey [1934] 1954: 10, and see below, pp. 261–2). Later philosophers who acknowledge a considerable debt to Bergson include Heidegger, Sartre, Teilhard de Chardin, Levinas and Deleuze; and in all of them the sense is that when they refer to specifically 'creative' processes they have Bergson in mind (see Mullarkey 1999: 1–16, 42–65). What is more, though Bergson's work is often ignored or dismissed out of hand by contemporary theorists of evolution (a simplistic reading of the 'vital impulse' seems to be the problem), there is a remarkable conceptual similarity between many of their ideas of 'emergence', 'contingency' and 'autopoiesis' and his notion of a specifically *creative* evolution. These are issues that will be picked up in Chapter 4.

Creatures: monsters, machines, wo/men

We finally turn to one of the most richly resonant and deeply problematic of the 'create' words: *creature*. Whether we think of 'creatures' in specifically religious terms, as what has been 'created by a divine Creator' (*OED*, 'creature' sense 1), or in popular cultural terms, as 'the creature from the black lagoon' or 'creatures from outer space' – or for that matter as 'creatures from inner space', the figures of our dreams and nightmares – 'creatures' of one kind and another have a great deal to tell us about the imagined worlds in which we operate. They thereby tell us a lot about other things, too: about how far humanity is conceived as a part of – or apart from – the rest of the natural and physical world; about what it is to be considered a woman and/or man (many of the most fascinating creatures are both); and about changing relations between organisms and machines (again, it is often the hybrid that intrigues). What we encounter, then, is a vast array of problems and possibilities very variously configured on a number of shifting interfaces: human–animal, natural–artificial and organic–mechanical – with spiritual–human for good measure. For in theological terms, certain kinds of crea*ture* presuppose certain kinds of Crea*tor* (usually with a capital C). And then it all depends upon the precise creature–Creator relations: whether the creature is dutiful or rebellious, wants to be a creator itself, or can do without a Creator altogether.

The orthodox Christian view, propounded by St Augustine and reinforced by St Thomas Aquinas, was that 'the creature cannot itself create' (*creatura non potest creare*). This was based upon the Biblical account in which Adam and Eve have the power of 'naming' the other creatures but not of actually creating them (Genesis 2.19). The same limitation was extended to humanity; though it is interesting to note that the orthodox version in Genesis was long shadowed by the ancient apocryphal account of 'the Golem', a legendary humanoid creature supposedly created by Adam and Eve as a servant, but which was itself infertile and could not create (see Kearney 1994: 53–61, and below p. 166). In other words, there are shades of the Frankenstein motif (considered shortly) even from the earliest days. The dominant Judaeo-Christian view, however, reinforced in orthodox doctrine to this day, is that *only God can create – not his creature, humanity*.

Meanwhile, the popular view of 'creatures' has tended to be much more capacious and accommodating. Thus for some six hundred years it has been possible to use the English word 'creature' as a term of endearment or contempt, approval or abuse – and sometimes all at once. Hence the persistence in common usage of a wide range of phrases that can refer to somebody, on a sliding scale, as a 'delightful/sweet/dear/ poor/wretched/vile/despicable . . . *creature*'. Counterparts of all of these can be traced back to before the fourteenth century (see *OED*, 'creature' sense 3 b–c). But whether the 'creature' in question is set up to be admired or deplored, the overall implication is that he or she does not exist on an equal footing with the speaker (and may even tend to be an 'it'). Either way, to be a 'creature' is in some sense to be patronised. Indeed, this usage may well be tied in with the practice of deliberately 'creating' aristocrats that became widespread in the later Middle Ages, as opposed to the earlier appeal to blood and land alone: 'the King's Grace . . . created him Duke', as an Act of the reign of Henry VII puts it (1495; see *OED* 'create' sense 3). From this arose the early and predominantly pejorative sense of 'creature' meaning 'one who is a dependent, instrument or puppet of someone or something else' (*OED* 'create' sense 5), as in *Timon of Athens* (I.1.118; *c.* 1604): 'This fellow here, Lord Timon, this thy creature.' This notion of dependence persists in a more generalised way to this day in such phrases as 'creature of habit' or 'creature of the night'. Both these senses express some misgivings about humans being *mere* creatures.

Mary Shelley's *Frankenstein* (1818), featured in Chapter 7, is a particularly famous exploration of the human creator–creature relationship. And there it is clear that 'the creature' (he is hardly ever in fact referred to as a 'monster' except in the film versions) is an object of general sympathy as well as anxiety. Indeed, in modern critical accounts, the 'creator', Baron Frankenstein, tends to be interpreted as an instance of the irresponsible power and unchecked privilege of the mad (typically male) intellect, while the 'creature' stands for the mangled body and constrained mind of an alienated and dispossessed underclass. More generally, from the Romantic period onwards, there is an increasing sense that fixed creator–creature hierarchies are disabling for all concerned. This model was also expressed in terms of the unequal relations obtaining between the artist (as creator), his model (as creature) and his art (as creation). The classic example is the Pygmalion myth, in which the artist both fashions a woman and falls in love with her.

In common usage and popular culture, too, the story of 'creatures/cratures/critters/kritters' (all these forms occur) has continued to unfold in complex and fascinating ways. The term 'critters', for instance, has been current in American usage since the seventeenth century (see Webster's *New American Dictionary*). It refers to wild and domesticated animals, from bears to livestock, but tends to exclude people, except as a joke or insult (e.g., 'He's an ornery critter'). There is clearly a nagging uncertainty about just how far people may be counted as animals and, conversely, how far animals may be counted as 'human'. This is attested by two very different contemporary films featuring 'creatures/critters'. One, the British animated television series *Creature Comforts* (1989–), uses film animations based on plasticine models of such figures as the homely working-class Northerner, Wallace, his faithful dog, Grommit, and the hapless Sean the Sheep. As the title and cast suggest, the emphasis is upon a cosily nostalgic image of 'creature comforts' that is both enduring and endearing; there is much brewing of tea, eating of toast and putting on of slippers. This is obviously an image of 'creatures' who belong to the endearingly 'dear/sweet/poor' category. At the other end of the scale we have the American fantasy horror film *Critters* (1990). This features small furry, half-humanoid creatures who at first seem likeable but soon turn out to be loathsome. They're a cross between cuddly pets and vicious poltergeists. These 'critters' may start off in the 'dear/sweet' category, but they quickly bare their teeth and are finally the very embodiment of malevolence and misrule. In short, they are *little monsters*.

There is now a substantial critical literature on monsters and monstrosity, both in relation to Gothic fantasy fiction and to popular cinema and culture at large (e.g., Rosemary Jackson's *Fantasy* (1988) and Fred Botting's *Gothic* (1999)). Sometimes the monsters are grotesquely organic creatures reappearing from a primordial past or arriving from a primitive planet (*Jurassic Park* is the classic example of the DNA cloning experiment gone wrong). Sometimes the monsters are purely mechanical devices, the robotic creations and 'brain-children' of more or less mad or misguided scientists; alternatively, they arrive from the future and a more technologically advanced civilisation (Hal, the suave and seemingly super-serviceable computer bent on 'personal' survival in *2001, A Space Odyssey*, is a teasing embodiment of both). Meanwhile, the various *Star Wars* and *Star Trek* movies, old and new, *The Hitch Hiker's Guide to the Galaxy* and TV series such as *Red Dwarf* are all populated with caricatured and more or less parodic versions of all these types – often many at once. For the basic appeal of these 'monsters' is precisely that they offer palpably hybrid forms embodying various permutations of the organic and the mechanical, flesh and electronics, biology and physics. What is more, as the type of the autonomous *Terminator* gives way to the more web-like *Matrix*, the trend is clearly away from crude mixtures towards subtle compounding and virtually seamless blends (where the emphasis is as much upon the 'virtual' system as the robotic or bionic individual). These creatures are 'bionic' at the *organic*-mechanical end of the scale and 'cyborg' at the *mechanical*-organic end. And it is the fact that they are part of a larger bionic/robotic organism/mechanism that makes them so elusive to grasp.

In terms of current science and technology, the two main poles between which such monstrous 'creatures' occur are genetics and computing. To these must be added bioengineering, which covers everything from spare-part and cosmetic surgery to genetically modified food and full-scale cloning. Meanwhile, artificial intelligence and artificial life range on a scale from the mechanical simulation of human intelligence to the quasi-biological evolution of computer-generated 'life-forms' such as neural networks (see Boden 1996, Bentley 2001 and, for the work of the designer of the artificial life programme 'Creatures', Grand 2000). There are historical precedents, too. The surgeon, La Mettrie, for instance, published his *L'Homme machine* ('Man a Machine') in 1747. It featured a body propelled by a *jeu d'esprit* that in some ways anticipated both Galvani's experiments with electrical nerve stimulation and even Bergson's energetic *élan vital* (see Smith 1997: 223–7). Babbage's mid-nineteenth-century 'analytical engine' was also a mechanically modest but conceptually ambitious precursor to Turing's mid-twentieth-century model for a 'universal' computer. As is now virtually a cultural commonplace – though its full implications and long-term consequences are only just being recognised – the descendants of this 'universal Turing machine' (i.e. potential as well as actual computers) offer apparently limitless possibilities in the areas of 'self-organisation' and 'emergence' because of their prodigious capacity to combine parallel processing with cyclic feed-back loops (see Brown 1998, Johnson 2001 and Boden 2004: 88–124, 305–22). Though it remains a moot point how far such 'machines' offer to supplement and enhance or dominate and degrade the life of their initial designers and 'creators'.

To illustrate the contemporary history of humans as monsters and/or machines (and vice versa), we pick up two contemporary accounts of 'creatures' in the popular sphere. Both are by women and both show how complex and contentious the question of 'who or what creates whom or what' continues to be. This is especially so in a society in which technology is so pervasive and, some would add, invasive. Susan Bordo begins the chapter '"Material girl": the effacements of postmodern culture', from her book *Unbearable Weight: Feminism, Western Culture, and the Body* (1993), with the following general observation (Bordo [1993] 2004: 142–58; also in Leitch 2001: 2360–76):

> In a culture in which organ transplants, life-extension machinery, microsurgery and artificial organs have entered everyday medicine, we seem on the verge of

practical realization of the seventeenth-century imagination of the body as a machine. But if we seem to have technically and technologically realized that conception, it can also be argued that metaphysically we have deconstructed it.

Here, by 'deconstruction' Bordo means that not only can we remove, replace or add on parts (as in a machine), we can also transform and develop the material itself (as in an organism). This new materiality she calls 'cultural plasticity'; and the capacity – or claim – to mould it she attributes to 'an ideology fuelled by fantasies of rearranging, transforming, and correcting, an ideology of limitless improvement and change, defying the historicity, the mortality, and indeed the very materiality of the body' (p. 142). This ideology, as the rest of the essay makes explicit, is based on an economics of capitalist consumerism and is articulated through a notionally democratic politics of individual freedom. Both converge in a 'rhetoric of choice and self-determination' similar to that of the Demos group featured in the previous chapter; while the 'fantasies of rearrangement and self-transformation' that they favour are predominantly those of whites and males. By way of example, Bordo points to the way in which contemporary advertising persuades people, especially women, to use cosmetic surgery to transform their bodies into a preferred shape (p. 142): "'*Create a masterpiece, sculpt your body into a work of art,*" urges *Fit* magazine. "*You visualise what you want to look like, and then you create that form . . . You become the master sculptress.*"'

The problem, of course, is that, for all the illusion of self-determination and self-transformation and the challenge of 'creating one's self', the results tend to be dully predictable and in a sense mass-produced: endless variants of black women with narrowed noses and white women with 'collagen–plumped lips'. In theory there may be a vision of 'life as plastic possibility and weightless choice'. In practice, far more often than not, 'we are surrounded by homogenizing and normalising images of . . . the "perfect" body' (p. 144). And naturally – and in this case one might just as easily say *un*naturally – the perfect body aimed at tends to be slim, youthful and firm (blonde hair, and blue eyes a cosmetic extra). Moreover, even this, as Bordo insists, is to overlook 'the dark underside of the practices of body-transformation and rearrangement': 'botched and sometimes fatal operations, exercise addictions, eating disorders'.

Ideological questions of agency and subjection ('creator–creature' relations, in the present terms) loom large here – and they are more vexed and complex than they may at first appear. After all, the injunction to 'create a masterpiece, sculpt your body into a work of art' presupposes a 'you' who may be compliant or at least interested. It trades on the potentially admirable aspiration to literally 'make something of one's self' and might, for example, be aligned with Foucault's positive notion of 'self-fashioning' (see Foucault 1986). Thus it would be simplistic – though it is certainly tempting – to see the 'creators' of these images as the usual suspects of false ideology (capitalism, patriarchy and 'whiteness') and to see the 'creatures' whom they address and in some measure 'create' in their own image as the usual victims (women and people of colour). Given the current configuration of power relations, such an analysis still has force and truth. But creator–creature relations, like all power relations, involve kinds of complicity as well as persuasion, and only on occasion downright coercion. At the very least, in Gramsci's terms, they involve 'hegemony', the internalising and embracing of values hostile to the person's own best interests. They may also involve a deep desire to be different, regardless of other people's values.

In any particular case, however, there is a moral and political imperative to assign responsibility and make a value judgement. And this applies whether the judgement is made in an archaic or a contemporary critical idiom: *Who is the creator and who is the creature?* or *Who or what is in active subject position, and who or what is in passive object position?* In the abstract, these may be unanswerable questions. But, on balance, Bordo's case against cosmetic surgery points to the 'creator' (i.e. the private surgeon and advertiser) as aggressor and the 'creature' (i.e. the patient and consumer) as victim. To look at an alternative scenario, with a different configuration of power and a radically reconceptualised sense of self–other and organism–machine relations, we turn to a writer with a contrasting – though potentially complementary – agenda.

In her 'A manifesto for cyborgs' (1985), Donna Haraway takes a quite different perspective on the kinds of 'creature' we currently imagine and may in fact be turning ourselves into. She offers a politically principled yet deeply ironic vision of 'the cyborg'. This she characterises as 'a cybernetic organism, a hybrid of machine and organism, a creature of social reality as well as a creature of fiction' (Haraway [1985] in Leitch 2001: 2266–99, the text cited here). The continuation of Haraway's title, 'Science, technology and socialist feminism in the 1980s', confirms her political alignment and cultural focus; while her subtitle, 'An ironic dream of a common language for women in the integrated circuit', cues us for a critique that is playful as well as re-visionary. It alludes to 'A dream of a common language', an influential essay by Adrienne Rich in a collection of the same name (1979), where Rich sought to promote women's consciousness of the possibility of a kind of organic, cross-cultural and transhistorical communication among women. Writing a decade later, Haraway offers 'a dream not of a common language, but of a powerful infidel heteroglossia' (p. 2267). This irreverent hybridity carries over into Haraway's mode of writing – part polemic, part academic review, part futurist fiction – and is continuous with her celebration and investigation of the hybrid cyborg.

As Haraway observes, 'Contemporary science fiction is full of cyborgs – creatures simultaneously animal and machine, who populate worlds ambiguously natural and crafted.' But there are routinely 'cyborg' elements in life, too. And she draws particular attention to the modern technologies and technical procedures of contraception, sterilisation and fertilisation: 'Modern medicine is also full of cyborgs, of couplings between organism and machine, [. . .] in an intimacy and with a power that was not generated in the history of sexuality' (pp. 2267–8). The implications and consequences, Haraway argues, are profound, not only for our cultural views of gender roles but for the biological functioning of sexuality itself. 'The cyborg is a creature in a postgender world' and 'the stakes [. . .] are the territories of production, reproduction and imagination' (p. 2268). Haraway may appear to be offering an apocalyptic vision of the end of humanity, especially human sexuality, as we know it. But in fact her emphasis is upon what she refers to as 'the utopian tradition of imagining a world without gender, which is perhaps a world without genesis, but may be also a world without end.' Conversely, recalling debates first prompted by the evolutionary biology of Darwinism but pushing them to their current technological limits, she suggests that 'Within this framework, teaching modern Christian creationism should be fought as a form of child abuse' (p. 2268). On a more positive note, Haraway insists that hers is 'an argument for pleasure in the confusion of boundaries and for responsibility in their construction' (p. 2266).

The kinds of boundary confused and redrawn in Haraway's vision of a new kind of 'cyborg creature' entail the rethinking of a whole range of cultural categories, 'natural' and 'automatic'. Indeed, it is precisely the renegotiation, reconstitution and revaluation of the 'natural–automatic' interface that is at issue. But many other traditional binary categories are challenged – and changed too. She characterises this process overall as 'a movement from an organic, industrial society to a polymorphous information system – from all work to all play, a deadly game.' And she goes on to distinguish a number of 'transitions' in which cyborg creatures (fictional and factual) are currently involved (p. 2272; note that again the > is a 'transforms into', 'becomes' sign):

Organism	>	Biotic component
Sex	>	Genetic engineering
Nature/culture	>	Fields of difference
Physiology	>	Communications
Mind	>	Artificial intelligence
Reproduction	>	Replication
Representation	>	Simulation
Functional specialisation	>	Modular construction
White capitalist patriarchy	>	Informatics of domination

Such transitions (transformations, becomings) require a distinctive conceptual vocabulary, too: 'one must think not in terms of essential properties, but in terms of design, boundary constraints, rates of flows, systems logics, cost of lowering constraints' (p. 2273). Responses to all of this will vary widely. For some, again, it may sound like the kind of utopian 'brave new world' that has all the makings of a nightmarish dystopia (the double-edged vision of *Blade Runner* or Le Guin's *Left Hand of Darkness*, for instance). It may also recall the bright vision of a radically hi-tech, corporate democracy – shadowed by techno-fascism and planned obsolescence – proffered by the projectors of *The Creative Age* and critiqued in Chapter 1. But Haraway is alert to such risks, and to the glib rhetoric of the quick fix. She acknowledges that the future presents threats as well as opportunities, divisively sub- and super-human options as well as other-than-human aspirations – especially for women (p. 2267):

> From one perspective, a cyborg world is about the final imposition of a grid of control on the planet, about the final abstraction [. . .] about the final appropriation of women's bodies [. . .]. From another perspective, a cyborg world might be about lived social and bodily realities in which people are not afraid of their joint kinship with animals and machines, not afraid of permanently partial identities and contradictory standpoints.

Similar arguments about the potential threats and promises of what they see as the radically 'deterritorialised body', 'the body without organs' are made by Deleuze and Guattari ([1980] 1987: 149–91). These are given a further feminist twist under the influence of Luce Irigaray by Rosi Braidotti (2002), notably in her complex refiguring of kinds of 'metamorphosis' ('metalmorphosis', 'metramorphosis', etc., see below p. 157). Meanwhile, we may observe that Haraway's capacity to embrace and explore 'contradictory standpoints' and her search for a fresh synthesis – without normalising reduction and premature resolution – are key ingredients in any definition of creativity that stresses its broadly paradoxical or specifically dialectical nature. So is a willingness to celebrate what she hails as 'permanently partial identities', without lamenting the apparent 'holes' or accepting an illusory 'whole'. It is with such playful – but also deadly – serious challenges in mind that we now venture on an extended attempt to define what creativity is or can be. A history of the 'create' terms has helped establish what they have meant so far. But only a sustained bout of theorising, itself informed by historical reflection as well as cross-cultural comparison, can offer to speculate convincingly about what they yet may mean.

3 Creating definitions theoretically

A good theory does not totalise, it is an instrument for multiplication and it also multiplies itself.

(Deleuze 1995: 208)

Ronald flung himself upon his horse and rode madly off in all directions.

(Stephen Leacock, *Nonsense Novels*, 1911)

Creativity is . . .

This chapter is an extended meditation upon a single sentence: **Creativity is extra/ordinary, original and fitting, full-filling, in(ter)ventive, co-operative, un/conscious, fe<>male, re . . . creation**. While the sentence may at first look odd, keeping it in mind throughout this chapter will help make cumulative sense of the various versions of creativity in play.

Meanwhile, it remains a moot point whether creativity *is* anything at all. Perhaps it would be better to open with '*creativities are . . .*', and recognise straight away the potential multiplicity of what is only a notionally singular term. (The first epigraph gestures to the desirability of a theory that multiplies itself as well as its objects.) Then again, perhaps we should grasp creativity functionally in terms of what it *does*; or frame it socially in terms of *who*, *where* and *how*; or simply develop the historical view of what being creative *has meant* opened up in the previous chapter. All these issues will be picked up here (and are examined in various ways by Csikszentmihalyi 1996, Boden 2004, Carter 2004). We of course have to start somewhere, though.

At first glance, the above sentence seems to go off 'in all directions at once' (like Ronald in the second epigraph). Thus, along with reflections on what may or may not be 'extra/ordinary', 'un/conscious', 'co-operative' or 'full-filling' about creativity, we shall explore 'invention' as a kind of 'intervention' and the connection between notions of what is considered 'original' and 'fitting'. We will also look to the complex relations between sexuality, gender and pro/creation ('fe<>male'). The sentence is in a sense a kind of snake: conceived perhaps as curled up with its tail in its mouth, as in 'Creativity is re . . . creation', and thus figuring either frustration or infinity; or perhaps as a shy and elusive creature that may slip off through an opening at any moment. It all depends how closely you follow its course and how you care – or dare – to pick it up: by its head or tail or, most dangerously, by the middle. Indeed, it is precisely in the spaces *between* the sections, and even the suspension dots *within* 're . . . creation', that there is an invitation for the reader to think otherwise: to respond creatively as well as reflect critically. After all, you may not entirely agree that creativity is

. . . extra/ordinary

This is the axis upon which many arguments about creativity rotate. Is creativity *extra*ordinary: the prerogative of a few individuals who are in some respects exceptional, whether through innate 'genius' or by chance? Or is creativity *ordinary*: a commonly available, essentially routine capacity latent in everyone? The specialist literature on this question has been and continues to be divided (for overviews, see Sternberg 1999: 3–34, 449–60 and Boden 2004: 256–76). Earlier studies of 'genius' such as Galton's *Hereditary Genius* (1869) and contemporary 'historiometric' (i.e. historical + psychometric) studies of famous creative individuals by Simonton tend to assert or assume the 'extraordinary' case (see Simonton in Sternberg 1999: 116–36). Thinkers from Rousseau onwards, however – including many of those involved in programmes of liberal or revolutionary educational development, from Rudolf Steiner to Paolo Freire – have tended to insist upon the 'ordinary' case. The dominant view in the nineteenth century was of the 'Genius' as 'Great Man' (with equal emphasis upon 'Great' and 'Man') and, in Thomas Carlyle's terms, 'The Hero' as successively 'Divinity', 'Prophet' and, latterly, 'Poet' (*The Hero as Poet*, 1841). But there were dissenting voices, notably from American populist and overtly 'democratic' writers and speakers such as Emerson, Thoreau and Whitman. Thus Ralph Waldo Emerson in *The Over-Soul* (1841) declares that 'genius . . . is a larger imbibing of the common heart. It is not anomalous, but more like, and not less like other men' (Baym *et al.* 1994, Vol. 2: 1066 ff.). Such views were to inform the work of later pragmatists such as James and Dewey, who also celebrated the essentially 'common' roots of kinds of creative and imaginative experience.

The twentieth century sees a less hierarchical, more overtly democratic society. Thus the previous chapter traced the ever-wider application of the term 'creative' to practically everyone – even if, as Christine Battersby shows in her *Gender and Genius* (1989), it took a while for 'everyone' to include 'everywoman' (see below pp. 165–6). On balance, the current orthodoxy among academic psychologists and educationists researching the area tends to support the 'ordinary' case. Michael Howe summarises it thus in his *Genius Explained* (1999: 179):

> [T]he mental operations that geniuses depend upon are not qualitatively distinct from the ones used by individuals whose expertise is not exceptional, [. . .] mental processes underlying the creative acts of geniuses follow broadly the same rules and principles as the mental processes that lead other men and women towards more mundane creative achievements, and involve no added magic ingredient.

Thus even if one accepts the distinctions between 'genius' (extraordinary creativity) and 'other men and women' 'not exceptional', 'more mundane creative achievements' (ordinary creativity), these are seen as operating on a continuum and following 'broadly the same rules and principles'. There is no mystifying difference: 'no added

magic ingredient'. This democratic and secular note is sounded in most public pronouncements on creativity by contemporary Western governments, especially in the
educational domain. 'Creativity is possible in all areas of human activity, including the
arts and sciences, at work and at play and in all other areas of daily life', observes the
UK National Advisory Committee on Creative and Cultural Education (Department
for Education and Employment 1999: 6). The message is at once inclusive and discriminating: 'All people have creative abilities and we all have them differently.' But
such a view of creativity is not discriminatory enough for some, as witnessed by the
appeals for exclusivity still heard in a substantial minority of the conservative media.
Thus John Tusa of BBC Radio 3 protests that

> to pretend everyone has it [creativity], to imply that everyone might have it, or
> even to hint that creativity should be spread more thinly in order to be more
> equal, is to delude ourselves and to diminish society's capacity for innovative
> imagining.
>
> (Tusa 2003: 12; and see above p. 33).

Much of the academic research on the ordinariness (or otherwise) of creativity has
spun off from intelligence quotient (IQ) testing, notably that pioneered in the US by
Terman and Cox and their successors during the mid-twentieth century. IQ testing
has always been a double-edged weapon. On the one hand it demonstrates that many
people conventionally recognised as creative have quite average IQs, so there is no
necessary correlation between 'intelligence' and 'creativity'. But on the other hand it
tends to measure analytical, logical and narrowly temporo-spatial capacity, and misses
many other, subtler dimensions of what Howard Gardner and others prefer to call
'multiple intelligences' (including kinetic, tactile and emotional capacities; see Policas-
tro *et al.* in Sternberg 1999: 213–72). Indeed, much work on creativity tries to have it
both ways, as the full title of one of Gardner's more popularising books reminds us:
*Extraordinary Minds: Portraits of Exceptional Individuals and an Examination of our Extraordinar-
iness* (1998). Moreover, tests and assessments generally, whether older IQ or newer
psychometric, are primarily associated with competitive and hierarchical grading for
educational, military and professional purposes. They are therefore chiefly concerned
with the recognition and reinforcement of socially normative or specifically required
behaviour. Their characteristic mode is that of problem-*solving*: providing answers to
given questions. This overlooks the fact that much creative activity takes place a stage
earlier, with problem-*posing*: asking questions about things previously assumed, abandoned or ignored.

   In fact, much of the most fundamental research exploring the extra/ordinariness of
creativity derives from work with young, often pre-school children. One reason may
be that such work tends to be therapeutic rather than assessment-driven: more concerned with stimulating and helping than with grading. Another reason – what
conservative critics such as Scruton would dismiss as 'the Romantic, Rousseauist view'
(see above p. 24) – is that small children may be more unselfconsciously 'creative'
than older people precisely because they have not been subjected to much formalised
schooling. An essential reference point for many practitioners in child therapy is the
work of Donald Winnicott, notably his *Playing and Reality* (1971). Based upon decades
of clinical practice with small children, Winnicott was convinced that: 'everything that

happens is creative except in so far as the individual is ill, or is hampered by ongoing environmental factors which stifle his creative processes' (Winnicott 1971: 79). And it was in the normal functioning of the healthy child that he saw the most profound and pervasive evidence of and basis for human creativity. Thus in the chapter devoted to 'Creativity and its Origins' (1971: 76–100, here 80–1) he insists that 'the creative impulse' can move 'anyone':

> The creative impulse is therefore [. . .] something that is present when *anyone* – baby, child, adolescent, adult, old man or woman – looks in a healthy way at anything or does anything deliberately, such as making a mess with faeces or pro-longing the act of crying to enjoy a musical sound. It is present as much in the moment-by-moment living of a backward child who is enjoying breathing as it is in the inspiration of an architect who suddenly knows what it is that he wishes to construct.

In this view the basic materials for creativity are widely available and almost anything might be turned into a tool for creative play. Winnicott calls the symbolic tools with which people play and thereby make sense of the world 'transitional' (and sometimes 'transactional') objects. They are transitional in that they allow change to take place, and transactional in that they involve exchanges with oneself and others. Over life, such transitional/transactional objects might range from a corner of blanket clutched by an infant to making tea, from relishing a single word to sharing the practices of language and culture at large. In this respect Winnicott is at one with Willis and others in the emphasis upon 'symbolic work at play in the everyday cultures of the young' and the kinds of 'grounded aesthetics' reviewed in Chapter 1.

Perhaps the most compelling example of a resource that is extra/ordinarily cre-ative is language: whatever the linguistic model, linguists agree that words are at once an utterly routine and fantastically rich resource (for an overview, see 'Language and creativity' in Burke *et al.* 2000: 330–72). Noam Chomsky, for example, talks of the prodigious 'generative' power of a few essentially 'deep' structures and their capacity to be 'transformed' into myriad 'surface' forms as virtually infinite realisa-tions of basically finite resources. He observes in *Language and Mind* (Chomsky 1972: 100), 'The normal use of language is, in this sense, a creative activity. This creative aspect of normal language use is one fundamental factor that distinguishes human language from any known system of animal communication.' In a similar vein, Steven Pinker's 'language instinct' is 'an extraordinary gift: the ability to dis-patch an infinite number of precisely structured thoughts'. This can only happen because of the interplay between game-like grammatical 'rules' and specific verbal items, 'words': 'Words and rules give rise to the vast expressive powers of language, allowing us to share the fruits of the vast creative power of thought' (Pinker 1999: 321). For Pinker and Chomsky, verbal creativity is an aspect of mental creativ-ity, and both define what it is to be distinctively human.

But there are accounts of creativity in language that emphasise its social and his-torical dimensions, and there are political directions in which an understanding of 'extra/ordinariness' can take us. Fundamental here is Bakhtin's view of the creatively 'dialogic' nature of language and the kinds of 'response-ability' that this requires from its users. What this means is that in so far as every utterance fully and freshly 'responds' to what has been said, it projects itself forward to an anticipated response and, more generally, to an as-yet-unrealised future (see Bakhtin 1990). Such, for Bakhtin, is the potentially deeply radical 'response-ability' (including 'responsiveness' as well as 'responsibility') that is entailed by ordinary language-use when its implications are fully grasped (the Russian term *otvetsvenost* carries the same pun and is sometimes alternatively translated as 'answerability'). Being fully 'response-able' in this complex sense is necessarily to be socially aware and, in that words are themselves acts with real consequences, to be politically engaged. An example is the decision to call someone – or oneself – a 'terrorist' or 'religious fanatic' or 'true believer', etc. Another would be switching the preposition in 'War *on* Terrorism' to 'War *of* Terrorism'. Such seemingly slight changes have potentially profound repercussions. At stake is what the functional grammarian M. A. K. Halliday refers to as 'a theory of language as choice', where 'any part of a language' is 'a resource for making meaning by choosing' (Halliday 1994: xxvii). Simply as a result of the words we choose, then, something potentially momentous can suddenly occur, or be made to occur. As Janet Frame puts it in her novel *The Carpathians* (1988: 11): 'The journey is one of choices, judgments, of logic – if . . . then . . . and also . . . therefore . . . – the small words that have little use become instruments of power.'

Language, then, is a constantly available resource for demonstrating the fundamentally extra/ordinary nature of human creativity. Crucially, this is not the exclusive prerogative of a special class of 'creative language users'. To be sure, poets, novelists and playwrights, along with political speech-makers, journalists and advertising copywriters, may all have more resource and facility or opportunity and practice in certain areas of language use, but even then many writers claim to represent commonly available experience in freshly accessible ways, not the esoteric experiences of an elite few. This is as true of a neo-Classicist such as Pope, who aspires to write 'what oft was thought but ne'er so well expressed', as it is of an arch-Romantic such as Wordsworth, who aims at an enhanced sense of commonly available experience in 'the language that men do use'.

For most people most of the time, though, the most extra/ordinarily creative language resource available to them is conversation, whether in the forms of passing banter and informal chat or of full-blown discussion and formal debate. Thus Ron Carter both opens and closes his ground-breaking study *Language and Creativity: The Art of Common Talk* (2004) with the uncompromising observation that 'linguistic creativity is not simply a property of exceptional people but an exceptional property of all people' (Carter 2004: 13, 215). An extended example of so-called 'ordinary' conversation featured in Chapter 7 below (pp. 215–17) demonstrates that 'the art of common talk' is not simply a matter of the occasional use of puns, metaphors and other kinds of overtly playful language, but also the ways in which group identity may be extended and enriched through kinds of communal pattern building and transformation. Such strategies range from bouncing a key word or metaphor back and forth till it assumes a particular shape and force, through variations on rhythm, syntax and intonation, such as picking up and extending one another's sentences, to strategic matters of taking turns and developing topics. These features, as Carter insists, are 'not a capacity of special people but a special capacity of all people' (p. 215). That is what makes all genuinely creative activity, not just language, fundamentally 'extra/ordinary'. It is also, arguably, what makes creativity

. . . original and fitting

Standard definitions of creativity in the specialist literature tend to turn on a conception of creativity as something 'new and valuable' or 'novel and appropriate'. This section offers to replace these definitions with another in which the key terms ('original and fitting') are defined in deliberately ambiguous and capacious ways. First we consider the standard definitions. All are drawn from the *Handbook of Creativity* (1999), in which many prominent academics, chiefly from American departments of psychology, survey the current state of play in their respective areas of creativity research. Typical is the definition offered by the editor, Robert Sternberg (Sternberg 1999: 3): 'Creativity is the ability to produce work that is both novel (i.e. original, unexpected) and appropriate (i.e. adaptive concerning task constraints)'. Similar definitions are underwritten by most of the contributors. Thus we have 'novelty and value' (Gruber and Wallace, Chapter 5); 'original and appropriate' (Martindale, Chapter 7); 'something new that people find significant' (Lumsden, Chapter 8); and 'novel and adaptive solutions to problems' (Feist, Chapter 14). Still further variations are listed by Mayer (Chapter 22).

But there are exceptions. Lubart (Chapter 17) adds a significant qualification: 'creativity from a Western point of view can be defined as the ability to produce work that is novel and appropriate' (p. 339). This draws attention to other, non-Western, broadly 'Eastern' conceptions of creativity in which re-creation of 'the old' is valued, not just the generation of 'the novel' (counterparts in the West include kinds of traditionalism such as 'neo-Classicism'). Meanwhile, Boden (Chapter 18) makes the important distinction that 'novelty may be defined with reference either to the individual concerned or to the whole of human history' (p. 351). This allows for the fact that someone may make a discovery or experience a personal break-through (what Boden calls 'P-creativity', new to the person) but that it may be already known or at some time have been known (what she calls 'H-creativity', new in history).

These qualifications about the *relative* 'newness' of creativity can be still further qualified. We might add 'from a Western *modern* point of view' to Lubart's definition, and 'new to the person or new to history *in some context of ex/change*' to Boden's. Such fine tuning is necessary because it is the very project of modernity (of which most of the above researchers are arguably a part) that by definition promotes 'the new' as modern and downgrades 'the old' as ancient; and because precisely what is judged 'valuable' depends upon a complex, often contentious sense of changing 'values' and variable rates of exchange. For these reasons, the definition of creativity offered now is couched more circumspectly, in terms of what is 'original and fitting', with several different senses in play.

'Original' here, by design, carries ambiguous and diametrically opposed senses (see *OED* 'original' senses 1 and 2, and Williams 1983: 230–1). That is, it can mean 'from the beginning, former, ancient', (as in the phrase 'the original inhabitants') *and* it can mean 'fresh, new, novel, unexpected' (as in 'what an original idea!'). The former, ancient meaning of original was dominant until the middle of the eighteenth century; the latter meaning became dominant thereafter. Edward Young's *Conjectures on Original Composition* (1759) marks the turning point. Drawing an essentially modern, Romantic distinction between 'Imitations' and 'Originals', he loads the valuation firmly in favour of the latter: 'Originals are, and ought to be, great favourites, for they [. . .] add a new province. [. . .] Imitations only give us a sort of duplicate of what we had, possibly much better, before' (Young [1759] 1968: 273). Hence, via Kant and Coleridge, the observation by Wordsworth that the 'great and original writer' must 'create the taste by which he is to be relished' (see above p. 38).

Both the ancient and modern senses of 'original' were to persist, however. Emerson in the middle of the nineteenth century talks freely of the dynamic interchange between the 'original' soul of the individual poet (lower case, modern sense) and the 'Original' Over-Soul of the divine energy within Nature and Humanity at large (upper case, ancient sense) (*The Poet*, 1841 in Baym *et al.* 1994, Vol. 2: 1073). Indeed, both senses of 'original' happily co-exist right up to the present day, with phrases such as 'original recipe' trading on the prestige of tradition as well as the glamour of innovation, often with a conveniently fuzzy appeal to both.

There is, then, a significantly divided yet subtly intertwined and ongoing history of the two senses of 'original'. It can still mean both 'from the origins' (the oldest) and 'innovative' (the newest). Grasping the distinctions *and* connections between these two senses is crucial if there is to be an understanding of creativity that is itself both 'old' and 'new': historically informed and theoretically aware, sensitive to ancient precedent as well as modern preference. The same may be said of the other term with which 'original' is here paired.

'Fitting' in the physical sense refers to the process of 'filling an appropriate space' and, by extension, 'fulfilling an appropriate role or function' (see *OED* 'fitting' senses 1 and 2). For example, we may say of an engine that 'that part fits there', or more generally that something 'fits the bill'. 'S/he's fit!' is a colloquial expression in the UK meaning that someone is reckoned physically attractive, not just healthy. In all these ways to be 'fitting' is to be *appropriate* and in some way *approved*. However, as the last examples attest, there is also a social, aesthetic and now slightly archaic sense of 'fitting' meaning *acceptable* and (in earlier usage) *decorous*. The same applies to 'appropriate' when we accentuate the sense of 'propriety', what is 'proper' (hence 'appropriate/ proper behaviour' reckoned 'fitting' for the context).

The more particular prompt for the present conception of 'fitting' is a chapter in *On Creativity* (1998: 62–101) by the theoretical physicist and educational philosopher David Bohm. Based on the general proposition that 'In this art of life we have to be both creative artists and skilled artisans' (p. 86), Bohm develops a conception of creativity drawing upon the notion both of 'fitting' into old patterns that already exist *and* of finding new patterns that will 'fit' current and constantly changing circumstances, needs and desires. In general terms, he puts the matter thus (p. 86):

> We are always in the act of fitting an ever-changing reality so that there is no fixed or final goal to be attained. Rather, at each moment the ends and the means are both to be described as the action of making every aspect fit.

Using a more precisely mathematical and philosophical term, he expresses this sense of 'fitting' as the recognition and re-fashioning of the *ratio*, where the latter means 'proportion' and 'measure' as well as 'reason' or 'intelligibility'. Invoking both senses, Bohm argues that 'As in science, the essence of the art [of living] is in flashes of creative insight into new forms of universal ratio'. Thus when we perceive a fresh 'proportion/measure/ratio' in the world we achieve a whole new conception of what it is to be 'intelligible/reasonable/rational' – and by extension human.

This insight resonates closely with one of William Blake's more provocative pronouncements on art. Blake attacked Sir Joshua Reynolds's *Discourses on Art* (1798) for maintaining the conservative Enlightenment position that there was a single universal 'ratio' based upon one controlling perspective and harmony. Instead, Blake insisted that 'Reason, or a Ratio of All we have Known, is not the Same it shall be when we know More' (Annotations to Reynolds, *c.* 1808; also in 'There is No Natural Religion' 1788; see Blake 1972: 475, 97). This is remarkably close to Bohm and Peat's observation that whatever we say about creativity there is always 'something more and something different' (Bohm and Peat 2000: 226, and see above, p. 35). It also chimes with ideas that we examine in Chapter 6, found in the history and philosophy of science and specifically in the work of Thomas Kuhn and Michel Foucault. Both these thinkers insist, albeit in very different ways, that at every major turn in intellectual history there is a radical rethinking of the epistemological (knowledge-knowing) bases of humanity. For Bohm, who refers to neither Kuhn nor Foucault but in this respect agrees with both, the more accessible term corresponding to the mathematical concept of the 'ratio' is the process and practice of 'fitting'. And 'fitting', for Bohm as for me here, applies not only to the whole range of 'creative work carried out by different groups', it also embraces aesthetic and functional aspects of creativity. Again, the insight is simple and foundational (Bohm 1998: 86):

> Each human being *is* artist, scientist and mathematician all in one, in the sense that he is most profoundly concerned with aesthetic and emotional fitting, with practical and functional fitting, with universal rational fitting, and, more generally, with fitting between his world view and his overall experience with the reality in which he lives.

Bohm's concept of 'fitting' may therefore be compared with the more dynamic, less determinist models of biological adaptation and, more generally, evolution. But these, it should be stressed, refer to processes whereby organisms do not simply adapt to their environment but actively adapt it and are in turn adapted by it (see Ridley 1997: 109–58; Rose 1997). In a similarly complex and flexible sense, Anthony Storr makes the case for 'adaptation' being essential to the creative psychological development of the individual in relation to others (1972: 137–50). Indeed, the present sense of 'fitting' is quite compatible with the Darwinian notion of 'the survival of the fittest' – as long as it is remembered that the phrase is Herbert Spencer's (not Darwin's) and that it refers to the survival of those species or varieties which *in the event* turn out to have been 'most fit for their roles and relations', not 'fit' in the crude sense of 'physically strongest'. Of necessity, this is a 'fitness' that can only be confirmed in retrospect, by the act of survival. It may be provisionally projected but it certainly cannot be predicted in advance (compare Darwin, *The Origin of Species* (1859), Chapters 3 and 4).

   If we now put together the two parts of this definition – 'original' and 'fitting' – we get a conception of creativity that is itself pretty adaptable. It might be formulated like this:

> Creativity may be 'original' in the sense both of drawing on ancient origins and of originating something in its own right; either way, the overall aim or end is a

'fitting' – an active exploration of the changing proportions, measure, ratios – between older modes of understanding and newer ones.

Of course individual readers might come up with a formulation that is fresher or more to the point – something 'original and fitting' in their own terms. Derek Attridge, for instance, in a chapter on 'Originality and Invention', adapts Kant's notion of 'exemplary originality' so as to designate 'a particular kind of difference from what goes before, one that changes the field in question for later practitioners' (Attridge 2004: 36). This can be compared with Boden's 'Historical' as distinct from purely 'Personal' creativity (Sternberg 1999: Chapter 18). Further, Attridge develops Kant's 'exemplary originality' so that those who are truly original tend, paradoxically, to find 'fresh ways to be original in response to [another's] originality'. In other words, true originality helps prompt originality – not just imitation – in others. By extension, if there is anything 'original' in the present argument, it will be because it prompts you to go still further and as you see fit. The same goes for the next proposition – that creativity is

. . . full-filling

Here the emphasis is on creativity as a process of making oneself 'full' (hence the spelling) or, on further reflection, finding oneself already to be so. Its necessary complement is a process of 'emptying out', or, on reflection, finding oneself already to be 'empty'. Such ideas sound strange to modern Westerners used to thinking of creativity in terms of 'the new' and 'innovation'. Creativity within modern capitalism is especially identified with the creation of new products (new art objects, new technologies); just as Ezra Pound's injunction to 'Make it new!' was a rallying call to the modernist avant-garde (*ABC of Reading*, 1934: 29). However, a conception of creativity as 'filling full' in one respect while 'emptying out' in another is fundamental to many areas of imaginative, meditative and therapeutic practice. This process may be conceived as an alternating cycle or a simultaneous motion. But such ideas should not be confused with casually 'New Age' notions of personal 'wholeness' as a kind of individual spiritual hygiene. Rather, one must try to see this whole issue – and this issue of 'wholeness' – in terms that are both differently Western and non-stereotypically Eastern.

One way of countering narrow characterisations of creativity as a restless pursuit of 'the new' is to appeal to the ancient Greek root of the Latin verb *creare*. Greek *krainein* meant 'to fulfil', and 'by this definition, anyone who fulfils his or her potential, who expresses an inner drive or capacity [. . .] may be described as creative' (Evans and Deehan 1988: 20–1). Another way is to appeal to broadly 'Eastern' models of creative fulfilment through 'being' or 'becoming' rather than 'doing' or 'making'. In an important essay on 'Creativity across Cultures', Todd Lubart characterises the 'Eastern' view as follows (Lubart in Sternberg 1999: 339–50, here 340):

> The Eastern conception of creativity seems less focused on innovative products. Instead, creativity involves a state of personal fulfilment, a connection to a primordial realm, or the expression of an inner essence or ultimate reality. Creativity is related to meditation.

Such an 'Eastern' conception of creativity prompts several observations but also some qualification. It depends upon a highly selective and partly archaic construction of 'the East' in terms of, say, Buddhist meditative practices and the fine arts rather than modern car manufacturing and electronics (all are current in modern Japan). None the less it can be argued that there is a more explicit tradition of attention to the potential creativity of everyday practices such as cooking or the organisation of living spaces in the East than the West. Examples that readily spring to mind are the Japanese 'tea ceremony' and *feng shui*; though it should be added that these spring to mind precisely because they now circulate in palpably exoticised and readily exportable forms.

In fact, television viewers and magazine readers the world over are currently urged to scrutinise and transform ('make over') just about every aspect of their daily lives by media cooks, gardeners, designers and fashion pundits. In this respect, creativity both as 'personal fulfilment' and as something deeply 'ordinary' has global appeal as never before. And yet, commercially recycled as 'lifestyle', it is as commodifiable as any other object, idea or practice. What might be hailed as *creativity as personal lifestyle* – what Joas calls 'this self-image of creative individuality' – may then be recognised as 'the new repression' (Joas 1996: 253–4). In its place, following the social psychologist Abraham Maslow, Joas argues for a socially participative and politically engaged form of 'integrated creativity' (pp. 254–8). Foucault (1984) also offers a critique of merely off-the-peg or customised lifestyles and in their place proposes a much more personally ascetic and discriminatingly ethical and aesthetic notion of 'self-fashioning'. ('I *am* a work of art', Oscar Wilde insisted.)

There is, then, more to the matter of being creatively 'empty' – and therefore 'fullfilled' – than idle gestures and vacuous thoughts. We can also do more than invoke stereotypes of 'Eastern' practices such as yoga and t'ai chi or philosophies and religions such as Taoism and Buddhism as correctives to modern Western conceptions of the 'new' as almost automatically valuable (invigorating and salutary though such perspectives are). In fact, one of the main benefits for Westerners in trying to get an 'Eastern take' on creativity is that it prompts a fresh look at obscured or ignored religious and philosophical traditions in the West itself; for many intellectual traditions and religious practices in the West also emphasise creativity through awareness of kinds of 'wholeness' and absolute 'being', or of 'non-being' and ceaseless 'becoming'. Examples in Chapter 7 include the mystical sense of oneness with Christ described in Julian of Norwich's *Revelations*, and the alternative 'negative way' to God enjoined by the author of *The Cloud of Unknowing*, stripping away all the illusions of what appears to be to get at what really is. Both bear comparison with the kinds of enlightening 'Non/Being' that are identified in Eastern philosophies and religions (further considered in Chapter 5).

In the Western philosophical tradition as such, the explicit theorising of 'awareness' and 'circumspection' as kinds of creative act can be traced back at least as far as Herder (1744–1803). Conceiving 'genius' as a generally available capacity, Herder defines it as 'any ability to awaken human gifts and encourage them to fulfil their purpose' (see Joas 1996: 84). Other German Romantic philosophers such as Schiller, Schelling and Schopenhauer make similar statements, and their influence can be traced throughout the early American philosophical tradition: in the 'transcendental', nature-based philosophies of Emerson and Thoreau, and on to the pragmatic philosophies of 'experience' and 'life' of James and Dewey. (See Wheeler 1993 on these intertwined lines of development.) We may also note the concern with kinds of 'becoming' in the vitalist philosophy of Bergson, and with kinds of 'being' in the phenomenology of Husserl and Heidegger. The latter, in particular, developed a philosophy of 'being there' (*Dasein*) configured around ideas of 'dwelling' and 'building' (see Heidegger [1952] 1993: 343–64). Later philosophies influenced by vitalist and phenomenological traditions range from Sartre's existentialism to Deleuze and Guattari's preoccupation with kinds of 'becoming'. To complicate issues further, many of these European thinkers (including Schopenhauer and Heidegger) also drew on their own visions of Eastern religious and philosophical traditions.

Meanwhile, at the very core of contemporary nuclear physics, there has long been a recognition that matter/energy as we know it is neither more nor less than the elusive flickering into and out of existence of virtual particle/waves. This happens in a 'quantum vacuum', the defining characteristics of which are precisely that it is both empty and full, simultaneously and by turns (see Ridley 1976: 100–18 and Thuan 2001: 208–11, 345). The striking resemblance between this perspective on existence and that of many Eastern philosophical traditions has been frequently remarked upon (see Capra 1983: 229–72 and Peat 2000: 89–114). In all these ways, then, creative awareness conceived as a kind of meditative 'being there' and, more dynamically, as a process of empathic 'becoming' or a trembling on the interface of 'non/being', can be traced along a number of intersecting routes that knit 'West' and 'East' in ways that defy absolute distinction and deny glib opposition. However one comes at it, the fact is that the notion of creativity as a kind of contented 'full-fillment' – or alternatively a pregnant 'emptiness' – has a rich array of intellectual traditions, Eastern *and* Western, to support it. (For extension of the argument to African, Polynesian and other cultures, and a similar 'note of caution' on Western stereotypes of the East, see Carter 2004: 42–6.)

The ideas of creativity treated in this section may be summarised in three observations: (1) that creativity can be conceived in terms of more or less ordinary kinds of 'fulfilment', including the experiences of being or becoming 'emptied out' as well as 'filled full'; (2) that 'Eastern' models of creativity are a useful corrective to 'Western' models, as long as we remember that both are simplified and to some extent stereotypical constructs; (3) that none of these insights is exclusive to either tradition and that, as one commentator puts it, 'a blend of Eastern and Western models involves knowledge of the person as a creative, spontaneous expression *within* specific cultural and historical manifestations' (Kasulis 1981: 37). None of this points to a single, simple answer to 'what creativity is', but it encourages us to keep reformulating the question, and perhaps de-forming and re-forming the words, too. That is why, it is suggested, creativity can also be

. . . in(ter)ventive

This is a combination of the words 'inventive' and 'interventive': the latter word 'intervenes' in the former. Taken together, they express the fact that *inventions* (things such as the wheel, telescope or microchip, but also ideas such as democracy, scientific truth, progress) always represent *interventions* in an existing state of affairs. They introduce some change into life. The tense and radically unstable concept that is *in(ter)vention* will help articulate a sense of creativity in some of its more restlessly innovative aspects. In fact, 'in(ter)vention' can be seen in extreme opposition to the concept of 'full-filling' creativity – as long as we remember that extremes may meet or prove complementary and that there are always more opposites than two.

The words 'invention' and 'intervention' have a common root in the past participle (*ventum*) of Latin *venire*, 'to come'. Both 'inventing' and 'intervening' therefore carry a radical sense of 'coming': the former a 'coming-in', 'in-coming', 'entry' (*in-venire*); the latter a 'coming-between' or 'between-coming' (*inter-venire*). The two processes are distinct yet intricately connected. 'Invention', however, had an early sense almost diametrically opposed to its currently dominant sense. It meant 'finding or discovering what already exists' rather than, as now, 'making or bringing into being what never before existed' (cf. *OED* 'invention' senses 1 and 3). In classical rhetoric, where it is first used in a technical sense, *inventio* comprised 'the preliminary tasks of collecting, exploring, discovering or creating materials' (see 'Invention' in Preminger and Brogan 1993: 628–9). Only one of these tasks, notice, involves 'creating' narrowly conceived; the other three all involve finding, gathering and generally discovering. Thus in the Middle Ages the ceremony of the 'Invention of the Cross' meant the unveiling, processing and ritual 'coming-in' of the cross. Indeed, all the very earliest senses of invention are closer to the modern sense of 'discovery', the dis-covering or un-veiling of that which already exists – hence 'inventory' as a list of things.

The crucial moment in the changed understanding of 'invention' is signalled in Francis Bacon's *The Advancement of Learning* (Book 3, 3a; 1605). Rejecting 'the invention of speech or argument' as 'not properly an invention', he insists that 'to *invent* is to discover that [which] we know not, and not to recover or resummon that which we already know'. This modern sense of 'invention' meaning discovering what is not already known has persisted to the present day; and it continues to cause some confusion with 'discovery', even when the emphasis is upon invention in the sense of technical or technological innovation. Indeed, any full grasp of 'invention' always entails trying to get hold of the equally slippery term 'discovery'. For, while 'discovery' also means discovering (i.e. revealing) what was not previously known, the question of *who* gets to discover *what* and *when* remains decisive. Thus, the so-called 'Discovery of the New World' opened up the Americas and Australasia to Western invaders, colonisers and settlers from the sixteenth to eighteenth centuries, but these worlds were certainly not 'new' to the peoples who already lived there, i.e. the 'discovered'.

The broader implication is that someone's 'discovery of the new' may turn out to be someone else's 're-invention of the old'. A technological example of this is the (re-)invention – or (re-)discovery – of steam power (for in the event the prefix might plausibly attach to either). Michael Howe illustrates the point in a chapter on the dynamic between 'inventing and discovering' (Howe 1999: 176–87, here 176):

> For example, George Stephenson and James Watt have both been credited with inventing the steam engine, although neither of them actually did. Nor, strictly speaking, did Thomas Newcomen, who made the first practical steam-powered machine with moving parts. Newcomen built upon earlier developments by Savery. [. . .] Savery's innovations, in turn, were preceded by the written description of a steam turbine made sixteen hundred years earlier by the Greek mathematician Hero.

'Invention', then, is hardly ever a making-up entirely from scratch. It is the 'coming-in' and in effect the 'coming-together' of potentialities already available. In many cases these potentialities have already been grasped, albeit in different forms, by other people at different moments: hence the complex interrelations between what Boden terms 'P-creativity' (new to particular persons and times) and 'H-creativity' (new to history at large) (see above p. 57). Thus, while every invention is in some respects an *inter*vention, it may also be to some extent a *re*-invention. We return to this point at the end of the chapter.

The fully deconstructive – and ultimately *re*-constructive – implications of the view of in(ter)vention proposed here are explored by Derrida in 'Psyche: invention of the other' (Derrida 1992: 310–43). Initially delivered as two lectures, Derrida's paper opens with the words 'What am I going to be able to invent this time?' (*Que vais-je inventer encore?*). As the editor of the English translation notes, 'a rendering closer to the collo-quial meaning would be "What am I going to be able to come up with this time?"; for, 'as Derrida goes on to suggest, the implications of *encore* are multiple: "again," "once more," "still," "this time," "else" ("what else am I going to be able to invent?")' (p. 311, n. 1). None of this is mere sophistry, for it is precisely the act of 'inventing', poised between the old and new senses of the term, to which Derrida draws attention in this paper and the performance that occasioned it. Indeed it is the tension between the written paper and the actual lecture – to be even more precise, between what was scripted in advance, what was improvised in the event, and what was subsequently re-drafted for publication – that is the mainspring of the piece. Derrida explains it thus: 'the improvised speech will constantly remain unpredictable, that is to say, as usual, "still" ["*encore*"] new, original, unique – in a word, inventive'. Here the fully *inter*ventive force of Derrida's stance appears. Though he does not use the latter term himself, the potentially disruptive and interrupting sense of 'invention' is strong (p. 312):

> And in fact, by having at least invented something with his very first sentence, such an orator would be breaking the [rhetorical and academic] rules, would be breaking with convention, etiquette, the rhetoric of modesty. [. . .] An invention always presupposes some illegality, the breaking of an implicit contract: it inserts a disorder into the peaceful ordering of things, it disregards the proprieties.

In this way, the act of invention is both a rehearsal and a refusal of what is familiar and expected, a contribution to and an intervention in the occasion. Put another way, in terms with which Derrida is famously associated (but often infamously misrepre-sented), such invention is a form of 'deconstruction'. Indeed, Derrida says 'Decon-struction is invention or it is nothing at all' (p. 320). We must be careful, therefore, to place equal emphasis upon all the elements of *de-con-struction*: negative and positive, dedicated to building as well as unbuilding. (Such complexity is arguably already there in Heidegger's basically Nietzschean notion of *Destruktion*, which is where Derrida picks up the term before giving it his own twist; see Wolfreys 2001: 297.) The richly ambivalent resource of such concepts is clearly drawn upon towards the end of the piece. There Derrida confirms that his complex sense of 'invention' extends to matters of similarity/difference and self/other, in the name of what he there, for his purposes, calls 'deconstruction' – but what I here, for mine, call 'in(ter)vention' (Derrida 1992: 341):

It is in this paradoxical predicament that a deconstruction [in(ter)vention] gets under way. Our current tiredness results from the invention of the same and of the possible, from the invention that is always possible. It is not against it but beyond it that we are trying to reinvent invention itself, another invention, or rather an invention of the other that would come through the economy of the same.

Derrida's editor and translator, Derek Attridge, picks up and develops this sense of 'invention' in his own work (Attridge 2004: 35–62) and emphasises its status as an 'event' that is lived through, not just a fact that is recorded: 'Invention is always the invention of the other. And the other does not exist as an entity, but is lived through as an event' (compare above, p. 19). ('Event' is another word with a root in Latin *venire*; it means an 'out-come' or 'coming-out', *e-ventum*). The closing words of Derrida's paper/lectures draw attention to its status as an event and its own ongoing processes of de- and re-construction. For, by the end, it too will have been 'only an invention, the invention of the other'. But even this is immediately countered and the piece concludes with a gesture to an alternative possibility: 'that the other is what is never inventable, and will never have waited for your invention. The call of the other is a call to come, and that happens only in multiple voices' (Derrida 1992: 343).

We too have come to the end of a section. *In the event*, we are 'coming out' at a point similar yet significantly different from where we 'came' in. There have also been various kinds of intervention ('coming between'), drawing on – and in – the words of people other than myself, though, clearly, I have de- and re-constructed their texts and arguments to serve as parts of the present one. Again (*encore*), it is up to you, the reader, to decide whether these various 'comings' amount to something worth developing in your own terms. After all, you may favour both or neither of the key terms on offer here: *de-con-struction* or *in(ter)vention*. In that case you are at liberty to invent and intervene in (discover, re-invent, find, make, . . .) or de-and re-construct (break down, make up, piece together, transform, . . .) any other term that for you is more fulfilling or seems more original and fitting (see previous two sections). In any event, you are still urged to keep yet other possibilities – including all sorts of possible others – very much in mind. For creativity, it is suggested, is also

. . . co-operative

Creativity is rarely, if at all, a matter of the individual creator creating in splendid or miserable isolation. Rather, in the terms of an important article by David Harrington on 'The ecology of human creativity', it is a matter of 'people working in intended or unintended collaboration' (Harrington in Runco and Albert 1990: 143–69, here 144). The corresponding term in the 'sentence' underpinning this chapter is *co-operation*, punctuated with a hyphen and pronounced with the stress on 'co-'. It basically means 'operating together' and can be more precisely defined as *working and playing with and with respect to others*. This picks up and extends the tail end of the preliminary definition of creativity in the 'before the beginning' section of this book.

Several things need to be emphasised in such a *co*-operative view of creativity. Firstly, it involves 'working and playing' and 'work as play', and vice versa, in the senses offered by Willis when talking about 'common culture' and Carse when talking about 'infinite games' (see above p. 12, below pp. 122–3). It is a shared, ongoing process of change through exchange. Secondly, co-operation entails action that is undertaken 'with respect to others': in relation to other people *and* with a recognition of the rights of others to their own voices and positions. Ethically, this requires that the latter do not inhibit those of others; psychologically, it embraces 'the other' within as well as beyond 'the self'. Thirdly, by extension, co-operation entails the recognition of differences and the right to express alternative preferences. It therefore acknowledges and even invites kinds of dissent and disagreement: not just 'co-operation' in the weakly expedient sense of 'going along with what is expected or required'; nor the kind of insistence upon 'co-operation' that comes with a veiled threat of coercion. Fourthly, *co*-operation in the presently preferred sense involves kinds of interaction indirectly and at a distance, in different spaces and times, not just direct collaboration in a shared space- and time-frame. It includes kinds of highly mediated production and reproduction as well as intertextuality and influence of a more or less indirect and perhaps unconscious kind. Finally, this whole conception of *co*-operation may be compared with Bakhtin's complexly dynamic notion of 'responsiveness/response-ability/ responsibility' (*otvetsvenost*); and more particularly with his notion of 'co-being' as a form of shared and evolving consciousness (*sobytie*; see Morris 1994: 246–9). Though even then, to follow the spirit and not just the letter of Bakhtin's project and to be consistent with my own, I would prefer to speak of '*co-becoming*'. In any event, such *co*-operation entails an ethics as well as an aesthetics of response, and a politics as well as a poetics of participation and engagement. To co-operate in this sense, you don't have to – and arguably shouldn't – agree with anyone completely!

Clearly, this view of creativity has little in common with the hyper-individualistic notion of the solitary genius: the lone artist in his garret or the isolated scientist slaving in his laboratory. Such stereotypes have a great deal to do with the late Romantic, especially mid-nineteenth-century, mythology of creation. But, as we see in Chapter 7, they have little to do with the actual creative practices of most scientists and artists, including the Romantics. Equally clearly, however, the present conception of co-operation recognises and celebrates the essential contribution of kinds of individual (but not necessarily individualist) input. As with a genuinely dynamic model of conversation, the whole thing depends upon there being spaces and opportunities for the expression of individual differences and alternative preferences without any single voice or point of view dominating (for an example, see pp. 215–17). In this way, being fully and creatively co-operative has as little to do with 'stealing the show' as it does with 'going with the flow'.

Other contemporary theories of creativity point in similar directions. The present view of co-operation corresponds to what Joas, prompted by the social psychologist Maslow, characterises as 'integrated creativity'. This occurs when 'the openness of self-articulation is wedded to the responsibility of self-control'; it underwrites a degree of personal 'autonomy' while precluding private 'anomie' and a sense of social 'alienation' (Joas 1996: 253–8). Bohm develops a relatable concept in his notion of 'participatory thought'. He developed this from an earlier notion of 'collective thought' and, by way of refinement, insisted that thought is only genuinely creative when one is capable of acknowledging and to some extent adopting the roles of other participants and observers (Bohm 1996: 48–60, 84–95). 'Participatory think*ing*', to emphasise its ongoing aspect, is very much in line with Bohm's notion of creativity as a process of dynamic and reciprocal 'fitting' considered above. It also draws on his experience as a theoretical physicist, where the observer is always a participant in the event and the very act of measuring affects what is to be measured. (In this respect every observation is also an 'intervention' in the sense traced in the previous section.) Further, the whole emphasis upon dual observer/participant status chimes with an ethnographic approach to social and cultural studies, where events are represented experientially from within and not just observed experimentally from outside. Meanwhile, in philosophical terms, we are talking about a radical reconfiguration of subject/object relations such that the subject can be conceived as a part of as well as apart from the object, and vice versa. We pick up these issues in the section on 'un/conscious'.

What is here called a *co*-operative approach to creativity is crucial, then, if we are to avoid mere self-expression on the one hand and sheer social subjectification on the other. The downside of the former is self-indulgence and solipsism ultimately leading to an audience of one (the performer alone); the downside of the latter is a hollow ventriloquism or politics of correctness in which one only speaks to represent the imagined many, never oneself. Co-operatively speaking, however, whenever there is genuine exchange there is always a potential for change, with alternatives beyond as well as between: simply 'being together' openly and responsively generates the possibility of 'becoming otherwise'.

To point up these issues, there follows an examination of an influential model of creativity drawn from systems theory. This, too, is offered in a spirit of creative *co*-operation: there are some fundamentally useful things about this model that should be more widely recognised, and others that may need to be modified and built up differently.

> [W]hat we call creativity is a phenomenon that is constructed through an *interaction between producers and audience*. Creativity is not the product of single individuals, but of social systems making judgements about individuals' products.
> (Csikszentmihalyi in Sternberg 1999: 313)

This is the definition of creativity offered by Mihalyi Csikszentmihalyi in his essay 'Implications of a systems perspective for the study of creativity' (Sternberg 1999: 313–35). The essay offers a refined and condensed theoretical re-statement of the 'systems approach' to creativity developed in the author's book-length study, *Creativity: Flow and the Psychology of Discovery and Invention* (Csikszentmihalyi 1996; espescially Chapters 1 and 2; cf. Gardner 1998). As with all systems approaches, the emphasis is upon the interrelations and interactions among physical entities and social identities, not the id/entities in isolation.

Csikszentmihalyi distinguishes two areas of the social system in which the creative person or product is realised and recognised: the *cultural domain*, the specific discipline or discourse in which an activity takes place (artistic, scientific, academic, commercial, etc.); and the *social field*, which is made up of the 'competent' judges and arbiters in that area (reviewers, specialists, editors, directors, etc.) 'Creativity', he insists, 'is a process that can be observed only at the intersection where individuals, domains, and fields interact' (Csikszentmihalyi in Sternberg 1999: 315). As a result, the criteria for what is creative vary from one domain to another. Partly this is because of the fairly obvious point that different activities draw on different materials, skills and knowledges. You might be able to compare one great omelette with another, and one great jazz riff with another – but how do you compare an omelette with a jazz riff, and either of them with a painted landscape? (It is just this problem that Scruton ignores in his comparison between Mozart and Emin; see above pp. 22–3.)

An important theoretical consequence of a systems approach is that to some extent we had better talk of 'systems of creativity' or simply 'creativities' rather than look for some singular 'creativity' common to every domain. This accords with a 'multiple intelligences' view of people's different capacities, rather than expecting everyone to be measurable according to a standard IQ test (see Gardner 1993a, 1998). Another consequence is that we need to view each form or mode of creativity in relation to the communities, social organisations and institutions whereby it is judged and promoted. Csikszentmihalyi focuses most of his attention in this latter area: 'What is meant by creativity is not a real objective quality, but refers only to the acceptance by a particular field of judges.' Moreover, this applies 'at every level, from considering Nobel Prize nominations to considering the scribbles of four-year-olds'. In each and every domain, therefore, 'fields are busy assessing new products and deciding whether they are creative or not' (Csikszentmihalyi in Sternberg 1999: 316). This would, for example, transfer attention from the intrinsic value of Rushdie's *Midnight's Children* to the panels of judges who chose it for the Booker Prize in 1981 and for the 'Booker of Bookers' in 1993, and beyond them to the complexes of commercial, artistic and academic interests in which such prizes are implicated. If one *were* to look for an overall mode or model of creativity in such a systems approach it is likely to come down to the *relative* valuing of the various domains within a given culture as a whole: how far cooking, say, is rated in relation to painting. That in turn might occasion a political-historical consideration of the whole matter of 'taste', 'discrimination' and 'judgement' across and between the domains of popular and high art culture, for instance, along with the gendered and ethnic dimensions of such domains and their respective fields. The system in which Csikszentmihalyi's particular 'systems approach' operates is more social and contemporary than political and historical, but a powerful exemplar of the latter kind of work is Pierre Bourdieu's *Distinction: A Social Critique of the Judgement of Taste* (1984).

This brings us to a critique of the systems approach as practised by Csikszentmihalyi. Firstly, for all his sensitivity to social networks and contexts, he still privileges the notion of the creator as a 'person' (singular). This plays down creativity as an overtly collective or collaborative activity, and presupposes a relatively stable and unified human subject. Secondly, he does not fully allow for activity *between* domains, or for the radically creative challenge of *inter*disciplinary or *cross*-cultural exchanges resulting in *hybrid* forms. Thirdly, though he recognises that the 'judges' who make up a 'field' may vary and differ, he does not tackle the fact that the really creative (or crazy) act may be ignored or suppressed by currently dominant judges, who may be inclined to dismiss everything beyond their ken as, say, dangerous or banal. In other words, he plays down the personal and political struggles that characterise the making *and breaking* of the authorities and institutions themselves. Thus, though it is socially aware, Csikszentmihalyi's model of authority – and by extension creativity – is finally consensual. Like Stanley Fish's account of 'interpretive communities', it is fine at explaining how those who share interpretive strategies come to share them, but not at how new interpretations, strategies and communities arise (see Fish [1980] in Leitch 2001: 2067–89 and compare Eliot and Williams below, pp. 96–7).

For similar reasons, the present *co*-operative understanding of creativity should be distinguished from the 'co-operative maxims' proposed for the analysis of conversation by the linguistic philosopher H. P. Grice (Grice [1967] in Jaworski and Coupland 1999: 76–88). These, too, are consensual and arguably normative in that for the purpose of logical analysis they presuppose that the ultimate aim of conversation is agreement. There are four basic maxims and they work on the premise that participants in conversation should seek to: (1) give adequate information; (2) tell the truth; (3) be relevant; and (4) avoid obscurity; to which later commentators have added, (5) be polite. Now, there is no problem with Grice's maxims as a kind of 'ideal world' analytical tool-kit, but applying them to naturally occurring language situations and expecting them to be met is another matter. 'Real world' exchanges are rarely in a simple sense a matter of telling 'the truth, the whole truth and nothing but the truth' (as English law requires of witnesses under oath); for one of the reasons for talking about anything with other people is that you do not share their experience of it, though perhaps you would like to.

Grice himself turns out to be more interested in the ways in which people accidentally 'violate' or deliberately 'flout' these maxims, as they consistently say more or less than is required, tell lies or part-truths, are irrelevant or obscure – and sometimes impolite. Despite the negative force of Grice's 'violate' and 'flout', though, being 'unco-operative' is not necessarily a bad thing. Indeed, we may speak more positively of, say, 'assertive principles', and thereby avoid the merely negative sense of *unco*-operative meaning 'awkwardly aggressive' or, conversely, 'submissive' (for further discussion, see Pope 1995: 127–30). All we need note here is that being creatively 'co-operative' in the present sense takes issue with the sense proposed by Grice in so far as it has been misapplied or over-extended. And that, *arguably*, is precisely what he and I are talking about. Indeed, *arguing* – which includes agreeing as well as disagreeing – is what I am also happy to do with Csikszentmihalyi's 'systems view' of creativity. The arguments he presents are stimulating to 'co-operate' with precisely because they help you sharpen your own. Thus I welcome his gesture towards the possibility that 'creativity can be seen as a special case of evolution' (Csikszentmihalyi in Sternberg 1999: 316) – but I suggest that he fails to grasp the *post*structural implications of a systems approach pushed to its logical and evolutionary limits. In radically evolutionary terms, such a system is itself both open and in process. (These issues I pick up in Chapter 4.) All that said, Csikszentmihalyi's systems-based approach offers a powerful corrective to notions of creativity focused exclusively on creators or on creative products. Though it tends to leave certain categories such as 'individual' and 'community' relatively undisturbed, there is much that is bracing or, for some, abrasive in the conclusion that 'In the last analysis, it is the community and not the individual who makes creativity manifest' (Csikszentmihalyi in Sternberg 1999: 333).

Creative co-operation also has its technological dimensions. Harrington's 'ecology of creativity', referred to earlier in this section, moves as freely across the human–machine as the human–nature interface. Working from the premise that 'life processes are sustained by functional relationships and interdependencies', he observes that 'the ecological study of human creativity will almost surely need to include a role for the concept of information and information flow that is in some respects analogous to but importantly different from the concept of energy and energy flow in biological ecosystems' (Harrington in Runco and Albert 1990: 151). In its emphasis upon 'flow' this recalls Bergson's view of 'creative evolution', and it is an insight and an image that informs Csikszentmihalyi's *Creativity: Flow and the Psychology of Discovery and Invention* (1996).

But at this point I must invite your co-operation, too, for I was unsure whether to put the section on 'un/conscious' or the section on 'fe<>male' next. Which comes first: being conscious or being conscious of being female or male? Or is there an undifferentiated unconscious state that is strictly neither female nor male? In the present context, the basic issue is whether we can think of human creativity without (1) thinking of thinking as itself a creative act; (2) thinking of sex. I have put the following sections in that order, but I ask you to co-operate by turning to whichever you have a mind to – or thinking of something else entirely

. . . un/conscious

It is a commonplace of contemporary popular thinking about creativity that it springs from 'unconscious' processes (see Ghiselin 1985 for examples). This is especially so where creativity is associated with stereotypically Romantic notions of 'inspiration' or 'genius'. Where once were inspiration by gods and muses and the spontaneous workings of natural genius are now, it seems, the unseen promptings and subterranean eruptions of unconscious desires, hopes, fears. Psychology has taken over the roles previously assumed by religion and myth in providing the dominant discourse for the more mysterious aspects of the creative process.

But what do we mean by 'the Unconscious'? Should it really be a singular noun prefaced with a definite article and graced with a capital letter, and treated as a specific 'thing'? (This, following Freud, was for long the dominant usage in psychoanalysis.) Or should it be treated in a lower key and in lower case – as in, say, 'unconscious' processes – where the term functions grammatically as an adjective and perceptually as an attribute of something else? (This is the form preferred here, because it keeps the concept fluid.) What is more, can we think about the term without at least some sense of its obverse: 'consciousness' (the noun) and 'conscious' (the adjective)? These are the concepts being negated, and historically they are prior to the 'un-' forms (see *OED* 'conscious', Williams 1983: 320–4 and Lewis [1967] 1990: 181–213). The relation between what is 'conscious' and what is 'unconscious' must be conceived as a dynamic and reciprocally defining process: you can't think about one without at least assuming the other. Nor can you get beyond merely binary thinking without developing a synthesis that includes and eventually exceeds both. That is why *un/conscious* is here offered as a slashed term, representing 'both/and more' not just 'either-or'.

The first recorded use of the phrase 'the unconscious' in English is by Samuel Taylor Coleridge in his *Biographia Literaria* (1817, Chapter 17), where it is expressly braced against 'the conscious'. Talking of 'Poesy or Art', he observes that 'In every work of art there is a reconcilement of the external with the internal; the conscious is so impressed upon the unconscious as to appear in it.' Coleridge is taking his cue from German idealist philosophers in that art is conceived as a kind of coming together ('reconcilement') of apparently contrary states or impulses: outer and inner, conscious and unconscious. Freud was also a direct heir to this tradition and, though he gave it a decisively psychoanalytic twist, he inherited both its residual idealism (notably the building of totalising intellectual structures) and its persistent dualism (especially evident in Freud's opposition between ego and id, 'self' and 'other' and, as we see now, 'conscious' and 'unconscious' processes).

In his *Note on the Unconscious* (1912) and *The Unconscious* (1915) (Freud 1986: 135–83), Freud made two observations that were to prove decisive in twentieth-century conceptions of the relations between what came to be seen as 'consciousness' and 'the Unconscious': (1) that much of the Unconscious is the result of an active *repression* of conscious awareness – the 'forgetting' of a traumatic experience from early childhood, for instance – and (2) that the workings of the Unconscious may be deliberately accessed through such techniques as hypnosis and psychoanalysis, or be incidentally revealed through such everyday activities as dreaming, day-dreaming or slips of the tongue. Either way, what is repressed in the Unconscious tends to get indirectly expressed in consciousness. We may therefore talk of *un/conscious* processes in terms of a dynamic interplay of *repression/expression*. Once again, you can't grasp the one without the other. This fact is crucial to most psychological understandings of creativity, whether the routinely unconscious creativity of what Freud called 'dream work' or the more conscious creativity of literature and art.

Freud had a complex attitude to literature and art. From the point of view of a cultivated Austrian intellectual, he revered great writers and artists. He also saw their project as fundamentally continuous with his own: 'The poets and philosophers before me discovered the unconscious. What I discovered was the scientific method by which the unconscious can be studied' (Freud [1908] in Lodge 1972: 35). Thus, just as he explored dreams and their systematic analysis as a 'royal road to the unconscious' in *The Interpretation of Dreams* (1900), so he hailed the extraordinary power of great artists such as Leonardo da Vinci, of whom he made a special study in 1910. Freud therefore both imbibed and endorsed the 'great man' view of 'genius' current in his day. Indeed, in his heroically individual labours as the self-appointed founder and acknowledged 'father' of psychoanalysis, he made a claim to being treated as just such a 'genius' himself (see Gardner 1998: 69–86).

However, in his attempts to apply a psychological model to literature, Freud's approach to creativity tends to look more reductive than reverential. In 'Creative writers and day-dreaming' (1908), for example, he conflates creative writing with day-dreaming, and both of them with a particular version of 'child's play'. He works on the assumption that 'a piece of creative writing, like a day-dream, is a continuation of and a substitute for what was once the play of childhood' (Freud [1908] in Lodge 1972: 35–42, here p. 41). This assumption depends upon a notion of day-dreams as 'fantasies' and 'castles in the air', and a concept of 'child's play' that is firmly braced against 'reality' conceived as adult, 'when the child has grown up and ceased to play'. What draws these things together is the notion that fantasies, child's play and creative writing are neither more nor less than forms of 'wish-fulfilment' and a compensation or consolation for a basically unsatisfactory reality: 'The motive forces of fantasies are unsatisfied wishes, and every single fantasy is the fulfilment of a wish, a correction of unsatisfying reality' (p. 38). From the reader's point of view, meanwhile, the chief attraction of fiction seems to be a kind of self-indulgent escapism: the opportunity 'to enjoy our own day-dreams without self-reproach or shame' (p. 42).

Freud's is basically a 'deficit' model of creativity. Art and literature seek to correct and compensate for a fundamentally unsatisfying reality, where reality is resolutely 'adult'. For better and worse, 'play' is what gets left behind in childhood; and there is an air of something suspiciously childish about creative writers and artists in so far as they persist in 'playing' into adulthood. To be sure, Freud's work in general, especially in its more mythic dimensions, supplies a rich mine for literary critics and cultural theorists. His version of the Oedipus complex helps inform Bloom's notion of the struggle between 'strong' poets and their poetic 'precursors' (see Chapter 4); and ego and id, usually in the company of the super-ego, continue to stalk many a critical discourse. Freud's case studies, too – of 'the Wolf Man', 'Little Hans' and 'Dora' – clearly recall the then-popular genre of detective fiction; and in Freud's case the culprit, tracked down by himself as master sleuth, is invariably revealed to be some traumatic event repressed from childhood. These are now widely recognised as 'creative' works in their own right.

But the dominant note in Freud's work is that *all* civilised life is a more or less (un)successful attempt to come to terms with a basically intractable, austerely adult reality. 'Beyond the pleasure principle' – to recall the title of one of his essays – it is also beyond play as such. Indeed, his *Civilisation and its Discontents* (1930) makes 'civilisation' virtually synonymous with its 'discontents'. At best civilisation offers a 'sublimation' of potentially harmful neuroses and psychoses by displacing and transforming them. At worst it causes them. For in Freud's model, while expression may offer a release from repression, it can also act as a mask for it. It all depends what 'wishes' are being 'fulfilled' and at what cost to the psyche. By a similar mechanism, consciousness may achieve temporary states of equilibrium with the unconscious; but it may just as often be disturbed and deranged by it. Indeed, and this is the gloomy tenor of the work, 'civilisation' may lead to the Unconscious being so comprehensively repressed that 'dis-ease' and 'discontent' become the apparent norm. Critics and theorists of art and literature are still drawn to Freud's work; but his appeal to creative practitioners is noticeably weaker.

The reverse may be said of the work of Carl Jung, Freud's one-time collaborator and subsequent critic. Sometimes summarily dismissed by academic critics, he is still widely read in artistic circles (see Ghiselin 1985, Ward Jouve 1998). The split between Jung and Freud opened up around their very different conceptions of the unconscious, and we might usefully consider their different understandings of the part played by unconscious processes in creative life. In *Psychology of the Unconscious* (1912) Jung criticises Freud for a narrowly individualistic notion of the psyche, as though the unconscious were formed almost exclusively from the repressed experiences of a person's childhood. Crucially, Jung distinguishes between what he terms the 'personal unconscious' (the part of the unconscious built up by each person individually) and the 'collective unconscious' (the reservoir of instinctual energies and the repertoire of persistent images shared by humanity at large). For Jung, then, 'Every creative person is a duality or synthesis of contradictory aptitudes. On the one side he is a human being with a personal life, while on the other side he is an impersonal creative force' (Jung [1912] 1976: 123). This makes for a very different conception of creativity to that of Freud.

We can trace the implications further in Jung's essay 'On the relation of analytical psychology to poetry' (1922). Here Jung accuses Freud of a 'pathological' view of creativity and insists that 'a work of art is not a disease' (Jung [1922] 1976: 301–21, here p. 308). Jung then identifies two contrasting yet complementary character-types ('introverted' and 'extraverted') and shows how both are essential to the creative process. The *introverted* attitude 'is characterised by the subject's assertion of his conscious intentions and aims against the demands of the object. [. . .] His material is entirely subordinated to his artistic purpose' (pp. 310–11). This is creativity as conscious design by the creator. The *extraverted* attitude, meanwhile, 'is characterised by the subject's subordination to the demands which the object makes upon him' (p. 311). This is creativity as an overwhelming of the creator by the unconscious: 'While his conscious mind stands amazed and empty [. . .] he is overwhelmed by a flood of thoughts and images which he never intended to create and which his own will could never have brought into being' (p. 310). It is important to observe, however, that for Jung *both* these attitudes are potential paths to creativity: 'He [the artist] is wholly at one with the creative process, whether he has deliberately made himself its spearhead, as it were, or whether it has made him its instrument so completely that he has lost all consciousness of the fact.' The ultimate aim or eventual result is the same: 'In either case, the artist is so identified with his work that his intentions and faculties are indistinguishable from the act of creation' (p. 310).

Jung's recognition of two sides to creativity – conscious design and unconscious force – in some respects recalls conventional distinctions between Classicism, which emphasises deliberate craft and rules, and Romanticism, which stresses spontaneous expression and impulse. It also finds a parallel in a pioneering work on creativity by Jung's contemporary Graham Wallas. In *The Art of Thought* (1926), Wallas proposes a (still influential) model of the creative process in terms of alternations of conscious and unconscious activity. Picking up insights first offered by the mathematician Henri Poincaré, Wallas distinguishes four stages through which most creative actions go (Wallas [1926] in Vernon 1970: 91–7):

- *Preparation* – 'when the problem is investigated in all directions'
- *Incubation* – a period of 'not consciously thinking about the problem'
- *Illumination* – 'the appearance of the happy idea'
- *Verification* – the conscious testing of the solution.

For Wallas, the periods of more or less unconscious Incubation and Illumination are central to the creative process, flanked by more or less conscious stages of Preparation and Verification. His is still basically a problem-*solving* model of the creative process, however, and its consecutively staged progression can seem rather mechanical. A version re-cast in terms of problem-*posing* would insist on at least one prior stage where the vague idea of a problem is sensed, and would treat the 'consecutive stages' as levels that might be accessed at any point, simultaneously or by turns, and on more than one occasion (see Sternberg 1999: 107–8). That said, Wallas's model of the interplay of conscious and unconscious factors in the creative process is a handy point of departure if not of arrival, which puts simply and schematically what Jung expressed more diffusely and discursively.

More problematic is Jung's emphasis upon a specifically 'collective' unconscious as the chief well-spring of creativity. This he expressly posits as a creative source 'not in the personal consciousness of the poet, but in a sphere of unconscious mythology whose primordial images are the common heritage of mankind' (Jung [1922] 1976: 319). Further, for Jung, 'The creative process [. . .] consists in the unconscious activation of an archetypal image' (p. 321). This has led to Jung being accused of vaguely universalising and patently unhistorical gestures; and there is some justification for such accusations. (Once he starts looking for them, Jung finds mandalas – a meditative device and symbol of power combining a cross and floral design – just about everywhere.) But to concentrate only on such excesses would be to miss the larger picture: Jung is careful to add that 'the social significance of art' is precisely that 'it is constantly at work educating the spirit of the age, conjuring up the forms in which the age is most lacking'. He also insists that the function of the artist is 'to discover what it is that would meet the unconscious needs of the age' (p. 322). In other words, this is a supplementary and potentially celebratory model of creativity, constantly retuned to historical and cultural circumstance and alert to the needs of the moment. Certainly it is not Freud's deficit model of creativity as a kind of sublimated pathology.

Jung particularly emphasises the process of finding one's 'personal unconscious' *through* the 'collective unconscious', not losing oneself *in* it. He terms this process 'individuation'. As Anthony Storr points out, this has nothing to do with the individual conceived as a notionally finished or self-sufficient entity, but rather, in openly evolutionary terms, the constantly 'fresh adaptation of individuals to and of their circumstances' (Storr 1972: Chapters 11 and 18, and here Storr in Abbs 1989: 183–97). In Jung's own definition, 'Individuation means nothing less than the optimum development of the whole individual human being [. . .] because the constant flow of life again and again demands fresh adaptation' (Jung [1933] in Abbs 1989: 184).

In later psychology and contemporary cultural theory there exist many more models of the relations between consciousness and the unconscious, many of which have a bearing on conceptions of creativity. In Chapter 4 we shall review the models and methods not only of post-Freudians and post-Jungians but also of psychoanalysts and psychotherapists who belong to different traditions altogether. For example, we observe how Lacan gives the whole matter a decisively linguistic turn by exploring 'the insistence of the letter [language] in the unconscious' and, further, opens it out to a poststructuralist critique by insisting upon 'the self's radical ex-centricity to itself'. We also note Kristeva's emphasis upon the 'revolutionary' potential of the specifically 'semiotic' unconscious and her insistence upon 'abject' positions radically alternative to those of conventional subject–object relations. Meanwhile, in connection with both 'genius' and 'genetics', we explore aspects of behaviour being brought to light by current work on neural networks and brain activity in neuro-psychology. All these have a bearing on the kinds of creativity that result from the constant crossing and redrawing of all sorts of boundaries (not just the un/conscious interface). They also show how these may be mapped in terms of overlapping 'fields' or traced through systems of 'parallel processing'.

In fact, many of these models of consciousness work perfectly well without an 'unconscious'. Instead, they involve levels or stages of *more or less* conscious processing. Dennett favours this model in his influential *Consciousness Explained* (1991). Shades or kinds of consciousness contribute to an overall effect through what Dennett calls 'multiple drafting' at sensory, emotional and cognitive levels. The result is complexly layered and subtly textured, but does not require any 'absent', 'hidden' or 'secret' ingredient such as 'the unconscious' to make it work. Comparable models are developed by Calvin (1997: 113–44) and Damasio (2000: 317–35). In none of these cases is it necessary to posit the working of an essentially ineffable, unknowable unconscious in order to explain the sense of being 'moved' from within by a power apparently beyond the self/ego. This can be accounted for by 'cognitive dissonance' and kinds of productive or disruptive 'mismatch' in the processing at various levels. These are *in principle* knowable, even if in practice they are difficult to gauge or control. Nor is the notion of multiple consciousness without an unconscious only the brainchild of contemporary cognitive psychologists. Philosopher and psychologist William James, also famous for coining the phrase 'stream of consciousness', was an influential proponent of a model that involved many stages and levels of consciousness, with no need for the 'unconscious' of his younger contemporaries Freud and Jung. In his *The Varieties of Religious Experience* ([1901] 1970: 221) James writes: 'the world of our present consciousness is only one of many worlds of consciousness that exist, and these other worlds must contain experiences which have meaning for our life also.'

This should not surprise us. 'Consciousness' had a long history in philosophy before it was introduced in psychology and then paired with the relative newcomer 'the unconscious'. Hegel, for example, saw all human history as the gradual, dialectical development of higher levels of consciousness, and assigned the Arts a crucial role in this process (notably in his *Lectures on Fine Art*, 1835). Marx gave that dialectic a materialist and social-historical twist in his preface to *The Critique of Political Economy* (1859) by maintaining that 'It is not the consciousness of men that determines their being, but, on the contrary, their social being that determines their consciousness' (Marx 1963: 67). As a result, notions of being or becoming conscious have been identified with the most sublime philosophical speculations and the most pressing political problems. Indeed, it is the recognition that the personal is not only psychological but also political and philosophical that makes debates on the dynamics of the (un)conscious both fraught and fascinating. A prime example is Macherey's *A Theory of Literary Production* ([1966] 1978), where the point at issue (as we saw in Chapter 1) is precisely the relation between what the text does *not* or can*not* say (its psychologically repressed or politically suppressed subject matter) and what it appears to say on the surface (its manifestly expressed subject matter). Fredric Jameson, in his *The Political Unconscious* (1981), also recognises the psychopolitical force of narrative as a double-edged act of repression/oppression and expression. The stories and histories we tell can serve to raise consciousness (by commemorating and celebrating, for example) but they can also plunge back into the unconscious (by omission or distortion) all that is uncomfortable to remember or convenient to forget.

We conclude this section with a review of two very different contemporary constructions of consciousness and the very different models of creativity they underwrite. One is from firmly within mainstream academic psychology and clinical psychiatry. The other is fiercely opposed to the dominant practices of both. The first is Kay Redfield Jamison's *Touched with Fire* (1994), which, its subtitle confirms, is a study of 'manic depressive illness and the artistic temperament'. Jamison is a professor of psychiatry who has both suffered from manic-depressive illness and co-written a standard medical text on the subject. The argument of *Touched with Fire* is that what is commonly known as 'the artistic temperament' (characterised by mood swings and erratic or eccentric behaviour) bears a close resemblance to what is currently called 'manic-depressive illness'. Earlier names for this condition include 'mania' and 'melancholia', and in the eighteenth and nineteenth centuries it was sometimes (mis)diagnosed as 'hysteria', especially in the case of women. Jamison's argument for the link between manic-depressive illness and creativity is supported by extensive clinical profiles of manic-depressive illness (milder states of which are known as 'cyclothymia') and by an array of historical case studies featuring writers, composers and artists, from Byron, Schumann and Van Gogh to Woolf and Sexton. A similar case is made by Storr (1972: Chapters 7 and 16) but on Freudian and Jungian grounds.

Jamison argues that there is 'a compelling association, not to say actual overlap, between two temperaments – the artistic and the manic-depressive', and that what is common to these temperaments is 'their contrary and oppositional qualities, their flux, their extremes' (Jamison 1994: 5). The book's extensive analytical tables and family-trees are particularly thought-provoking. The tables list hosts of 'Writers, artists and composers with probable cyclothymia, major depression or manic-depressive illness', and include a key to those who had periods in asylums or psychiatric hospitals as well as information on suicides and attempted suicides (pp. 267–70). Family-trees for the Byrons, Tennysons, Jameses and Woolfs chart the course of these (in part hereditary) diseases over several generations (pp. 191–237). What in Jamison's view distinguishes the various members of these families is how far they managed to cope with manic-depressive illness by turning it to creative account. Evidently most of them experienced wide swings of mood; but only some of them realised and in some measure resolved these tensions in kinds of 'art' or 'creation', broadly conceived: 'creating chaos, forcing order upon that chaos, and enabling transformation' (p. 5).

The differences between more and less creative responses to adversity are crucial. For, Jamison is keen to insist, it is far from the case that all artists are 'successful manic-depressives' or, conversely, that all manic-depressives are 'potential artists'. Rather, it is the different ways in which people constitutionally prone to kinds of mental illness respond to their condition that distinguish them one from another. Moreover – though Jamison tends to play down this point – it is clear that the nature and strength of that response will in part depend upon the opportunities and support (both emotional and economic) that are available. It obviously makes a difference whether you are locked away in seclusion or nurtured by friends and family, have private care or are put in a public institution. The contrasting cases of the mid-nineteenth-century 'peasant poet' John Clare and the late nineteenth- and early twentieth-century novelist and activist Charlotte Perkins Gilman (not cited by Jamison) help underscore this point. Clare was locked up in Northampton General Lunatic Asylum for the last twenty years of his life, where he eventually stopped writing altogether. Gilman, unlike the unfortunate heroine of her *The Yellow Wallpaper*, managed with the support of friends to avoid becoming yet another 'madwoman in the attic' and later became an influential figure in the early women's movement (see below p. 227). Temperaments vary, of course, but so do circumstances. At least part of the 'madness' of the 'madwoman in the attic', as of the 'madman in the asylum', is caused by being put in the attic or asylum in the first place.

The overall situation is, then, complex. Being judged 'mad', like being hailed an 'artist', is a matter of social conditions and institutions, not just biological conditioning and personal temperament. The stereotypically Romantic image of the genius as 'obsessed artist' or 'mad scientist' is therefore doubly vexed (see also Chapter 7). That said, Jamison makes a convincing, if not conclusive, case for at least some creators being 'creative' precisely in so far as they respond to their conditions, biological and social, in ways that are healthful and 'healing' rather than harmful and destructive. What distinguishes them, it seems, is a capacity to handle contrary states and to achieve at least a temporary sense of balance, often through their work. As Jamison puts it, 'It is the interaction, tension, and transition between changing mood states, as well as the sustenance and discipline drawn from periods of health, that is critically important' (p. 6). Thus, though the basic premise of Jamison's study may appear to be gloomily determinist, its overall emphasis is positive and emancipatory. It presents not so much a 'deficit' model of creativity as 'pathology' (the charge laid against Freud by Jung), as a celebration of 'the use of art by artists to heal themselves' (p. 6). This argument is endorsed by Daniel Nettle in his *Strong Imagination* (2001); only there it is made on anthropological as well as genetic grounds (see below, Chapter 4). In any case, the conviction that creative activity is a potentially 'healing' response to all kinds of mental illness and dis-ease, actual or imminent, is shared by most people who work with kinds of creative play, whether formally therapeutic or otherwise. Nor does it apply only to 'artists': as we see in Chapter 8, 'Healing: making whole' can apply to the distressed individual mind or the dis-eased mentality of the age.

Deleuze and Guattari take a very different view of health and illness; though arguably their conclusions tend in partly the same directions. They argue for a reconceptualisation of consciousness that virtually does away with a Freudian 'unconscious', and present a radical critique of academic psychology and clinical psychoanalysis from philosophical and political points of view. Deleuze was a professor of philosophy who professed a highly energetic and eclectic mix of what he termed 'bastard philosophy', while Guattari was a political activist who worked at a psychiatric clinic renowned for its innovative group therapy practices. Neither of them would have much time for Jamison's correlation of 'the artistic temperament' with 'manic-depressive illness'. They had as little patience with artists conventionally conceived as with conventional psychiatry and psychology institutionally framed. In fact, they complain of repression *by* orthodox Freudian psychology and point to its complicity with forms of oppressive individualism current under late capitalism. This twin target was the object of Deleuze and Guattari's idiosyncratic and iconoclastic *Anti Oedipus: Capitalism and Schizophrenia* ([1972] 1982). There they reject any notion of desire premised on a sense of 'lack'; this, they say, plays into the hands of a consumerism always ready to 'fill' – but never really 'fulfil' – that lack. Instead, they see the body as an assemblage of 'desiring machines' bristling with energies all its own, always in search of fit objects for desire but never strictly lacking in desire in the first or last place. As Michel Foucault writes in his preface to *Anti-Oedipus*,

> To be anti-Oedipal is to be anti-ego as well as anti-homo, wilfully attacking all reductive psychoanalytic and political analyses that remain caught within the sphere of totality and unity, in order to free multiplicity and desire from the deadly neurotic and Oedipal yoke.
>
> (Deleuze and Guattari [1972] 1982: xx)

Deleuze and Guattari's name for this restlessly anarchic and endlessly resourceful project is 'schizoanalysis' (the root is Greek *schiz*, meaning 'split'). Schizoanalysis constitutes an attack on 'splitting', and by extension on dualisms, of all kinds. Philosophically, it is premised upon an abstract notion of continuous 'becoming: 'That's what we call "schizoanalysis", this analysis of lines, spaces, becomings' (Deleuze and Guattari [1991] 1994: 34). Psychologically, it depends upon a deeply politicised notion of the psyche constituted in terms of such concepts as 'de- and re-territorialising', 'nomadism', 'lines of flight' and 'rhizomatic growth': 'We're saying there's a schizoid process of decoding and deterritorialising, which only revolutionary activity can stop turning into the production of schizophrenia' (Deleuze [1991] 1995: 22–3). Embracing a 'schizoid process', in this healthful sense, is what enables people to overcome the 'splitting' effects of 'schizophrenia' in a harmful sense. Deleuze and Guattari over-extend the term 'schizophrenia' by applying it to both the specific mental illness and a general social sense of fragmentation – schizoanalysis was born of frustration in the aftermath of the failed 1968 'revolution' in France. But they gradually drop the *term* and keep what is most powerful about the *concept* so as to infuse a host of other terms that carry through their project. Foremost among these are 'chaosmos' and 'heterogenesis', introduced in Chapter 1. These terms help inform the reconceptualising of 're . . . creation' at the end of the present chapter. All that need be noted here is that we are no longer talking of being 'repressed' or of being 'conscious' or 'unconscious'. In fact, it is not a matter of *being* at all and the 'human being' had perhaps better be conceived as a series of *human becomings*. This returns us to the complex and vexed matter of what it is to *become human*, including man and woman. For creativity is also

. . . fe<>male

Women and men, female and male principles, are often at the core of the creative process: physically in sexual procreation; symbolically in creation myths (see Chapters 4 and 5). Here we concentrate on the psychological interplay of 'female' and 'male' as creative principles *within* people of either sex as well as *between* people of what is loosely and deceptively called 'the opposite sex'. This helps us better appreciate the complementary, not just conflicting, nature of what is here designated the 'fe<>male' principle of creativity. The <> symbol attempts to register the complexly dynamic nature of this relationship. Seen as two arrows or two forks, it points to the recipro-cally defining *movement* of the relationship; how far it is motion from or towards, an opening or a closing, depends upon which 'arrow' or 'fork' you take to be attached to which of the two components.

We must also recognise that there may be kinds and configurations of sexuality *beyond* as well as *between* and *within* the 'fe<>male'. This accords with the observation that creative activity not only explores but exceeds simple binary thinking, reaching out towards states that are 'more than' and 'other-wise' not just 'similar to' and 'different from'. We might add further arrows or forks to either side: perhaps '<fe<>male>', or '>fe<>male<'. Whatever device we use, the general point should be clear. This section is concerned with the deeply *hetero*sexual nature of creativity, where *hetero*- carries its primary etymological sense of 'various' and 'different' rather than its reduced sense of 'opposite'. As Stephen Heath puts it, we must 'take seriously at last the *hetero* in heterosexuality, which means the heterogeneity in us, on us', and to do that we may need to 'give up [. . .] that oppressive representation of the sexual as act, complementarity, two sexes, coupling' (Heath in Jardine and Smith 1987: 22). Such a radical *hetero*sexuality can embrace, without merely assimilating, yet further complementarities based on notions of *homo*sexual (i.e. 'same-sex') creativity. More-over, this 'sameness' is constituted by differences (man–man and woman–woman) and in any given instance is never merely the 'self-same' (in the sense of identical) but always open to and in process of becoming 'other' (complicated by matters of age and ethnicity, for example). In sum, we are concerned with the radically hetero- and homo-sexual dimensions of creativity in process of becoming 'other', even while in some sense finding its 'self'.

Also pushed up to and beyond the limit is the distinction between 'sex' as biologically conceived ('male' and 'female' distinguished by genitals and reproductive capacities) and 'gender' as socially constructed ('masculine' and 'feminine' distinguished by dress and social roles). The continuous breaking and re-making of this mould is essential if we are to grasp the richly sexual dimensions of creativity and, conversely, the richly creative dimensions of sexuality. This applies whether we see creativity in a narrow sense (with Freud) as the sublimation or displacement of sexual drives, in a broader sense (with Jung) as the celebration of the 'collective unconscious', or as various expressions and embodiments of 'lack' or 'desire' (with Lacan and Kristeva; see previous section). The work of psychologist and cultural critic Erich Fromm offers a useful way into these issues. A fundamental principle informing his *The Art of Loving* (1957) is that the female–male polarity 'is the basis for all creativity'. This informs a conception of love as a practised 'art' of change and exchange and of a true 'labour of love' as that which far exceeds any casually romantic notion of 'falling in love' or reductively sensual notion of 'sex'. Fromm sets up the female–male 'polarity' as 'the basis for all creativity' not just *between* people but *within* each person:

> The polarity between the male and female principles exists also *within* each man and each woman. Just as physiologically man and woman each have hormones of the opposite sex, they are bisexual also in the psychological sense. They carry in themselves the principle of receiving and penetrating, of matter and of spirit. Man – and woman – finds union within himself only in the union of his female and his male polarity. This polarity is the basis for all creativity.
>
> (Fromm [1957] 1975: 33–4)

For Fromm, then, there is a bisexuality at the core of every person, and creativity is realised through the coming together of the 'male' and 'female' polarities. This premise is shared by a number of psychologists. Winnicott, for example, observes that 'creativity is one of the common denominators of men and women' precisely because there are 'male and female elements in men *and* women' (Winnicott 1971: 85, 89). One may wonder, however, about Fromm's precise emphasis and assumptions. For one thing, he privileges 'Man' throughout, adding ' – and woman – ' in passing. He also appears to be operating with stereotypical notions of the male principle 'penetrating' and the female 'receiving', and of male as 'matter' and female as 'spirit'. This extends to talk of 'the polarity of the earth and rain, of the river and ocean, of night and day, of darkness and light, of matter and spirit' (p. 34). Distinctions based on biological *sex* (males 'penetrate', females 'receive') are being extended in terms of culturally constructed notions of *gender* (male as 'darkness' and 'matter', female as 'light' and 'spirit', etc.). Such binary oppositions have a long history in accounts of the respective 'characters' or 'genius' of men and women (see Battersby 1989: 88–102, 117–31). They are also, as we see shortly, the object of concerted de- and re-construction by feminist critics such as Cixous.

Further, when Fromm talks about relations *between* people it becomes clear that a basically binary model of heterosexuality is being asserted: 'The male–female polarity is also the basis for *interpersonal* creativity [. . .] in the love between man and woman each of them is reborn' (p. 34). Homosexuality is explicitly conceived as a 'deviation' and a 'failure' resulting in permanent 'separateness': 'The homosexual deviation is a failure to attain this polarised union, and thus the homosexual suffers from the pain of never-resolved separateness' (p. 34). Overall, then, there are problems as well as possibilities in the model of (hetero)sexuality that underpins Fromm's concept of creativity. Premised upon a union of opposites, it implicitly privileges the male, favours the conventionally heterosexual, and expressly disables the homosexual.

Such a narrowly heterosexual and palpably hierarchical conception of creativity is deeply rooted in the Western tradition. It extends from the classical notion of male semen as 'seed' sown in the receiving and nurturing 'earth' of the female womb to the Aristotelian notion of the *logos spermatikos* as a specifically masculine principle of creativity (see Battersby 1989: 88–103). The latter idea continues into Jung's conception of 'the *logos spermatikos*, the spermatic word' whereby 'a man brings forth his work as a complete creation out of his inner feminine nature' (Jung [1943] 1976: 209), or Ezra Pound's more virulently, violently male celebration of 'an upsurt of sperm [. . .] sperm, the form-creator, the substance which compels the ovule to evolve in a given pattern' in his Introduction to Remy Gourmont's *The Natural Philosophy of Love* (1957). Jung's position is much more subtle and moderate, but his characterisation of the woman as 'the *femme inspiratrice*' who 'brings forth creative seeds which have the power to fertilize the feminine side of the man' (p. 209) clearly recalls the figure of the female muse beloved as a source of creative inspiration by predominantly male poets and artists. The precise nature and direction of such inspirational flows often turn out to be far more complex than they first appear, but in general terms it is hard to see such male appropriations of female creativity as other than a kind of 'womb envy' (to invert Freud's more familiar phrase): men abrogating the procreative power of women for their own purportedly superior 'creative' ends. In Chapter 7, Philip Sidney's sonnet is an example in this long and vexed tradition, and Edna St Vincent Millay's is an arresting rejoinder from a woman. But it is now time to look at some theoretical alternatives.

Christine Battersby in her *Gender and Genius: Towards a Feminist Aesthetics* (1989) is committed to a recognition of women's creative powers in and on their own terms. But this, she insists, can only be achieved through fundamental changes in the social and economic order. It cannot be derived from a feminist aesthetics premised on a view of 'Woman' as ultimately and absolutely 'Other'. In particular, Battersby resists the notion of an exclusively 'feminine' mode of writing (*écriture feminine*) based on the biological sex of the writer. Such writing is supposedly characterised by fragmented, discontinuous, recursive structures and a preoccupation with emotions and relationships (for a fuller discussion, see Toril Moi's *Sexual/Textual Politics* 1985). Here is how Battersby frames the issue of fe/male creativity – with the emphasis firmly but not exclusively upon the female:

> Women creators still have to struggle (both socially and inwardly) against dispersing into kinds of Otherness now endorsed as 'feminine' by many of those who look to *l'écriture feminine*. To be seen as an individual – with an *œuvre* that persists

coherently through the (apparently incoherent) fragments that make it up – a woman creator has to be positioned within male *and* female traditions of art. But female traditions of art will not emerge via a revaluation of supposedly 'feminine' characteristics of mind or body. [. . .] Being female involves not some collection of innate or acquired psychological or biological qualities. It is rather a matter of being consigned – on the basis of the way one's body is perceived – to a (non-privileged) position in a social nexus of power.

(Battersby 1989: 210)

In rejecting psychological *and* biological determinants of 'being female', and acquired *or* innate notions of a specifically female *or* feminine creativity, Battersby here rejects current conceptions of both sex and gender as bases for a specifically feminist aesthetics. Instead, as her conclusion to the book confirms, it is to *future* acts of self-creation and to a *yet-to-be-created* tradition grounded in critique of the past that we must look for an alternative resolution of these issues: 'A female genius is a construct created as we, the feminist consumers and critics, look back at the past, create a new tradition, and project ourselves and our values towards the future' (p. 232). A similar backward-glancing but basically forward-looking concept of 'women's creativity' is projected by Lesley Saunders in her introduction to the wide range of experimental work in the critical-creative anthology *Glancing Fires: An Investigation into Women's Creativity* (Saunders 1987: x):

> What is common, I think, to these practices of making, connecting and risking is that they enlarge our conception of what is possible. They show us ways from what we are supposed to be towards what we, pluralistically, could be. The women here are making a space to go on exploring both immediate and long-standing meanings of creativity.

These are, then, future-directed, women-driven visions of creativity. Crucially, the key concepts – 'creativity' and 'women' – are characterised more by what they *can* or *may yet* be in the future (their potential meaning) than by what they *do* or *are* in the present (their actual meaning).

One of these futures, ten years on, is represented by Nicole Ward Jouve's *Female Genesis: Creativity, Self and Gender* (1998). Taking a more personal and spiritual, less publicly political line, this study focuses on 'sexual identity and creativity', and finds 'food for thought in Jung and Winnicott and Klein rather than in Freud and Lacan' (Ward Jouve 1998: 27). The book opens with a critique of the Biblical story of creation and closes with a re-writing of it. The key passage is Genesis 1.27: 'So God created man in his own image, in the image of God created he him: male and female created he them.' Creation myths will be considered at length in Chapter 5. Here we examine questions posed by Ward Jouve about a specifically 'female' construction of 'genesis':

> 'Male and female created He them'. Does that mean that all created beings, both males and females, were made with masculine and feminine components, with both principles active in them, the offspring of both? Or that He made one male and one female, but as related components of His creation? Male relative to female, female to male, each finding itself and its fulfilment in relation to the

other? There are over the ages countless human meditations on this theme, from Pausanias's story of the androgyne in Plato's *Symposium* – the double beings having been forcibly separated, each half seeking for ever after for its other half – to Virginia Woolf's notion that the true, the full creator is both male and female, and needs to achieve a lyrical state of balance.

(Ward Jouve 1998: 3)

Woolf fictionally embodies her 'notion' in the sexually enigmatic hero/heroine of *Orlando* (1928). Along with allusions to androgynous figures in Plato, this gestures towards conceptions of radical *hetero*sexuality that embrace kinds of *bi-* and *homo-* sexuality. The kinds of religious creation and secular creativity in play (both are covered by Ward Jouve's notion of 'female genesis') can, then, be very variously conceived: generated within each person (primarily but not exclusively women); generated between people of either or both sexes; and generated by each person's relation to the 'god' within and without (whether Jung's *animus/anima*, a Christian god-made-flesh or some other divinely human incarnation). Indeed, the last lines of *Female Genesis* expressly issue 'a call to sexual, or gender, inclusiveness. To a bisexuality more fundamental than the sex/gender of whom we desire. A call to wholeness . . .' (p. 249).

Ward Jouve is committed – like Battersby but in a different key – to a vision that exceeds current definitions of sex and gender. She embraces what was here provisionally termed a 'fe<>male' principle of creativity, but which on further inspection had perhaps better be designated as, say, '>fe<>male<' or '<fe><male>' creativi*ties*. No such term, of course, will definitively establish what creativity *is*, but they do help point towards what it *can* be. In any event, some reformulations are required if we are to register the myriad permutations and potential transformations opened up by an infinitely various and extendable array of intra-, inter- and extra-personal dynamics. These particular formulations may be refined or rejected (they only use a limited number of symbols, after all, and tend to privilege a central pair rather than an extensive multiplicity). But they do attempt to model a radically *hetero*sexual array of creativities, potential as well as actual; and they gesture to at least some of the richly 'other' ways of relating – and ways of relating to the 'other' – between and beyond the notions of bi- and homo-sexuality as currently conceived.

One of these 'other' ways of configuring creativity and sexuality is articulated by Hélène Cixous. Her critical-creative tour de force, *Sorties* (1975), plays with the various possible meanings in French of its title ('exits', 'escapes', 'assaults', 'outcomes') and may be teasingly translated as 'Way(s) Out!'. It begins by exploring and exploding the kinds of conventional male/female polarities assumed by Fromm and others: activity/passivity, sun/moon, culture/nature, head/heart, form/matter, etc. Once she has exposed the systematically divisive and hierarchical nature of these binary oppositions, notably their tendency to privilege the male even while venerating the female, Cixous proceeds to articulate a view of 'invention' that depends upon 'an abundance of the other' in 'the inventing subject' (Cixous [1975] in Lodge and Wood 2000: 269). Crucially, Cixous's 'invention' involves an 'other' that is ultimately unnameable and unknowable, and in this respect can be compared with Derrida's notion of creative 'invention' as the 'coming-in' of an 'other', considered earlier in this chapter. Cixous, however, insists upon the primarily sexual nature of this creative resource. In a simple sense this is 'homosexual'; but it is homosexuality understood in a particular way and as part of a complex configuration. Thus Cixous opposes 'the relentless repression of the homosexual component [in everyone]', but also seeks to celebrate men *and* women as 'complex, mobile, open beings' who by 'admitting the component of the other sex' become 'richer, plural, strong' (p. 269). She is careful to point out that 'This does not mean that in order to create you must be homosexual', but she also insists that 'there is no invention possible [. . .] without the presence in the inventing subject of an abundance of the other, of the diverse' (p. 269):

> [T]here is no invention of other I's, no poetry, no fiction, without a certain homo-sexuality (interplay therefore of bisexuality) making in me a crystallized work of my ultrasubjectivities. I is this matter, personal, exuberant, lively, masculine, feminine, or other in which I delights and distresses me.

The wrenching of personal pronouns and conventional grammar, as in Rimbaud's 'I is an other' (*Je est un autre*), attests to an attempt to reach beyond the limits of current language for a formulation as yet inexpressible.

Current proponents of 'queer' reading and writing attempt something similar, yet also radically different. For example, Eve Kosofsky Sedgwick in her *Epistemology of the Closet* (1990) and *Tendencies* (1993) argues for what she calls 'queer performativity' in the acts either of 'coming out' or of guarding the secrets of 'the closet'. The former especially is the defining movement and moment in which the person publicly declares 'I am queer' – or 'gay', or 'lesbian', etc. Here the choice of term is a highly specific social-historical as well as deeply personal-political act. For instance, Alan Sinfield writes in his *Cultural Politics: Queer Reading* (1994: 204) in the context of the re-appropriation of the term by homosexuals in the mid 1990s, that '"Queer" says, defiantly, that we don't care what they call us'. Sedgwick, too, draws attention to the 'performative aspects of texts . . . as sites of definitional creation' (Sedgwick [1990] in Leitch 2001: 2436–45; and for discussion see Wolfreys 2001: 224–41).

It is the capacity of much homosexual practice to mock and mimic – and to travesty and transgress – dominantly heterosexual practices that makes it powerful in the de- and re-construction of models of creativity no less than of sexuality. Obvious examples are cross-dressing and kinds of 'camp' or 'butch' behaviour; but there are also subtler matters of gesture, intonation and inflection. Thus Jonathan Dollimore, recalling Derrida's notion of 'iteration' as 'alteration in repetition', endorses Judith Butler's emphasis in her *Bodies that Matter* (1993) and insists upon 'the importance of *repetition* in the process of resistance and transformation'. He – as does she – 'sees deviant sexualities [. . .] as parodic, subversive repetitions which displace rather than consolidate sexual norms' (see Wolfreys 2001: 234–5). The seriously playful aspect of this carni-valised and sexualised vision of creativity is emphasised in Isobel Armstrong's *The Radical Aesthetic* (2000: 214–15), as will be examined in Chapter 4. What may be emphasised here is the radically *performative* nature of such speech (and other) acts as they bring complexly reconfigured realities into being. In this respect, 'Queer' ways of seeing and saying, being and doing, stand for any ongoing attempt to renegotiate categories and exceed current perceptions of what is ab/normal. 'The relations of the closet', as Kosofsky Sedgwick sees them, embody a specific, insistent exploration of 'the relations of the known and the unknown, the explicit and the inexplicit around homo/heterosexual definition' (Sedgwick in Leitch 2001: 2444). But the same broad principle applies to all radically creative attempts to rearticulate sexuality – and all radically sexual attempts to define creativity. It applies, for instance, albeit often fundamentally transformed, to attempts to articulate specifically black (white, coloured) configurations of sexuality and creativity (those by bell hooks and Trinh T. Minh-ha, for instance) and to the various kinds of 'cyborg' and 'metamorphic' identity projected by Donna Haraway and Rosi Braidotti on the human–animal–machine and sex–gender interfaces (see above pp. 49–50 and below pp. 157–8, 265). In any event, *by definition*, the resulting definitions need doing and over and over again (differently) if they are to remain fresh and valuable.

Yet again, then, we are concerned as much with the creation of definitions as we are with the definition of creativity. Again we are engaged in an evolving cycle of repetitions with variations. There remains, however, just one more act to complete this particular movement: the end of the sentence on which all these definitions are strung; the noun to which all the preceding adjectives incline; the last flourish of this particular snake's tail. *Creativity is extra/ordinary, original and fitting, full-filling, in(ter)ventive, co-operative, un/conscious, fe<>male*

. . . re . . . creation

Re . . . creation can be provisionally defined as 'the ongoing process of making afresh'. It must be distinguished from the quasi-divine notion of 'creation from nothing' (*ex nihilo*): in the present view there is never 'nothing', nor is creation ever a once-and-for-all act. It must also be distinguished from the relatively weak and increasingly commodified notion of 'recreation' as leisure or pastime, because creation involves 'making' and active participation rather than purchase and relatively passive consumption. The suspension dots within the word *re . . . creation* are a considered device, as are those between words in the sentence that spans this chapter. They remind us to pause and reflect upon the potential meanings and interrelations in play. Here, for instance, the suspended prefix '*re . . .*' can mean 'afresh' as well as 'again', and denotes repetition with variation, not just duplication. In this respect we should recall that processes of *re*production, whether sexual or technological, never result in the production of identical copies but always involve some transformation of form or function, however slight or apparently accidental.

At the same time, ' *. . . creation*' is an invitation to review the many meanings of the 'create' words considered so far. Historically, these include such figures as 'God the Creator', 'the creative artist' and the various 'creatures' of the imagination, along with such processes as 'creative evolution' and 'heterogenesis'. In the present chapter, more theoretically and speculatively, they range over everything that creativity is or may yet be – from 'extra/ordinary' to 'fe<>male' and beyond. We are in part of that 'beyond' now. It all turns upon the relation between what has happened so far and what may happen now and now and now (i.e. 'next' conceived as an unfolding series). In the present terms, it depends upon the perceived relation between what may be gathered from the process up to this moment (*re . . .*) and what may come out of it and be projected forward from this moment on (*. . . creation*). Both are entailed by the compound concept *re . . . creation*. Moreover, though the relation between its elements is in principle wide open, in practice it is always partially closed. Though permanently held in suspension, the exact articulation of the idea always depends upon the specific points of reference to which it is attached at any particular moment in history.

The suspension dots of *re . . . creation* invite us, then, not only to 'mind the gap' (as on the London Underground), but also, each in our own way, to 'jump' and thereby 'bridge' it. First used in this way by the philosopher Eugene Gendlin in his *Experiencing and the Creation of Meaning* (1962), suspension dots are a crucial strategy in his development of a particular blend of pragmatism and phenomenology. Gendlin explains the device thus: 'We can let a . . . . . come in any spot where we pause, and we can think from it' (Gendlin 1997: 7; notice that he uses five dots not three, of which more shortly). Slightly more complexly, he proposes that 'The . . . . . is not the mere combination of existing elements; it is rather a situation (an experience, a slot in a sentence)'. For Gendlin, situation and words are part and parcel of the same reciprocally defining and dynamically evolving complex: 'the situation gives the word a new life' just as 'a situation changes itself in response to the words' (p. 8). Meaning-making is therefore a cumulative matter of an unfolding text in a developing context, not just a sequence of words in a social-historical vacuum. Gendlin summarises the matter thus: 'Situation and words *cross*, so that each becomes part of the meaning of the other. As word after word *comes*, the situation *reads* . . . . . in its own way' (p. 8, his emphasis).

Gendlin's philosophy of language as the creation of meaning in context can be aligned with a number of pragmatic and phenomenological approaches. In the West, we can trace a (somewhat wavy) line from James and Dewey through Bergson and Heidegger to the later Wittgenstein and Ricoeur (see above pp. 43–4). This intertwines at various points with both speech act and reception theories in so far as these stress the continuously *performative* aspect of speaking/writing and listening/reading: the way words actively articulate possible worlds rather than simply refer to a world that already exists (see Burke *et al.* 2000: Part Four). It also anticipates Alain Badiou's notion of philosophy that 'opens up an active void within thought' and 'seizes truth. The seizure is its act' (Badiou 2003: 165). Meanwhile, in Eastern Europe, close parallels can be drawn with aspects of work by Vygotsky and Bakhtin. The crux of Lev Vygotsky's *Speech and Thinking* (1934) is expressed thus: 'Speech does not merely serve as the expression of developed thought. Thought is restructured as it is transformed into speech. It is not expressed but completed in the word' (Vygotsky [1934] 1987: 257; and see Holzman 1999). This clearly resonates with Bakhtin's notion of the vibrantly 'dialogic' utterance that is constantly 'response-able' (i.e. both responsive and responsible) with respect to current conditions and surrounding people (see above p. 66). To be fully 'response-able' is inevitably to be involved in *re . . . creation*.

The fact that I have adapted – and not simply adopted – Gendlin's practice helps demonstrate what is here meant by *re . . . creation*. That is, I have changed his typographical device to fit the present con/text and to serve present purposes. Firstly, I have reduced Gendlin's five dots to the usual three in order to be consistent with the linkages between the words that make up the single sentence upon which this section is strung. Secondly, I have placed them *within* an existing word so as to make another word with a relatable yet distinct sense (Gendlin does not do this). Crucially, however, that still leaves you, the present reader, with the responsibility of deciding exactly what kind of *re . . . creation* you take this to be. Merely verbal tinkering or the promise of a genuinely fresh concept? Perhaps almost everything is changed – or almost nothing! Partly it depends how you respond to the above explanation. Partly it depends how far you yourself are prepared to read and write – explore and fill – the '. . .' in *re . . . creation*. And that in turn depends upon how you engage with the larger sentence (*'Creativity is . . . extra/ ordinary . . . original and fitting . . . full-filling . . . in(ter)ventive . . . co-operative . . . un/ conscious . . . fe<>male . . .'*) which *'re . . . creation'* offers to conclude but not completely close down. That is the beauty and terror of *re . . . creation* fully grasped. We never have the last – nor for that matter the first – word.

We may align the present concept of *re . . . creation* with a number of other cultural projects. One is that of *re-vision*, as articulated by Adrienne Rich in her paper, 'When we dead awaken: writing as re-vision' (1971): *'Re-vision* – the act of looking back, of seeing with fresh eyes, of entering an old text from a new direction – is for women more than a chapter in cultural history; it is an act of survival' (Rich [1971] in Bartholomae and Petrosky 1999: 603–20, here 604). Though framed as part of an expressly feminist project, Rich's concept of re-vision resonates with many other historically aware and politically interventive critical and creative endeavours, particularly those identified with kinds of *re-membering*. These span the politics and histories of colour, class, gender and sexuality, and draw on the rich ambiguity of 're-membering' meaning: (1) calling to memory, 'recalling' in its routine sense; (2) recognising and celebrating the 'members' of a previously neglected or misrepresented community (e.g., slaves, factory workers, 'gays'); (3) putting back together a vision of 'the body' that has been physically 'dismembered' through criminal or clinical practices or metaphorically 'dismembered' by analytical regimes of categorisation and control. Kinds of 're-membering' in these senses are central to a number of theoretical and historical projects, including new historicism, cultural materialism, feminism and post-colonialism.

Precursors of the poetic and political dimensions of *re . . . creation* can therefore be discerned in a wide range of work by individual theorists: Walter Benjamin's ([1930s] 1970) notion of a 'political memory' which, like Foucault's (1984), draws attention to the disjunctures and contradictions as well as the continuities and consistencies of historical change; Linda Hutcheon's (1988) model of 'historiographic metafiction' as the dominant postmodern political aesthetic, where the past is recast in openly knowing and telling ways; and Richard Kearney's (1998, 2002) notion of 'narrative imagination' as 'the testimonial capacity to bear witness to a forgotten past' coupled with a 'critical utopian' openness to possible futures (see above p. 15). *Re . . . creation* also bears comparison with a clutch of concepts developed by Derrida. Chief among these are the general notion of 'iterability' or 'iteration', which he glosses as 'alteration in repetition', and the more specific notion of writing as 'counter-signing' (Derrida 1992: 62–6). Derrida uses these terms to characterise his own distinctively critical-creative practices of reading and writing (p. 61):

> I wrote a text which, in the face of the event of another's text, as it comes to me at a particular, quite singular moment, tries to 'respond' or to 'counter-sign' in an idiom which turns out to be mine.

Relatable concepts can be traced in Derrida's ideas of 'inspiration' as 'dictation by an other', and 'invention' as the 'coming-in of the other' (see above pp. 17–18, 64–5).

All these ideas complement the notion of *re . . . creation* as an ongoing transformation of past-through-present-to-future and self-through-other-to-otherwise. They do not depend upon the illusion of absolutely determined beginnings or end; though they do (importantly) require provisional and preferential points of opening and closure. Neither do they presuppose an absolute distinction between the processes of reading and writing and, by extension, of re-reading and re-writing; though, again, they recognise that agency and responsibility must still be assigned at various stages of communication and transformation, and that 'writer' and 'reader' are roles that can be distinguished as well as exchanged. Put another way, it is recognised that *re . . . creation* is a 'critical' as well as 'creative' activity, whether simultaneously or by turns. The goal is to get beyond the current impasse whereby the one is seen as opposed, rather than complementary, to the other and, I would suggest, to recognise that you need to be and do both – perhaps not simultaneously, but certainly by turns.

The final figures I wish to 're-member' here are Deleuze and Guattari. These two had a way of jumping the gap between 're' and 'creation' that inspired some and irritated others. They are, then, just the kind of awkward round pegs in square holes (or vice versa) that will help show what kind of 'hole' we are dealing with. One of the early jumping-off points for their approach is Deleuze's *Difference and Repetition* ([1968] 1994), a concerted exploration of the matter of how 'differences' arise from 'repetition' and, conversely, how 'repetition' tends to erode 'difference'. In his Foreword, Deleuze sets out to articulate his project: 'I make, re-make and un-make my concepts with a view to a moving horizon, a centre that is always off-centre, a periphery that is always out of place, and which repeats yet differentiates them' (Deleuze 1968: 3, my translation; cf Deleuze 1994: 3). But it is Deleuze and Guattari's *What is Philosophy?* (1991) that provides the main launch-pad for the present conception of *re . . . creation*. There they pick up on Nietzsche's notion of 'the eternal recurrence': like many cosmologies, ancient and modern, this is characterised by ceaselessly varying *cycles* rather than perfectly repeated circles. In a similar vein, Deleuze and Guattari invoke what they call 'the Great Refrain' of 'co-creation', which they characterise as: 'the constantly renewed suffering of men and women, their re-created protestations, their constantly resumed struggle' (Deleuze and Guattari [1991] 1994: 173–7). They identify its modes of expression with a peculiarly dynamic version of what other writers refer to as 'intertextuality': 'It is in this way that, from one writer to another, great creative affects can link up or diverge, within compounds of sensations that transform themselves, vibrate, couple, or split apart.' (p. 175). Thus, while recognising that artists are 'the inventors and creators of affects' through processes of 'co-creation', Deleuze and Guattari insist that 'They not only create them in their work, they give them to us and make us *become* with them, they draw us into the compound' (1994: 174–5). In other words, in the terms of the present argument, they – and we – engage in kinds of *re . . . creation*.

More boldly, *re . . . creation* is here offered as at least one alternative to postmodernism – and to all the other 'posts-', including 'post-theory'. While the prefix 'post-' can mean 'after and a continuation of' as well as 'after and in place of', and has prospective as well as retrospective dimensions, it still presupposes an essentially backward-looking gaze and there is little sense in the main stem (e.g. modernism) that anything really fresh can come of it. There are comparable problems with postcolonialism, poststructuralism and postfeminism; and in each case the legacy may be conceived as liability as well as asset. 'Re . . . creation', I suggest, carries very different baggage and can be very differently unpacked. The prefix 're-', for example, can mean 'afresh' as well as 'again', as already argued, and can signify repetition with variation (to be more precise, 'iteration with difference') not just – or indeed ever – absolute replication. 'Creation', meanwhile, brings all the rich potential as well as problematic resonances of its still living history. On its own, its links with divine or artistic creation narrowly conceived make it a mixed blessing, but together with 're' and with the all-important ' . . .' in the middle, the concept as a whole is dynamised. Part of its appeal is precisely that it is a whole with a hole in the middle: the concept does not resist closure, but insists upon reserving a space for what, since Aristotle, has been called 'the excluded middle'. The 'excluded middle' is basically all that does not fit into a neatly polarised notion of difference conceived as opposition (body/soul, subject/object, inside/outside, etc.); and quite rightly it has come in for some criticism in genuinely energetic and materialist conceptions of aesthetics and ethics (see Armstrong 2000 and above pp. 82–3).

The great strength of the concept *re . . . creation* (which is therefore its greatest potential weakness) is that it draws attention to the possibility of missing or excluded terms. It invites us to *see through* the existing possibilities to words and worlds beyond as well as between; and it encourages a view of 'difference' that is genuinely otherwise. Put another way, it is an invitation to keep on jumping or bridging the gap; for it cannot be permanently filled in, and simply ignoring and then falling into it gets us nowhere. At the very least, *re . . . creation* is an attempt to revive the dialogue on creativity: to reassure those who are weary of debates about 'Theory' (as if 'Theory', singular and capitalised, were really the point at issue) and to encourage those who wish to get past the 'post-s' (with their perpetual sense of belatedness) and get on with the important business of theorising practice and practising theory – and seeing where else that gets us.

Finally, I would argue that a concept such as *re . . . creation* offers a more responsive and responsible vision of 'creativity' than that provided by the standard definitions in the specialist literature. There the emphasis tends to be upon the 'new', the 'novel' and the 'original' in their narrowly 'modern' senses (see above p. 57). *Re . . . creation* leaves more room for conserving and sustaining as well as recasting and refreshing, while resisting conservative, reactionary impulses of an unthinking and merely reflexive kind. Put another way, this is an attempt to articulate a socially sensitive and ecologically sustainable rather than technologically driven and economically determined model of creativity. It is emphatically not some kind of quick-fix, 'New Age' or 'third way' paradigm underwritten by the notion that we would all recognise ourselves as creative if we simply signed up to the latest movement in individual therapy or social engineering (for a critique of such tendencies, see Chapter 1). It is harder work and more fun – and requires far more social participation and political engagement – than that. Rather, to recall Raymond Williams's words, 'creativity and social self-creation are both known and unknown events, and it is still from grasping the known that the unknown – the next step, the next work – is conceived' (Williams 1977: 212; see above p. 11).

To take that 'next step' and proceed to that 'next work' again, afresh, we must move beyond the terms *create, creative* and even *re . . . creation*; for it will be abundantly clear by now that, however we define it, creativity will always be 'something more and something different' (Bohm and Peat 2000: 226). Creativity *as a concept* constantly demands to be reinterpreted and re-written (counter-signed, re-invented, re-visioned, re-membered, . . . and thereby itself re . . . created) in terms current at the time. Those terms, in turn, will necessarily work some change in what the concept can possibly mean in future – not just what it has actually meant so far. At this point, then, we turn to 'alternative terms and emerging debates'. The matter at issue is precisely *how* alternative, *where* they are emerging from, and into *what* . . .

4 Alternative terms, emerging debates

The successful theory predicts that there are things that it cannot predict.

(Barrow 2000: 368–9)

A person with one theory is lost. We need several of them – or lots. We should stuff them in our pockets like newspapers.

(after Bertolt Brecht [*c.* 1945] in Makaryk 1993: vii)

In moving beyond the 'creativity' terms as such, we expressly recognise that any term can only be defined through terms that it is not. In a simple sense this is because all attempts at dictionary definition lead from one entry to another and another and usually at some point back to the entry you started with (look up 'word' and 'language' to see such circular logic in action). In a rather more complex sense it is because language is composed of an interplay of differences ('differences without positive terms,' as Saussure put it) so any encounter with absolute sense is ultimately deferred (hence Derrida's pun upon *différance* meaning both 'deferral' and 'difference'). Such problems and possibilities are especially acute with a concept as elusive and pervasive as 'creativity'. If the latter is always, in Bohm and Peat's phrase, 'more than and different from' whatever we expect it to be, it is imperative that we get beyond the dominant constructions (and constrictions) of the *term* so as to enrich and extend the potential range of the *concept*. It is also important, as intimated in the above epigraphs, that we develop a way of theorising that is principled and yet flexible: aware of the historical force and current sense of our key terms, but also open to the possibility that they may need to be refined or be replaced by others as the occasion arises. In the present chapter, therefore, the question is what are the 'alternative terms', where are they emerging from – and what and where next?

We begin with a historical review of notions of *inspiration* and *ecstasy* and trace their counterparts in contemporary accounts of *intertextuality* and *influence*. The common denominator is a sense of being moved or motivated by some 'other' (person, or text, or whatever), and the underlying question is 'who or what informs the drive to create?' In the second section the history of notions of *genius* leads into the problems and possibilities of modern *genetics*, picking up issues of *gender* (and *genre*) along the way. All these words have a common root in '*gen–*' meaning birth or growth, and there is a recurrent concern with creativity as procreation, literally as well as metaphorically. The third section opens with a consideration of contemporary notions of *emergence* and *complexity*, and it closes with a reprise of them. In between we trace changing conceptions of *game* and *play* which, in the fourth section, modulate into corresponding notions of *order* and *chaos*. Creativity is here understood in terms of game-like constraints and the kinds of rule-making and rule-breaking activity that more or less 'free' play may entail. The discussion then folds or loops back into consideration of the various kinds of *order* and *chaos* identified in theories of complex and emergent systems. In fact, 'folding', 'loops' and recursive processes of all kinds are central to the manner as well as the matter of the present chapter; and following these various lines of thought through we get increasingly involved in debates on much more than 'creativity' conventionally conceived. Reformulating what might currently be meant by creativity when working across the sciences as well as the arts is a particular concern of this chapter and of Chapter 6.

Inspiration and influence, from ecstasy to intertextuality

There are many terms used to express what prompts, informs and drives the creative process. **Inspiration** carries the general sense of being moved and stirred by a powerful force other than oneself (divine, natural, human, or otherwise). Its root sense, from Latin *in-spiratio*, is of 'breathing into'. **Ecstasy** suggests an even more intense experience of being taken over, transported and in some way transcended. Its root is Greek *ek-stasis*, meaning 'standing outside', and is perhaps best registered by such colloquial phrases as 'being carried away', 'beside oneself' – 'far out', 'way out'. But there are other less extravagant ways of conceiving of the process. **Influence**, for instance, initially meant a 'flowing-into' (rather like the 'breathing-into' of inspiration), but now more commonly refers to 'influences' in the sense of sources, models and exemplars (Shelley's influence on Yeats, Hegel's influence on Marx, etc.). More recently, the concept of **intertextuality** has been introduced to cover all sorts of relations 'between texts': direct and indirect, conscious or otherwise – from quotation and allusion to the fact of belonging to the same genre or discourse or culture.

Writers and artists have claimed to be 'inspired' by everything from a god or a landscape to a chance word or brief encounter. They have also been 'influenced' by – or created 'under the influence of' – alcohol, drugs, a powerful model, a patron, and one another. Often 'love' of someone or something – and equally often lack of it – is in the picture somewhere. (See Allott 1959: 111–160 and Ghiselin 1985 for copious examples.) Meanwhile, not for nothing is 'ecstasy' the name of a perfume and a narcotic, as well as a word for something that happens during sexual orgasm, religious revelation, or any other state of unusually heightened perception. Some of this turns out to be a very old story retold in new ways. Some of it opens up new ways of saying and seeing the world entirely. Where once were the gods and demons of ancient mythologies and the muses of archaic arts and sciences are now the tools and techniques of modern psychology and pharmacology. And even poststructuralist philosophy. Inspiration conceived as what Derrida calls 'dictation by an other' has already been considered in the first chapter. Here we take a historically longer and culturally wider perspective.

In classical terms, **inspiration** is usually attributed to a divinity or muse and reckoned to be a good thing. If the influence is judged malign, it is more usual to talk of

being 'possessed' (by a devil or evil spirits, for instance); though in shamanistic religions being 'possessed' by an ancestor or animal spirit is reckoned beneficial. Either
way, there is potential danger as well as delight in being inspired or possessed. Both
senses can be found in the classical Roman notion of the *furor poeticus* (poetic madness),
where one may stress the *furor*/madness or the *poeticus*/making. The notion of the
divine *afflatus*, meanwhile, like *inspiratio*, recalls the radical sense of 'breathing in' or
being 'breathed into' and thereby achieving a kind of fulfilment. Such a sense of being
'filled full' may be attributed to an otherworldly spirit ('spirit' is another word that
shares a root with *spiratio*, breathing); but it may also be induced by the kinds of
breathing exercise practised in yoga and other forms of meditation. In that respect
'inspiration' as 'breathing' is as 'extra/ordinary' and 'full-filling' as any of the other
routinely creative practices referred to in the previous chapter. It has literal and physio-
logical as well as symbolic and spiritual dimensions to it. So in that sense 'inspired'
creation is as simple – and difficult – as breathing properly. Though it should be
straightaway added that such apparent ease only tends to be achieved after much
practice and not a little *per*-spiration/'through-breathing' – i.e. sweat. (The '90 per
cent perspiration and 10 per cent inspiration' rule is commonly invoked by expert
practitioners of all kinds.) Indeed, to complete the cycle, 'spiration'/'breathing' taken
as a whole obviously requires a capacity for *ex*-piration, 'breathing out' and 'letting
go', too. Ultimately, this includes the 'art of dying' (*ars moriendi*): being in the fullest
sense prepared to 'give up one's last breath'.

Typically, appeals to inspiration are couched in terms of 'breath', 'breeze', 'wind',
'spirit' or 'fire'; and they draw on the rich ambiguity of literal and metaphoric senses.
Plato, however, offers his own highly influential analogy for this process in the *Ion*
(*c*. 360 BCE). There he speaks of *enthusiasmos* (a kind of divinely inspired 'enthusiasm'
or 'energy' equivalent to Latin *inspiratio*) in terms of magnetic power as it passes from
one iron ring to another and another and another. In just such a way, he suggests,
poetic energy is communicated from the divinity to the poet and so on through the
performer (here the rhapsode) to the audience:

> Then know that the member of the audience is the last of those rings which I
> describe as getting power from each other through the magnet. You the reciter
> and actor [rhapsode] are the middle ring; and the first is the poet himself; but
> God through all these draws the soul of men whithersoever he will, by running
> the power through them one after another.

> (Plato [*c*. 360 BCE] 1956: 20)

But other, very different kinds of 'inspiration' can be imagined. In Billy Marshall-
Stoneking's *Passage*, for example (which we look at more closely in the next chapter),
an Aboriginal elder is moved to sing by the spirits in the landscape; but his song also
gives back to the spirits, the landscape and his people by reaffirming the living bond
among all of them: 'This is the power of the Song. / Through the singing we keep
everything alive; / through the songs the spirits keep us alive'. The distinction is an
important one. Plato's image of the magnet suggests a one-way transmission of energy
from a divine source through physical and human intermediaries to the audience. His
is essentially a monologic, top-down model of the inspirational process. That of the
Aboriginal elder is more dynamic and dialogic. It involves two- and many-way flows

of energy and, through them, kinds of reciprocal support and inter-animation. Clearly, then, a lot depends upon the precise process of inspiration: who or what is reckoned to be 'breathing into' whom or what, through what means and with what effects.

A couple of influential distinctions about kinds of inspiration were made by Friedrich Nietzsche in *The Birth of Tragedy* (1872). Drawing on a powerful and to some extent idiosyncratic vision of ancient Greek drama and ritual, Nietzsche distinguished between two kinds of creative impulse: the Dionysian (ecstatic) and the Apollonian (rational). The former he identifies as a primitive source of inspiration associated with the festivals of the nature god, Dionysus. Such festivals were characterised by drunkenness, wild dancing, sexual licence and bodily excess in general. Partial parallels can be found in the Roman Bacchanalia and medieval carnivals, and in contemporary popular culture in 'partying', 'raves', and that persistent threesome 'sex, drugs and rock 'n' roll'. For Nietzsche, however, the image of such revels was quickly intellectualised and made to stand for a general attitude to life: 'the Dionysian'. (Bakhtin was to do something similar when conceptualising the comparable notion of *carnival* as 'the temporary liberation from prevailing truth and the established order [. . .] the suspension of all hierarchical rank, privileges, norms and prohibitions'; see Bakhtin [1949] 1968: 10.) Thus Nietzsche applied 'the Dionysian' to a whole way of being in the world. 'Under the charm of the Dionysian not only is the union between man and man reaffirmed, but Nature, which had become estranged, hostile, or subjugated, celebrates once more her reconciliation with her prodigal son, man' (Nietzsche (1872) complete in Hofstadter and Kuhns [1964] 1976; here p. 501). A result of this renewed communion and reconciliation of humanity with nature is that 'man feels himself a god, he himself now walks about enchanted, in ecstasy. [. . .] He is no longer an artist, he has become a work of art' (pp. 501–2).

The Dionysian impulse, then, is above all ecstatic and embodied: it celebrates creation as an act of sublime becoming. Especially identified with 'the powerful approach of Spring, penetrating with the joy of nature' and sometimes intensified by 'the influence of narcotic potions', such 'Dionysian stirrings' tend to lead the individual 'to forget himself completely'. But we should not be misled by Nietzsche's characteristic emphasis upon the male. As Carlo Ginzburg shows in his monumental cross-cultural and historical study *Ecstasies* (1990), gangs of deliriously inspired and crazily prophetic 'wild women' were central figures in the early festivals of Dionysus, as in the Orphic rites before and the Bacchanalia afterwards. Indeed, from the Greek and Roman maenads, furies and bacchantes to the witches' sabbaths of the late medieval and early modern periods, there is a strongly feminised and distinctly collective feel to many of the expressions of ecstasy in the popular imaginary (see Plant 1999: 89–98).

In contradistinction to the Dionysian impulse, Nietzsche saw an alternative in the festivals, rituals and world-view he identified with Apollo, the Greek god of reason and wisdom. The latter, he maintained, is the necessary obverse of all that is Dionysian. 'The Apollonian' is thus ultimately characterised by 'higher truth and inner calm': 'the deep consciousness of nature healing and helping in sleep and dreams' along with 'measured restraint' and 'freedom from the wilder emotions' (Hofstadter and Kuhns [1964] 1976: 500). At once tranquil and stable, the Apollonian offers a more quietly interior and disciplined vision of the creative process. It infuses a sense of reason, proportion and intellectual order, and is the very antithesis of the Dionysian emphasis upon wild passion and bodily excess. The Apollonian is also emphatically gendered as masculine. Nietzsche's Dionysian and Apollonian principles are often represented as though they were merely contrary. Properly speaking, however, like so many apparently opposed aspects of the creative process, they turn out to be complementary. As Nietzsche himself insists, with characteristic portentousness: 'And lo! Apollo could not live without Dionysus! The "titanic" and the "barbaric" were in the last analysis as necessary as the Apollonian' (p. 509).

Counterparts of such a 'titanic' struggle over the sources and nature of inspiration can be traced in modern psychology. In fact they occur from its inception in the dramatic and often mythopoeic realisations of the psyche as a site for the clash between 'conscious' and 'unconscious' forces. These were outlined in the previous chapter. All that need be added here is that much later in life Freud developed a frankly dualistic image of two primal forces struggling for control of the psyche: *Eros* (the desire for life and regeneration) and *Thanatos* (the drive to death and destruction). Jung, meanwhile, with his notion of archetypes drawn from the collective unconscious, had always tended to be openly mythopoeic in his view of what drives the psyche. Indeed, both Freud's and Jung's views of the psychic well-springs of creation and destruction often appear to owe more to the dramatic, poetic and philosophical traditions of German Romanticism (including Goethe and Wagner as well as Nietzsche) than they do to clinical practice and empirical observation.

There are numerous variations on and alternatives to these classic psychological views of the 'inspirational' role of the unconscious. Jacques Lacan, for instance, in his 'The Insistence of the Letter in the Unconscious' (1957) endorses Freud's commitment to a project whereby '*I* must come to the place where *it* was' (*Wo* Es *war, soll* Ich *werden*). But for Lacan it is above all what he calls 'the self's radical ex-centricity to itself' that is the main dynamic driving the psyche (Lacan [1957] in Lodge and Wood 2000: 60–88, here pp. 82–3). Moreover, it is precisely at the point where the 'I' senses this 'lack' that language ('the letter') intervenes with both the promise and threat of consolation and compensation on a symbolic level. For, as the title of Lacan's essay itself insists, it is 'the *insistence* of the letter in the unconscious', along with his famous assertion that 'the unconscious is structured like a language' (p. 60), which confirm his commitment to a fundamentally linguistic and symbolic construction of desire. By extension, it is 'language' – not experience – which must be the locus and focus for inspiration. This is the so-called 'linguistic turn' in much post-Freudian and poststructuralist thought. Barthes, for instance, in his 'The Death of the Author' (1969), famously insists, echoing Heidegger, that 'it is language which speaks, not the author; to write is [. . .] to reach that point where only language acts, "performs", and not "me"' (Barthes 1977: 143; cf. Heidegger [1937] 1993: 42).

There are specifically gendered and sexual aspects to inspiration, too. These follow from the 'fe<>male' dynamic of creativity considered in the previous chapter. Hélène Cixous, for instance, in her *Way(s) Out* (1972) argues that it is precisely a person's openness to the interplay of differences, especially inner sexual differences, that ensures that there will be 'the presence in the inventing subject of an abundance of the other [. . .] a springing forth of the self that we did not know about' (Cixous [1972] in Lodge and Wood 2000: 269). Something similar is said by Julia Kristeva, another feminist critic with a strong interest in the relations among sexuality, textuality and psychoanalysis. For Kristeva, the key terms are 'ecstasy', 'intertextuality' and 'the abject'. **Ecstasy**, as already mentioned, comes from Greek *ek-stasis* meaning 'standing beyond' and already had the general sense of 'beside oneself'/'out of it' when Kristeva picked it up and gave it a further twist. The other two terms she coined herself. What precisely she meant by 'intertextuality' is confirmed shortly. The concept of the **abject** (*l'abjet*) may be less familiar and require preliminary explanation. Kristeva coined the word as a noun by analogy with 'subject' (*sujet*) and 'object' (*objet*), drawing on the same Latin root (*jectum*, from *iacere*, to throw). For Kristeva, 'the abject' is that which is 'thrown away' or 'cast aside' from conscious perception, and is strictly neither a perceiving 'subject' nor a perceived 'object'. Here is how Kristeva extrapolates this third, previously excluded state that is strictly neither subject (as self) nor object (as other): *the abject*. Kristeva puts it thus in her *Powers of Horror* (1982):

> There looms within *abjection*, one of those violent, dark revolts of being, directed against a threat that seems to emanate from an exorbitant outside or inside, ejected beyond the scope of the possible, the tolerable, the thinkable. [. . .] that spasm, that leap, is drawn towards an elsewhere as tempting as it is condemned. Unflaggingly, like an inescapable boomerang, a vortex of summons and repulsion places the one haunted by it literally *beside himself*.
>
> (Kristeva [1982] in Cazeaux 2000: 542)

The link with ecstasy is confirmed in Kristeva's comments on Dostoyevsky later in the same essay. For it is above all in the latter's work that she recognises 'the *ecstasy* of an ego that, having lost its Other and its objects, reaches, at the precise moment of [this] suicide, the height of harmony with the promised land' (p. 553, Kristeva's emphasis). This project is elaborated in Kristeva's *Strangers to Ourselves* (1988). Two further things need to be observed historically about this ab-ject/ec-static vision. One is that there clearly – or, perhaps better, opaquely – 'looms within abjection' the shadow of images of the sublime, the grotesque and the monstrous (see above pp. 46–9). This is ecstasy induced by a blend of the awesome and the awful. Secondly, in Kristeva as in Cixous, we may recognise a philosophy as well as a psychology of what the latter calls 'the mad Nietzschean sort', in which the 'creators of new values' are hailed, ambiguously and ambivalently, as both 'inventors and destroyers of concepts' (Cixous [1972] in Lodge and Wood 2000: 269). This is inspiration fraught with dangers as well as delights: the Classical *furor poeticus* pushed to the Romantic limits of 'madness' *and* 'making'.

There are a couple of further twists in the tale of inspiration and its modern counterparts. One relates to 'the linguistic turn' in general, and to **intertextuality** in particular. Barthes puts the general point clearly when he characterises 'a text' as 'a tissue of quotations drawn from the innumerable centres of culture' (Barthes 1977: 146). This, then, is inspiration as 'intertextuality' (see the entry in Makaryk 1993: 568–71). Kristeva was evidently the first to coin the term in the 1960s, when she used it to describe the way in which any text is the 'absorption and transformation of another'. The concept was clearly influenced by Bakhtin's specifically 'dialogic' approach to utterances as 'another's words in one's own language' and by his general concept of 'response-ability'. At the same time, as with her notion of 'the abject', Kristeva adapted these ideas so as to address her own project. In Kristeva's hands, intertextuality is more about the psychological destabilising of conventional subject–object relations (resisting and recasting the idea of a unitary 'author' 'text' or 'reader', for instance) than the retracing of literary sources, allusions and influences as such.

This brings us to the apparently simple but remarkably rich observation that writers and artists (like everyone else) do indeed ***influence*** one another. That is, to pick up a term introduced in the previous chapter, we are all involved in various kinds of 'co-operation', directly or indirectly, consciously or otherwise. Put yet another way, there are various communities, traditions and, ultimately, entire cultures to which each of us belongs and contributes. But whatever frame of reference or 'sphere of influence' we decide to focus upon, several preliminary observations must be made:

- For each of us there are *many* and *various* communities, traditions and cultures to which we relate – not just one and the same.
- These span the dead as well as the living, the remotely absent as well the immediately present.
- Influences therefore exist on a continuum that, in principle, is intrinsically plural and infinitely open.
- And yet, habitually, each influence tends to be treated as if it were singular and finite.

Related issues have been signalled elsewhere (pp. 86–7) in connection with the concept of creativity as *re . . . creation* and, more specifically, as a form of *re-membering*. Here we consider a clutch of writers whose work helps us to both historicise and theorise what may be meant by such concepts as 'tradition' and 'influence'.

T. S. Eliot's classic essay 'Tradition and the individual talent' (1919) is a telling place to start and more complex than a casual reading suggests. To be sure, Eliot offers a version of tradition that is notoriously Eurocentric and potentially nationalist in scope; it is also overtly intellectual, male and depersonalised. Thus 'He [the poet, individual talent] must be aware' of 'the mind of Europe – the mind of his own country – a mind which he learns in time to be much more important than his own private mind' (Eliot [1919] in Lodge 1972: 72–3). Moreover, this is clearly a version of tradition that depends upon 'the appreciation of his [the individual talent's] relation to the dead poets and artists'. Put crudely, this is the tradition of the 'Dead White European Male'. But that is by no means all. Eliot is also sensitive to the possibility of neglected yet potentially significant contributions ('the main current, which does not at all flow invariably through the most distinguished reputations'); and he is careful to emphasise that such a tradition evolves and even progresses: it is 'a mind which changes' and 'this change is a development'. As a result, 'the individual talent' both draws on and in a sense exceeds previous materials, models and insights: 'the conscious present is an awareness of the past in a way and to an extent which the past's awareness of itself cannot show' (p. 73). Thus what from one point of view looks to be a highly conservative, cautiously neo-Classical view of tradition, from another may be aligned with a radically dynamic re-creation of it.

Raymond Williams in his *Marxism and Literature* (1977) says something partly similar to T. S. Eliot about 'tradition', but with a more critically vigorous, overtly class-based edge: 'Most versions of "tradition" can be quickly shown to be radically selective. [. . .] What has then to be said about any tradition is that it is in this sense an aspect of *contemporary* social and cultural organization, in the interest of the dominance of a specific class' (Williams 1977: 115–16). This leads Williams to talk of tradition*s* (plural) in so far as they express the coalescence or collision of three social-historical tendencies: what is 'dominant' and privileged at the time; what is 'residual' and left over from earlier practices; and what is 'emergent' and expressive of potential future directions (pp. 121–7). An example would be Shakespeare's *Hamlet*, where residual feudal models of society are challenged by emergent forms of individualism, and both are set in the context of a dominant contemporary model of the nation state. ('Emergence' of many kinds is picked up later in the chapter.)

Finally, we recognise that *influence* may be very variously construed. Probably the most famous (or infamous) modern attempt at definition is Harold Bloom's *The Anxiety of Influence* (1973). This, along with the three books that followed devoted to this theme, draws together an intriguing yet highly idiosyncratic blend of Freudian psychology and Jewish mysticism. The essential idea, Bloom insists, is that 'strong' poets experience a kind of Oedipal struggle with their god-like 'precursors' in which the latter are subject to a creative 'misreading' or 'misprision'. The result is that 'poetic influence is necessarily misprision, a taking or doing amiss of one's burden', as he puts it in the second book in the series, *A Map of Misreading* (1975; also in Lodge and Wood 2000: 217–29). In more esoteric language, Bloom speaks of the 'ephebe' (the aspiring poet) poised anxiously between 'poetic incarnation' and 'the Return of the Dead' (p. 224). George Steiner uses a similarly archaic idiom when talking of creation as the 'incarnation', literally 'making flesh', of the words of one's literary predecessors (Steiner 2001: 139–40). In both Bloom and Steiner the generally religious and specifically Jewish antecedents of their models of 'influence' are declared. What is not declared, though it can hardly be ignored, is the fact that almost all the writers and artists they cite are men; also that the primal scene of creation is the Oedipal struggle of the son with the father or the originary act of creation of a father-god. In so far as any female principle is recognised, 'she' is the poetic or artistic creation itself (not the struggle that brings it into being) or some relatively conventional version of the woman as ancillary muse or guide (Steiner appeals repeatedly to the role of Beatrice in Dante's *Divine Comedy*).

For a critique of Bloom's predominantly male 'anxiety of influence' we may turn to Sandra Gilbert and Susan Gubar's equally classic and in its own way even more influential study of nineteenth-century women writers, *The Madwoman in the Attic* (1979; 2nd edn 2000). There Gilbert and Gubar argue that so pervasive and insidious was the power of 'patriarchal poetics' in the nineteenth century and earlier that

> the 'anxiety of influence' that a male poet experiences is felt by a female poet as an even more primary 'anxiety of authorship' – a radical fear that she cannot create, that because she cannot become a 'precursor' the act of writing will isolate or destroy her.
>
> (Gilbert and Gubar [1979] 2000: 48–9)

Accentuating the positive, the aim for Gilbert and Gubar was 'to trace the difficult paths by which nineteenth-century women overcame their "anxiety of authorship", repudiated debilitating patriarchal prescriptions, and recovered or remembered the lost foremothers who could help them find their distinctive female power' (p. 59). Thus if the basic challenge for male writers was to overcome the influence of other males, that for female writers was to overcome those of males *and* to find or fashion a female tradition.

The most pressing task for feminist literary historians of the late 1970s and early 1980s, then, was to retrace what Elaine Showalter (also influentially) dubbed *A Litera-ture of Their Own* (1977). In both title and substance this book recalled and celebrated Virginia Woolf's (even more influential) early sketch of a distinctly female tradition of writing and writers in *A Room of One's Own* ([1929] 1992). In this way we can discern not only the unearthing and revaluing of a previously obscured tradition of women's writing but also the consolidation and development of a highly influential academic tradition of women writing on women's writing. The creative influence of the one cannot finally be disentangled from the critical influence of the other. Indeed, as both novelist and essayist, Virginia Woolf fairly stands as a critical-creative 'foremother' crucial to the development of both.

Gilbert and Gubar have been charged by some of their critics with an unduly neg-ative concentration on a female 'anxiety of authorship'; also with a naively essentialist construction of a distinctly 'female power'. Gayatri Spivak, for example, points out that they make a certain version of white individualist feminism complicit with colo-nial privilege. None the less, Gilbert and Gubar succeeded in clearing the way both for more ideologically complex work and for a recognition of the tremendous achieve-ments of later, twentieth-century women writers. Attempting to chart 'how women have won through disease to artistic health' (p. 59), the vision they offer finally exceeds rather than merely extends that offered by their own critical 'precursors', whether Harold Bloom or Virginia Woolf:

> In recent years, for instance, while male writers seem increasingly to have felt exhausted by the need for revisionism which Bloom's theory of the 'anxiety of influence' accurately describes, women writers have seen themselves as pioneers in a creativity so intense that their male counterparts have probably not experi-enced its analog since the Renaissance or at least since the Romantic era.
>
> (Gilbert and Gubar [1979] 2000: 50)

To be sure, questions still hang over the accuracy or adequacy of Bloom's model in the first place (even for male writers), and one may wonder precisely how the exhausted 'revisionism' of male writers differs from the energetic 're-vision' of female traditions so enthusiastically championed by Rich and endorsed by Gilbert and Gubar (pp. 97–9, and see above p. 86). However, proof of such energy – critical as well as creative, in theory and in practice – can be found in the work of Haraway (1991), Ward Jouve (1998), Armstrong (2000) and Braidotti (2002), among many others. And there, as the earlier discussion of 'fe<>male' creativity confirmed, it is precisely the complementarity and heterogeneity – not just the binary opposition – of a radically reconstituted tradition of women's *and* men's writing that is at issue.

Also at issue is the whole notion of the individual, of whatever sex or gender, as the primary locus and focus of *any* kind of influence or tradition. For one thing, attention should perhaps be shifted to the collaborative relationship as such and, beyond that, to the whole 'co-operative' ecology of support networks. Indeed, in the preface to the initial edition of *The Madwoman in the Attic* (1979), Gilbert and Gubar drew attention to the specifically collaborative aspect of their own practice as writers: 'Redefining what has so far been male-defined literary history in the same way that women writers have revised "patriarchal poetics," we have found that the process of collaboration has given us the essential support we needed' (Gilbert and Gubar [1979] 2000: xiv). As a commentator notes, 'Their own collaboration breaks with the model of the isolated, individual scholar' (Leitch 2001: 2022). This strain is expressly maintained in the envoi with which they close the introduction to the second edition of *The Madwoman in the Attic* (2000). There they see themselves as addressing '[n]either our progeny nor our replicants but very much our confederates' (p. xlv). None the less, Gilbert and Gubar are still committed to the idea of individual autonomy and responsibility. They are guarded about 'poststructuralist' critics who are 'less interested in individual writers as originators of meaning and more focused on textual production as a complex and powerful set of meaning-effects with political implications.' They are prepared to acknowledge that for some critics (naming Lacan, Derrida and Foucault) 'it is language that constitutes subjectivity not vice versa'. But they themselves are loath to relinquish their own 'myth of an autonomous subject' – even while recognising that it may indeed be a 'myth' (p. xxxviii).

Clearly, then, when it comes to identifying what 'inspires' or 'informs' or 'influences' the creative act or actor, the precise choice of terms is important. Equally clearly, however, the meaning and force of these terms change as do their relations to one another. So it can never simply be a matter of making a choice between, say, 'language' and 'intertextuality' on the one hand and 'the author' and 'the autonomous subject' on the other. Depending upon the precise context and use, the one may virtually stand in for the other or, alternatively, mean something entirely different. Thus Nietzsche's 'Dionysian' principle may be compared but it should not be casually conflated with Cixous's notion of 'way out' (*sortie*) and Kristeva's notion of 'the abject' and 'ecstatic'. Similarly, there are convincing cases that can be made for both T. S. Eliot's and Raymond Williams's notions of 'tradition'; but so fundamental are the differences in politics that you could not easily combine both perspectives in the same frame for long. Further, you might resist the notion of both a female 'anxiety of authorship' and a male 'anxiety of influence' in a contemporary context; you might have an altogether more celebratory or 'co-operative' vision of the creative process at large. But you would be unwise to discount both totally in a historical view of literary 'influence' in the late nineteenth and early twentieth centuries; or, for that matter, the influence of the critical institutions themselves in the later twentieth century.

And of course you don't have to favour *any* of the terms and concepts highlighted in this section. But you do have to weigh the changing relations among them: to observe the fact that historically one concept may turn into or resemble another, even as a new term appears to displace or replace an old one or an old term returns with a transformed meaning. There are no once-and-for-all answers. But there are more or less historically aware and linguistically sensitive ways of posing the questions and reviewing the possibilities. The same applies – differently – to the cluster of terms, old and new, gathered in the next section.

'Gen–': genius, gender, genetics

All the terms featured in this section have a common root: ***gen–***. In ancient Greek this meant 'birth' in particular and 'beginning' in general: the root is *gennaein*, meaning 'to give birth', 'to begin'. ***Genesis***, for example, the first word of the Bible from which that particular book derives its name, can be translated 'At the birth . . .' as well as the more usual 'In the beginning . . .'. This clearly makes a considerable difference to how we might 'conceive' this most famous of creation stories (which is examined at length in Chapter 5). More generally, we may observe that all the *gen–* terms ultimately have something to do with processes of 'giving birth' and/or 'beginning', whether conceived literally or metaphorically, as sexual procreation or symbolic creation, a one-off act or an ongoing activity. We shall concentrate on just three *gen–* terms central to creativity debates, ancient and modern: **genius** and **genetics**, with **gender** as a crucial link. As we shall see, *gen*etics turns out to be the modern *gen*ius of the age in far more senses than one; while changing conceptions of what it is to be socially constructed as feminine or masculine (in terms of *gen*der) or biologically constructed as female or male (in terms of sex) have crucial roles to play in both processes. A brief review of a couple of other familiar *gen–* terms will help set the scene.

Generation – as in such phrases as 'the older/younger generation', 'your parents' generation' – refers broadly to all those members of a social group or species born around the same time. Latterly, this sense has been much extended to include all those machines and models (computers, programmes, cars, etc.) developed according to the same design and production process. Thus both human and the artificial 'generations' are implied in the sub-title of the various *Star Trek* follow-up series: *The Second Generation, The Next Generation*, etc. Meanwhile, from the early nineteenth century onwards it has been increasingly common to talk of the 'generation' of everything from wealth to ideas and electricity (see *OED* and Williams 1983: 140–2). This is a powerful reminder that 'generation' (like 'reproduction') can now readily designate processes that are mental as well as material, mechanical as well as biological. Indeed, as so often in crucial areas of contemporary discourse, all these categories tend to be unstable and permeable. 'Generative linguistics', for example, is an approach to language learning and grammatical transformation that has much in common with systems-based and computer-assisted modelling (see above p. 55). Following Chomsky, the basic idea is that all language has the capacity to 'generate' potentially infinite and highly complex strings of words from essentially simple resources according to finite rules. This is an approach to codes and sign-systems that now informs models ranging from cognitive linguistics to artificial intelligence (see Pinker 1999 and Boden in Sternberg 1999: 351–72). Indeed, as biology and technology converge in neural networks and genetic engineering, the question of 'who or what *creates* whom or what?' increasingly tends to be reframed as 'who or what *generates* whom or what?'

Genres, too, are crucial areas of 'beginning' and 'birth'. They designate 'kinds' of literature and art and, by extension, cultural practice at large: kinds of poetry, prose, music, painting, film, advert, news story, clothing, hair style, etc. At root the term is a French variant of the plural *genera* of Latin *genus*, which also gives us the biological term for related groups of species. Thus humanity (*homo sapiens*) is a part of the genus that includes apes and chimpanzees (the anthropoids). All this is a reminder that, in an evolutionary perspective, the study of 'genre' is ultimately concerned with the ways in which the various 'kinds' of cultural form change, grow and evolve over time and vary from culture to culture. Genre is never a matter of absolutely fixed or universal categories. The genre known as 'the novel', for instance (as we see in Chapter 7), not withstanding its apparent claim to a kind of once-and-for-all 'newness', grew out of earlier forms of narrative in verse and drama as well as prose journals and letters, and has since grown into yet other forms influenced by film and TV as well the other printed media. So in this respect, aspects of it are both immemorially old (as old as story-telling) and ceaselessly renewed (as new as the latest story-line in a video game or a soap opera).

The more general point is that *all* genres, in so far as they continue to be alive and vibrant, are as 'old' as we find them and as 'new' as we (re-)make them. This fact is often obscured by the persistently neo-Classical tendency to treat genres as fixed, pure and distinct categories: approaching Shakespeare's plays as 'comedies' *or* 'tragedies' *or* 'histories', for instance, or as 'poetry' *or* 'prose'. Such an approach may be initially convenient but is grossly distorting and fundamentally limiting. *Hamlet* (nominally a tragedy), *Henry IV* (nominally a history) and *The Merry Wives of Windsor* (nominally a comedy) all carry elements of the other two 'genres' in various configurations; and each includes poetry as well as prose. In fact, none is purely or absolutely anything. Moreover, all of them can be realised in very various ways depending upon the moment, medium and aim of the production. The character of Hamlet, for instance, can be played as brooding or flippant, while 'the clowns' who play the gravediggers can be solemn philosophers, social subversives or just plain 'clownish'. In fact, genres that didn't constantly change, grow and 'give birth' to other genres wouldn't be proper 'genres' at all. They would be merely after-the-event critical categories rather than ongoing creative resources. As Bakhtin puts it, talking of literature in particular but in terms that apply to any cultural form, 'Genre is reborn and renewed at every stage in the development of literature, and in every individual work of a given genre' (Bakhtin 1981: 321; also see Bakhtin 1986 and Duff 2000).

Clearly, then, stretching from *gen*esis to *gen*re, there is an enormous amount of *gen*erative power packed into that tiny element *gen–*. Having grasped that, we may now trace the roots that bind – and the routes that join – the ancient concept of *gen*ius to the recent science of *gen*etics. And to do that, as already mentioned, we must pick up issues of *gen*der (and sex and much else) along the way.

In its earliest Latinate usage, '**genius**' has remarkably little to do with the modern sense of exceptionally creative individuals. Rather, it is closely associated with the collective identity of the tribe, kin or family (Latin *gens*, *ingens*) and more particularly with tribal or family spirits (*genii*) (*OED* 'genius' sense 1); hence the modern sense of other *gen–* words such as *gen*ial and *gen*erous, meaning 'sociable' and 'giving'. Hence, too, the etymological as well as cultural link with Asian notions of the 'genie' or *djinn*. Most familiar in the West from *The Thousand and One Nights*, a genie could be a power for good or ill depending how it was invoked and handled (*OED*, sense 2). The same applied to the Greek notion of a personal spirit as a *daimon*. This too could be a beneficial guardian spirit; but it was literally 'demonised' by Christianity to give us the utterly diabolical notion of a 'demon'. Meanwhile, a sense of 'genius of place' (*genius loci*) identified many of these 'spirits' not only with people but with the places where those people were born and brought up: houses, gardens, farms, territories and regions. In this respect, genius was conceived as a guarding and guiding 'tutelary' spirit or as a 'familiar' identified with familiar haunts and family. It sprang from a sense of place as well as race, something in the soil as well as the blood. It therefore expressed a collective resource rather than an individual capacity. This archaic view of genius is the one recalled and celebrated by William Blake in his *The Marriage of Heaven and Hell* (1793, Plate 11):

> The ancient Poets animated all sensible objects with Gods or Geniuses, calling them by the names and adorning them with the properties of woods, rivers, mountains, lakes, cities, nations, and whatever their enlarged & numerous senses could perceive. And particularly they studied the genius of each city & country, placing it under its mental deity.

Typical of Blake, his appeal to a classical 'genius of place' ran counter to the increasingly individualistic notions of genius that were developing at the time, and which have since become Romantic clichés. Thus in the Proverbs of Hell Blake urges 'When thou seest an Eagle, thou seest a portion of Genius; lift up thy head!' (Plate 9, l. 15) and insists 'Improvement makes strait roads; but the crooked roads without Improvement are roads of Genius' (Plate 10, l. 6). In modern terms we might call this an 'ecological' view of genius; and it is interesting to note that the general classical sense had been maintained in learned discourse throughout the Middle Ages. The figure of 'Genius' in Gower's *Confessio Amantis* (*c.* 1385), for example, like its precursor in *The Romance of the Rose*, is a guiding presence expressing the larger design of Nature and Reason within humanity. Meanwhile, in more general parlance, genius for a long time simply meant what was 'natural' to a person: an expression of their characteristic disposition but not necessarily an exceptional quality. 'Every man has his genius', says Dr Johnson (1780) (see *OED* sense 4).

But a decisive shift in the meaning of 'genius' began to take place during the late eighteenth century. Thenceforward 'genius' steadily moved away from its spiritual and collective senses associated with kith and kin and from its routine sense of characteristic disposition, towards its dominant modern sense of 'an exceptionally creative or clever individual', 'intellectual power of an exalted type' (*OED*, sense 5). The reasons for such a shift are complex. In narrowly linguistic terms it seems to have been facilitated by a partial confusion and conflation of sense with the recently introduced and distantly related word 'ingenious' (from neo-Classical Latin *ingenium*, where it meant 'ability' or 'capacity'). In English the latter quickly came to mean 'clever' and 'cunning', and may have pushed the sense of 'genius' in that direction too. More generally, however, the overall trajectory of 'genius' can clearly be associated with the rise of individualism and humanism from the sixteenth century and, from the eighteenth century, with the particular forms this took under the pressure of Romanticism. Significantly, both the 'old' and 'new' senses of 'genius' can be observed in the work of Joseph Addison, an early eighteenth-century writer recognised for his sensitivity to changes in social taste and aesthetic value. In pieces written for *The Spectator* in the same year (numbers 29 and 160; 1711), he observes on the one hand that 'A Composer should fit his Music to the genius of the People' (older, collective, generalised sense) and on the other that 'there is no Character more frequently given to a Writer than that of being a Genius' (newer, individual, elevated sense) (see *OED* senses 3b and 6b). Such changes in the English sense of 'genius' seem to have both anticipated and influenced later changes in the other main European languages (see Williams 1983: 143). The German Romantic movement known variously as *Genieperiode* ('Genius-period') and *Sturm und Drang* ('Storm and Stress') is the most famous manifestation of this tendency. But whatever the precise order of influence, the overall situation in terms of literary and cultural history is clear:

> *Genius* is the crucial middle term developed mainly in the eighteenth century, in the millennial transition from theories which view the sources of poetic originality and creation as *external* (i.e. concepts of divine inspiration and poetic madness) to theories which posit them as *internal* (i.e. as processes of imagination or of the sub-conscious).
>
> (Preminger and Brogan 1993: 455–6, my emphasis)

To be sure, there continued to be intense argument about what may be conceived as 'external' or 'internal', and whether genius is inspired by nature at large or gener-ated from within a specifically human nature. Indeed, contrary to stereotypes of the Romantic artist as a kind of divinely inspired visionary on the one hand or a nat-urally spontaneous 'genius' on the other, it is usually the sense of a dynamic relation *between* external and internal sources and resources – and especially the apprehension of the external *as* internal (and vice versa) – that acts as the main locus of imaginative work at this time (see 'Real Romantic Writers', Chapter 7).

There are several aspects of the 'genius' debate that were prominent through the eighteenth century and beyond, and continue to have resonance in creativity debates today. One is the question 'How far is genius (creativity) *innate?*' The other, related, is 'Can genius (creativity) be *learnt?*' Yet another relates to the persistent but by no means universal distinction between (mere) *talent* and (sheer) *genius*. The answers turn out to be more complex and vexed than one may expect.

'Genius is the innate mental disposition through which nature gives the rule to art', declared Immanuel Kant in his *Critique of Judgement* (1790; section 46; in Hofstadter and Kuhns [1964] 1976: 314). This clearly aligns genius with 'nature' and recalls many a neo-Classical insistence that art is informed by nature (e.g. that of Alexander Pope; see below p. 232). However, Kant, goes on to give the whole thing a number of distinctly modern twists. He makes 'originality' the primary defining quality of genius; he comes down against the applicability to it of rules, and he insists that ultimately it cannot be learnt: 'We thus see that genius is a *talent* for producing that for which no definite rule can be given; it is not a mere aptitude for what can be learned by a rule. Hence *originality* must be its first property' (p. 315, Kant's emphasis). This clearly favours the modern sense of 'original' meaning 'new/novel' rather than its ancient diametrically opposed sense of 'from the origin/beginning' (see above p. 57). Impor-tant qualifications need to be made, however. Kant expressly limits his conception of genius to the arts, and to 'beautiful' art at that; he does not extend it to the sciences: 'Nature, by the medium of genius, does not prescribe rules to science but to art, and to it only in so far as it is to be beautiful art' (p. 315). Georg Hegel, however, writing half a century later, will have little to do with the supposedly superior 'genius' of the artist, even if it is allowed to be 'natural'. This is how he sums up the issue in the Introduction to his *Lectures on Fine Art* (1835–8):

> All that is essential is to state the view that even if the talent and genius of the artist has in it a natural element, yet this element essentially requires development

by thought, reflection on the mode of its productivity, and practice and skill in producing. For, apart from anything else, a main feature of artistic production is external workmanship, since the work of art has a purely technical side which extends into handicraft.

(Hegel [1835–8] in Leitch 2001: 637)

Hegel thus sounds a deeply sceptical note echoing many others before and since. Longinus, for instance, in his treatise *On the Sublime* (which was written in the first century CE but not rediscovered until the sixteenth) reports the generally held view: 'Genius, they say, is innate; it is not something that can be learnt, and nature is the only art that begets it' (Chapter 2, Longinus 1965: 101). But for his own part he argues 'a case for the opposite point of view', that 'although nature is in the main subject to her own laws where sublime feelings are concerned, she is not given to acting at random and wholly without system'. In fact, in a whole string of writers from before Longinus to after Hegel, whenever the notion of a supposedly natural 'genius' arises, it is rarely let pass without a series of counter-appeals: to the sheer materiality of processes of production; to the crucial importance of acquired technique; and to the essential continuity between 'art' and all forms of 'workmanship' and 'handicraft' (see Preminger and Brogan 1993: 455–7 and references in Leitch 2001: 2586).

In a similar vein, there are periodic attempts to distinguish 'talent' as an inferior, more mechanical facility from 'genius' as a superior, more innovative capacity. Thus Samuel Taylor Coleridge in his *Biographia Literaria* (Chapter 2, 1817) defines 'mere talent' as 'the faculty of appropriating and applying the knowledge of others' and distinguishes it from 'the creative and self-sufficing power of absolute genius'. And latterly Harold Bloom bases his 'personal definition' of the talent/genius distinction upon a 'rough but effectual test: however I have been entertained, has my awareness been intensified, my consciousness widened, and clarified?' And he concludes, 'If not, then I have encountered talent, not genius' (Bloom 2002: 12). But Kant and Hegel use the corresponding terms interchangeably, and the talent/genius distinction always proves easier to assert theoretically than demonstrate in practice. Indeed, most contemporary researchers into creativity leave it well alone and, like Michael Howe, content themselves with the observation that 'the mental operations that geniuses depend upon are not qualitatively distinct from ones used by individuals whose expertise is not exceptional' (Howe 1999: 179; and see above p. 53).

None the less, in common parlance and the language of the popular media, the stereotype of the Romantic 'genius' proves remarkably tenacious. To be sure, it is often given a homely or ironic twist ('You're a genius!' I say to my twelve-year-old son, who in two minutes – without the manual, of course – has succeeded in tuning the video I had been struggling with for an hour), but it continues to feature regularly as a blanket term of approval for individuals who are supposedly outstanding in some way. It is widely used in advertising and journalism, and at the moment frequently crops up in TV cookery and home improvement shows: 'Jamie's a genius with the herbs!' (of TV cook Jamie Oliver), and 'That fence was a stroke of genius' (of garden handyman Tommy Walsh). In fact, 'genius' is still far and away the most common epithet used for all kinds of individuals reckoned to be outstanding in their field: a Shakespeare in literature, a Mozart in music, an Einstein in science, and more recently Stephen (*A Brief History of Time*) Hawking and Bill (Microsoft®) Gates.

In popular culture, then, the concept of 'genius' is alive and well. In ideological terms, its most common function seems to be to promote some supposedly outstanding individual (and often by implication some product) while at the same time ignoring the routine process and all the detail that goes into the making – whether the product in question be a theory of physics or a computer empire. In this respect 'genius' is the personalised quintessence of a highly individualised brand of creativity. It is 'creativity as hero', with an overwhelming emphasis on the male. Meanwhile, the notion of 'the evil genius' – who often turns out to be a 'mad scientist' or 'master criminal' or both (Moriarty, Dr No, Hannibal Lecter, the parodic Dr Evil of *Austin Powers*) – is the personified embodiment of all that is *wrong* with the world. He is the secular counterpart of 'the devil incarnate'. And again the ideological effect is to simplify, personalise and exoticise what otherwise might have to be faced as highly complex, deeply vexed and substantially impersonal issues to do with knowledge, power and responsibility. This may be no problem in the area of popular entertainment and fiction. But it begins to look distinctly dubious – and downright dangerous – when extended to such figures as Osama Bin Laden (frequently depicted as the 'evil genius' and 'mastermind' behind the atrocities of 11 September 2001), just as historically it has been regularly applied to such figures as Napoleon, Stalin, Hitler and Pol Pot. All these names are dramatically appealing but perilously reductive ciphers for highly involved political-historical processes and ethical issues. 'Evil geniuses' – like their more virtuous counterparts – are never solely responsible for anything.

It is also abundantly clear, as the above examples attest, that the concept of 'genius' is deeply gendered. It is the ultimate embodiment, of 'the great man as creator' – or 'destroyer'. Either way, the emphasis falls equally upon 'great' and 'man'. Indeed, throughout its history the concept has been almost indelibly marked as masculine. Thus, whether identifying tutelary deities, territorial holdings, tribal or national allegiances, the nature of people in general or of specially creative persons in particular, 'genius' has referred primarily to men. Conversely, at its crudest, it underwrote the view that 'there are no women of genius; the women of genius are men', as the Goncourt brothers said and Cesare Lombroso endorsed in his *The Man of Genius* (1863). Such statements belong to what Christine Battersby in her *Gender and Genius: Towards a Feminist Aesthetics* (1989) identifies as 'the Virility School of Creativity' (Battersby 1989: 60, 115). The typical 'member of the Virility School', says Battersby, 'makes art *dis*placed male sexuality [. . .] but *mis*placed female sexuality' (p. 60). Ezra Pound's aggressively male celebration of the *logos spermatikos*, referred to in the previous chapter, is a classic modernist example. And there are many more, from before Aristotle to after Mailer.

But the presumed 'maleness' of genius has often been hotly contested and itself shown to be misplaced. Elizabeth Barrett Browning, for instance, addressed sonnets both of 'Recognition' and 'Desire' to George Sand, a female writer who in contemporary gender terms was shockingly unconventional (she wore suits like a man, for example): 'True genius, but true woman! Dost deny / Thy woman's nature with a manly scorn, / And break away the gauds and armlets worn / By weaker women in captivity?' ('To George Sand – A Recognition', ll. 1–4, 1844; and see Chapter 7 below p. 209). The logic of this is vexed (Barrett Browning is not prepared to say 'True genius *and* true woman', for instance) and the tone is questioning, even querulous. But there is no doubt that both she and George Sand are openly challenging a male monopoly on 'genius', and that the concept is seen, along with decorative dress codes, as an instrument for keeping 'weaker women in captivity'. In fact, Barrett Browning is one of the literary 'foremothers' who prompts Virginia Woolf to observe in *A Room of One's Own* that 'genius of a sort must have existed among women, as it must have existed among the working class' (Woolf [1929] 1992: 63). Though again we may sense a note of reserve or a need for qualification ('genius *of a sort*'). This is a sentence and a sentiment expressly picked up and amplified by Alice Walker in her *In Search of Our Mothers' Gardens* (1974). And there it is cued by a question that leaves little doubt about the politics of reappropriating the term for a specifically black and female consciousness – 'Did you have a genius of a great-great-grandmother who died under some ignorant and depraved white overseer's lash?' Walker's glossing of Woolf acts as both endorsement and challenge:

> 'Yet genius of a sort must have existed among women as it must have existed among the working class.' [Change this to 'slaves' and 'the wives and daughters of sharecroppers.'] Now and again an Emily Brontë or a Robert Burns [change this to 'a Zora Hurston or a Richard Wright'] blazes out and proves its presence.
> (Walker [1974] in Gates and McKay 1997: 2385)

To be sure, at first glance, neither Woolf's nor Walker's statement appear to fundamentally subvert the notion of the 'genius' as outstanding named individual. They simply – albeit crucially – open up the possibility of individual named geniuses who are female, black and poor (as opposed to male, white and privileged). It should be observed, however, that both writers go on to acknowledge the potential significance of anonymous work: 'Indeed, I would venture to suggest that Anon, who wrote so many poems without signing them, was often a woman', says Woolf ([1929] 1992: 63). And Walker takes this as the cue for an open celebration of the kind of 'creative spark' that is nurtured and passed on through work of a collaborative, often manual and non-verbal kind: 'And so our mothers and grandmothers have, more often than not anonymously, handed on the creative spark, the seed of the flower they themselves never hoped to see; or like a sealed letter they could not plainly read.' Significantly, Walker's central examples of this are gardening and quilt-making, neither of which is conventionally considered a 'high art' form of creativity. This, then, is 'genius' not as great individual artist but as collaborative and anonymous artisan: a matter of skilled and patient handiwork rather than grandly imposing gestures. It gets its hands dirty, has its feet on the ground, and its roots in the soil. It is therefore what Willis and others would call a 'grounded aesthetic' (see above pp. 12–13). And in a curious way it both recalls and reconnects with that ancient conception of genius as 'the spirit of place' and 'tutelary deity': in archaic terms, kith and kin (literally, 'the familiar and the family'); in contemporary terms, identity and belonging. In any event 'genius' has in some measure been re-claimed and re-freshed. *Re . . . created*, if you like.

To *re . . . create* the concept of 'genius' in yet other ways, however, we need to take a fresh line of enquiry. And to do that we shall pick up that other *gen–* term: *genetics*. Equipped with some basic information on the latter (drawn from such standard references as Jones 1994, Ridley 1997 and Coen 1999), we shall be in a position to grasp a complexly interconnected *gen–* agenda that spans the arts and sciences, from 'genius' to 'genes' with 'gender' as a crucial link. This opens the way to a further, radically re-configured conception of creativity.

Genetics is the study of genes, and genes are the basic elements of biochemical codes passed on in reproduction. Clustered together in chromosomes, genes are what tell the cells of an organism to make a flower, a fish, an insect, a cow or a human being. This information is crucial because in many fundamental respects the cells of all organic life, whether animals or plants, are substantially similar: all have a central nucleus, mitochondria for respiration, and ribosomes for making proteins (though only plant cells have chloroplasts for photosynthesis and only animal blood cells have haemoglobin). Humans, for example, share 98 per cent of their genetic material with chimpanzees and 40 per cent with lettuces. All this points to the fundamental inter-relatedness of all organic life, notwithstanding differentiations of structure and function. 'Life', meanwhile, may be provisionally defined as *the capacity to reproduce and grow, where growth includes adaptation and variation not just reaction and identical replication* (see Boden 1996: Introduction). Clearly, 'life' in this sense has a great deal in common with what in the previous chapter was defined as 'creativity'. For instance, it is at once deeply ordinary, because shared by many organisms, and highly extraordinary, because extremely diverse and ultimately unique in each case – hence 'extra/ordi-nary'. And by the same token, like creativity, life is always in various senses 'original and fitting' (i.e. adapting and adaptive). In fact, many of the other criteria used to define creativity – 'full-filling', 'in(ter)ventive', 'co-operative', etc., – can also be applied, with due modification, to life. For this reason, very different philosophers of 'life' who have been deeply mindful of evolution – from Bergson to Deleuze and from Dewey to Dennett – have often been in every sense 'vitally' concerned with matters of creativity (see Joas 1996: 126–44 and Ansell Pearson 1999). Further, as we now see, a genetically informed account of the specifically reproductive aspects of life offers a working model – not just a catchy metaphor – for creativity as an evolving process. In these senses, creativity *is* – not just is like – life.

In order to explore the life/creativity relation more closely, we shall begin by reviewing the three basic kinds of biological reproduction: viral, cellular, and sexual. We shall treat each in turn, beginning with the simplest. *Viruses* are parasites that can only exist and grow within some 'host' cell that they invade and in effect 'colonise'. Viruses cause everything from foot and mouth disease in cattle and sheep to the common cold in human beings. A virus does this by injecting a host cell with its genetic material and taking over the reproductive system to work on its own behalf. Viruses are not cells in their own right (they have no nucleus of their own, for example) and they exist on the borderline between organic life and inorganic chem-istry. A second, more complex mode of reproduction is by *cell division*: a process called 'fission' or 'mitosis'. In this a single cell 'replicates' itself and splits into virtually identi-cal cells; the most famous single-celled organism that does this is amoeba. The third and most complex mode of reproduction is the one in which human beings (along with mammals, insects, fish and many plants) are all involved. This is *sexual reproduc-tion*. To reproduce sexually, cells from two organisms of the same species, typically distinguished as 'female' and 'male', come together in a process called 'fusion' or 'meiosis'. They thereby produce a cell related to but different from each of the parents' cells. Thereafter the cells divide and multiply through processes of fission, as in the second type of reproduction, and the organism develops from there.

Clearly, it is the third, sexual form of reproduction that is the most dynamic and complex. It entails the combination of different entities to produce another that is similar yet different (e.g. a child as distinct from yet related to its parents) rather than just the splitting of the same (as in amoeba) or the taking over of the one by the other (as in viruses). For that reason sexual reproduction is the naturally favoured form for comparatively complex and highly differentiated organisms, both in plants and animals. It is worth pointing out, however, that the specifically 'sexual' dimension of genetic coding is relatively limited and localised. In humans, for instance, of the twenty-three pairs of chromosomes (gene clusters) found in each cell, only one pair is distinguished as male or female. In this respect the modern 'genetic' answer to the ancient question of 'How different is the "genius" of men and women?' is 'Not very much.' That is, genetically speaking, members of both sexes have far more in common (in a proportion of 22:1) than not. The sexual difference is crucial, of course (women can have babies, men can't); but it is still less pervasive than many people expect.

The fundamental significance of all this for actual processes of *procreation* is obvious enough. However, as already intimated, it has a profound significance for processes of *creativity*, too. For instance, at the level of both biological *and* cultural reproduction we can engage immediately with matters of difference and similarity, fission and fusion, female and male ('fe<>male' in the terms of the previous chapter). Indeed, humanity is chiefly, if not exclusively, distinguished by virtue of the fact that it reproduces and develops itself *culturally* as well as biologically, through all the tools and institutions it creates and communicates (including language, symbolic systems and knowledge of all kinds), not just its capacity to procreate itself. And this applies whether we define humanity as *homo sapiens* (knowing) *homo faber* (making) or *homo ludens* (playing). Human sexual activity, for example, has been developed as an 'art' as well as a 'science', as attested by the countless manuals on the techniques for sex and love, ancient and modern, and the virtual obsession with the subject in the modern West. And yet, at the same time, it should be observed that these are properties that we share, at least to some extent, with the rest of the animal world. Elaborate 'courtship' and 'mating displays' are evidently – superabundantly – not just the prerogative of humans: all sorts of other organisms – from peacocks and butterflies to orange blossom and orchids – also go to extravagant lengths to attract and secure the attentions of their sexual mates and go-betweens.

Our general dilemma, then, is precisely that we are very much *a part of* the rest of life on this planet, however much we may appear to be *apart from* it. Indeed, it may be argued that the models and materials of biological reproduction (especially sexual reproduction) are the very building-blocks and informing principles of *creative life in general* – not just *human creativity in particular*. None the less, for humanity (i.e. us) a couple of crucial questions still remain: how far do our unusually highly developed modes of *cultural* life differ fundamentally from those of our *sexual* life? And are these *differences in kind* (setting us apart from aspects of ourselves as well as animals which thereby become inaccessibly 'other') or *differences in degree* (recognising our fundamental continuity and, indeed, community with what can then be acknowledged as 'other animals'). Either way, *human creation as a cultural activity* (including the ongoing creation of what we know as 'humanity') has a fundamentally unresolved – if not necessarily irresolvable – connection with *human procreation as a biological activity* (including our ongoing relations with 'other animals' – or 'animals as other' – on this planet). Something similar might be said about the relations between human (re)production and the (re)production of what it is to be human.

The mythic and metaphorical relations between (cultural) creation and (sexual) procreation are explored at length in Part 2. Here we shall simply observe that even to posit such a relation requires us to draw on the resources of language, metaphorical and otherwise. In the present case, therefore, we need to take a closer look at the 'language' of genetics. For even among scientists it is common to talk of genetics as a specialised chemical 'code' and, in common parlance, a kind of 'language'. At a basic level this is not surprising. DNA (deoxyribonucleic acid), the essential chemical ingredient of genetic material, is organised in terms of just four basic elements: adenine, guanine, thymine and cytosin (A, G, T and C, for short). Each part of the gene may therefore be 'spelt', and in the scientific literature actually recorded, in terms of permutations of just four letters: AGTC, TCGA, CATG, etc. In this respect the analogy between genetics and language is quite compelling. Both are concerned with kinds of selection and combination. Genes can be broken down into 'letters' and built up into sequences, just as words can be. We may even be inclined to think of strings or clusters of genes (chromosomes) as 'sentences' and the overall genetic make-up of a particular organism (the genotype) as a kind of 'text'. From there it is a comparatively easy leap to conceive of the genetic resources of a particular species (its gene pool or genome) as a specific 'language', which itself exists as one among many other more or less interconnected 'languages' (i.e. more or less shared gene pools/genomes). These are all analogies explored by the geneticist Steve Jones in his *The Language of the Genes* (1994).

But the 'genetic code/language' analogy, as Jones recognises, needs to be applied with caution, and with a sense of what actually goes on in language as well as genetics. For instance, the precise way in which strings of genes actually reproduce ('replicate') involves the unravelling of a linked, ladder-like chain into two strands and the attraction of materials from the surrounding biochemical 'soup' in order to make up two new and virtually identical strings. This process is facilitated by a simpler form of nucleic acid (ribonucleic acid, RNA) which acts as a kind of 'messenger', 'mediator' or 'catalyst' between the DNA and the surrounding material. It's as if the two parts of a zip were to come apart and draw on the surrounding materials to make two new zips. This is the famous 'double helix' structure of DNA and, as the preceding description demonstrates, it can be explained by other analogies than 'language' alone: 'string', 'chain', 'ladder', 'soup', 'zip', etc. Or rather, to be more precise, genetics can be explained drawing upon the metaphorical resources of language at large (including algebraic formulae), not just 'language' as itself a metaphor. 'Gene', for example, was coined in the late nineteenth century from the Greek root *gen–* (meaning 'beginning', 'birth') featured throughout the present section. 'Chromosome' was coined in the early twentieth century from the Greek for 'coloured body' (*chromos + soma*) because that was precisely how it appeared when first observed under high-powered microscopes.

But there is a deeper and more structural way in which genetics and language can be conceived as related. Both involve the ceaseless recombination of existing elements to make new configurations. Indeed, it is precisely because ostensibly 'the same thing' constantly gets 'put' in slightly – sometimes very – different ways that both language and genetics are fundamentally 'generative' processes: they are ceaselessly engaged with the one thing that becomes, two, three . . . and eventually many. As far as language is concerned, this may be put in the terms of 'generative linguistics' introduced earlier. Language is a system informed by rules that are in principle simple but which in practice are capable of generating highly complex, fresh and potentially infinite instances (including blends, mutations and 'mistakes'). As a result, every language (English, for example) can be seen as a system in process, never completed, always open to change. In short, it evolves.

Very much the same can be said of a genome (i.e. the gene pool for a particular species). Genes, too, are simple in principle (at base they involve just four elements, represented by the letters ACGT); but in practice, when permutated and 'translated' into specific materials, they can result in forms as different as a sea anemone, a tree and a chimpanzee. Indeed, it is modern genetics that has helped relate the inner workings of the organism and the development of species to the overall processes of natural selection and evolution observed by Darwin. Further, in an evolutionary perspective, it is to genetics that we look for the 'mistakes' (mutations, deviations) that ensure that the genome will remain open and capable of change. Thus we now know, as Darwin did not, that genes 'are continually being shuffled down the generations into new arrangements by sex and re-combination', and that this is the way in which 'nature is continually testing out different combinations of genes' (Gribbin 1998: 115). Further, because 'all of this copying that goes on when cells divide is not perfect [. . .] nature is also "inventing" new genes – or, at least, variations on old genes'. In fact, it is precisely this aspect of the copy that is 'not perfect' (i.e. not absolutely identical) that is the essential – not the incidental – feature in a system designed to support variation and 'mutation'. Gribbin summarises the matter thus:

> Evolution (at the level of individual animals and plants) depends on the way genes are copied and passed on to the next generation (heredity), and the fact that this copying process is (as we have seen) very nearly, but not quite, perfect. It is the 'very nearly' that ensures that offspring resemble their parents, and are members of the same species; it is the 'not quite' that allows evolution to work, sometimes leading to the establishment of new species.
>
> (Gribbin 1998: 116)

Such observations are common in the literature. 'It is imperfection that drives evolution – without variation due to genetic mutation or miscopying, there is no heritable differentiation on which the environment can work' (Ede 2000: 117). 'It is upon the *flaws* of Nature, not the Laws of nature, that the possibility of our existence hinges' (Barrow 1995: 37). More positively, the emphasis is upon the capacity of genes to 'create' new configurations, not just 'copy' old ones. And this is precisely how the plant geneticist Enrico Coen frames it in his *The Art of Genes: How Organisms Make Themselves* (1999). Drawing upon a broadly artistic and specifically pictorial analogy, Coen insists that the whole process whereby genes contribute to the formation of an organism is much closer to the activity of an artist 'creating' than 'copying' a picture. He explains the distinction thus:

> By *creating*, I mean the highly interactive process that goes on when, say, an artist paints an original picture. Unlike *copying*, the final aim is not there in front of

the artist to begin with. The picture emerges through an interaction between the artist, the canvas and the environment. [. . .] the process by which a DNA sequence eventually becomes manifest in a complex organism has many more parallels with the interactive process of creating an original than with making a replica or copy.

(Coen 1999: 34)

Thus, in broad outline, whether the analogy is with language or with art, the basic genetic mechanisms of evolution are generally agreed. There are, however, still many questions about the precise how and why. In particular: *How 'determined' or 'free' are these systems? and how fundamentally competitive ('selfish') or collaborative ('co-operative') is the behaviour they embody?* For convenience, the main lines of these debates will be traced in the opposed views of two professors of biology (Steven Rose and Richard Dawkins), interspersed with other comparisons in passing.

In his *Lifelines: Biology, Freedom, Determinism* (1997), Steven Rose operates with a model in which 'Organisms are open systems in which continuity is provided by a constant flow of energy through them' (Rose 1997: 306). In general terms this recalls both Bergson and Csikszentmihalyi in their conceptions of creative 'energy' as kinds of 'flow'. More specifically, Rose observes that 'lives form a developmental trajectory, or lifeline, stabilized by the operation of homeodynamic principles' (p. 306). The latter are principles that maintain both continuing 'sameness' (from Greek *hom(e)o*, 'same') and variable difference (dynamically). Philosophically, this idea bears comparison with Deleuze's concept of creative activity on 'lines of flight' constituted by the interplay of 'difference and repetition' (see above pp. 87–8). Another term Rose uses to refer to this process is *autopoiesis*, from the Greek elements for 'self' (as in *auto*nomy and *auto*biography) and 'making, fashioning' (the initial sense of *poiesis*). Life in this view is at least in part *autopoietic* in that it is 'self-fashioning' and 'self-determining'. Interestingly, Csikszentmihalyi makes a similar claim for creative persons being at least in some measure *autotelic*, responsible for discerning and pursuing their own goals (from Greek *auto* plus *telos*, 'aim', 'goal', 'end'; see Csikszentmihalyi 1996: 113). Rose is particularly keen to counter those who see 'the genes' as some kind of pre-determined force: a template or blueprint from which the organism cannot and must not diverge. 'Rather,' insists Rose,

life [. . .] is an autopoietic process, shaped by the interplay of specificity and plasticity. In so far as any aspect of life can be said to be 'in the genes', our genes provide the capacity for both *specificity* – a lifeline relatively impervious to developmental and environmental buffeting – and *plasticity* – the ability to respond appropriately to unpredictable environmental *contingency*, that is, to experience.

(Rose 1997: 306, my emphasis)

The key terms here are 'specificity' and 'plasticity' and 'contingency', all of which feature prominently in arguments against what Rose and others term 'genetic reductionism' (see Pfenninger and Shubik 2001: 90, 94). Stephen Jay Gould also makes 'contingency' central to his theory of evolution, and points to a pattern of 'punctuated equilibrium' (i.e. highly variable rates of change) rather than the even and gradual change assumed by Darwin or the unrelenting and virtually determinist change proposed by some contemporary evolutionists (see Gould 2002: 1332–43). 'Genetic reductionism', which both Rose and Gould oppose, is the tendency to reduce agency to single, all-controlling causes. In the case of genetics this means that everything is imagined to be 'in the genes'. In extreme form this amounts to the claim that there is a single gene which determines each physical feature: one for blue eyes; another for cancer of the liver; yet another for a certain intelligence, etc. In scientific terms, as all experimental geneticists agree, this is simply not true: physical characteristics result from the dynamic interplay *between* genes (not particular genes in isolation). Further, what actually gets 'triggered' in a particular organism is influenced by all the other materials and conditions that go into the process of living, from the presence or absence of certain nutrients to immediate levels of stress, and conditions in the environment at large. As a result, having a gene associated with cancer or with diabetes in no way guarantees that you will get these diseases. There may be a slightly higher probability; but there is absolutely no certainty. The general problem, as Rose points out, is that 'Reductionism ignores the paradox' – of same–difference, continuity–change and self–making – 'and freezes life at a moment. In attempting to capture its *being*, it loses its *becoming*, turning processes into reified objects' (Rose 1997: 306).

In this respect it is important to distinguish Rose's concept of 'autopoiesis' (self-making) from Richard Dawkins's notion of 'the selfish gene'. The latter phrase was popularised by the 1976 book of that name, substantially and significantly revised in 1989 (Dawkins [1976] 1989). Dawkins, a theoretical geneticist, initially gave the impression, qualified in the second edition, that genes are both highly determinist and intrinsically 'selfish'. They drive the organisms that carry them, which in Dawkins's view are little more than 'vehicles', and do virtually anything to maintain the continuance and identity of the 'gene pool'. This leads to a potentially highly deterministic and instrumental vision of life. Indeed, recalling the clockwork model of eighteenth-century deists and the title of another of Dawkins's books (1986), it resembles the mechanistic work of a 'blind watchmaker'. Life keeps on ticking away more or less regardless of the particular 'watches' (i.e. organisms) through which it is registered. Indeed, to revert to Dawkins's initial metaphor, each organism is propelled by genes that are not only blind but 'selfish'. By the time of his *Unweaving the Rainbow* (1998), however, Dawkins is refining his terms if not quite changing his tune. Now he hails genes in terms of what he calls 'The selfish cooperator' (Chapter 9), and, as he expressly signals at its close (p. 233), 'This chapter has used the metaphor of the personified gene to explain a sense in which "selfish" genes are also "co-operative"'. Dawkins thereby acknowledges the need for genes, through the organisms that carry them, to interrelate and in effect 'collaborate' with other organisms in order to survive and flourish. A classic and familiar example is the collaboration/co-operation of bees with flowers, swapping nectar for the dissemination of pollen. Another example, less familiar but still more fundamental, is the fact that individual cells are themselves 'teams' whose constituent parts have gradually evolved from the collaboration of previously separate agents such as ribosomes and mitochondria. Lynn Margulis (1998) develops this into a thorough-going view of evolution as 'co-evolution' and life as 'symbiosis'.

The debate between the 'co-operative' and 'competitive' views of evolution is of long standing. In general terms, it is a continuation of the Enlightenment debate on how 'selfish' or 'altruistic' is human nature. Mark Ridley, the editor of an anthology of key documents in the history and theory of evolution, summarises the overall trend thus:

> One conception is (more in nineteenth-century language) 'racial'; it supposes that selection is between competing groups. In the age of power philosophies [. . .] there was more stress on selection in the form of an offensive struggle between nations; more recently group selection has been used to explain how selection favours co-operation by its benefit at the group level.
>
> (Ridley 1997: 4)

In short, whereas the nineteenth-century emphasis was upon evolution as *competition*, the twentieth-century emphasis was upon evolution as *co-operation*. This is a timely reminder that even our most cherished beliefs about what is apparently natural – precisely because they *are* cherished and because they *appear* so natural – may turn out to be in every sense 'partial'. And, *a fortiori*, this applies as much to the present work as any other. For it should be observed that my own proposition in the last chapter that 'Creativity is co-operative' evidently goes along with the recent trend in emphasising evolution as co-evolution. It may therefore turn out to be no more – nor less – than a product of its time. But then again, I would never claim that the present book can be completely above or to one side of its own history; any more than evolutionists could claim that they are themselves – as human be(com)ings – above or to one side of the processes of evolution. We may not be able to get out of this double bind. But we can at least give it some further twists.

Another genetically grounded but non-determinist approach to creativity is developed by the anthropologist Daniel Nettle in his *Strong Imagination: Madness, Creativity and Human Nature* (2001). His central argument, based on cross-cultural studies, is that creativity and kinds of 'madness' (notably psychotic illnesses such as manic depression and schizophrenia) are twin aspects of a genetic configuration that is essential to the human genome. For better and worse, this dual capacity predisposes us to image-building and projection of possible worlds ('imagination') as well as risk-taking and pushing boundaries in general ('creativity'). The crucial difference is whether this potential is manifested constructively as 'creativity' or destructively as 'madness', and that in turn, Nettle argues, depends upon the cultural framework and immediate situations in which it is expressed. This is basically an anthropological response to the link between creativity and schizophrenia proposed by Jamison and reviewed in the previous chapter.

Some societies, it seems, are much better than others at accommodating people with apparently odd or unusual imaginations: they assure their place in the community rather than alienating them, and nurture rather than thwart their creativity. Nettle compares the Inuit favourably in this respect (where such persons tend to function as shamans, singers, dancers and story-tellers as well as having simple tasks set aside for them) with dominant Western ways of treating mental illness (where most people suffer social stigma, exclusion and ultimately institutionalisation, and only the privileged few get support, protection and perhaps 'therapy'). For Nettle, then, 'strong imagination' is a pervasive, essential and genetically predisposed aspect of being human (there is no human society without it); but the precise form that it takes is in large measure socially and culturally dependent not biologically predetermined.

Depending on whether it is stigmatised or assimilated, and ultimately rejected or respected, it may issue as 'madness' or 'creativity'. Stressing that overall 'the conclusion . . . should be a positive one', Nettle summarises his view of 'the genetic-creativity argument' thus:

> The major psychoses are basically genetic in origin, though the genetic liability may need triggering by unfavourable aspects of the environment. [. . .] These personality traits are not wholly negative. As well as madness, they are associated with great creativity. Great creativity is highly attractive, and so the traits, and the genetic variants behind them, persist in the gene pool.
>
> (Nettle 2001: 201–2)

In some ways all this is simply a restatement in modern terms of the ancient insight enshrined in the double-edged notion of the *furor poeticus* ('the madness of making') or, as Dryden put it, 'Great Wits are sure to Madness near allied / And thin Partitions do their Bounds divide' (*Absalom and Achitophel* 1681). The difference, however, is that contemporary genetic research is giving us detailed insights into the workings of 'nature' (including 'human nature') that is complexly dynamic, driven by internal predispositions as well as interacting with external conditions. As a result, it is not only unwise but virtually impossible to take a reductively determinist view of genetic make-up in relation to creativity. The organism in/and/as its environment always operates multidirectionally and multidimensionally: it involves many more agencies and interactions than one.

The same applies to attempts to trace and map creativity in terms of specific neural networks and changing brain chemistry. The neurologist Antonio Damasio, for example, flatly resists any notion that creativity can simply be found *either* in the genes *or* the neural networks: '[creative] artifacts cannot be reduced simply to the neural circuitry of an adult brain and even less to the genes behind our brains' (Damasio in Pfenninger and Shubik 2001: 59). Instead, he insists, it is '[f]rom the interactions between individuals and environment' that 'the social and cultural artifacts that we talk about when we discuss creativity *emerge*' (emphasising a term to which we return shortly). Damasio sums up this complex and dynamic situation thus (pp. 59–60):

> the sort of brain activity that leads to creative behavior involves three functional levels: a genome-specified level of brain circuitry, an activity-specified level of brain circuitry, and then something that results from the interactions of the brain with physical, social and cultural environments. That is why extremely reductionist views cannot capture all the issues we wish to understand when we discuss creativity.

This recalls a number of long-running debates in cultural theory that span both the arts and sciences: on the relation between 'nature' (the capacities we are born with) and 'nurture' (what we are encouraged or enabled to do with them); and on the relation between 'the individual' (organism, person or whatever) and 'the environment' (physical, social, cultural, etc.). But once more the precise techniques and terms in play (here drawn from the approaches and apparatuses of neurology and the contemporary life sciences) make for a distinctive outcome. For one thing, the inner workings

---

Myths of 'right' and 'left' brain, and 'divergent' and 'convergent' thinking

It is still common in casual conversation about creativity to talk of two supposedly distinct capacities corresponding to the brain's two hemispheres: 'right brain' as the creative and imaginative side; and 'left brain' as the critical and analytical side. This often gets mixed up with equally casual, and similarly binary, appeals to two supposedly distinct styles of thinking and, by extension, thinker: 'divergent' (creatively open) and 'convergent' (critically focused). Such terms may be handy as a crude and largely symbolic shorthand; but they derive from early behavioural and substantially superseded studies of learning styles in the 1960s and 1970s (see Vernon 1970: 371–84 and compare Sternberg 1999: 48–9, 145–9). Certainly they bear little resemblance to the complexly integrated workings of the brain as described in the foregoing pages. Nowadays, cognitive psychologists would tend to talk of brain activity in terms of *multilevel, parallel and recursive processing*. And the kinds of electronic and chemical 'mapping' referred to above are increasingly showing that the brain has *complex networks of complementary activity all over*, as well as localised response to stimulus in a specific area (see Dennett 1991, Calvin 1997, Damasio 2000, Boden 2004, Geake and Dodson 2004 and Greenfield 2004).

---

of 'nature' (human and animal) can now be studied through such brain-scanning techniques as 'positron emission tomography' (PET) and 'functional magnetic resonance' (fMR). And what such research reveals is 'images' and 'patterns' of brain and neural activity characterised both by reassuring regularity and remarkable diversity. While some patterns are relatively predictable, especially in the sensory-motor areas, others, chiefly to do with the 'higher' cognitive functions of intelligence and judgement, vary widely – even wildly. Moreover, in any instance the precise results depend upon the particular task and occasion and the immediate demands and desires (the 'soft information') not just the given apparatus and established patterns (the 'hard wiring'). As another neurologist puts it, 'To scientists who use brain-imaging devices to watch the brain as it remembers, imagines, and desires, it is awe-inspiring' (Etcoff in Brockman 2002: 281).

But even this is only part of the picture to date. Indeed, once we introduce genetic *engineering* into the picture, the whole thing changes at a dizzying rate; for we may then become part of the object engineered as well as the subject doing the engineering. To be sure, the fully 'bionic' being or the 'cyborg' may still be a creature of science fiction or of theoretical speculation (as we saw in Chapter 2). But science fact is rapidly making its own way in areas ranging from genetic screening and cloning to electronic implants and other prostheses. So there are increasingly urgent reasons to engage with an evolutionary biology in which we are already putting ourselves in the driving seat – even if we haven't yet learnt to drive! Here is how Csikszentmihalyi sees the problems and possibilities, looking back over human evolutionary history and trying to project ahead for the next fifty years:

In the past, we were like passengers on the slow coach of evolution. Now evolution is more like a rocket hurtling through space, and we are no longer passengers but its pilots. What kinds of human beings are we going to create? Flesh-and-blood copies of our machines and our computers? Or beings with a consciousness open to the cosmos, organisms that are joyfully evolving in unprecedented directions?

(Csikszentmihalyi in Brockman 2002: 102–3)

For cultural theorists and critical philosophers such as Haraway, Deleuze and Guattari, and Braidotti, the question would perhaps be re-posed as 'What kinds of *becoming* (human/animal/machine . . .) are we to engage in?' (see above pp. 49–50). And for each of them the answer would probably be an array of genuinely hybrid and as-yet unimaginable multiplicities – rather than the conventionally hierarchical dichotomy maintained by Csikszentmihalyi: organic (good)/mechanical (bad). ('What immortal hand or eye / Dare frame thy fearful symmetry?' springs to mind from Blake's *The Tyger.*) But however we frame the questions and answers, the issue is increasingly how far humanity has a hand and mind in evolution – and whether we are taking it for a ride or it is taking us. At the moment, genetics and the neurosciences offer themselves as the controlling 'genius' of the age. But in the future who – or what – knows?!

Emerging complexity

In his *Complexity: the Emerging Science at the Edge of Order and Chaos* (1994) Mitchell Waldrop cues some more terms and concepts that prove invaluable when trying to articulate a contemporary understanding of creativity. To these – namely 'emergence', 'complexity', 'order' and 'chaos' – will be added a couple of others: 'play' and 'game'. Taken together, all these ideas help push the debate in yet further directions and dimensions. In fact they themselves prove 'complexly emergent' in that they issue in a variety of configurations that exceed the possibilities of either 'games-playing' or 'chaos-ordering' simply and separately conceived. Other accessible and influential books that introduced these issues to a wider audience include Gleick's *Chaos: Making a New Science* ([1988] 1994) and Coveney and Highfield's *Frontiers of Complexity: The Search for Order in a Chaotic World* (1995). These in turn drew on the more specialised work of Prirogine, Mandelbrot and others referred to shortly. So do subsequent studies that bring the story, itself still emerging, up to date (e.g. Johnson 2000, Thuan 2001 and Atkins 2003: 1–40).

Waldrop's central concern in *Complexity* is the capacity of all kinds of system (physical and biological, natural and human) to engage in kinds of 'spontaneous self-organisation' and 'adaptive' behaviour. Drawing attention to systems as various as stock-market fluctuations, patterns of bird migration, multicellular organisation and brain activity – along with genetic mutation and the evolution of species (considered in the previous section) – Waldrop observes that 'all these complex systems have acquired the ability to bring order and chaos into a special kind of balance' (Waldrop 1994: 12). The usual name for this point of balance or area of interplay is 'the edge of chaos', which he defines thus: 'The edge of chaos is where life has enough stability to sustain itself and enough creativity to deserve the name of life' (p. 12). The phrase was given further currency by such books as Lewin's *Complexity: Life and the Edge of Chaos* (1992) and Davies's *The Cosmic Blueprint: Order and Complexity at the Edge of Chaos* (1995). These are accessible introductions written by authoritative scientists. The problem is that in casual, especially radical chic conversation, 'chaos theory' and 'complexity' tend to be bandied around without any real understanding of the concepts. (The same happens with vague appeals to 'relativity' and 'quantum' effects.) Mindful of this danger, the aim of the present section is to unpack these ideas as clearly and accurately as possible, and to bring the account up to date in the light of what is currently understood about 'emergence' as a form of creativity. The underlying questions may be put as follows:

- Is 'complexity' an order or pattern that in some sense already exists and simply has to be recognised? (This is basically creativity as *discovery*.)
- Or is 'complexity' – perhaps better described as 'complexifying' – an ongoing process of 'coming-to-be' and 'becoming' that is never wholly predictable in advance and only ever fully graspable in the event? Hence 'emerg*ing*'. (This is basically creativity as *invention*.)

As usual, there are no pat answers. But there are more or less revealing ways of posing the questions and developing the definitions.

'Emergence', for example, according to Horst Hendriks-Jansen, may be defined in two interrelated senses, theoretical and historical: "The first [theoretically] implies that properties at higher levels are not necessarily predictable from properties at lower levels' (Hendriks-Jansen in Boden 1996: 283–4). A relatively straightforward example from physics is what happens to water when it boils, becomes turbulent and turns into clouds of steam. A much more complicated example from biology is what happens to a leaf when it is eaten by a caterpillar which spins a cocoon from which emerges a butterfly which lays eggs from which emerge caterpillars that eat leaves – and the whole cycle goes round again. For Hendriks-Jansen, 'the second [historical sense of emergence] draws attention to the fact that simple traits and forms of organisation give rise, in the course of evolution, to more complex and irreducibly novel traits and structures'. Here, looking back into the depths of time, we may think of the gradual build-up of living organisms from atoms and molecules to single and multicellular organisms (a process that defies absolute distinctions between 'physics' and 'biology'); and more particularly of the gradual evolution of present-day humanity from ape-like creatures, and before that from amphibians and amoeba-like organisms. Alternatively, looking forward into the future, we may wonder what kinds of species will eventually emerge on the planet – with or without the species currently called *homo sapiens*, and therefore with or without the intervention of genetic engineering, drugs, machines, computers, and so on. Who – or what – knows . . .? That is precisely the gradually emergent but not absolutely predictable point raised at the end of the previous section. We may or may not be part of some final solution. But we are certainly part of a most pressing question.

Meanwhile, as Hendriks-Jansen goes on to point out, the most powerful and flexible models of emergence tend to combine theoretical and historical perspectives. They take both a short-term and concentrated (synchronic) and a long-term and comparative (diachronic) view of the matter. For what is at issue is often a tissue: relatively 'simple matter' that transforms into relatively 'complex life'; something more or less living that in certain basic respects is what it always was (e.g. atoms and sub-atomic particles) but which is constantly changing and may yet become something different again (e.g. an organism that reproduces life and yet itself dies). Such conundrums are only confusing if we insist on fixing on a single state or staying at a single level or stage. But as argued by a host of life scientists in specifically 'evolutionary' terms in the previous section, the most comprehensive and convincing approach to adopt is at once multistaged *and* multilevel, synchronic *and* diachronic, theoretically principled *and* historically sensitive. Moreover, as many commentators would insist, room has to be left for kinds of *contingency* (chance interconnection), if only because we can never know the full nature and structure of all the properties and processes in play within, around and beyond a given system (see Rose 1997: 231–3, Gould [2003] 2004: 201–2). 'Contingency', it should be observed, comes from Latin *con*, 'with', and *tingere*, 'to touch', and so carries the general sense of 'being in touch with'.

Ultimately, what we are dealing with is all the ways in which one system not only dynamically interacts with but actually transforms into other systems. In terms of physics this involves the interrelations between, say, light and heat, or energy and matter, or time and space – and all of them not just in time but over time, and not just in one place but from one space to another. In terms of biology, it might involve not just the cycle of a particular species of caterpillar–cocoon–butterfly–egg–caterpillar . . . , but also how that species itself came to evolve from others – and may evolve again into yet others. Moreover, in so far as butterflies *are* energy and matter and absorb or generate light *and* heat, and move around in time *and* space, what we are also dealing with is the area where physics and biology blur or blend into one another. Hence the increasing significance of such 'life sciences' as biochemistry and molecular biology and in/organic chemistry. These were once seen as strangely hybrid and marginal but are now recognised to be both central and in a new sense 'normal'. In all these ways what used to be called 'evolution' (with an organic emphasis and a base in the biological sciences) or 'complexity' (with a mechanical emphasis and a base in physics, mathematics and computing) are coming together to form fresh syntheses in words and worlds – and certainly in disciplines – previously unknown. One of these wor(l)ds and (inter)disciplines goes by the name of 'Emergence'.

Steven Johnson opens *Emergence* (2001), his book-length study of the topic, with a fairly straightforward definition: 'The movement from low-level rules to higher-level sophistication is what we call emergence' (p. 18). But he eventually works round to a number of definitions and questions framed far more specifically, in his case with an emphasis upon games and games theory. For Johnson (like Hughes 2000) is a designer of computer games as well as being a theorist of dynamic systems. Thus he observes that 'Emergent behaviors, like games, are all about living within boundaries defined by rules, but also using that space to create something greater than the sum of its parts' (Johnson 2001: 181). And he is particularly exercised by the question: 'Is there a way to reconcile the unpredictable creativity of emergence with the directed flow of gaming?' (p. 184). His answer to this is 'a resounding yes'. But to see why, and to gauge how all this relates to complex – not just simple – notions of creativity as a kind of 'organised chaos', we need to take a step sideways and backwards. (Complexity never emerges in a straight line; it always involves non-linear and recursive dynamics.) And to do this we need to look at changing theories of 'games' and 'play'. To be precise, we must

play . . . . **game**

Is creativity basically a form of play? And if so, at what point does 'playing the game' mean bending or breaking the rules – or making up a new game entirely? There are related questions to do with chaos and order. If creating things involves a kind of ordering, where does this order come from, and when and how does it break down – or up?! Is chaos, for example, merely *dis*order (i.e. absence of order), or is it simply the name for a form of order we have not – or at least not yet – learnt to perceive? Alternatively, perhaps there is something intrinsically and inevitably random, unknowable and unpredictable (the colloquial sense of 'chaotic') about *all* behaviour, animate and inanimate, human and otherwise. Maybe there is some essential 'play' in all systems – whatever the 'games' we think are being played. In this section we explore changing concepts of play and game. This modulates, in the next section, into a more specific consideration of contemporary theories of chaos and order. (Creation myths involving chaos and order are the subject of Chapter 5.)

The dominant ancient Greek view of the relation between play and game is articulated by Plato. In his *Phaedrus* (*c.* 360 BCE), he firmly distinguishes 'play' (*paedia*) from 'game' (*ludus*) and ranks them hierarchically. 'Play' he sees as unstructured and lacking in rules and goals, and as basically an activity for children – *mere* child's play. 'Games', however, have structured rules and roles, and have some determined end in view. They are therefore appropriately instructive activities for the young and acceptable diversions for adults. 'Child's play' (*paedia*), for example, would include playing with dolls and other toys; whereas 'grown-up games' (*ludus*) would include athletic competition and military exercises (the original Olympic Games had elements of both).

But this is not the modern, especially the Romantic and post-Romantic, view. In the eighteenth century a change set in that effectively inverted Plato's hierarchy, revaluing play and often putting it above game. As Slethaug notes in two articles on 'Game Theory' and 'Play/free play' (in Makaryk 1993: 64–9, 145–9, here 145), 'The work of Immanuel Kant is often taken as the critical turning point in the conceptualization of play, for he linked aesthetic judgment and art to play. [. . .] As a form of play, art is spontaneous, free and pleasurable in itself, liberated from the necessity of having to be about reality, of having to be representational, or of having to *say* anything at all.' Thereafter it became increasingly common to talk of play in positive terms as a form of liberation and creative fulfilment. This is the position expressly adopted by Winnicott in his *Playing and Reality* (1971) where creativity is a 'naturally playful' aspect of a 'normally healthy' life, and in that sense 'ordinary'; also in Willis and others' work on 'symbolic work at play in the everyday cultures of the young' (as discussed in earlier chapters).

Two important modern theorists of game and play are Johan Huizinga and Roger Caillois. Huizinga's *Homo Ludens: A Study of the Play Element in Culture* (1944) offers a vision of play as virtually synonymous with culture and civilisation: 'Civilization arises and unfolds in play' (Huizinga [1944] 1970: 9). Indeed, he actually suggests that play is *the* defining human quality; hence the title, *Homo Ludens*, variously translatable as 'Man the Player' or 'Playing/Playful Humanity' (by analogy with *homo sapiens*, humanity the knower and *homo faber*, humanity the maker). It should also be observed that Huizinga's equation of 'ludic' activity with 'the play element in culture' inverts Plato's distinction between *paedia* as unstructured play and *ludus* as rule-governed game. Care therefore needs to be taken with these terms, for confusion can easily arise, especially given the tendency among contemporary writers to use 'ludic' casually to mean any more or less freely playful activity.

Caillois in *Man, Play and Games* (1961) is more precise and discriminating. He insists on seeing *paedia* on a continuum with *ludus*, but at opposite ends of the same spectrum. For Caillois, recalling Nietzsche's *The Gay Science* (1882), *paedia* (play) expresses 'the primary power of improvisation and gaiety' while *ludus* (game) represents 'rules . . . institutional existence' and 'civilising power', also 'the taste for gratuitous difficulty' (Caillois 1961: 24). Caillois's model is particularly useful in that he offers four basic categories that may be applied to all sorts of activities of play *and* game. It all depends how far the activities are undertaken in improvisatory (playful) or rule-governed (game-like) ways. I shall draw on and slightly modify the summaries of these in Guy Cook's *Language Play, Language Learning* (2000: 114–16), where there is a clear exposition of Caillois's ideas. The four kinds of play/game, called by their Greek names, are:

agôn where competition is dominant (cf. ant*agon*ism): pitting one person or team against another (e.g. football, tennis, chess)
alea where chance is dominant: submitting oneself to fate or fortune (e.g. roulette, the lottery, spinning a coin)
mimicry where simulation is dominant: assuming the personality or taking on the role of another (e.g. role-play, charades, 'pretend')
ilinx where vertigo is dominant: aiming at giddiness or, in extreme cases, ecstasy (carousels, driving fast, raves)

Moreover, as Caillois insists, none of these four kinds of play/game is absolutely exclusive. They can be combined in various permutations and with varying emphases. Rather, it is that certain ways of playing the game tend to emphasise one aspect more than the others. Thus football or even chess (primarily *agôn*/competition) can be played in a devil-may-care manner (*alea*); players may pretend or fantasise they are their favourite 'star' player (*mimicry*); and it may be the thrills and spills of the experience (*ilinx*) rather than competing to win (ant*agon*istically) that are the main appeals of the game. But whatever the precise mix or motive there will be a sliding scale, and to some extent a tension, between relatively *'free' play* and more or less *'rule-governed' game*.

The same continuous dynamic characterises any system in so far as it is both structured, determinate and complete (game-like) and structuring, determining and ongoing (playful). Language, for example, is just such a complete yet ongoing system. And so is any semiotic (sign) system in actual use and therefore in process of evolving and emerging, even though it may in the abstract and for analytical convenience be conceived as a totality (see Cook 2000: 97–148). Indeed, this is the basic difference between structuralist and poststructuralist understandings of systems. Structuralism conceives each system as a provisionally finished totality, a complexly interconnected object with a notional centre. Poststructuralism conceives systems (plural) as ongoing partialities or fragments, tenuously continuous processes with multiple, indeterminate or even absent centres. Put another way, as I suggest elsewhere, 'structuralists tend to emphasise the system as a *closed* "whole"' whereas 'poststructuralists tend to emphasise the "holes" within and around *open* systems' (Pope 2002: 129). Moreover, it is precisely the tension between the two – the fact that every system is a whole with holes in – that makes this 'w/hole' thing dynamic!

Derrida explores similar possibilities, and in terms specifically related to play, in his influential essay 'Structure, Sign and Play in the Discourse of the Human Sciences' (1966). His overall project is 'the joyous affirmation of the play of the world and of the innocence of becoming'. For Derrida, this is undertaken in a distinctly 'deconstructive' mode in so far as 'Play is the disruption of presence. [. . .] Play is always play of absence and presence, but if it is to be thought radically, play must be conceived of before the alternative of presence and absence' (Derrida [1966] in Lodge and Wood 2000: 88–103, here 102). Clearly, then, 'play' is a highly charged and deeply positive concept for Derrida. It is identified with 'joyous affirmation' of something that precedes and exceeds division and distinction, and is not just disruptive or destructive in a negative sense. (This follows from the radically *re*constructive side of deconstruction noted elsewhere; see above p. 64.) In fact, Derrida doesn't even talk about 'game' in the sense that Plato uses it. Rather, he expressly situates himself in relation to the 'Rousseauistic side of the thinking of play whose other side would be the Nietzschean affirmation' (p. 102). His is therefore a basically Romantic conception of what has come to be approvingly called 'free play', a valuation that is diametrically opposed to the Classical rule-governed and goal-directed version of 'game'.

Key influences on modern notions of 'free play' can be found in Nietzsche's conception of the ecstatically 'Dionysian' impulse in art and in his *The Gay Science* and *Thus Spake Zarathustra*; also in Bakhtin's notion of 'carnival' as a kind of holiday release from workaday cares and routine norms of official behaviour (see above pp. 93–4 and below p. 262). Both are not just releases of excess energy but forms of productive disruption and transgression that can have political implications and even revolutionary effects. They are therefore, at least potentially, forms of 'free*ing*' (i.e. liberat*ing*) play.

Related possibilities are opened up in the politicised aesthetics of what Isobel Armstrong refers to as 'ludic feminism' (Armstrong 2000: 214–15). Featuring the designedly disruptive, transgressive and, in terms of writing, often generically hybrid work-as-play of writers such as Judith Butler and Hélène Cixous, ludic feminism is characterised as having a common concern with exploring 'the performative iterability of heterosexual identity along with the possibility of its alterability' (p. 214). Thus all these writers sport with repetition, often parodically, and point playfully to the as-yet unrealised but virtually conceivable possibility of productive change. Crucially, such change extends beyond, not just between, the polarities of male and female, and even bi- and homo-sexuality as conventionally conceived. Indeed, with a radically *hetero*sexual (i.e. sexually various and varying) conception of both gender roles and sexuality, the rules of the 'game' change or get made up as you go along. This most obviously happens where, as argued by Haraway and discussed in Chapter 1, wo/men meet machines and the engineering of genes, with the result that 'life' and 'love' get 'played' in radically different ways.

Yet other prospects are opened up by Ludwig Wittgenstein in his later vision of philosophy as it aspires to the condition of 'language games'. The key works here are his aphoristic, designedly fragmentary and seriously witty *Blue and Brown Books* (1958) and *Philosophical Investigations* ([1953] 1967). An example of one of Wittgenstein's 'language games' from the latter appears in Chapter 8 (see below pp. 258–9). Jean-François Lyotard also develops his own ideas of 'language games' and inflects them in a distinctly social-scientific idiom. Thus in his *The Postmodern Condition: A Report on Knowledge* (1979, section 10), Lyotard suggests that 'there are two kinds of "progress" in knowledge: one corresponds to a new move (a new argument) within the established rules: the other, to the invention of new rules, in other words a change to a new game'. Indeed, one such 'new game' is the arrival on the scene of 'Game Theory' itself as a fully recognised and respected area of academic activity. The 1994 Nobel Prize for economics was awarded to John Harsanyi, John Nash and Reinhard Selten for their application of a particularly 'complex' model of Game Theory to systems of international trade and monetary flow (see Coveney and Highfield 1995: 336–7).

Finally, we shall consider one of the main ways of expressing the dynamic between 'free play' and 'bound game': the relation between *creativity* and *constraint*. For it is precisely through game-like constraints – as long as these are not too many and too inhibiting – that playful creativity is stimulated to emerge. But there is a delicate balance and, in practice, a moving point of equilibrium. Too little constraint and nothing happens (because there is no pressure for change) – or it just occurs haphazardly. Too much constraint and again nothing happens (this time because the system is seized) – or it all happens in a rush, willy-nilly. Either way, it's a miss or a mess. On the one hand, as A. N. Whitehead warns, 'Unlimited possibility and abstract creativity can procure nothing' (see *OED* 'creativity' and Whitehead 1926). And on the other hand, as Bohm and Peat caution, 'without proper free play of the mind, the context [. . .] will be far too limited for the perception of new orders' (Bohm and Peat 2000: 130). This predicament is explored at length by Mike Sharples in *How We Write: Writing as Creative Design* (1999), especially Chapter 3, 'Constraint and Creativity'. The crucial thing, he suggests, is to grasp creativity *as* constraint (not in opposition to constraint); just as the way to develop one's 'game' is to play it in every sense *to the limit*. Sharples summarises the constraint/creativity dynamic thus:

> Constraints allow us to control the multitude of possibilities that thought and language offer. There are so many ideas that we might have, and so many possible ways of expressing them, that we have to impose constraint to avoid thinking and writing gibberish. Constraint is not a barrier to creative thinking, but the context within which creativity can occur.
>
> (Sharples 1999: 41)

Margaret Boden makes a similar point. Observing that what is commonly called 'constraint satisfaction' is just one, narrow and instrumental approach to problems (that of problem-*solving*), she insists that 'Constraints map out a territory of structural possibilities which can then be explored and perhaps transformed to give another one' (Boden 2004: 95). In this respect, constraints fully understood should also be grasped as opportunities for problem-*posing* (including the re-*posing* of the initial problem); for only then can they lead beyond the mere shuffling of immediately apparent options. That is, in terms of Boden's three main categories of creativity, we may then move beyond 'Combinatorial Creativity' through 'Exploratory Creativity' to fully 'Transformational Creativity' (pp. 3–6, 95–101).

A comparable perspective is opened up by the philosopher and educationist James Carse. In his *Finite and Infinite Games: A Vision of Life as Play and Possibility* (1987), Carse poses the problem in terms of a tension between 'finite play' and 'infinite play': the former tends to be more constrainedly game-like and the latter more creatively playful. For Carse, however, the crucial difference is the ways in which players participate in the game and why. 'Finite players' play competitively, for themselves, to a desired or required end. 'Infinite players', on the other hand, play with and for others; they play co-operatively and with no determinate ends in view. Carse summarises the distinction thus:

> The contradiction of finite play is that the players desire to *bring play to an end for themselves*. The paradox of infinite play is that the players desire to *continue the play in others*. [. . .]. The joyfulness of infinite play, its laughter, lies in learning to start something we cannot finish.
>
> (Carse 1987: 26, his emphasis)

Such 'laughter' resonates, albeit in different keys, with that of Nietzsche in *The Gay Science*, Bakhtin in *Rabelais and his World* and Cixous in 'The Laugh of the Medusa'. For all their manifold differences, as with Carse, what is being urged is a version of play as collaboration rather than competition, and participation rather than observation. And ultimately, as A. N. Whitehead maintains in *The Aims of Education* (1950, Chapter 4), echoing the words of George Bernard Shaw in *John Bull's Other Island* (1904), 'It is a commonwealth in which work is play and play is life.'

Further – much further – all these processes of collaboration and participation and work-as-play may be perceived as ongoing and open-ended. They involve 'players' before and after who take part in and contribute to a 'game' that freely evolves, in principle to infinity. And in that consists Carse's 'vision of life as play and possibility'. In a productively utopian sense, to quote the words of the 1970s Peter Gabriel song, they are 'Games without frontiers, war without tears.' Put yet another way (for there are always other ways of putting ostensibly the 'same thing' differently, that's the whole point), it is a matter of how far we can

order - - - - - - - - - - - - - - - - *fold here* - - - - - - - - - - - - - - - - **-chaos**

Is there already order existing in the universe, or is order something we perceive and in effect impose? Put another way, is order found or made, discovered or invented? Naturally enough, the answers we give to such questions are also likely to depend upon what we mean by 'disorder' and, in extreme form, 'chaos'. For 'chaos', in a casual and colloquial sense, is apparently the very antithesis of 'order'. As usual, then, from the outset, we need to be careful about the terms we choose and how we apply them. Chaos, for example, can be conceived in at least two quite different ways: (1) as disorder or absence of order in some absolutely negative sense (in which case it is intrinsically undesirable); or (2) as a state from which order emerges and to which it returns (in which case it is properly a kind of pre- or post-order).

A similar issue arises with *anarchy*, another term which, like 'disorder' and 'chaos', tends to carry broadly negative connotations but which can have a more neutral or precise sense. In casual usage it tends to mean 'utter disorder' or 'mere lawlessness' and is definitely a bad thing. But its more precise sense is 'without control' or 'without a ruler' (from Greek *an-archê*). Hence the neutral designation, and for some people the positive appeal, of 'anarchism' as a nineteenth- and twentieth-century political movement opposed to all forms of centralised power but supportive of all kinds of free association among individuals (see Woodcock 1986: 11–31). An-archically speaking, therefore, to be 'without a ruler' (i.e. no one ordering you around) is not necessarily to be 'disorderly' (i.e. causing a public nuisance). In fact, anarchists in a strict political sense would maintain that being without leaders could only be for the public good. That said, the fact remains that with both 'chaos' and 'anarchy' we are still left asking what we meant by 'order' (or 'orders') in the first place; and we may still be unsure about the precise relations between 'order' and 'chaos' (or 'anarchy') in any given instance.

Take the words '*order - - - - - - chaos*' as they appear in the present section heading, for instance. (We'll leave the 'fold here' to one side for a moment.) How exactly is this to be read and understood? Do we read it as two nouns, 'order' and 'chaos', which represent two quite separate 'things' suspended at either end of the intervening dashes? The sense might then be something like 'Order here - - - - - - Chaos there', but with an uncertain sense of how the two states relate, and whether they are in con-flict or balance. Alternatively, do we read 'order' as a verb, 'chaos' as a noun, and the intervening dashes as a kind of dynamic flow; which would turn the whole thing into an active process of transformation rather than just a perception of difference? The sense then might be an imperative 'Go on, order chaos!' or even an exclamatory and interrogative 'Order chaos! How?'

Clearly, the very framing of the topic(s) – as one or many, as distinct particles or continuous flow – is itself part of the matter at issue. Indeed, being alert to such possi-bilities is what theorists of both chaos and complexity refer to as 'sensitivity to initial conditions': even the slightest change in how an event is initiated (here an argument, but it could just as well be how you set about preparing a meal or laying the founda-tions for a building) can result in major differences in how it eventually turns out. In a similar vein, the rich ambiguities and teasing indeterminacies that we find and make in language are also crucial, not incidental, to the material (words) in which we are working. We always need to be alert to potentially remote and indirect effects as well as immediate consequences and obvious implications. Bearing all this in mind and to bring some provisional 'order' to this particular configuration of 'chaos', we shall explicate each of the key terms, now including 'fold here', in the order we meet them: 'order' in relation to concepts of 'folding' and both of them in relation to 'chaos'.

Of particular relevance for the present conceptualising of order is Bohm and Peat's work on *implicate* and *explicate orders* in their *Science, Order and Creativity* (2000). The basic principle is very simple. It all depends upon the notion of 'folding' and, to be precise, the complementary motions of '*en*folding' and '*un*folding'. Either way, the core sense of 'folding' is fundamental in that the Latin root *plicare* (meaning 'to fold') is common to both 'im*plic*ate' and 'ex*plic*ate', as it is to the more familiar and related words, 'implicit' and 'explicit' (whence, too, the English words 'pliable', bendable, and the French ballet term *plié*, a 'folded-leg' pose). For Bohm and Peat, an *im*plicate order is one which is 'folded within' or 'enfolded', like the petals within a closed rose-bud or the rings of an onion. Conversely, an *ex*plicate order is one which is 'folded out' or 'unfolded', like a flower when it blooms or an onion when its layers are pulled apart. If we take these two processes together, we see that notionally 'the same thing' can be grasped at different moments and, as it were, caught in different movements: *enfolding* (the *implicate* order) and *unfolding* (the *explicate* order). This corresponds to the general idea of things being more or less *implicit* (i.e. intuitively understood but hidden and un- or under-stated) and more or less *explicit* (i.e. openly declared and there for all to see and say). A partial optical equivalent is *the hologram*, in which the image of the whole is refracted in each part, whichever way you look at it. Genetically, it is the capacity of *the clone*, in principle at least, to generate a whole organism from the DNA of a single cell.

Bohm and Peat are theoretical physicists as well as theorists of creativity. The scale on which they project things therefore tends to range from the universe at large to the universe at small: from the macro-structures and long-term processes of deep-space astronomy and deep-time cosmology to the micro-structures and instantaneous processes of subatomic particles and wave patterns. Crucially, these two perspectives come together in the perception, increasingly common in contemporary science, that the 'universe at large' can be seen as an *un*folded version of the 'universe at small' (which is therefore its *en*folded counterpart). This can be illustrated in general terms with a couple of related observations. Looking into deep space, with the naked eye or a radio telescope, and looking into a drop of water, with the naked eye or an electron microscope, will both produce images of worlds beyond and within worlds. The one, opened up by astronomy and astrophysics, is as it were *un*folded over vast tracts of space and – given the fact that the light from distant stars takes millions of years to reach us – vast tracts of time, too. The other image, opened up by microscopy and nuclear physics, is as it were *en*folded within highly condensed points and – given the fact that most activity in atoms takes place in billionths of a second – highly concentrated bursts of time.

Some such awareness of the infinitely large and the infinitely small, the seemingly eternal and the seemingly instantaneous, has been with humanity as long as *homo sapiens* (or *faber* or *ludens*) has been around and capable of being conscious of the fact. It was massively increased from the sixteenth century with the development of ever more powerful telescopes and microsopes, for looking both 'far' (Greek *tele-*) and in miniature (Greek *micro-*). But now the development of advanced electronic and computer-assisted technologies, along with increasingly sophisticated and specialised terminologies, has enabled us to push such insights and outsights (including what were previously oversights) to utterly unforeseen limits. The idea of a simultaneously unfolding and enfolding perspective – a bifocal vision of worlds within and beyond worlds – is fundamental to this process. Bohm and Peat put the overall situation thus:

> [T]he entire universe in space and time is enfolded within each region and can then be unfolded with the aid of lenses and cameras. [. . .] Indeed, it is just this process of enfoldment and unfoldment that allows scientists to learn about the whole of the universe, no matter where they may be in it.
>
> (Bohm and Peat 2000: 179)

Further – again, much further – we may speak of this intricately interrelated yet infinitely extendable 'process of enfoldment and unfoldment' as the crucial *complication* in any attempt to understand the universe 'as a whole'. For com*plic*ation is another word with the same 'folding' root as im*plic*ate and ex*plic*ate. Latin *complicare* means 'to fold together'. Indeed, though this is not a step that Bohm and Peat themselves take, there

Fold here

> this stage invents itself   a blue and shadowed edge
> bordered   as a mask   edged like air   shadings
> a place to dance across the fold
> > (Opening of Helen Kidd's 'Origami', 2003: 27)

Take a single flat sheet of paper. Fold it once. You now, to state the obvious, have a folded piece of paper that is no longer flat. Rather more teasingly, what from one side is evidently unfolded, from the other side is evidently enfolded. Indeed, you can change and even invert the relation by folding the paper one way or the other, backwards or forwards, thereby making what was previously enfolded unfolded, and vice versa. But the fact is that the inverse relation between the two planes obtains: enfolding one way means unfolding the other. The same applies in a slightly more complicated fashion to a book (this one, for instance). As you open the pages out, you close the covers in, and vice versa. This becomes especially obvious if you open the book till the covers meet at the back and the pages fan out in front. Again, enfolding one way means unfolding the other. What's more, with a book there's a further particular complication. (There is with every object in so far as it has a range of specific shapes or forms, its topology.) Because the pages of a book are all glued or stitched together on one side, the spine, when you slowly leaf or quickly flick through it the pages 'fan' out to make a highly mobile array of overlays and gaps organised round a 'fixed' axis. In other words, there's a built-in constraint to the way in which a book opens and closes, and therefore particular ways in which we tend to use it. (There are significantly different constraints – and therefore significantly different possibilities – with, say, loose-leaf folders or boxes or with rolls of parchment or clay tablets.)

But even if we stick with a conventionally made modern book, there are obviously yet further complications that arise as you move it around in your hand. The spine/axis is only relatively fixed in time and space. Try moving it slowly in a horizontal or a diagonal direction in front of you – or even waving it around wildly above your head! Again, there will be different kinds and rates of unfolding and enfolding (along with all sorts of swishing, rustling and crackling), and now these are going on in a variety of directions and dimensions. In the most general sense, then, to recall the lead term of this section, there will be a number of 'orders' and, to be more precise – in so far as these are dynamic and changing – 'orderings' in play. In this respect, even though it is an apparently simple and highly constrained physical object, a book has a remarkably complex array of possible dynamics. Though it is far from 'chaos' in a casual sense – unless you rip the covers off and pages out and scatter them all over the place – it is none the less many not just one form(s) that paper(s) may take. In its own beguiling and remarkably portable way, it is a kind of multiverse as well as a universe: a 'manifold' that may turn out – or in – to be considerably more than the sum of its parts.

As intimated in the opening lines of the above poem, all these principles have long been known to practitioners of origami. By a few judicious and practised folds, they can turn a plain sheet of paper into an exotic bird or a highly abstract design in a trice. Roger Penrose, one of the most adventurous and influential of contemporary mathematicians, traces his own grasp of the subject to early experiments in nothing more – or less – complicated than 'paper-folding' (see Penrose in Lightman and Brawer 1990: 415–34).

is something suggestively fitting yet still teasingly open about a vision of universal order(s) that ends where it began – with *complication*. For in that sense it may be grasped in a redefined and refined sense, at another level of understanding: as a complex 'folding together' not simply an unresolved difficulty. Related insights arise when we recognise that every *uni*verse is also in some sense a *multi*verse (i.e. is both 'one' and 'many'), especially if we recall that the '-verse' bit means 'turn' (from Latin *vertere*, to turn), as in 'reverse' or 'obverse' or 'verse' (i.e. poetry), because lines of verse 'turn' at more or less regular intervals.

Such insights on 'folding' are common in many areas of modern mathematics (see Peat 1992 and Penrose 1994). They result in geometries very different from the familiar flat-surface, single-sided geometry of Euclid. Such 'non-Euclidean' geometries (and their corresponding algorithms) explore the curved-space and time-phased properties of shapes ranging from regular spheres to irregular orbits. They also explore the complex and changing shapes of natural objects and processes such as snowflake and cloud formation and plant growth. An apparently simple yet remarkably complex example is the inverted loop known as a 'Möbius strip'. To make this, you take a strip of paper, twist it back on itself and fasten the ends so that the 'outside' becomes the 'inside' in a continuous loop. (Again, doing is knowing.) Particularly when you bend and flex this self-involved loop, the result plays happy havoc with all sorts of Euclidean axioms designed for single-plane, flat surfaces: with the notion of fixed points and shortest distances between them (here they move and vary with the shape); with the notion of lines being straight *or* curved (here they can be both depending whether you look at them from above or at an angle); and with the notion of fixed and precise angles (they constantly vary at every turn). The whole thing also makes a 'nonsense', in a quite strict sense, of fixed notions of inside and outside, and up and down. As you run your finger along a 'single' plane, it doubles back and round – inside-out, upside-down. This, then, is geometry in three dimensions – four if you add the dimension of time – not just one. And again, we are presented with an apparently self-enclosed universe that none the less has the properties of an infinitely flexible multiverse: the basic form is the same but constantly transforms depending how it is handled and viewed.

In fact, theoretical physicists are currently arguing whether there are ten or even twenty-six dimensions – not the usual three of length, breadth and depth and the 'fourth', of time, that we experience. They are also, again, teasing at a model that has been in and out of theoretical fashion for the past thirty years and more: the possibility that the universe is organised in terms of 'strings', 'super-strings' and latterly 'branes' (short for membranes). What all these approaches have in common is the notion that matter-as-energy is stretched out as incredibly fine strands (or incredibly fine surfaces in the case of 'branes') in a kind of interlocking net or web stretching from one end of the universe to the other. Moreover, as with the 'folded' and 'curved' view of space-time, the 'ends' are interconnected one with another and therefore in principle 'end-less' (i.e. non-finite). But whichever model is preferred, the fact is – and experimental observed facts are evidently much harder to come by than mathematical speculations in these matters – we are everywhere confronted by the possibility that there may be many more dimensions and, indeed, many more '-verses' than our routine perceptions and our current conceptions of either 'uni-verse' or 'multiverse' can even recognise let alone deal with. We revisit these issues at various points in the next two chapters. Before that, however, we take a look at some of the other areas in which similar kinds of *complication* occur as a result of processes of 'folding together'.

'Folds' and 'folding' have a particularly crucial role to play in Gilles Deleuze's idea of philosophy as concept creation. Following Spinoza and Leibniz, Deleuze sees nature as being 'explicated and implicated' through and through (see Marks 1998: 46). He develops this idea particularly elaborately in his study of the various swirling and involved 'folds' (*les plis*) disclosed by Leibniz's baroque philosophy of life. Thus in *The Fold: Leibniz and the Baroque*, Deleuze observes that 'A fold is always folded within a fold, like a cavern in a cavern. The unit of matter, the smallest element of the labyrinth, is the fold.' Cumulatively, therefore, the overall effect is of an 'unfolding' that 'follows the fold up to the following fold' (Deleuze [1988] 1993: 11–12; also see 'The Deleuzian fold of thought' in Patton 1996: 107–13). This process extends to the notion of 'waves', whether in water, air or some other medium, visible or invisible, electromagnetic and otherwise. For there are many areas of life in which 'folds' (or more dynamically 'waves') are crucial, and their forms and functions always entail some sense of bending backwards and forwards, gathering up and pressing on. Classic examples from science include the densely rippled physiology of the brain cortex; the double helix structure of DNA; plate tectonics and the bending, buckling and layering of the earth's surface; also the Einsteinian notion of curved time-space as a continuum folded back on itself. More routinely, however, as already pointed out, we are constantly engaging with the possi-bilities of folds and folding every time we open a book – or put on clothes or fold our arms or bend our legs and walk.

Now that we have got a basic grasp of 'order' and 'folding', we can turn back to the third and final term in this section: 'chaos'. Strangely enough, in 'chaos theory' there are individual figures hailed as 'creators' of the subject, whether as inventors or discoverers. This is especially odd and ironic in that 'chaos', even more than most areas of emerging interest, is a catch-all term for a loosely multidisciplinary and often highly collaborative set of discourses. To mention only the most obvious, it draws on ecology and economics and the sciences of natural and artificial life, as well as math-ematics and computing. So a few of the 'stars' of chaos theory will be mentioned, if only because their names and basic ideas may be familiar. But what will be empha-sised are their contributions to essentially common insights and endeavours.

First there is Benoit Mandelbrot (b. 1924) and the concept of 'fractals' that he articulated in his *The Fractal Geometry of Nature* (1982). Fractals (from Latin *fractus*, 'irregular, broken up') are highly irregular objects which can none the less be broken down into components that are 'self-similar'. The degree or kind of 'self-similarity' is itself the point at issue. In a naturally irregular object such as a coastline the similarity of one bay or beach or cliff to another is only loosely generic. In a snowflake or salt crystal, however, the self-similarity is greater: all snowflakes or all salt crystals share many structural principles and each replicates its own unique 'lattice' at various scales. Computer designs, too, may use exactly repeated or more loosely recursive for-mulae. The self-similarity that results may then vary from absolute identity (every feature is reduplicated at every level, as happens with the so-called 'Mandelbrot set') to subtly varying evolutions – including convolutions and involutions – of elaborate shapes and patterns. In the latter case, it should be observed, Mandelbrot himself now prefers to talk of a flexible 'self-affinity' rather than a rigid 'self-similarity' (see Mandelbrot in Pfenninger and Shubik 2001: 191–212). Philosophically, it all depends upon how much 'play' is allowed within, between and around the concepts of 'self' and 'similarity': how far 'self' confronts or becomes 'other', for example, and 'similarity' turns out to be more or less 'different'.

The same applies to the playful – or game-like – aspects of what is now called 'computer art'. Interestingly, those computer-generated designs commonly considered most mathematically significant and aesthetically beautiful tend to derive not from exact replication at every level (i.e. absolute self-similarity) but from a degree of mutation and variation generated by occasional 'seeding' with selected as well as random numbers (that is, they exhibit what Mandelbrot now calls 'self-affinity' and what Wittgenstein would probably hail as 'family resemblances'). Indeed, only by some kind or degree of human input do such designs tend to 'evolve' into more 'complex' structures that are considered satisfying by human observers rather than just repeating themselves or, conversely, degenerating into arbitrary and undifferentiated patterns without discernible design. Ian Stewart, for example, talks of such processes in terms of the need to balance periods of sustained 'symmetry building' with bouts of 'symmetry breaking' (Stewart 1995: 72–92). Margaret Boden, meanwhile, along with many others, practitioners as well as theorists, observes that the most successful computer-assisted art is precisely that: *assisted* but not wholly generated by computer (Boden 2004: 9):

> In each case the selection of the 'fittest' at each generation [of the program] is done by a human being who picks out the most aesthetically pleasing patterns. In short, these are interactive graphics-environments in which human and computer can cooperate in generating otherwise unimaginable images.

Conversely, computer-generated designs that aim to be substantially untouched by human hand or mind (i.e. without periodic human input and intervention) may be reckoned interesting but are rarely judged satisfying. This is what Boden calls the 'evaluation bottleneck that lies in the way of automated transformational creativity', and it means that 'evaluation typically has to be done by people not programs' (Boden 2004: 320; also see the comments on 'Artificial–artful–intelligences–lives' in Chapter 8 below).

Ilya Prirogine (b. 1917), a chemist, is another of the stars of chaos theory. He won the Nobel prize for his work on 'dissipative structures' and 'self-organisation'. Prirogine showed that most systems in the universe are 'far from equilibrium' in that they are highly unstable, and that they need to be so in order to change and exchange materials with other systems. In fact, it is often at moments of greatest 'dissipation' that a new order sets in, and it can do this so rapidly and apparently autonomously that it appears to 'self-organise'. Again, however, as with Mandelbrot's notion of fractal 'self-similarity', there are tensions within and between the key terms. The apparent *self*-organisation may in fact involve the invisible and perhaps remote influence of another system; so the 'organisation' may itself be more of a 'dissipated' (i.e. diffuse, diverse and multicentred) nature and not be concentrated in a localisable organism/organisation as such. Moreover, for Prirogine, notably in his and Stenger's book *Order out of Chaos* (1984), it is precisely the *irreversibility* of certain processes which ensures that matter will in fact 'get organised' and not simply keep on dissipating into amorphous and undifferentiated processes. Thus he observes: 'Far-from equilibrium studies led me to the conviction that irreversibility has its constructive role. It makes form. It makes human beings' (see Sardar and Abrams 1999: 69–77).

Edward Lorenz is famous for two highly memorable and connected contributions to chaos theory made at the Massachusetts Institute of Technology during the early 1960s and the 1970s (see Gleick 1997: 11–31). One is the 'Lorenz attractor', which is a diagrammatic representation that looks like a butterfly, with the two 'wings' of the butterfly made up of spiralling lines crossing a common axis (the butterfly's 'body'). Its geometric and mathematical function is to model the most common forms of turbulence in 'fluid' systems (systems which in principle include fluctuations in anything from population change and bird migration to patterns of stock-market trading and brain activity). This whole class of diagrammatic and mathematical representation goes by the popular name of 'strange attractors', a phrase first introduced by David Ruelle, Professor of Theoretical Physics, in the early 1970s. The name has a science-fiction ring to it and is problematic in that it suggests there are 'strange' forces in the universe (sometimes with a butterfly shape to them!) and that, like 'Black Holes', they are somewhere 'out there' waiting to drag in or 'attract' unsuspecting matter (e.g. us). In fact, the mathematics of 'attractors' is not that strange, nor is their geometry; but both are striking when plotted in multicoloured movement in three-dimensional (again, non-Euclidean) space changing over time. It should be observed, however, that many are rapidly being familiarised through visual effects in advertising, films and computer screen-savers. So they are getting less 'strange' by the minute.

Still more famous, at least for its catchy title, is Lorenz's paper of 1972: 'Does the flap of a butterfly's wings in Brazil set off a tornado in Texas?' (see Gleick 1997: 20–3, 246–9). This is the source for the so-called *butterfly effect*, more technically known as 'sensitive dependence on initial conditions'. As a phrase at least, 'the butterfly effect' is familiar in popular 'New Age' discourse and media chat about chaos: it tends to be invoked to justify anything from a blandly holistic 'one-world' view (everything connects to everything else) to a more cynically laissez-faire attitude (anything goes anyway). Perhaps surprisingly, then, Lorenz hardly answers his own question; he is more interested in the maths. Instead he offers a non-committal aside to the effect that, yes, a single flap could eventually help generate a tornado – but it could just as easily prevent one. In any case there would be all sorts of other things going on at the time, each with its cumulative effects, so you could not possibly know about the effect of that particular butterfly wing. More significant, perhaps, is the seemingly incidental fact that the title of Lorenz's paper confirms the perennial anxiety in North America about the effects of what may be going on in South America. Perhaps the really significant political implication of this particular butterfly is that it was in America's 'backyard'!

There are many technical definitions of chaos in the scientific literature. Some of these are reported and discussed by Gleick in his classic study *Chaos: Making a New Science* ([1988] 1994: 303–17): 'A kind of order without periodicity' (Hao Bai-Lin); 'The complicated, aperiodic, attracting orbits of certain (usually low-dimensional) dynamical systems' (Philip Holmes); 'The irregular, unpredictable behavior of deterministic, nonlinear dynamical systems' (Bruce Stewart). For all their technical differences, what all these definitions have in common is a model of chaos as both unpredictable and yet far from disorderly – in short far from 'chaotic' in the casual sense. Currently, as already observed, the tendency is to talk of *complexity* and *emergence*:

with the emphasis upon complexity that 'emerges' from lower orders and apparent chaos (see Johnson 2001 and Gould [2003] 2004). But that is where we came into this section. So we shall go out with a number of complex and even apparently 'chaotic' gestures. The first three are drawn from some philosopher-poets (arguably all are both). And the final series (over the page) is an attempt to demonstrate as well as define the matter in hand. What may emerge from all of this is very hard – perhaps impossible – to say in advance. For my part, the first and last line of defence is that the person who never made a mistake never made anything. For your part, please make of it what you wish.

> To see a world in a grain of sand
> And a heaven in a wild flower
> Hold infinity in the palm of your hand
> And eternity in an hour.
>
> (William Blake, *Auguries of Innocence*, c. 1792)

> Those thinkers in whom all stars move in cyclic orbits are not the most profound; whoever looks into himself as into vast space and carries galaxies in himself also knows how irregular all galaxies are: they lead into the chaos and labyrinth of existence.
>
> (Friedrich Nietzsche, *The Gay Science*, 1882, no. 322)

> Chaos has three daughters, depending on the plane that cuts through it: these are the Chaoids – art, science and philosophy – as forms of thought or creation. We call Chaoids the realities produced on the planes that cut through the chaos in different ways. [. . .] A concept is therefore a chaoid state par excellence; it refers back to a chaos rendered consistent, become Thought, mental chaosmos. And what would thinking be if it did not constantly confront chaos?
>
> (Gilles Deleuze and Félix Guattari, *What Is Philosophy?* [1991] 1994: 208)

Emerging -

- sensitivity to initial conditions, which are always multiply determined and in some respects unique in each case -

- emergence rather than imposition of order, generation of evolving structures rather than replication of existing structures, repetition with variation - - - - - - - - - - - - -

- kinds of 'mis-copying' resulting in productive but rarely deliberate or predictable 'mistakes' -

- self-organisation as an apparently 'internal' response, though always in some measure a response to 'other-organisation' (i.e. other systems around and beyond)- - - - -

- operating far from equilibrium, at the edge of chaos, with the possibility of moving – often suddenly – to another 'order' -

- non-linearity, feed-back and recursiveness – 'folding', 'waves', 'loops' – which result in cyclic but never absolutely circular motion -

- irreversibility as a principle of 'formation' (including 'trans-formation' and 'in-formation'), in that irreversible processes tend to result in determinate products (i.e. something) rather than indeterminate or non-existent products (anything or nothing) -

- an ongoing awareness of apparent chaos as potential order or, conversely, of apparent order on the point of chaos, and either way a fresh recognition of the complex principles informing the 'w/hole' (including the 'holes' from and into which the 'whole' emerges) -

whatever else you happen to find

and that

a
d
h
o
h
r

- - - Creativity

- - - -*   creating 'from the beginning' with a full awareness that this is the continuation of other things and will bring yet other things into being

- - - - *   feeling for and thinking about an appropriate shape, form, design – 'fitting' for your immediate aim and need but also capable of full-filling a broader, even if initially obscure, purpose

- - - - *   being open to the apparently chance or accidental event, including 'mistakes' – that in the event may turn out to be crucial in avoiding mere repetition of the predictable and help usher in the freshly different, singular and arresting

- - - - *   becoming able to articulate and sustain a viable and valuable sense of 'self' through ongoing openness to the 'other' within that self, between that self and others, and beyond conventional self-other constructions altogether

- - - - *   being prepared to 'tolerate ambiguities', 'suspend disbelief', sport with both 'negative' and 'positive' capabilities, and to look for closure without foreclosure

- - - - *   going with the flow – but only so far as it brings you back transformed and enriched; holding to a line – and yet appreciating how it bends and flexes

- - - - *   making something (of yourself for and with others), going for provisional completion (but not absolute conclusion), making a difference (by expressing a preference)

- - - - *   finally as at first – but differently – a celebration of being 'in the middle' and yet gradually – sometimes suddenly – gaining a fresh sense of awareness and purpose and value, even if you are no longer sure precisely where they came from or to which new ends they tend, or whether it matters in the same way any more

or care to make

of this

n
t
e
t
e

Part 3

Creation as myth, story, metaphor

Man is the symbol-using (symbol-making, symbol-misusing) animal.

(Burke 1966: 16)

In this part we examine ancient creation myths and contemporary scientific accounts of the beginnings of the universe and of life, along with some of their counterparts in early materialist science and idealist philosophy. As we shall see, the poetical makings of the most ancient *cosmogonies* (i.e. 'birth of the cosmos', from Greek *kosmos*, meaning both order and beauty, plus *genesis*, birth) sometimes curiously anticipate the scientific findings of the most recent *cosmologies* (i.e. 'study of the cosmos', where *logos* means both word and study). Science fact has a way of resonating as well as jarring with mythic fiction. Further, recalling that Greek *mythos* could mean 'truth' of many kinds and had a range of senses spanning 'design' and 'world-view' as well as 'story' and 'fable', 'science' itself turns out to be one of the most powerful of modern 'myths'. With this in mind, 'creation myth' is capaciously defined as 'a narrative that describes the original ordering of the universe' (Leeming and Leeming 1994: vii); so the precise nature and status of the 'truth' each myth offers can be provisionally left open.

Creation myths offer a fascinating perspective on questions that exercise us throughout this book. In particular, they help us to ask who or what *has created and is creating* whom or what. They also remind us that creation can be identified with a wide range of sources, causes or agencies: *people* in some shape or form, whether as individuals or groups ('who'); *things other than people* – gods, natural or supernatural forces, evolution, science and technology viewed impersonally ('what'); and, most often, some dynamic configuration of *things-in-people* or *people-become-other* ('who and/as what'). This last relates to creation conceived as a kind of *metamorphosis* (from the Greek for 'across-shape'), *transformation* (its exact Latinate counterpart) or *shape-shifting* (the closest Germanic equivalent). In any event, a vision of creation as metamorphosis/transformation/shape-shifting tends to underwrite a version of creativity as continuous *becoming* rather than once-and-for-all being. Alternatively, to pick up a term from Chapter 3, it means we are concerned with creativity as *re . . . creation*. Though again, as we shall see, it is the precise ways in which the gap between the 're' and the 'creation' can be jumped, bridged, filled in or even fallen into that make all the differences: the difference between one version of a creation myth and another (Chapter 5); and the difference between ancient and modern myths of science (Chapter 6).

5 Re-creation myths, ancient and modern

Whence this creation has arisen – perhaps it formed itself, or perhaps it did not – the one who looks down on it, in the highest heaven, only he knows – or perhaps he does not know.

(*The Rig Veda* [*c.* 1500 BCE] 10, 129, in Hamilton 2001: 26)

All myths of creation are strictly *re*-creation myths, and in two crucial respects. Firstly, contrary to initial appearances, every creation myth involves creation from something (whether a prior state of order, chaos, the void or notionally 'nothing'); for even 'nothing' requires that we imagine 'some-thing' in order to negate it. In this sense, so-called 'creation from nothing' (*ex nihilo*) is a rhetorical trick and a sleight of mind. Secondly, every telling or presentation of a creation myth is in some measure a re-telling or re-presentation of a version or vision that is held already to exist. In that sense, to claim any kind of authority, a creation myth *must* be a re-creation myth. However, it is never sufficient merely to 'decode' a myth, as though it has some 'message' embedded within that is simply waiting to be extracted. (This is the besetting problem in all sorts of naïvely allegorical approaches to mythology, ancient and modern.) Rather, it is the very words, stories, images and associated actions of a myth which themselves *in the event* – *through* the processes of narration and dramatisation – *realise* the moment of creation. They *bring* its truth *into being*. The telling or performance of the myth (in words and images, music and dance, for instance) can then be grasped as an *embodiment* and an *enactment*, not simply the record or rehearsal of a prior state.

We must also bear in mind that most creation myths were embedded in particular ritual occasions, typically associated with spring or birth or the founding of some institution. They had social functions as well as aesthetic forms, and they often involved a degree of public participation. It is important to remember this because many of the myths that follow are reproduced in apparently 'finished', written texts that may be read privately; they have little or no indication of social context or ritual occasion. Moreover, on closer inspection, the record is often fragmentary, and the surviving versions turn out to be highly assorted, often inconsistent, and sometimes downright contradictory (for a good overview, see Coupe 1997).

For all these reasons, the versions of myths reproduced here are *not* offered with any claim to absolute authority or essential authenticity. They are *not* 'the original myths' because, strictly, no myth can be. That is, no extant version of an ancient myth – simply by virtue of being extant *and* ancient – can be completely 'original', either in the archaic sense of 'going back to some primitive origin' or the modern, diametrically opposed sense of 'novel, innovative' (see Chapter 3). Rather, the myths represented here are 'original' in both archaic *and* modern senses: recalling earlier versions and realising them in new ways; translating and thereby transforming them; adopting but also adapting. The use of current retellings of older materials is therefore recognised as an opportunity not just an obstacle. In fact, this has always been the way with myths, as with stories and histories of all kinds. They only really live in the re-telling. As the structural anthropologist Claude Lévi-Strauss puts it, 'A myth truly always consists of all its versions' and, as a commentator on his work adds, 'The "meaning" of mythology [. . .] must take account of the potential for transformation that such a combination involves' (Hawkes 1977: 43–5). By extension, the system of myth-building is open and ongoing, and new performers and audiences – along with whole new media – have their parts to play too. That includes us and ours. Comic Batmans no less than the cosmic Brahman go through many 'incarnations'.

Something must also be said about the nature of metaphor. As conceived here, *all* language is fundamentally metaphorical in that it involves constantly talking of one thing in terms of another. The most familiar aspect of this is the use of physical terms with an abstract sense: 'standing up for oneself', 'not taking things lying down', 'sticking one's neck out', etc. Indeed, the word 'metaphor' is itself metaphorical in that Greek *metapherein* means 'to carry across'; and so does its Latinate equivalent 'transfer' (from Latin *trans-ferre*), the past participle of which (*translatum*, 'something carried across') underpins the general sense of 'translation'. Conversely, there can strictly be no 'literal' meanings in language if by 'literal' we understand a meaning completely uncoloured by the resources of imagery and comparison. Thus the word 'literal' itself derives from Latin *littera* (meaning 'letter of the alphabet'), and that in turn derives from an early form of *litor* meaning 'shore' or 'edge' (as in the modern geological term 'littoral'). The root sense is obviously of letters being 'outlines' or 'edges', carved out from or marked on some material. Nietzsche, in a note from the 1870s, puts the general point with characteristic force: 'The drive toward the formation of metaphors is the fundamental human drive which one cannot for an instance dispense with in thought, for one would thereby dispense with man himself' (see Cazeaux 2000: 53–63, here 59). Percy Shelley makes a similar observation in his *Defence of Poetry* (1821), insisting that 'language is vitally metaphorical . . . because language itself is poetry' (Shelley [1821] 1991: 206–7). In fact, the view that language is essentially metaphorical can be found as far back as Bacon's *Novum Organum* (1620), where it is perceived as a major problem, and Vico's *The New Science* (1725), where it is perceived as a major potential (both are examined in the next chapter). And nowadays it is virtually axiomatic among philosophers of language that, for better and worse, metaphor plays a central and quite routine role in processes of symbolisation and signification. It is one of those crucial aspects of linguistic creativity that, in Carter's words, is 'not simply a property of exceptional people but an exceptional property of all people' (Carter 2004: 13, 69–72 ; also see Carter 1997: 140–53).

However, as already intimated, the pervasively metaphorical nature of language has 'up' as well as 'down' sides to it; for metaphors can be in varying degrees 'live' or 'dead'. (These are themselves, of course, metaphorically loaded terms.) The linguistic philosopher Paul Ricoeur accentuates the positively life-enhancing aspects of metaphor in his *Living Metaphor* (*La Métaphore vive*, 1975). Recalling the overall rationale for this influential study, he insists that: 'The term *vive* (living) in the title of this work is all important for it demonstrates that there is [. . .] a linguistic imagination which generates and regenerates meaning through the living power of metaphoricity' (Ricoeur, 'The Creativity of Language' [1978] in Kearney 1995: 218). However, as Kenneth Burke reminds us, 'Man is the symbol-using (symbol-making, symbol-misusing) animal' (Burke 1966: 16). Metaphors are there to be ab/used and it is this double-edged capacity, along with their tendency to flicker between 'live' and 'dead' states, that is the central concern in Lakoff and Johnson's classic study *Metaphors We Live By* (1980). For when metaphors become routine and over-familiar they dull rather than sharpen experience, and they tend to inhibit rather than enable creativity. Shelley sounds the warning note as a kind of wake-up call to the 'poet' in all of us: 'if no new poets (in the most universal sense of the word) should arise to create afresh the associations [. . .] language will be dead to all the nobler purposes of human intercourse' (Shelley [1821] 1991: 206–7). While Nietzsche, more laconically, observes that 'to be truthful means to employ the usual metaphors' and that 'truths are illusions which we have forgotten are illusions; they are metaphors that have become worn out' (Cazeaux 2000: 59). 'God' and 'man' were just such illusory truths and worn-out metaphors for Nietzsche – which is why his counter-claims for 'the Superman' (*Übermensch*) and that 'God is dead' are themselves so bracingly and abrasively metaphorical.

A grasp of the essentially metaphorical nature of language is especially necessary with creation stories. They bring worlds into being through narrative and dramatic means, so they are themselves highly charged acts of wor(l)d-creation. What's more, they are dealing with matters that can *only* be realised metaphorically, by talking of one thing in terms of another. For how else is one to bring into being that which previously did *not* exist except by making images of and comparisons with what already *does*? Conversely, how else except by kinds of 'metaphor' are we to imagine the 'nothing' before there was 'something', the 'void' before it was 'filled'? 'No mountains then. No rivers then. No forests then', as it is put in a Native American creation story we consider shortly. Thus only by invoking potential presences ('mountains', 'rivers', 'forests') and systematically negating them ('No . . . No . . . No . . .') can absences be established. (The same technique is used extensively in the mystical 'way of negation' practised in *The Cloud of Unknowing*; see below, pp. 204–5.) More generally, we may observe that only by an *act* do we establish a *fact* (we *say* it was so) and only by telling a *story* do we establish a *history* (we *tell* it how it was). As we see repeatedly in the creation myths that follow, the resources of metaphor and story are crucial – not incidental – to the processes of myth-making. Ricoeur, insisting upon 'the capacity of language to open up new worlds', summarises the matter thus:

> Poetry and myth are not just nostalgia for some forgotten world. They constitute a disclosure of unprecedented worlds, an opening on to other *possible* worlds which transcend the established limits of our *actual* world.
>
> (Ricoeur [1978], in Kearney 1995: 243, his emphasis)

Kinds of creation, kinds of creator

Creation myths worldwide can be provisionally grouped into a few basic types. David and Margaret Leeming in their *A Dictionary of Creation Myths* (1994) identify just five and, with some qualification, these are useful places to start (p. viii):

1   'creation from chaos or nothingness (*ex nihilo*)' – though it should be added that chaos can be a form of 'everything' (not 'nothing') and that, as just mentioned, the imagining of a 'no-thing' invariably requires the negation of a 'some-thing';
2   'creation from a cosmic egg or primal maternal mound' – which like many such things in creation myths is 'just there' in a state which is itself unexplained;
3   'creation from world parents who are separated' – i.e. whose separation into female and male, mother and father, is itself the constitutive act of creation;
4   'creation from a process of earth-diving' – e.g. going down to the bottom of a lake or ocean and bringing up a lump of earth from which land is formed;
5   'creation from several stages of emergence from other worlds' – i.e. a gradual unfolding or enfolding of worlds beyond or within worlds.

Clearly, then, there are very many ways in which creation can be conceived. Equally clearly, there are at least as many impersonal forces ('what') as there are personalised figures ('who') responsible for the process. Significant, too, is the fact that only a relatively small proportion of myths feature creation that is notionally 'from nothing'. The vast majority involve creation 'from something' and some involve creation 'from everything' (i.e. it's all already there, it's just in a particularly 'chaotic' state). In other words, even in the simplest and most obvious sense, most creation myths are really *re*-creation myths. Characteristically, therefore, many of the processes represented are cyclic and recursive rather than linear and unidirectional; and some suggest open 'multiverses' rather than a closed 'universe'. Interestingly, these are all possibilities we encounter in contemporary models of emergence, complexity and chaos (see Chapter 4).

Particularly striking is the fact that very few (re-)creation myths depend upon a single Creator figure. Most involve multiple creators or creative forces (often it is unclear whether we are dealing with fully personified figures or dramatised forces); and many proceed from some specific material (e.g. an egg, a drum) or some generalised state (e.g. chaos, the void). These last are usually presumed to 'just be there' – in a poststructuralist idiom, 'they always already are'. Meanwhile, following Leeming and Leeming (1994: viii), it is convenient to identify four main kinds of creative figure or force:

1   *a creator or creatrix* – the primal ordered form that wrenches cosmos from chaos;
2   *the trickster*, who is sometimes a negative force and sometimes a culture hero;
3   *a first man and first woman*, who continue the process of creation in human time and space, and sometimes fall from the creator's grace and are punished;
4   *a flood hero*, who, floating free of the general destruction, represents the possibility of a new beginning.

Some of these creator figures/forces will already be familiar to readers of the Biblical story of Genesis. It is important to observe, however, that the accounts in the Bible are not the only and are far from the first versions of these motifs. As witnessed by the Sumerian and Babylonian accounts, they are found earlier in different combinations, and the figures and forces are of a totally different order. Meanwhile, the creative trickster figure appears late on in the Biblical apocrypha (as Satan); but in the creation stories of the Native American Coyote, s/he is in on the creative act from the beginning. For all these reasons, we gradually work our way round to and through the Biblical accounts. But they are neither a natural nor a necessary place to start.

In each of the following sections we examine an instance of a particular creation myth, occasionally more than one. Each has its own story to tell and each has its own metaphorical ways of seeing and saying the world. But it should be emphasised at the outset that, taken together, they do not add up to a single, global narrative of creation and, still less, a single discourse on creativity. That is, there is no 'grand narrative', as Lyotard would put it; nor is there any 'Key to all Mythologies' such as that sought by Casaubon, the deluded scholar in George Eliot's *Middlemarch*. It is argued, however, that these materials give us rewarding insights into a rich multiplicity of visions of creation, and that the lights they throw on a contemporary understanding of creativity are both obliquely revealing and refreshingly bright. Certainly, they encourage us to exceed and explode some of the more casual orthodoxies that persist in narrowly modern and predominantly Western creativity debates: the myth of a single creator or a one-off act of creation, for example. That aside, seeking to approach them in their own terms and according to their own lights, these accounts serve as so many brightly particular 'small narratives'; and they may be pieced and patterned into whatever larger design and fitted to whatever informing purpose the reader cares to find or dares to make. For that, in the end as in the beginning, is what this chapter is all about: myths *of* creation and creating *through* metaphors and stories; seeing what others have made of such things and, in the process, grasping what we ourselves may make of them now.

A drop of milk, a word made flesh

Here is how the Nigerian novelist, Chinua Achebe, introduces a story of creation related by the Fulani, a Muslim people of West Africa. Achebe has much to say about stories *as* creation as well as stories *of* creation:

> The universal creative rondo revolves on people and stories. People create stories create people; or rather, stories create people create stories. Was it stories first and then people, or the other way round? Most creation myths would seem to suggest the antecedence of stories – a scenario in which the story was already unfolding in the cosmos before, and even as a result of which, man came into being. Take this remarkable Fulani creation story:
>
> > In the beginning was a huge drop of milk. Then the milk created stone, the stone created fire; the fire created water; the water created air. Then Doondari came and took the five elements and moulded them into man. But man was proud. Then Doondari created blindness and blindness defeated man.
>
> (Achebe [1988] in Thieme 1996: 21–2)

Whichever way the issue is grasped ('stories first and then people, or the other way round'), Achebe sees narration as itself a fundamentally creative act – not merely a vehicle for some prefabricated reality. There is an ongoing and potentially endless continuum of ' . . . stories create people create stories create people create . . .'. Turning to the Fulani myth in particular, Western readers may be initially surprised by an act of creation prompted by an inanimate, albeit organic object ('a huge drop of milk'). They may also be surprised by the fact that it seems just to 'be there': materialising from nowhere, creating yet itself apparently uncreated ('In the beginning was . . .'). They may even, if they've a mind to be literal, begin to wonder where the milk came from: from what udder or breast or, for that matter, pail, bottle or pack. In a sense, then, from the very outset this story strains belief. Or rather, in Coleridge's phrase, it requires us to engage in 'that willing suspension of disbelief for the moment which constitutes poetic faith' (see *Biographia Literaria* 1817, Chapter 14).

And yet, for those familiar with the opening of the Biblical Gospel of St John (1.1, 14), perhaps such a straining of belief or suspension of disbelief is not that difficult: 'In the beginning was the Word, and the Word was with God, and the Word was God. [. . .] And the Word was made flesh, and dwelt among us.' For not only is the opening formula the same (as it is in countless creation myths worldwide), the more literal-minded may just as well ask from which mouth did 'the Word' proceed as ask from which udder or breast the 'drop of milk' issued. That is, there is nothing more inherently fantastical about milk creating stone and by extension fire, water and air (as in the Muslim account) than a word making flesh (as in the Christian account). In both cases what is at stake is a particular way of saying and seeing the world. Further, we may say that a full 'grasp' of each of these 'ways of saying/seeing' requires not only what Heidegger would call a particular sense of *being in the world* (*Dasein*, a reconnection with the essence of things) but what Deleuze and others would call an intense sense of *becoming through the world* (a participation in the continuing flow of things) (see above pp. 87, 116). Rolling all this together, we may therefore say that what is at issue is a complex sense of *wor(l)d be(com)ing*, where *words* bring *worlds* into being (and vice versa), and apparently static *being* is realised as fluid *becoming* (and vice versa). The paradox is sustained – though it can hardly be explained – by the fact that, as Achebe puts it, ' . . . stories create people create stories . . .'.

Crucially, then, all these operations of understanding and 'grasping' are dependent upon two fundamental modes of apprehension: narrative and metaphor. We may thus accept mythic explanations as 'stories' in the broadest sense, even if we reject them as 'histories' in the narrowest. And we may also accept them as kinds of richly 'metaphorical' thinking, even if we reject them as strictly 'literal' references. In fact, like the fairy-tale opening 'Once upon a time . . .', the mythic formula 'In the beginning . . .' ushers us into a make-believe world where words offer 'a truth' (indefinite and contingent) and, spell-like, during the time of the telling, conjure it into 'the Truth' (definite and absolute). One of many possible beginnings is thereby instituted as '*the* beginning' – at least for the duration of the narration. Conversely, it is clear that one beginning tends automatically to exclude another. To be precise, you cannot properly attend to two 'beginnings' *at the same time* (listening to the Muslim myth and the Biblical myth together, for example). Crucially, however, you *can* attend to each beginning *at different times*. The more general point is that while no creation myth can have a monopoly on how and why things get created (though many claim to do just that), each has something to offer *in its own time* and *on its own terms*. We are thus left with a potential multiplicity of highly singular beginnings: what may be called *extensive multiplicity* composed of *intensive singularities*. Nor is this simply a matter of respecting the differences between palpably distinct accounts. It is also about recognising variation within nominally the same account.

Within the Fulani myth alone, for instance, there are not just one but many moments of creation. There are many distinct yet connected beginnings. The first three are a series involving organic and inorganic matter: 'the milk created stone; the stone created fire; the fire created water; the water created air'. The fourth involves the god-figure Doondari, who just came from we know not where and 'took the five elements and moulded them into man' – so that is a fifth moment of creation. And then there is yet another in which 'Doondari created blindness' in punishment for man's pride. This last act of retribution is what can be called the 'creation-of-destruction' and is a widespread, though far from universal, motif in creation myths. Typically, the god-figures have second thoughts about the advisability of their creation. Counterparts can be found in the Babylonian and Biblical stories of the Flood and Babel (treated below) and in Frankenstein's attempt to destroy his 'creature'. In any event, it is often with the creation of humanity that the main problems begin. Though it should be observed that this is invariably preceded – and sometimes succeeded – by other moments of creation in which everything and everyone else (including gods) get created, and some of them (like the Fulani drop of milk and Doondari) just happen to be there already. Moreover, all of this may be yet further complicated by the fact that the particular version of the myth one has in mind or to hand is far from the only one. Achebe's version of the Fulani myth, for instance, is significantly different from that reproduced in *Voices from Twentieth-century Africa: Griots and Towncriers* (Chinweizu 1988: 321, my emphasis). The latter opens with: 'At the beginning there was a huge drop of milk. / *Then Doondari came and he created the stone* . . .'.

If there is a single lesson to be learnt from all of this, it is that there are always more mythic beginnings and moments of creation than one – and that sometimes humanity is not the central attraction. This is an exhilarating as well as sobering prospect, and it has fascinating implications for our understanding of creativity. Perhaps creativity, too, is always necessarily plural and multiple (creativi*ties*), and always involves an interplay of the organic and inorganic, the divine and the human. (Maybe it is not primarily or exclusively 'human' at all.) Perhaps creativity also inevitably entails kinds of destructive-creation (de/con/struction?), of one's own work along with that of others. In any event it is clear that one moment of creation is never the be-all and end-all. For there is always another beginning unfolding at some stage or level of what is notionally the same text (milk, stone, Doondari, human) even as there are always others that can be accessed elsewhere (word, flesh, etc.). In this respect the comparison between these particular Muslim and Christian creation myths is suggestive but arbitrary; many others could have been made – and will be now.

'Aboriginal' dream-time

Here is part of an Australian Aboriginal creation myth as re-told in his poem 'Passage' (1990) by the American-born poet Billy Marshall-Stoneking. The myth is cast in the form of a dramatic and poetic monologue in which an Aboriginal elder, described as 'the oldest man in the world', explains and 'names' features of the bush landscape to the poet, who describes himself as 'the newest man in the world'. One such feature prompts the Aborigine to 'name Names' and to make the following observation about the surrounding landscape (Marshall-Stoneking 1974] in Murray 1991: 387–8, ll. 22–32):

> 'Here [are] the bodies of the honey ant men
> where they crawled from the sand –
> no, they are not dead – they keep coming
> from the ground, moving toward the water at Warumpi –
> it has been like this for many years:
> the Dreaming does not end; it is not like the whiteman's way.
> What happened once happens again and again.
> This is the power of the Song.
> Through the singing we keep everything alive;
> through the songs the spirits keep us alive.'

Clearly, this is not a one-off event, a single act of creation. It is part of a continuing activity ('they keep coming . . . moving toward the water at Warumpi'): cyclic, recurring, perennial ('like this for many years'). Moreover, as the elder goes on to reveal – and through his own words demonstrate – this is not an activity which simply takes place regardless of humanity, in some free-standing time and space. Rather, the very recital by the speaker of the histories and figures that identify this particular place is itself an activity that both recognises and re-creates the landscape: 'Through the singing we keep everything alive; / through the songs the spirits keep us alive.' This is speech that acts and is acted upon: created, it creates in return.

Such a view of creation as ceaseless re-creation and of life itself being crucially dependent upon a mutually informing exchange of spirit and song, can seem strange and even unsettling to Western readers brought up in 'the whiteman's way'. Certainly it is experienced and expressed as such elsewhere in the poem by the American interlocutor ('The oldest man in the world speaks / to the newest man in the world; / my place less exact than his', ll. 33–5). For one thing, such a radically symbiotic model of re-creation may be almost incomprehensible to those who hold narrowly individualist and humanist views of creativity as a product of purely human genius or personal talent. It is also diametrically opposed to the notion of the artist as 'outsider' or 'rebel'; this Aboriginal elder is very much a speaker-singer from and on behalf of the heart of his community (compare the Anglo-Saxon poet 'Deor' in Chapter 7). Moreover, the complexly integrated wor(l)d of the poem plays havoc with hard-and-fast distinctions between story and history, and fiction and fact; for the landscape recorded in and realised through this poem is both literal *and* metaphorical: a routinely recognisable 'historical' time and place *and* a mythically conceived and invoked state of 'the Dreaming'. The latter, also called 'the Dreamtime', is 'a time in the past whose values are still active in the present' (see Hodge and Mishra on 'Aboriginal Place' in Ashcroft *et al.* 1995: 415); and for Aborigines it is the period 'when their heroic ancestors roamed the world and created it as they now know it'. More particularly, '[t]hese forebears shaped the landscape by giving parts of themselves to it, e.g. their eyes for waterholes, their tails for trees' (Goring 1992: 17). Bruce Chatwin's travelogue *The*

Songlines (1987) is an extended account of another white Westerner's attempt to come to terms with this Aboriginal way of mapping time and narrating place. Chatwin sees this as 'a trail of song' and elaborates it into 'a vision of the Songlines stretching across the continent and the ages' (Chatwin [1987] 1988: 314).

But perhaps such grand gestures are unnecessary and, in a strict sense, 'out of place'. Perhaps all we should do is attempt to attend to the specificities of this particular myth of creation in its own time and place, and be mindful that most of us, like the poet Billy Marshall-Stoneking, are far less in tune with it than Aboriginal elders. For the fact is that for most readers of this book what we are likely to perceive is a model of creativity that is suggestively, even seductively, 'not the whiteman's way'. And for that reason we should be wary of making too much of a song and dance about it in and on our own terms ('How wildly exotic! How wisely universal!' even 'How radically ecological!'). After all, both the song and the dance are more likely to be our own than those of real Aborigines. And in this respect we do well to recall that the name 'Aborigine', like 'Australia', is a distinctly Western label for the peoples and place involved (hence the inverted commas in the heading of this section). The former was the collective name indiscriminately applied to the various indigenous peoples by the white colonisers and settlers of the late eighteenth and early nineteenth centuries: it derives from Latin *ab origine*, 'from the origin', and exactly expresses the European view of the natives as a more primitive species. Their own tribal names for themselves were – and are – many, including Koori, Worora and Ngarinyin. In a similar vein, 'Australia' (from Latin *auster*, 'east'), was so named because of the prevailing easterly winds that blew Europeans there. An alternative European name was 'New Holland'.

But there appears to have been no single name for the whole of the Australian land-mass used among the earlier indigenous peoples. For they neither perceived nor conceived it in those terms at all. Indeed, to know the multifarious names by which the native peoples knew this land – a land which they mapped not in outline as a 'whole' land-mass (as did the Europeans through their cartography) but in intensively 'local' yet still 'wide-ranging' ways (through practices and discourses of their own) – we would really need to know far more of the kinds of myth and metaphor, story and history merely gestured to by the above text. And even then, like Marshall-Stoneking, we would still be likely to re-create them as much in our own images as theirs. Then again, we can do no other. And the attempt to attend sensitively – but not sentimentally – to the particularities of the text in hand might just make all the difference (for a full text and a fuller but far from comprehensive attempt of my own, see Pope 2002: 151–4, 304). So may sensitive attention to the myth of creation and, by extension, the model of creativity considered in the next section. It, too, is 'not the whiteman's way'.

Coyote makes 'a BIG mistake'

The idea that creativity partly depends upon chance, anomaly and even 'mistakes' is widely recognised. It figures prominently in contemporary theories of chaos and play, as in evolutionary biology and genetics, too, as discussed in the previous chapter. But the idea is evidently not new. There are many myths that see the creation of the world as the result of randomness and accumulated accident: the accounts of the Greek Presocratics and Roman Epicureans and Stoics are examples we pick up later.

But there are also examples of creation myths that see the whole thing as a kind of 'big mistake' or 'huge joke'.

Common in such myths is the figure of the creator as 'trickster' or 'joker'. A classic example is the character Coyote in the Native American myths and stories of the Pueblo and Papago. Coyote is a kind of irrepressible anti-hero and life-force, somewhat like Anansi the Spider in African story and Reynard the Fox in European story. And, like them, he is a cross between the indigenous animal of that name, mystic shaman, and mischievous ne'er-do-well. A particularly rich and suggestive instance appears in the work of the Californian writer Thomas King. His collection *One Good Story That One* (1993) contains the story of how 'Coyote Goes West' in search of things to create. The catch is that some of them have already been created, or have simply created themselves; and in the event the first thing that Coyote makes is 'a Big Mistake'!

As King handles it, the narrative draws on a blend of Native American oral story-telling technique and absurdist (or postmodern) metafictional devices. Either way, the telling is as important as the tale, for the process of narration is foregrounded and becomes central in the narrative design. Thus a great deal of the point and humour of the story depends on the cunning adaptation of a traditional narrative frame. This features a fictional narrator, 'Grandmother', and has 'Coyote' sitting in the audience as well as taking part in the story. We thus get a story within a story, and a narrator and character who freely move across both. Though initially confusing, the overall effect is both highly significant and deeply amusing. The opening of the tale will be quoted at length so as to establish the dramatic and comic significance of teller and audience. (If you get lost, try reading the passage out loud and feeling for its oral pace.) We begin with Grandmother, the 'I' who speaks, settling her audience down:

> – All right, I says. Pay attention. Coyote was heading west. That's how I always start this story. There was nothing else in this world. Just Coyote. She could see all the way, too. No mountains then. No rivers then. No forests then. Pretty flat then. So she starts to make things. So she starts to fix this world.
> – This is exciting, says Coyote, and she takes her nose out of my tea.
> – Yes, I says. Just the beginning, too. Coyote got a lot of things to make.
> – Tell me, grandmother, says Coyote. What does the clever one [i.e. Coyote herself] make first?
> – Well, I says. Maybe she makes that tree grows by the river. Maybe she makes that buffalo. Maybe she makes that mountain. Maybe she makes them clouds.
> – Maybe she makes that beautiful rainbow, says Coyote.
> – No, I says. She don't make that thing. Mink makes that.
> – Maybe she makes that beautiful moon, says Coyote.
> – No, I says. She don't do that either. Otter finds that moon in a pond later on.
> – Maybe she makes the oceans with that blue water, says Coyote.
> No, I says. Oceans are already there. She don't do any of that. The first thing Coyote makes, I tell Coyote, is a mistake.

> (King [1993] in Thieme 1996: 420–8)

Before seeing what the mistake is, we shall briefly review what has happened so far. For all its beguiling simplicity of expression, this is a complex tale with far-reaching implications for our understanding of the activity of creation. Perhaps the first thing to say is that, if Coyote is supposed to be a Creator, then she hasn't done much so far! In fact she hasn't been allowed to claim full credit for creating anything at all. At most Grandmother has allowed that 'maybe' Coyote has made 'that tree', 'that buffalo', etc. But as soon as the Coyote in the audience chips in with a suggestion of her own ('that beautiful rainbow', 'that beautiful moon', 'that blue water'), Grandmother slaps her down with an emphatic 'No'. She then points out to Coyote that 'Mink makes that', 'Otter finds that moon in a pond later' and 'Oceans are already there'. As a result, the would-be-omnipotent creator-figure is cut down to size. At best, she is *maybe* responsible for creating some things. But for the most part it has all either been created by somebody else or is simply 'already there'.

But as far as the story goes the whole matter of who or what is responsible for creating whom or what is even more complex than that. In narrative terms, the answer on one level is 'Grandmother': it is *she*, the story-teller, who is in control of the action and has the power to direct it and to correct Coyote's attempts at intervention. In that sense Grandmother is the creator. But on another level it is the story as such, the myth as an insistent ritual, that exercises control over what must be told. It all depends how you inflect the statement 'That's how I always start this story': with the emphasis upon the 'I' or 'this story'; upon the immediate moment of narration ('All right, I says', begins Grandmother) or the expectation of how it is 'always' told. As Achebe observes, 'people create stories create people . . .'; but he's not quite sure whether it was 'stories first and then people, or the other way round'.

Meanwhile, on yet another level, it is obviously the named author, Thomas King, who is responsible for telling this particular tale in this particular way. Perhaps it is tempting to identify *him* as the creator. But then again the same problem arises as with the fictional figure of Grandmother, and Achebe's observation holds 'outside' as well as 'inside' the particular tale in hand. King is re-telling tales based on Papago and Pueblo myths and on traditional practices of oral story-telling. While from one point of view he tells the story in his own way to his own end, from another point of view they tell themselves through him for theirs (' . . . stories create people create stories . . .'). It all depends at what point you choose to cut the continuum, and to *whom* or *what* you attribute immediate or ultimate agency: people and/or stories? The simple answer may be *both*. But that still leaves the matter of the precise relation between tellers and tales, and the more complex issue of how far people *are* in some sense stories. How far, say, are our identities formed as well as informed by the 'stories' we circulate and which are circulated through us? Put like that, the most telling and teasing answer might be 'people and/or/*as* stories'. Put more formally, but still paradoxically, it is a matter of how far the creator creates and is in turn created by his or her creation. Alternatively, we might say that the creation re-creates itself through its creatures. In any event, the story goes on. So it's now time to get back to it and find out what Coyote's 'big mistake' was (King [1993] in Thieme 1996: 420–8):

> The first thing Coyote makes, I tell Coyote, is a mistake. Big one, too, I says. Coyote is going west thinking of things to make. That one [i.e. Coyote] is trying to think of everything to make at once. So she don't see that hole. So she falls in that hole. [. . .]
> – Ho, that Coyote cries. I have fallen into a hole. I must have made a mistake.
> – And she did.

This, then, is 'creation as mistake', and the joke turns on the fact that Coyote here makes nothing else. She is so completely bound up with grandiose ideas of what she *might* create ('trying to think of everything to make at once') that she doesn't notice what is right under her nose and her feet. And the result, literally as well metaphorically, is that Coyote experiences 'a fall'. In one sense, of course, all this is simply a variant on the comic 'slipping on a banana-skin' motif, and illustrates the moral that 'pride comes before a fall'. In another sense, however, it is altogether more complex and sophisticated. What happens to Coyote is that she is disabused of an overweening belief in her own, sole capacity to create things. First, as the Coyote in the audience, she is carefully instructed by Grandmother that there are already many other creators, creations and creatures in the world apart from herself, however it may initially appear to Coyote. Then, as the Coyote in the tale, she is rudely reminded that the world really does have its own reality, whatever lofty or ill-informed illusions she may entertain to the contrary.

Thus an apparently simple, cautionary folk-tale is made to embody a number of profound insights. And, depending upon one's critical frame of reference, it may be interpreted in a wide variety of ways. Ecologically and ethically speaking, it urges the respect due to other creators and creatures in their own rights. Psychologically, it gives a sharp knock to the over-inflated ego and insists upon a reality principle that very definitely includes significant others. Meanwhile, a poststructuralist might argue that Coyote's attempts to think the 'whole' lead to her falling into a 'hole', thereby suffering the classic *aporia*; and, as already intimated, a postmodern narratologist might greet this as a fine instance of traditional oral story-telling strategies combined with a distinctly absurdist sense of metafictional complexity. But whatever we, in turn, 'make of' this myth/fable/short story (and such categories are far from exclusive or exhaustive), we can be sure that it has the power to go on creating new possibilities even while re-creating old ones.

Finally, you may be pleased to hear that Coyote gets out of the hole and gets over her 'big mistake'. But of course, being Coyote, she gets into fresh scrapes and makes new mistakes. For Coyote is, as you may recall, a type of shaman, trickster or joker. She is irrepressible. She just keeps on coming and going, rising and falling and rising again. Here, then, as a kind of 'creative coda', is a snippet of just one of her many subsequent escapades. She is still wandering round speculating about things to create, and still deluded about her exclusive rights as a mighty Creator. Suddenly she hears the sound of ducks quacking! (King [1993] in Thieme 1996: 423–4):

> – Hey, she says, where did them ducks come from?
> – Calm down, I [Grandmother] says. This story is going to be okay. This story is doing just fine. This story knows where it is going. Sit down. Keep your skin on. Coyote look around, and she see them four ducks. In that lake.
> – Ho, she says. Where did you ducks come from? I didn't make you yet.
> – Yes, says them ducks. We were waiting around, but you didn't come. So we got tired of waiting. So we did it ourselves.

To Coyote's persistent surprise, then, there are still more creators, creatures and acts of creation. What's more, there is now the alarming – or perhaps exhilarating – possibility that creatures can engage in spontaneous acts of *self*-creation! The humour, of course, hinges on the fact that the ducks must already have been around in some shape or form to create themselves; also their evident nonchalance about the whole thing. In fact, rather like the two tramps in Beckett's *Waiting for Godot* (where the titular God/Boss figure doesn't show up), the ducks simply get on with things themselves: 'We were waiting around, but you didn't come. So we got tired of waiting. So we did it ourselves.' The evolutionary biologist, Steven Rose, might refer to this process as *autopoiesis* (see above p. 111). But perhaps the ducks put it better.

Buddhist origination, Taoist non-being

'What I teach is dependent origination, that all knowable things are dependently originated: this is the way things are, the regularity of things'. Such, according to the *Samyutta Nikaya* (*c*. 300 BCE; II.25, in Hamilton 2001: 48), was the teaching of the Buddha known as Siddhartha Gautama, and in the West simply known as 'Buddha' (*c*. 563–*c*. 463 BCE). 'Dependent origination' corresponds to what in the West would be variously called a 'conditional', 'contextual' and 'contingent' model of origins (compare above pp. 67–8). The basic concept can be explained thus: 'nothing at all, of whatever nature – material or mental, sensory or conceptual, concrete or abstract, organic or inorganic – occurs independently of conditioning factors' (Hamilton 2001: 49). Dependent origination, Buddha maintained, is the reason for the pervasive impermanence of things. It is also why many of the questions about 'what is' or 'is not', as though each thing were a distinct and independent entity, are strictly irrelevant. The *Samyutta Nikaya* (IV.93) is unequivocal on this point: 'Understanding dependent origination means one will no longer ask questions about the existence of the self, [or questions] such as Is it? or Is it not? What is it? Why is it? [. . .] Where has it come from? Where will it go?' (Hamilton 2001: 53). But for Buddha the problem is not that we should wish to know things: knowledge he sees as crucial. It is rather that we should treat anything as an independent 'it' in the first place. If everything is always already connected to (dependent on, involved with, contingent upon) everything else, such questions simply don't make sense.

In Western philosophical terms, the notion of dependent origination offers a kind of cross between pluralism and monism as described in the next section: 'the many' are immediately as well as ultimately 'the One'; the 'universe' is always already a 'multiverse'. As a result, enlightenment about 'the whole' was potentially immediately available from any of its 'parts' (though, again, the whole/part distinction proves permeable rather than absolute). Further, crucially, such enlightenment was potentially available to all. Mahayanna Buddhism, for instance, in every sense the most 'popular' form of Buddhism, taught that *everyone* has 'Buddha nature' within, and that it is not the exclusive prerogative, and still less the property of any supposedly great individual. In this respect it extended the recognition, central to all Buddhism, that 'the Buddha' (Siddhartha Gautama) was simply the latest – but assuredly not the last – of a continuing series of prominent Buddha figures (Boddhisatva). There were others before and would be others after. And in principle this capacity was common to all; though in each person it might be realised in various ways. In Buddhist terms, there were many 'ways to enlightenment' and 'ways of liberation', and they were in no sense exclusive.

Similar observations have been made about the 'common' and at the same time 'extra/ordinary' nature of creativity (in Chapters 1 and 3). And this is no accident, because in many respects the various ways of enlightenment/liberation are the Eastern counterpart of what in the West is called creativity. The notion of 'full-fillment', in particular, has already been considered as an aspect of creativity especially, but not exclusively, associated with the East (see above pp. 60–2). There it was observed that 'being fulfilled' puts the emphasis upon the process of connecting with and discovering what is already within (Buddha nature is an example), not striving to invent some new object in the outside world (the dominant Western view of creativity). It was also observed that 'filling full' is commonly complemented by a sense of 'emptying out'. In doing the one, you also do the other. (Filling a glass with water, you also empty it of air, for example.) This leads us to engage with a number of paradoxes that are at the very core of a number of Eastern religions and philosophies, including Zen Buddhism and Taoism. The fact that this is strictly an 'empty' core filled with 'non-being' is itself the paradox at issue. The *Tao Te Ching* (*c.* fourth century BCE), one of the foundational books of Taoism attributed to Lao-Tzu, puts it thus (Chan 1963: 139):

> The way (*tao*) that can be spoken is not the constant way.
> The name that can be named is not the constant name.
> The nameless was the beginning of Heaven and Earth.

The *Tao Te Ching*'s insistence that the beginning of Heaven and Earth was 'nameless' is characteristic of the Zen approach to Buddhism. So is the emphasis upon the 'way' (way of liberation, way of enlightenment) that, properly speaking, cannot be spoken, and a 'name' that cannot be named. But some potential misconceptions need to be avoided. The *Tao Te Ching* is not simply registering the fairly obvious fact that spiritual principles are ultimately inexpressible, nor rehearsing the common taboo on naming the godhead (as in the Jewish and Islamic religions, for example). Rather, it is suggesting that there is a fundamental power in 'not-saying' and 'not-naming'. In Taoism, this extends to the concepts of 'not-doing' (*wu-wei*), 'non-being' (*wu-yu*) and 'no-mind' (*wu-hsin*). In all these cases, what is in play is not some merely negative inversion of 'saying', 'naming', 'doing', 'being' or 'thinking' (felt as a kind of lack or deficit), but rather a positive grasp of the capacity to refrain from conscious and deliberate action in order to let activity arise in its own time and terms. The Taoist vision is one of 'letting be' and being open to what arises, rather than striving to impress one's will (and words and names and thoughts) on experience before it has had a chance to form fully.

The Taoist conception of 'not-saying', 'not-doing' and 'non-being' are therefore ways of 'emptying out' in order to be 'filled-full'. The nearest, though inadequate, analogy in Western psychology is a refraining from conscious action in order to release the powers of the unconscious (though this would probably be in Jungian rather than Freudian terms; see above pp. 72–4). In contemporary Western philosophy, the closest analogy is probably Derrida's argument for the *productive* power of 'absence' (which is not just a lack of 'presence') and the *joyful* affirmation of perpetually 'deferred/different' meanings (which is not just a desire for the security of the same). Both make for a *de/con/struction* (with equal emphasis upon all elements) that is far more than the sophistically destructive exercise it is sometimes made out to be. In fact, in the dominant terms of Western humanist rationalism, it is almost as easy to misconstrue and misrepresent Derrida's alternative Western philosophical project as it is to fail to grasp what is at issue in Eastern Taoism. So-called 'negative theologies', like 'philosophies of negation', tend to get treated simplistically and uncritically, and merely stigmatised or celebrated accordingly. Certainly it is difficult for those who set store by some fixed rational orthodoxy to handle the play of poetic paradox in such statements as those by Lao Tzu. Here he is enunciating the Taoist belief in a kind of multiply generative unity, and of 'non-being' as the creative source of 'being' (in Kasulis 1981: 31):

> From the *Tao*, one is created;
> From one, two: from two, three;
> From three, ten thousand things [. . .]
> Ten thousand things in the universe are created from being.
> Being is created from non-being.

By definition this is not the first word on the matter. Nor is it the last. Nor perhaps is it properly a matter of words at all. (Remember: 'The way (*tao*) that can be spoken is not the way'.) None the less, against the odds, and even despite their own avowed premises, such words still continue to conjure a kind of world into being. Or non-being. It all depends in what ways we are prepared to go along with – or push – the text in hand. Or in mind. More pointedly, how far is this a vision of creation and, by extension, a version of creativity that *you* are happy to co-operate with (continue, re . . . create)? If so, how? If not, why not? The same questions may be asked, differently, about the myths that follow.

Idealists *v* materialists: universe or multiverse(s)

All these creation myths are by Greek and Roman authors. Some, such as those by Socrates and Plato, are broadly 'idealist' in that they are premised upon the belief that 'ideas', divine and otherwise, are prior or superior to the realities humans routinely sense and perceive. Others, such as those of the Presocratics and Lucretius, are broadly 'materialist' in that they set store chiefly by what can be directly sensed and perceived and they regard divine agencies as illusory. However, on closer inspection it turns out that 'idealists' necessarily have quite specific senses of what the material world is made of, just as 'materialists' have their own ideas about how it all works. So, as usual, such oppositions are convenient as points of departure, not of arrival.

For Plato in the *Timaeus* (*c.* 360 BCE), the answer to the question 'Are we then right to speak of one universe, or would it be more correct to speak of a plurality or infinity?' is simple and emphatic – 'ONE is right': 'the maker did not make two universes or an infinite number, but our universe was and is and will continue to be his only creation' (I.4.31; Plato, 1971: 43). Moreover, in principle and design this is a geometrical universe. It is modelled on the idea of a single, perfect sphere revolving round a fixed centre from which emanates the soul or spirit: 'So he [the maker] put soul in the centre and diffused it through the whole [. . .] So he established a single spherical universe in circular motion' (I.5.34; p. 45). It is also a universe in which there is a neat division and distribution of what Plato calls 'the Same' and 'the Different': the Same is conceived as eternal and perfect; the Different is conceived as changeable and imperfect. Drawing on the imagery of Ptolemaic (pre-Copernican) astronomy, Plato identifies the outer 'sphere of the Same' with the supposedly fixed stars, and the inner 'sphere of the Different' with the moving planets, here including sun, moon and earth. Earth-bound humanity is therefore conceived as belonging to the inferior, imperfect and changeable sphere of the Different. Clearly, this is a tightly hierarchical and totally circumscribed version of creation. It is emphatically a *universe*.

Plato's universe is also characterised by a strict order of priority in which whatever is created is always inferior to its creator. To this end, the supreme 'maker' (whom Plato styles 'the Demiurge') avails himself of the services of gods whom he has created as inferior to himself; and they in turn create humans who are inferior to them. Thus there are marked gradations between levels or kinds of creative power, even though everything is in principle pervaded by the same spirit or soul (to be more precise, 'the spirit of the Same'). As a result, while everything may ultimately be inspired by and aspire to 'the Same' (perfection), some things are more or less 'Different' (imperfect) than others. Humanity may derive its creative powers, via the gods, from the supreme maker, but in themselves those powers are markedly weaker and very far from perfect.

A comparable model of divinely informed but humanly inferior inspiration is developed in Plato's *Ion*. There Plato likens this process to the transmission of attractive power from a magnet to an iron ring, and through that to another iron ring – and so on until the magnetic power is negligible: 'So the Muse not only inspires people herself, but through these inspired ones others are inspired and dangle in a string' (Plato 1956: 18). As observed in Chapter 4, this is basically a 'one-way', 'monologic' model of inspiration. Further, Socrates criticises the 'rhapsode' Ion (a reciter and performer of poetry), for being no more than an 'interpreter of interpreters' (p. 15). This is unsurprising from a philosopher who banned poets from his ideal Republic on the grounds that, in his view, they offered mere imitations of imitations, illusions of illusions (see *The Republic*, Book X).

Plato's views of the derivative nature of human creativity and of the inferiority of the creation (or creature) to its creator were to prove influential. They blended relatively easily with the dominant 'fallen' view of humanity developed in the Bible (see below pp. 165–6). So did Plato's model of a single, hierarchically ordered universe organised in terms of perfect Sameness (above) and imperfect Difference (below), linked by ascending and descending chains of superior and inferior creators and their creations. All these features were further systematised in subsequent Platonism, notably in medieval and Renaissance models of the universe as 'a great chain of being' which linked God to humanity, creator to creatures. (Though it should be observed that in the work of Plotinus and some later Neoplatonists humanity was allowed a more actively creative role and a potentially more direct access to the sublimity of divine perfection; see Hofstadter and Kuhns [1964] 1976: 139–70.) In any event, the Platonic model of creation inevitably entails a *universe* (not a multiverse). It is also uncompromisingly *idealist* in that it is premised upon the *idea* of unity, totality and wholeness and entirely subordinates material reality to that vision. For Plato, ideas *are* reality, whereas matter and observable life are merely shadowy derivatives. This is consistent with Plato's famous image of the cave in *The Republic* (Book VII), where life is likened to shadows cast on the walls of a cave by the pure light of the sun outside.

For a very different view of material reality and a correspondingly different model of creation we must turn to the work of a number of philosophers who preceded Plato and his master Socrates by a century and more. The Greek Presocratics and their Roman successors such as Lucretius were emphatically *materialist* in outlook. They began with what they reckoned to be going on in the material interactions of observable experience. Instead of privileging ideas of the constancy of the Same and the One, they celebrated difference and change, conflict and transformation. This sense of an insistently 'chaotic' cosmos is all the more pronounced in that the work of the Presocratics survives in fragments reported by later commentators. The most comprehensive collection in English is Jonathan Barnes's *Early Greek Philosophy* (1987), and that is the translation cited here.

A good place to start is with one of the earliest Presocratics, Anaximander of Miletus (*c*. 610–540 BCE). Anaximander argued that there are infinite worlds produced by the alternating generation and destruction of the universe according to a principle of endless renewal: 'the infinite is the universal cause of the generation and destruction of the universe', and results in 'all the worlds, infinite in number [. . .] from time immemorial, all the same things being renewed' (Barnes 1987: 72). Anaximander also proposed a crude but remarkably suggestive version of what two and a half thousand years later would be called 'evolution theory': 'from hot water and earth there arose fish, or animals very like fish, [that] humans grew in them. [. . .] Humans originally resembled another type of animal, namely fish' (p. 72).

Another Presocratic, Pythagoras (born *c*. 570 BCE), held similar views on the cyclic and interdependent nature of existence: 'whatever has happened happens again, there being nothing absolutely new; [. . .] all living things should be considered as belonging to the same kind' (Barnes 1987: 86). With Pythagoras, however, perhaps under the influence of Indian notions of reincarnation, this came out as the mystical belief that 'the soul is immortal' and 'that it changes into other kinds of animals' – a doctrine later to be called *metempsychosis* ('across-spirit').

It is to Heraclitus, however, that we must turn for the vision of material creative processes that did much to inspire Renaissance alchemists and, later, generations of radical Romantic writers. Heraclitus flourished *c*. 500 BCE and was sometimes hailed as 'Heraclitus the Obscure' because of his highly metaphorical and paradoxical mode of writing. Perfectly clear, however, is his total opposition to any notion of an external, especially divine, creator or creative force. He was adamant that 'the created universe is itself the maker and creator of itself' (Barnes 1987: 104). According to Heraclitus, it did this through the constant interplay of opposites and the ceaseless transformation of everything into that which it is not through a process of 'flow': 'The things that exist are fitted together by the transformation of opposites [. . .] All things come about through opposition, and the universe flows like a river' (pp. 106–7). Heraclitus became famous for this concept of 'flow': to him was attributed the observation, also attributed to Taoist writers, that 'it is not possible to step twice into the same river' (p. 117). 'Flow', it should be observed, is also central to several modern models of creativity, notably those of Bergson and Csikszentmihalyi.

Heraclitus is also identified with the view that the primal element and ruling principle of the universe – what Greeks called the *archê* – is 'fire'. The belief that, in Hopkins's phrase, 'Nature is a Heraclitean fire' rages throughout Heraclitus' work: 'Fire is an element and all things are an exchange for fire.' 'The universe [. . .] is generated from fire and it is consumed in fire again' (Barnes 1987: 107 ff.). It is initially tempting to read such a 'fiery' view of the fundamental nature of matter as it under-goes ceaseless ex/change in a distinctly modern, even 'nuclear' way: as a metaphorical anticipation of Einstein's famous formula for the transformation of energy into matter, $E = mc^2$. But this would be a wildly anachronistic reading and wise after the event. Other Presocratics held that water or air or earth were the *archê* underpinning their very various visions of creation and versions of the universe. 'Fire', to Heraclitus, may have simply seemed a more dramatic alternative. Certainly it was attractive to Romantic poets such as Byron and Shelley. Similarly, it was Heraclitus' energetic materialism – disdainful of conventional appeals to gods and men and insistent in its claims for a kind of commonly observable science – that made his work so attractive to the early Marx and Nietzsche: 'The world, the same for all, neither any god nor any man made; but it was always and is and will be, fire ever living, kindling in measures and being extinguished in measures' (Barnes 1987: 122). This notion of 'measures', kindling and being extinguished, also recalls the concept of the ever-varying *ratio* so crucial to Blake's aesthetic (considered above p. 59).

In the ancient world, the most obvious heir of the Presocratics was the Roman Lucretius. His *On the Nature of Things* (*c.* 55 BCE) articulates what is in every sense the 'classic' case for a materialist vision of creativity. Drawing on the teachings of his master Epicurus, who in turn drew on the Presocratics, Lucretius offers a view of nature that emphasises the 'free', 'measureless' and 'unfathomable': 'Nature is free and uncontrolled by proud masters and runs the universe by herself without the aid of gods. For who can rule the sum total of the measureless? [. . .] Who can hold in coercive hand the strong reins of the unfathomable?' (Lucretius 1951: 92). Lucretius also works on the explicit principle that 'Nothing can ever be created by divine power out of nothing' (p. 31). In particular, he proposes 'to reveal those *atoms* from which nature creates all things and increases and feeds them and into which, when they perish, nature again resolves them' (p. 28). Lucretius calls these 'atoms' (which still carried the archaic Greek sense *a-tome*, 'un-cuttable', 'in-divisible') by various names throughout the book: 'raw material', 'generative bodies', 'seeds of things' and 'primary particles'. But whatever the term, the universe he projects is characterised by ceaseless motion and continuous conflict. Indeed, this happens to such a degree and with such intensity that it constantly threatens to transform into a *multi*verse. Thus for Lucretius the whole of nature, including humanity, is shot through and in effect constituted by the interplay of elementally opposed forces: of construction and destruction, generation and decay, life and death:

> The destructive motions can never permanently get the upper hand and entomb vitality for ever more. Neither can the generative and augmentative motions permanently safeguard what they have created. So the war of the elements that has raged throughout eternity continues.
>
> (Lucretius 1951: 76–7)

And what it continues to and through is a whole host of later models premised upon the concept of creative – and destructive – opposition. William Blake's, in the significantly titled *The Marriage of Heaven and Hell* (1793), is one of the more notable: 'Without Contraries is no progression. Attraction and Repulsion, Reason and Energy. Love and Hate, are necessary to Human existence' (Plate 3). Another is the rallying cry of the anarchist Mikhail Bakunin in his *Reaction in Germany* (*c.* 1841): 'Let us put our trust in the eternal spirit which destroys and annihilates only because it is the unsearchable and eternally creative source of life. The urge to destroy is also a creative urge' (see Woodcock 1986: 14–15, 125–6). We can also trace the lineaments of such elemental struggles all the way from Heraclitus, Epicurus and Lucretius through the German materialist traditions: to Marx, who wrote a doctoral dissertation on Epicurus; to Nietzsche, whose Dionysian and Apollonian principles owe a lot to Presocratic philosophy as well as early Greek tragedy; to Freud, whose later psychology included the Life and Death encounters of Eros and Thanatos. Bakhtin's vision of 'carnival' is shot through with it, too, for Rabelais was also a great reader and re-writer of the early materialists. And so were the other Classical writers we consider next.

Metamorphoses

Here we turn to two ancient accounts of creation expressly featuring kinds of metamorphosis – transformation, shape-shifting. Both show traces of the kinds of 'materialist' *and* 'idealist' attitudes treated in the previous section; and both, as it happens, were called 'Metamorphoses'. Ovid's *Metamorphoses* (*c.* 10 CE) is best known as the classic source for stories about interchanges between the world of the gods and spirits and that of human beings (Venus and Adonis, Orpheus and Eurydice, etc.). Many of these involve kinds of transformation in which a god or goddess assumes human or animal form to trick a human or explore some other human–animal–object permutation. One such myth recorded by Ovid is that of Pygmalion and Galatea, the statue that turns into a woman. George Bernard Shaw's play *Pygmalion* (1912) and the musical based on it, *My Fair Lady* (1956), are the most widely known modern adaptations of it. But there are others – by H. D., Angela Carter and Alasdair Gray, for example – that demonstrate the perennial fascination and challenge of the story (see Miles 1999: 332–449 for an invaluable overview). Philip Terry's *Ovid Metamorphosed* (2000) is a fascinating collection of contemporary fiction that responds to Ovid in a wide range of modes, and includes work by Atwood, Byatt, Namjoshi, Roberts, Ward Jouve and Warner.

Two main observations will be made about Ovid's *Metamorphoses*, which will here be cited in the version by Ted Hughes, *Tales from Ovid* (1997). Firstly, Ovid was perfectly happy to blend broadly 'materialist' and 'idealist' versions of the universe: natural and supernatural forces mix freely in his vision of creation from the outset. Thus, as the opening lines of the poem make clear, he is 'ready to tell how bodies are changed / Into different bodies' and also prepared to 'summon the supernatural beings / Who first contrived / The transmogrifications / In the stuff of life' (Hughes 1997: 3). The resulting vision of primordial 'Chaos' resembles that of Heraclitus and Lucretius in the emphasis upon 'flow' and the ceaseless warring of 'opposites': 'Everything fluid or vapour', 'Each thing hostile / To every other thing'. But Ovid is still non-committal as to who or what was responsible for whipping it all into an ordered cosmos in the first place: 'God, or some such artist as resourceful, / Began to sort it out' (p. 4).

Secondly, all the myths and stories Ovid recounts were far from original with him: all had circulated in some shape or form – often many – before. What he brought to their telling was a blend of eroticism and urbanity, passion and stylistic panache. These are qualities that were to prove perennially appealing. In the present terms, Ovid had a 'genius' for *re . . . creation*. And it is in the spirit of skilled and spirited adaptation that his writing has encouraged and enabled the development of such skills in others. In English the earliest, most influential and itself quite 'free' translation is that of Arthur Golding (1567), and it is this that Shakespeare drew upon, again 'freely', for his *A Midsummer Night's Dream* (Pyramus and Thisbe) and *Venus and Adonis*, for example. As Ted Hughes observes in the introduction to his own highly distinctive and spirited *Tales from Ovid*:

> As a guide to the historic 'original' forms of the myths, Ovid is of little use. His attitude to his material is like that of the many later poets who have adapted what he presents. He too is an adaptor. He takes only those tales which catch his fancy and engages with each one no further than it liberates his own creative zest.
>
> (Hughes 1997: viii)

Here, for instance, is how Jo Shapcott's *Thetis* (1998) begins to slip under the skin and into the limbs of the shape-shifting sea nymph of that name from Ovid's Book XI:

> No man can frighten me. Watch as I stretch
> my limbs for the transformation, I'm laughing
> to feel the surge of other shapes beneath my skin.
> It's like this: here comes the full thrill of my art
> as the picture of a variegated
> lizard insinuates itself into my mind.
> I extend my neck, lengthen fingers, push
> down toes to find the form. My back begins
> to undulate, the skin to gleam. I think
> my soul has slithered with me into this
> shape as real as the little, long tongue in my mouth,
> as the sun on my back, as the skill in absolute stillness.
> My name is Thetis Creatrix and you,
> voyeur, if you looked a little closer, would see
> the next ripples spread up my bloody tail, to bloom
> through my spine as the bark begins to harden
> over my trunk.
>
> (Shapcott [1998] 2000: 87)

The other *Metamorphoses* we shall consider is that of a slightly later Roman writer from North Africa, Lucius Apuleius (born *c.* 125 CE). The book is also popularly known as *The Golden Ass*, because that is what his hero finds himself magically transformed into at one point. Unlike Ovid's, however, Apuleius' *Metamorphoses* begins not so much with a myth of cosmic creation as a comic apologia for literary creation. He opens, as though in mid-conversation, by observing that he intends to write in a deliberately *mixed* narrative form: the 'Milesian mode', famous for its intertwining of elegant and erotic stories. He also makes no secret of his seductive designs on his listeners' attention: 'What I should like to do is to weave together different tales in this Milesian mode and to stroke your approving ears with some elegant whispers' (Apuleius

1994: 1). And he adds, clearly recalling Ovid, 'I want you to feel wonder at the transformations of men's shapes and destinies into alien forms, and their reversion by a
chain of interconnection to their own.'

The last point Apuleius makes in his opening relates to the very language(s), litera-
ture(s) and culture(s) in which he is composing. Born in the Roman colony of Madauros
in North Africa (modern Algeria) and educated in Carthage and Athens, Apuleius
wrote in varieties of Latin and Greek that he acknowledges range from 'provincial' to
'cosmopolitan' and 'colloquial' to 'literary'. With this in mind, Apuleius declares he is
going to make a virtue of a necessity and use all the language varieties at his disposal,
even if they don't add up to single coherent whole or match the imperial standard preferred in the Roman law schools:

> I beg your indulgence for any mistakes which I make as a novice in the foreign
> language in use at the Roman bar. This switch of languages in fact accords with
> the technique of composition which I have adopted, much as a circus rider leaps
> from one horse to another, for the romance on which I am embarking is adapted
> from the Greek.
>
> (Apuleius [*c.* 170 CE] 1994: 1)

Apuleius's *Metamorphoses* is thus in every sense a classic piece of 'hybridised' and 'heteroglossic' (varied-tongued) writing; and it is expressly recognised as such by Bakhtin
in his work on the prehistory of the novel (Bakhtin 1981). It also exactly expresses the
intimate and intricate interrelations among kinds of (Greek) meta-morphosis and
(Latin) trans-lation one would expect to be 'carried over' in a writer operating so
knowingly on the intersection of both cultures. Further, Apuleius' 'technique of composition' as 'a switch of languages' corresponds closely to what Deleuze and Guattari
would term a 'minor' literature. For them, Kafka is the classic modern instance of a
writer working from the margins of a nominally dominant 'major' language (in
Kafka's case German inflected by the Czech and Yiddish of his native Prague) in such
a way as to 'de- and re-territorialise' it in a productively 'bastardised', 'minor' way
(Deleuze and Guattari [1980] 1987, Deleuze 1995). Indeed, as one commentator
remarks, the appeal of Kafka's work for Deleuze and Guattari is precisely that he
offers a 'hypcrrcalism' that 'deals with metamorphosis rather than metaphor' (Marks
1998: 135–7). Nor is it an accident that Kafka's most famous story, *Metamorphosis*
(1915) is a wittily grotesque account of a man who wakes up one morning to find he
has turned into a beetle.

The cultural theorist Rosi Braidotti pushes such insights yet further and in dimensions all her own, though openly taking directions from other writers too. Her
Metamorphoses: Towards a Materialist Theory of Becoming (2002) articulates both a radical
philosophy and a sexual politics of 'becoming'; and to do so it draws together the work
of Deleuze and Guattari with that of the feminist psychoanalytic theorist Luce Irigaray.
One of the many striking results is a further transformation of the term and concept
of 'metamorphosis' itself so as to embody two specific modes of becoming: 'Met(r)a-
morphosis' ('becoming Woman/Animal/Insect', Chapter 3) and 'Meta(l)morphosis'
('the Becoming-Machine', Chapter 5). In a curiously uncanny and appropriately paradoxical way, these specifically 'materialist' transformations of 'metamorphosis' have
no precise precedent in the classic versions but are given ample warrant by them.

Braidotti thus expresses some of the current possibilities taken to their properly (il)logical extremes: metamorphoses that themselves carry on metalmorphosing, metra-morphosing . . .

Cosmic law and order: gods and wo/mankind

These are creation myths that revolve around family feuds and dynastic strife. They also contain some of the earliest invocations of muses in the Western tradition. Both these features resonate interestingly with modern models of creativity conceived as the result of tensions between generations and between women and men (especially the 'fe<>male' dynamic explored in Chapter 3). All these materials also reaffirm the value of an approach to myth which emphasises its performative as much as its repre-sentational character. For each of these songs and stories brings a reality into being at a particular time, it does not simply record it forever. Hesiod's *Theogony* (*c.* 730 BCE), the most influential ancient Greek account of the 'birth of the gods' (which is what theogony means), is typical in this respect. It opens not just with a description of the Olympian muses but with an invocation of them; they are Hesiod's source of inspira-tion as well as his object of attention:

> Now let us begin with the Olympian Muses who sing for their father Zeus and delight his great soul, telling with harmonious voices of things past and present and to come [. . .] Daughters of Zeus, I greet you; add passion to my song, and tell of the sacred race of the gods who are forever, descended from Earth and starry Sky, from dark Night, and from salty Sea. [. . .] Relate these things to me, Muses!
>
> (Hesiod [*c.* 730 BCE] in Caws and Prendergast 1994: 25–6)

In effect, then, Hesiod 'relates' what he has to say in a number of dimensions. He relates a story, he relates to the muses, and he relates to his audience and readers. At the same time, he clearly indicates that the inspirational flow proceeds in a partic-ular direction (female muse to male poet) and operates in a particular family hierarchy (the muses are the daughters of 'father Zeus'). As a result, though crucial, the role of the muses is ultimately supporting and secondary. This is an emphatically patriarchal acknowledgement of female power. We consider variations on and alter-natives to this dominant dynamic of female muse/inspiration and male poet/artist – and vice versa – at various points in the present book (notably in the sonnets of Philip Sidney and Elizabeth Barrett Browning featured in Chapter 7). Though readily dis-missed as 'merely conventional' – or downright sexist – by modern readers, such relations often turn out to be more complex and vexed than they first appear.

Also complicated and contentious are the various ancestries and 'births' of the gods reported by Hesiod; for he evidently knit together several accounts current at the time, and not always neatly. There is, for instance, a recognition of female and male powers far more primeval than anything available on Mount Olympus. Hesiod indi-cates that there were three and perhaps four stages before the gods of Olympus took over: 'First of all, the Void came into being, next broad-bosomed Mother Earth, the solid and eternal home of all' (p. 27). After that, Mother Earth (Gaia) gives birth all by herself to one Father Sky (Uranos) who then lay with his mother to produce 'the great Chronos, the cunning trickster', later known as Father Time and in the Roman pantheon as Saturn. It is Chronos/Time who heads the race of Titans (including Prometheus) before being deposed by his son, Zeus. And it is Zeus who heads the Olympians until such time as (depending upon the precise myth in play) he in turn is deposed either by Prometheus or by one of his own sons. (For a handy overview of the variants, see Miles 1999: 20–35.)

Now, in some ways all of this is simply ancient Greek history writ large. As is often observed, it is a caricature of dynastic politics and family feuding in the period before the development of the Greek city states. The gods just do what people did but on a grander, cosmic scale. What's more, they do it along predominantly patriarchal lines; though it should be pointed out that, as in many creation myths, there is a primordial 'Mother Earth' in the background who gives birth to all. Firmly in the foreground, however, is a vision of creation – and by extension a version of creativity – that is readily recognisable: one built on a model of socially dysfunctional families ruled over by tyrannical father figures threatened by aspiring sons. As discussed in Chapter 4, Harold Bloom (1973, 2002) takes such an Oedipal model as the basis for his broadly Freudian as well as specifically Hebraic and mythopoeic approach to the creative process.

There are, however, other models of the creative process that have been extrapolated from these Greek creation myths. One is that of the proverbial and primordial 'Earth Mother', 'Gaia'. 'She' has been adopted as the emblem of a fundamentally female principle of all-embracing creative as well as procreative power (see Saunders 1987). Gaia is also the name for a principle of 'deep ecology' given currency by James Lovelock's *Gaia: A New Look at Life on Earth* (1979), a book which argues for a 'whole earth' vision of radical global interdependence.

But the aspect of these creation myths that most appealed to Romantic radicals such as Goethe, Byron, Percy Shelley and, later, Elizabeth Barrett Browning was the myth of Prometheus. In Greek mythology Prometheus is the Titan credited with taking revenge on the Olympians by creating human beings from clay or by stealing fire from heaven for them. He was punished for this by Zeus and the Olympian Gods by being nailed to a rock. But on balance, Prometheus (whose name in Greek means 'Fore-thought') was seen as the bringer of all sorts of humanising and civilising capacities, including counting, writing, mining for metals and the interpretation of dreams. As Aeschylus puts it in his *Prometheus Bound*, 'All human science and skill was Prometheus's gift' (Aeschylus [*c.* 440 BCE] 1961: 31). In this respect 'Prometheus's gift' offers a far more positive view of human knowledge than that in a number of creation myths, including Genesis (of which more shortly).

For Percy Shelley, above all, Prometheus stands for the archetype of the justified rebel struggling against tyranny and oppression; also, finally, as the creative power of love to transform life. As its title confirms, Shelley's verse drama, *Prometheus Unbound* (1820) is dedicated to the potentially *un*bounded nature and significance of Prometheus. It is his creative contribution to human well-being that is stressed: 'He gave man speech, and speech created thought, / Which is the measure of the universe' (II.4.72–3). And for Shelley what is clinching is the fact that 'chaos [is] made calm by love, not fear' (IV.171). The overall tenor of Shelley's treatment is therefore increasingly positive: 'We will take our plan / From the new world of man, / And our work shall be called the Promethean' (IV.156–8). Even so, the conclusion leaves no doubt that the struggle with oppression is ongoing, and always fraught with a sense of inner turmoil; for by this stage Prometheus has become a symbol of resilient life, not simply a figure in an archaic myth: 'To defy Power, which seems omnipotent / To love, and bear; to hope, till Hope creates / From its own wreck the thing it contemplates' (IV.572–5).

On a specifically historical note, it should be added that Shelley was writing in the wake of the perceived failure of the French Revolution. In *Prometheus Unbound* we see him struggling to re-articulate his politics and poetics while still maintaining a commitment to human emancipation, justice and love. As he observes in his preface, he sees 'the great writers of our own age' as 'the companions and forerunners of some unimagined change in our social condition or the opinions which cement it'. But he is also realistic enough to recognise that even the most exalted images of creativity and the most energetically reworked myths of creation are grounded in their own times and terms. His words on this might properly preface any myth of creation and, for that matter, any model of creativity: 'Poets, not otherwise than philosophers, painters, sculptors, and musicians, are in one sense, the creators, and in another, the creations, of their age. From this subjection the loftiest do not escape' (Shelley [1820] 1991: 56).

To use contemporary theoretical terms, what this clearly means is that all models of creativity are inescapably ethnocentric and ideological. They are centred on particular cultures (and thereby marginalise or ignore others) and they present power relations favourable to certain sections of society (and thereby mis- or under-represent alternatives). As a consequence, we are always the acted-upon subjects ('creations') as well as the active agents ('creators') of our history, and of all the ideologies, discourses and narratives (in the present terms, myths, metaphors and stories) through which it is constituted and challenged. What's more, as Shelley insists, this is a 'subjection' from which 'the loftiest do not escape'. With this in mind, we turn to the creation stories in the Bible, and we approach them historically and in context.

Babble . . .

For many (though by no means all) readers of the present book, the account of creation in Genesis may be that with which they are already most familiar. So as to prompt a fresh and informed look at this account (which in any case may be familiar in outline rather than detail), it will be approached in two ways. First we look at one of its precursors, a Babylonian creation epic. Then we read the Genesis account backwards in time from the story of Babel through the Flood to the Garden of Eden. This helps highlight the fact that the Biblical account is composed of a linked and many-layered series of stories (not just one), and that it draws on multiple sources which result in a complex and, in places, discontinuous narrative. The text used is that of the King James or 'Authorised' version of 1611, as this is the most historically influential Bible for English language and literature (here in the edition by Carroll and Prickett, 1997). Meanwhile, as with the other myths featured, the question of the factuality or fictionality of these accounts – whether they are to be treated as history or story, and as objects of faith or superstition – will be left in abeyance. You don't have to believe or disbelieve the account of creation in Genesis to grasp its narrative structure and historical significance.

Enuma Elish is a Babylonian creation epic, written in Akkadian and dated around

1500–1200 BCE, some five hundred years before the first Biblical accounts (see Caws and Prendergast 1994: 10–21 for text, and Leeming and Leeming 1994: 23–9 for commentary). It gets its name from its first two words which in Akkadian mean 'When [skies] above', just as Genesis gets its name from its first word in Greek, meaning 'In the beginning' or 'At the birth'. *Enuma Elish* opens with a primordial state of chaos in which the male and female principles, represented by Father Freshwater (Apsu) and Mother Ocean (Tiamat), are not yet differentiated and named as such. None of the other parts of the world is differentiated by name either: 'When skies above were not yet named, / Nor earth below pronounced by name, / Apsu, the first one, their begetter / And maker Tiamat, who bore them all, / Had their waters mixed together' (Tablet 1.1–5). The originary creative act therefore has a strong emphasis upon differentiation through naming. Only when named do gods come into being: 'When yet no gods were manifest, / Nor names pronounced, nor destinies decreed, / The gods were born within them' (Tablet 1.7–9). From the offspring of these gods there emerges a certain Marduk who becomes the hero-king and founding father of the Babylonians. His word has the power to destroy as well as re-create: 'Command to destroy and to recreate, and let it be so! . . . He spoke, and at his word the constellation vanished. / He spoke to it again and the constellation was recreated' (Tablet 4.22–6).

All this is both like and unlike the accounts in Genesis. It is similar in that creation is seen as a series of mighty speech acts and acts of naming (cf. 'And God said, Let there be light: and there was light [. . .] and God called the light Day, and the darkness he called Night . . .'; 'And whatsoever Adam called every living creature, that was the name thereof' (Genesis 1.3–5; 2.19)). And it is different in that the Babylonian account presents the gods (plural) as the product of material, natural and sexual processes that are prior to them, whereas the Biblical account presents God (singular) as already there, creating but himself uncreated. The difference between Babylonian polytheism and Biblical monotheism is of fundamental significance. It is crucial, for instance, when it comes to presenting creation as an ongoing process or a one-off act; and it dramatically affects the concept of divine power as something dispersed across several figures or concentrated in just one. For instance, in the Biblical account when God decides to punish or destroy a portion of his creation that displeases him (as with the destruction of Babel, the infliction of the Flood and the expulsion of Adam and Eve from Eden) he just gets on and does it on his own. In the Babylonian account, however, such things are managed differently. When Father Freshwater (Apsu) has had enough of the unruly gods who are his children and resolves to get rid of them ('Their ways have become very grievous to me . . . I shall abolish their ways and disperse them'), he has his wife and their mother, Mother Ocean (Tiamat), to contend with: 'How could we allow what we ourselves created to perish? / Even though their ways are grievous, we should bear it patiently' (Tablet 1.37–46). As a result, where the Biblical account tends to *impose* cosmic law and order, the Babylonian account tends to *expose* it. There is, in every sense, a *dramatic difference* between the two modes of creation (and destruction) in play. Basically, the Babylonian account tends to dialogue and debate, and the Bible tends to monologue and diktat.

But there is nothing democratic about the world-order – and the capacity of the word to order – in *Enuma Elish*. As commentators note, especially in its latter portions it shows clear signs of being developed as 'a propaganda piece, written to justify

Marduk's glory and control over the natural forces of the universe and Babylon's supremacy over the Fertile Crescent Region' (Leeming and Leeming 1994: 25). In fact, like the Pharaohs and some of the later Roman emperors, Marduk and his dynasty are clearly being set up as gods in their own right. Thus Marduk is expressly presented as creator of the human race at large and as the founder and namer of Babylon in particular: 'I hereby name it Babylon, home of the great gods. / We shall make it the centre of religion' (Tablet V.86–7). The ethnocentrism of creation myths is rarely expressed in more naked terms. Meanwhile, there are obviously many other subject peoples and their respective gods that are expected to knuckle under to the power and glory of Marduk. Thus, though it may be residually polytheistic and ostensibly accommodating towards other religions ('Come let us call him by his fifty names'), it is clear that *Enuma Elish* is finally set on monotheism and the imposition of a virtual monopoly: 'Let mankind be mindful of him, and name him as their god' (Tablet VI.113–21). In other words, it is an attempt to impose a basically monocultural model (an ideological 'universe') on what was evidently a much more complex and contentious mix of peoples and religions (a 'multiverse'). Conversely, it is obvious that there were other ways of responding to the imperious injunction of the *Enuma Elish* to 'Create Babylon! / Let its mud bricks be moulded and build high the shrine!' (Tablet VI.57–8). One of them, famously, happens to be recorded in the Bible.

The Biblical story of Babel (Genesis 11) is strictly an 'un/creation myth'; and so are those of the Flood (Genesis 6–10) and the Garden of Eden (Genesis 1–5). That is, for each act of creation there is a corresponding act of uncreation: the building of the mighty Tower is confounded and abandoned; the Flood drowns all the people and creatures except those on the ark; Adam and Eve are put in a paradisal garden only to be expelled from it. The close connection between the activities of creating and uncreating, building up to knock down, has already been observed in several myths (the African myth of Doondari, for example, and the Greek myth of Prometheus). In the case of the Babel story this dual aspect of un/creation is memorialised in the words 'tower of Babel' and 'babble'. To begin with, 'Babel' (as the capital of Babylon) is clearly conceived as a symbol of human solidarity and aspiration: 'And the whole earth was of one language and of one speech. [. . .] Go to, let us build us a city and a tower whose top may reach unto heaven, and let us make a name lest we be scattered abroad upon the face of the whole earth' (Genesis 11.1–4). This clearly recalls the ambitions of *Enuma Elish*, where 'Babel' is glossed in Akkadian as 'Gate of God'. 'Babble', however – meaning 'a confusion of tongues' – is what these ambitions are reduced to when the project collapses through divine intervention and the consequent failure to communicate: 'Therefore is the name of it called Babel; because the Lord did there confound the language of all the earth' (11.9). The precise political and historical circumstances of all this are unclear. But what is certain is that there was a massive Babylonian building project that was not completed. Thereafter 'Babel/babble' became a by-word in the region: a sore point for the Babylonians in power, and a point to be pressed home by peoples subject to them such as the Hebrews. As the editors of the most recent edition of the Authorized King James version of the Bible observe, 'The story of the Tower of Babel [. . .] is a nice example of how an oppressed people [the Hebrews] can make fun of their imperial overlords by word-play and mock the grandiose projects of world-famous Babylon' (Carroll and Prickett 1997: 327).

Three other observations may be made about this particular un/creation myth. First, it involves the common motif of a fearful and angry divinity who opposes human attempts at creation and, in this case, seeks to divide and rule:

> And the Lord said, Behold, the people is one, and they have all one language; [. . .] and now nothing will be restrained from them which they have imagined to do.
>
> Go to, let us go down, and there confound their language, that they may not understand one another's speech.
>
> So the Lord scattered them abroad from thence upon the face of all the earth; and they left off to build the city.
>
> (Genesis 11.6–8).

Further, the Biblical account of Babel is an extended joke, a black-comic poke at grandiose plans that eventually come to nothing (as do Coyote's plans for creation in the Native American myth). Finally, as usual, precisely how one interprets and in effect re-tells the tale greatly affects its meaning. The present interpretation/re-telling is no exception. For, as we have seen time and again, creation myths are only ever available through later re-creations (adaptations, editions, interpretations). By way of further illustration, here are some hypothetical 'news headlines' representing the Babel story in a range of modern journalistic idioms. They were generated by students on the 'Changing Stories' course, Oxford 1999: 'Dream in ruins', 'Act of God halts major building project', 'Still no agreement between bosses and workers', 'Unions fail to ensure unity', 'Talks break-down threatens tower', 'Multiculturalism undermines the Monolith', 'Babylonians reject "Babble" smear', 'Jews vote with their feet and head for Promised Land'. Clearly, yet again, it all depends who is re-creating the creation myth in question – with what ends as well as beginnings in view.

. . . and Flood . . .

Similar problems and possibilities of interpretation (who re-creates the creation myth?) apply to the Biblical story immediately before that of the Tower of Babel, the story of Noah's ark (Genesis 6–9). In outline the events are straightforward enough. God is unhappy with the conduct of the human part of his creation, resolves to destroy nearly everyone by a flood, and then start over again almost from scratch. Only Noah and his wife and their three sons and their wives (along with a male and female of every species) are to be spared by being reserved a place in the ark which Noah is instructed to build. The dual constructive and destructive sides of this particular un/creation myth are clearly signalled from the outset:

> And the Lord said, I will destroy man whom I have created from the face of the earth; both man, and beast, and the creeping things, and the fowls of the air; for it repenteth me that I have made them.
>
> But Noah found grace in the eyes of the Lord.
>
> (Genesis 6.7–8)

Now, not surprisingly, ancient 'Flood' myths that save as well as destroy were common to many peoples who lived by and depended upon the deltas of the Nile, Euphrates and Tigris – Babylonians and Egyptians as well as Hebrews. In *Enuma Elish* it is referred to as 'the flood weapon' of the gods, and one of Marduk's claims to divinity is his commissioning of dams and waterways that seek to control the meeting of 'Father Freshwater' and 'Mother Ocean' at flood time. *The Epic of Gilgamesh* (*c.* 1200 BCE), from the same region, also includes an extended Creation and Flood narrative particularly close and again prior to that in the Bible. We are thus firmly reminded that creation and other myths are rooted in particular geographies and economies; also in the ebb and flow of seasonal cycles, here drought and flood. But there are always local fluctuations and often residues of previous versions. One of those rarely noted in orthodox retellings of the story of Noah's Flood but plainly there in Genesis (6.4) is the persistence of a story relating to 'giants', 'the sons of God' and 'daughters of men': 'There were giants in the earth in those days; and also after that, when the sons of God came in unto the daughters of men, and they bare children to them, the same became mighty men which were of old, men of renown.' Evidently this is an outcrop of an earlier or alternative heroic cosmology embedded in the dominant Hebrew version.

Moreover, like any other narrative, Noah's Flood can be read 'against or across the grain': in terms of what is absent or in the background rather than present and at the centre. In this case we may concentrate on who and what is destroyed rather than saved. For the fact remains that the vast majority of humanity (including presumably not a few 'giants' and 'sons of God') as well as most of the animals are wiped out. One such alternative perspective is opened up by a comic interlude in a late medieval mystery play, the Chester version of Noah's Flood (*c.* 1400 onwards; see Abrams *et al.* 2000: vol. 1: 313–17). There the close friends and drinking companions of Noah's wife are briefly brought centre-stage; she only leaves the warmth and jollity of their company when physically forced to by her sons. None of this is Biblical in origin; it is apocryphal. But the whole scene offers a telling as well as entertaining exposé of what, at one moment of its representation, was felt to have been left out of the official, heavily patriarchal account. Yet other alternatives are opened up by modern novelistic versions of the Noah's Ark story such as Jeanette Winterson's *Boating for Beginners* (1985) and the opening of Julian Barnes's *A History of the World in 10½ Chapters* (1989). All these remind us that the version of creation favoured depends upon the precise moment and medium in which it is re-presented – by whom, for whom, and why. For all their claims to timelessness and universality, there is always something timely and culture-specific about the truths such myths offer.

. . . back to the Beginning

We now turn to the central stories in Genesis 1–4, and those of God's creation of humanity in particular. Again the emphasis is upon stori*es* (plural), each with its own beginning, notwithstanding the apparent insistence of the opening words on a single beginning: 'In the beginning . . .', as it has it in the Authorised version (Hebrew *Bereshith*, Greek *Genesis*). For the fact is that there are at least three stages of composition discernible in the ancient Hebrew version (for much of the following information, see Caws and Prendergast 1994: 31–42 and Carroll and Prickett 1997: 326–7). The two earlier ones (*c.* 980–700 BCE) are the 'Yahwistic ' and 'Elohistic' stages, from the different names each used for God, *Yahweh* and *Elohim*; the latest is the so-called 'Priestly' stage (*c.* 500 BCE) and represents a more concerted attempt at institutional control by the priests. Together, these three stages show a clear trend of reworking initially polytheistic stories in a monotheistic direction. Where once were many gods and elemental forces, increasingly, officially, there is just one. Though even then it should be observed that vestiges of further creation stories can be traced elsewhere in the Old Testament: in Job 38, Isaiah 51. 9–10 and some of the Psalms. These include episodes in which God apparently has to contend with still earlier elemental forces. A further twist is that the first chapter of Genesis – the one with the beguiling beginning 'In the beginning . . .' – was written last. It was clearly an attempt by the priestly revisers to set the monotheistic seal on the whole book, and also introduce it as a 'whole' rather than a collection of bits. As Carroll and Prickett observe (1997: 326), 'each Bible is a palimpsest of the history of its own production'. We shall concentrate on the creation of Adam and Eve.

There are in fact two accounts of the creation of humanity in Genesis, not just one. And they especially differ with respect to the creation of male and female. The first account, associated with the priestly stage of composition, suggests that male and female were created in the image of God more or less simultaneously: 'So God created man in his own image, in the image of God created he him; male and female created he them. And God blessed them, and God said unto them, Be fruitful, and multiply . . .' (1.27–8). The apparently abrupt or inconsistent transition 'created he him, . . . created he them' is explained by the fact that *adam* in Hebrew means 'mankind' (i.e. humanity of both sexes) as well as 'man' (i.e. male). This point is clarified in an explicit restatement of this version of creation later: 'Male and female created he them; and blessed them, and called their name Adam, in the day they were created' (Genesis 5.2). This less famous and sometimes substantially ignored account of the creation of wo/mankind is the one preferred in Nicole Ward Jouve's *Female Genesis* (1998: 1–31, and see above pp. 81–2). The second account of the creation of humanity is associated with the 'Yahwistic' stage of composition. It is the far more (in)famous one of Eve being drawn from Adam's rib. In this case God first forms man from 'the dust of the ground' and inspires him with 'the breath of life' (2.7). Then, confirming that 'Adam' here primarily means 'male', 'the LORD God [Yahweh] caused a deep sleep to fall upon Adam, and he slept: and he took one of his ribs, and closed up the flesh instead thereof; And the rib, which the LORD God had taken from man, made he a woman, and brought her unto the man' (2.21–2).

All this leaves us with some pointed questions: simultaneous creation of male *and* female – or successive creation of male *then* female? both of them created in the image of God – or he created from divinely inspired dust and she created from a man's spare rib? Such questions are of more than theological interest. They even go beyond sexual politics narrowly conceived. For what they reveal is the fact that the most influential creation myth in the West for some two thousand years – and probably the most ubiquitous creation story ever – is fraught 'from the beginning' with fundamental complications and potential confusions. And the problem is precisely which beginning?!

We may also be left wondering, as we were in the stories of Noah's Flood and the Tower of Babel, just what kind of Creator it is who first creates then punishes a large part of his creation. After all, the crucial hinge of the story is the Creation and Fall of Adam and Eve: the fact that they are put in a paradisal garden, forbidden to eat the fruit from one of its trees and, when they do, summarily expelled. To say the least, they are put in a tight spot! For the tree is 'the tree of the knowledge of good and evil' (2.17), and the man and woman are caught between a clever serpent who urges them to eat and 'be as gods, knowing good and evil' (3.5) and an omnipotent deity who has categorically laid down 'thou shalt not eat of it' (2.17). Faced with such a predicament, even firm believers have, in Milton's phrase, sometimes felt compelled 'to justify the ways of God to man' (*Paradise Lost* I.22).

Indeed, in the English-speaking world, it is arguably Milton's version (published in 1667 and gradually turned into a national and literary institution) that has done more to influence understanding of this creation story than close attention to Genesis itself. Certainly, to Milton may be imputed the particularly energetic and darkly attractive figure of Satan as half-justified rebel. For this he drew on apocryphal Biblical sources and infused them with some Promethean potential that William Blake was among the first to detect (see below p. 234). Meanwhile, and still more contentiously, it is to Milton that many modern readers owe the abiding image of an emphatically gendered hierarchy of power stretching from God through Adam to Eve: 'He for God only, she for God in him', as it is (in)famously put in *Paradise Lost*, IV.299. None of this makes for a neatly ordered vision of the cosmos: Milton's world-view was neo-Classical as well as Christian; authoritarian as well as republican. But it does make for some fascinatingly 'chaotic' possibilities, as we see in Milton's vision of 'eldest Night and Chaos' featured in Chapter 7.

Finally it should be observed that there are yet other, more or less apocryphal stories woven into and around those of the Biblical account of the creation of humanity. One features a woman called Lilith. According to an ancient Sumerian tradition passed down in Jewish lore and medieval Christian legend, Lilith was created from the dust of the earth at the same time as Adam (see Isaiah, 34.14 and Goring 1992: 301). Lilith was created Adam's equal in all respects. Though she was subsequently demonised as a voracious seducer of men and slayer of children (apparently because she had the nerve to leave Adam), she offers yet another, alternative 'beginning' to the orthodox one(s) offered in the Biblical account of Adam and Eve.

Another twist in the Biblical tale is the story of the 'Golem'. According to Kabbalistic and especially Hasidic tradition, the Golem was 'a quasi-human creature constructed by man in imitation of his divine Creator' (see Kearney 1998: 53–61). Accounts of and attitudes to the Golem vary widely. For most people it was an abomination and an affront to the powers of the true creator, God. It was also an example of humanity's lack of skill and forethought as creators: most Golems could neither speak nor procreate and were in every sense sterile. But a few accounts of the Golem suggest it was a credit to its creator (humanity) and even, by extension, to humanity's creator (God). At the very least it proved serviceable in menial tasks such as running errands, and was treated as a kind of labour-saving device. Indeed, in one rabbinical text, the roles of creators and creatures get so conflated that Adam himself is seen as a kind of Golem – and judged none the worse for that (see Kearney 1998: 54–5).

Excitement about the conflation and anxiety about the confusion of established creator–creature roles are a recurrent concern in many other kinds of creation story. They are as central to versions of the Pygmalion myth as they are to that of Frankenstein (see above p. 46 and below pp. 238–40). Indeed, in a world increasingly formed and informed by the sciences and technologies of robotics, genetics and other 'man-made' practices and apparatuses, the problems and possibilities are becoming ever more pressing. We may therefore ask not just whether the world is being serviced by 'Golems' (cars, computers and other 'labour-saving devices') but whether humanity is itself, for better and worse, becoming a Golem – the creature of its own making. These are possibilities we explore in the next chapter.

6 New sciences for old

> To him who is a discoverer in this field, the products of his imagination appear so necessary and natural that he regards them, and would like to have them regarded by others, not as creations of thought but as given realities.
>
> (Albert Einstein [1948] in Gregory 1990: x)

Modern sciences have their own preferred ways of seeing and saying the origins of the universe and of life. They have their dominant metaphors (Big Bang, Cosmic Soup, Double Helix) and their more or less grand narratives (quantum theory, evolution, genetics). Before reviewing some instances of the accounts of origins ('creation myths') offered by contemporary science, we shall briefly consider the origins of modern science itself. For in some respects the modern scientific project is arguably far more radically 'creative' than any project in the arts traditionally conceived. That is, science ceaselessly seeks to prove and promote 'new' kinds of knowledge even as it seeks to extend and refine – and, if necessary, disprove and supersede – 'old' kinds of knowledge. This is clearly both a 'creative' and 'destructive' process. It proceeds by successive stages of proof and disproof, doubt and refutation. Indeed, according to Karl Popper, it is the very capacity of science to be *dis*proved by systematic experiment and observation as well as argument that sets it apart from sheer belief or mere opinion (see Popper in Kearney 1995: 196–210). In the latter respect all the preceding accounts of creation in the present chapter are strictly neither provable nor disprovable. In a modern sense they are 'non-scientific'.

But modern science does have its 'myths' in the capacious and neutral sense of 'truths' proposed at the beginning of Part 2 (i.e. widely shared and ritually rehearsed discourses, designs, stories and world-views). The most potent and seemingly natural of these myths is the belief in the overall 'advance' or 'progress' of science itself. This is the idea, widespread but by no means universal since the seventeenth century, that knowledge is always on the increase and is in every sense 'improving' (i.e. getting better and good for you, as well as the archaic sense of being amenable to 'proof'). This was one of the founding principles of the Royal Society (1662), as confirmed in its full title 'The Royal Society of London for the Improving of Natural Knowledge'. Such a view underpins popular appeals to the ultimate truth of 'Science' (capitalised and singular) and a belief in 'scientifically established facts' arrived at by 'the scientific method'. We shall consider all of these shortly.

But first it should be observed that there are plenty of modern counter-myths cautioning against the excesses or abuses of science. Especially persistent are those of Faust (notably in versions by Marlowe and Goethe), who sold his soul for universal knowledge that he used wildly or unwisely, and of Frankenstein (from Mary Shelley's tale to Hollywood films), who in attempting to make a marvel only succeeded in creating a monster (see Chapter 7). Such stories haunt the artistic and popular imaginations from the sixteenth century to the present; and in many respects they pick up from the Biblical and Classical myths featured in the previous chapter. For many of those are concerned with the appeals and perils of knowledge: of the tree of life whose fruit, when plucked, gives 'knowledge of good and evil' and leads to expulsion from the garden state of Eden; of grandly ambitious human projects that tend to fall apart, Babel-like, through failure of communication into a 'babble' of mutually incomprehensible languages; of the Promethean gift of fire and arts and sciences to humanity that is also a punishable theft from the gods; or, according to an alternative scenario also recycled by Hesiod in his *Theogony*, the myth of Pandora (whose name means 'All Gifts') from whose 'box' all the ills of humanity poured (see Miles 1999: 37–8). To these we may add the tale of Icarus (most famously retold in Ovid's *Metamorphoses*, Book VIII), who tried to escape captivity on waxen wings of his own fashioning but flew too close to the sun and, when they melted, fell into the sea and drowned. There is clearly no shortage of cautionary myths about knowledge in general and science in particular. At the very least they encourage a circumspect and sceptical approach to new knowledge. In extreme form, taken literally, they are an excuse for any old superstition and ignorance.

It was precisely to dispel the mists – and myths – of superstition and ignorance that Francis Bacon wrote *The Advancement of Learning* (1605) and its Latin continuation *Novum Organum* ('The New Instrument', 1620). These are widely recognised as defining documents of early modern science (many of the most relevant parts can be found in Abrams *et al.* 2000, Vol. 1: 1529–52). Bacon insists upon working from concrete particulars to general principles (i.e. inductive reasoning) and proposes that this be combined with empirical 'experiment' based on rigorously controlled observation. Bacon is also vigorously opposed to what he sees as 'the bewitchment of reason by language' and a correspondingly misguided concern with 'words rather than things' (*Novum Organum*, section 60). At the same time he especially attacks what he calls 'four classes of Idols which beset men's minds', where 'Idol' carries its Greek sense of *eidolon*, 'image'. In large measure, this is an attack on the metaphorical capacity of language to *create* a kind of spectral but strictly non-existent reality rather than *record* a substantial and supposedly pre-existent one. As Bacon puts it, 'The idols imposed by words on the understanding [. . .] are either names of things which do not exist, [. . .] or they are names of things which exist, but [are] yet confused and ill defined and hastily and irregularly derived from realities' (*Novum Organum*, section 60).

But there is a catch. As Bacon's own argument demonstrates, it is possible to be aware of the abuses of metaphor and yet be oblivious to the implications of one's own use of them. Thus, in his own highly metaphorical turn of phrase, Bacon identifies the four chief kinds of 'Idol/image' responsible for misunderstanding: 'Idols of the Tribe' (common to human nature); 'Idols of the Cave' (specific to the individual); 'Idols of the Marketplace' ('derived from 'the commerce and consort of men'); and 'Idols of the Theatre' ('which have migrated into men's minds from the various dogmas of philosophies and also from wrong laws of demonstration'). It is these last that most concern us here. In principle they consist of all the philosophical and religious systems featured so far. But in practice, characteristically, they exclude the writer's own religion and 'dogma of philosophy' (for Bacon was an orthodox Christian gentleman). They also overlook the fact that Bacon's argument is, by his own account, a 'wrong law of demonstration' in that it palpably depends upon an 'Idol/image' of 'the theatre' (i.e. the very metaphorical use of language he is attacking!): 'These I call Idols of the Theatre, because in my judgment all the received systems are but so many stage plays, representing worlds of their own creation after an unreal and scenic fashion' (*Novum Organum*, section 44). In other words, while quite properly counselling others to be cautious of the potential deceptions of received language and ideas (what we now call 'dead metaphors'), he quite improperly ignores his own (which are very much 'alive'). We may therefore be left wondering whether or not we are to include Bacon's as an instance of a 'world of *his* own creation after an unreal and scenic fashion'!

None of these complications and potential confusions should really surprise us. Bacon, like every other, was very much a man of his own time, even while helping prepare the way for a different future. Accordingly, for all his signal contributions to the development of a modern philosophy of science (his image of 'Salomon's House' in *The New Atlantis* (1626) supplied a blueprint for the Royal Society), Bacon did not himself contribute to any 'advancement of learning' through experiment. Nor did he show much awareness of the major scientific breakthroughs of his own age: Galileo on the earth's movement round the sun; Harvey on the circulation of the blood, for instance. None the less, as one commentator puts it, 'Bacon is a primary creator of the myth of science as pathway to Utopia' (Abrams *et al.* 2000, Vol. 1: 1530). And as the above analysis indicates, we should be careful to stress 'creator', 'myth' and 'Utopia' as well as 'science'.

We should also be alert to the richness and potential inconsistency of Bacon's views of 'creation'. Much depends upon the particular genre in which he is writing. All his works referred to so far (*The Advancement of Learning*, *Novum Organum* and *The New Atlantis*) belong to the genre of philosophical treatise of a more or less 'utopian' kind. They describe a world, a method and an institution of science as it might or should be – not as it was or even could be. They offer idealised images of science as progress and, conversely, demonised images of ignorance and superstition. Significantly, if we turn to work by Bacon in other genres we get quite different views. His *The Wisdom of the Ancients* (1619), for example, is a collection of essays interpreting classical myths in precisely those ways that one would have thought utterly inimical to the 'advancement of learning'. Thus in his essay 'Cupid, or the Atom' he declares that 'The fable relates to the cradle and infancy of nature, and pierces deep', and he interprets 'Cupid, or Love' as 'the most ancient of all the gods; the most ancient therefore of all things whatever, except Chaos'. He goes on to explain his subject thus: 'This Love I understand to be the appetite or instinct of primal matter; or to speak more plainly, the natural motion of the atoms; which is indeed the original and unique force that constitutes all things out of matter' (Kermode and Hollander 1973, Vol. 1: 1454). Clearly, then, Bacon is quite prepared to engage in the (then fashionable) invocation and interpretation of classical myth. He is also happy to relay the still received version of 'atomic' theory, even though it rehearses what he elsewhere calls a 'dogma of philosophy' derived from Greek and Roman materialists such as Lucretius.

Further, as both a Christian gentleman and an enlightened humanist, Bacon assumes it is perfectly proper and reasonable to interpret the Biblical creation story along broadly rationalist lines. Thus in his essay 'Of Truth' (*Essays or Counsels, Civil and Moral*, 1625), he observes 'The first creature of God, in the works of the days, was the light of the sense; the last was the light of reason' (Kermode and Hollander 1973, Vol. 1: 1436). Meanwhile, in his essay 'Of Innovations' what we meet is emphatically *not* some programme for the utopian reform of knowledge, science or anything else. Instead, we are treated to a cautious and commonsensical restatement of the need for balanced and gradual change: 'It were good therefore that men in their innovations would follow the example of time itself, which innovateth greatly, but quietly and by degrees scarce to be perceived' (p. 1440). This is the vision of a conservative statesman not a progressive scientist.

Overall, then, we come from a reading of Bacon's work *as a whole* with a distinctly divided, even multiple, message: about the relations between science and learning, ancient and modern; about the perils and appeals of myth and metaphor; and above all about language as both an utterly unreliable and absolutely indispensable tool with which humans attempt to grasp kinds of truth. None of this should perhaps surprise us. As seen in the previous chapter, Nietzsche, Ricoeur and many others have since alerted us to the inevitable double- and treble-binds of language as it constantly remakes – never just finds – the world. To recall Percy Shelley's words in his Preface to *Prometheus Unbound* (1820), all writers are the 'creations' as well as the 'creators' of their age: 'From this subjection the loftiest do not escape' (see above p. 240). Sir Francis Bacon, one of the brightest lights of the Enlightenment conception of science, was no exception. Nor was the next figure whose very different 'New Science' we now turn to.

The New Science (*La Scienza Nuova*) by the eminent Italian jurist Giambattista Vico (1668–1744) was first published in 1725 and revised in 1730 and 1744. In the words of a later commentator, '[this]was a momentous occasion, although it passed virtually unnoticed at the time. For the "science" Vico proposed was nothing less than a science of human society' (Hawkes 1977: 11–5, here 11). More particularly, and in his own words, Vico articulated a 'physics of man' based upon the premise that men have 'created themselves' and that 'the world of civil society has certainly been made by men, and that its principles are therefore to be found within the modifications of our own human mind' (Vico [1744] 1968: sections 331, 367). By extension, as his editors point out, Vico argues that 'humanity itself was created by the very same processes by which institutions were created' (p. xliv). Conversely, 'not only does man create societies and institutions in his own mind's image, but these in the end create him'. Where Bacon's emphasis, notionally at least, is upon science as the rational and dispassionate empirical study of nature independent of human language and belief, Vico's emphasis is upon a thoroughly engaged science in which humanity is the fit object as well as subject of study. Basically, Bacon is for 'Science *minus* Humanity' (i.e. the pure sciences) and Vico is for the 'Science *plus* Humanity' (including the human sciences). These are crude but initially serviceable oppositions; they will be refined shortly.

Vico's alignment with the view that science and knowledge are a part of – not apart from – humanity is confirmed by his emphasis upon what he calls *sapienza poetica* ('wise making', 'poetic wisdom'). By this he meant the 'wisdom' or 'understanding' (*sapienza*) of humanity as 'maker' or 'fashioner' (from the Greek root *poiesis*). Percy

Shelley in his *Defence of Poetry* (1821) has a similarly capacious and radical view of 'poesie' as any kind of 'making', in the sciences as well as the arts. For both Vico and Shelley, *homo sapiens* is always in effect *homo faber* ('humanity the maker'). A related key concept for Vico is that of the *verum factum*: the principle that what humanity believes to be 'true' (*verum*) is always substantially a construct, 'something made' (*factum*). Vico summarises his position succinctly thus: 'the true and the made convert into one another (*verum et factum convertuntur*)' (see Singer and Dunn 2000: 140–53). As a result, whether talking of *sapienza poetica* or *verum factum*, Vico's emphasis is firmly upon dynamic processes of human becoming and continuing self-creation, rather than a static, essentialist notion of the 'human being' or once-and-for-all creation by a divinity. (Though publicly a pious Catholic, there are signs that in private Vico questioned many aspects of orthodox dogma; see Smith 1997: 341–2.)

Especially significant in the present context is the fact that, for Vico, all these processes of human becoming and self-creation are expressed and apprehended through metaphor and symbol. Indeed, for him, language and human communication are fundamentally metaphorical and symbolic by nature: 'Words are carried over from bodies and from the properties of bodies to signify the institutions of the mind and spirit' (Vico [1744] 1968: section 237); and as he says of the manifestations of *sapienza poetica* later: 'The most luminous and therefore the most necessary and frequent is metaphor' (section 404). Vico was also interested in myth and story as symbolic articulations of human powers of 'making' and kinds of 'truth', and he was intrigued by 'myths of origins' in particular: 'It follows that the first science to be learned should be mythology or the interpretation of fables; for, as we shall see, all the histories of the gentiles have their beginnings in fables' (section 51). This insistence upon the primarily metaphorical and communicative (rather than literal and referential) dimension of human behaviour is carried through into Vico's view of history. Like story, history was above all something made and told; it entailed participant-observers: 'history cannot be more certain than when he who creates the things also narrates them' (section 349). The historian of the human sciences, Roger Smith, sums up the significance of Vico thus:

> [he] reinterpreted ancient history as the empirical basis for the science of humanity's self-creation – or, in modern terms, for the science of culture. [. . .] there is no thought, no life of the mind, except through symbols, and the record of myth and poetry is the record of human consciousness.
>
> (Smith 1997: 344)

The basic differences between Bacon's and Vico's conceptions of science are of fundamental and enduring significance. They represent two poles in the philosophy and history of modern science. Later counterparts can be traced in the very different attitudes to science adopted by respectively Carnap (logical positivist) and Heidegger (metaphorical phenomenologist) (see Critchley 2001: 90–111). Christopher Norris characterises such perennial differences as, respectively, Realist (or Rationalist) and Culturalist (or Relativist) (see Norris in Payne 1996: 485–96). For the Realist-rationalist (e.g. Bacon) the emphasis is upon science as it offers insights into natural and physical objects and processes, and ultimately rational 'laws', as these exist apart from and, in principle, independent of human observation. For the Cultural-relativist (e.g. Vico) the emphasis is upon science as it offers insights into cultural and historical objects and processes that exist as a part of and, in practice, dependent upon human participation. The Realist-rationalist attempts to avoid the deceptions of metaphor and ordinary language and the habits of merely received ideas ('myths') at all costs – even if in the event this proves ultimately impossible. The Cultural-relativist readily embraces metaphor, ordinary language and myth as key objects of enquiry – precisely because these prove immediately accessible.

It is tempting (and certainly common) to push the differences between Realist-rationalists and Cultural-relativists to extremes and to see their proponents in utterly opposing camps. This opposition may then underwrite a simplistic division between the supposedly 'hard', 'pure' 'physical and natural' sciences (e.g. physics, chemistry, biology) on the Realist-rationalist side, and the correspondingly 'soft', 'impure', 'human and social' sciences (e.g. law and sociology) on the Cultural-relativist side. To do so, however, would be to miss or mangle the point. In particular, what such a crudely binary opposition utterly fails to register is the ways in which these various forces interact to produce new models of science entirely, including new developments of old models. It also obscures the sudden revolutions and gradual evolutions of the sciences (pure, human and otherwise), especially the ways in which the one may turn away from or into the other. It is to these r/evolutions that we now turn. And as we shall see again, the creativity of science and scientists cannot be finally distinguished from the social and historical creation of the disciplines and institutions that sustain or constrain them.

Revolutionary science

In his *The Structure of Scientific Revolutions* (1962, 2nd edn 1970) Thomas Kuhn makes a now classic distinction between 'normal science' and a 'revolution in science'. For Kuhn, '"normal science" means research firmly based upon one or more past scientific achievements, achievements that some particular scientific community acknowledges for a time as supplying the foundation for its further practice' (Kuhn 1970: 10). An example of 'normal' science is Newton's laws of motion and causality, which displaced Aristotelian notions of essentially intrinsic force and supplied the conceptual and experimental foundation in many areas of physics from the mid-seventeenth to the early twentieth centuries (and for most practical purposes still supplies them in mechanics). Another example is Darwin's concept of 'natural selection', which displaced the religious notion of 'special creation' and has informed most aspects of evolutionary biology since the late nineteenth century. As these examples demonstrate and as Kuhn's careful qualifications confirm, 'normal science' is only *relatively* stable within *specific* limits of time, place and persons ('some particular community . . . for a time').

In many respects Kuhn's concept of 'normal science' is similar to Csikszentmihalyi's concept of a 'field' of judges competent in recognising and evaluating creativity in a certain 'domain'. It also corresponds to Fish's notion of an 'interpretative community' (see above p. 68). However, these concepts only acknowledge the fact that there are *varieties* of scientific model and community. They do not account for the dynamic process of *variation* within and between models and communities, nor the precise ways in which one not only displaces but utterly *replaces* another.

The question, then, is what happens when the 'foundations for . . . further practice' are not simply built upon (*evolution* conceived as gradual change) but swept aside and replaced by a structure built on quite different lines (*evolution* conceived as abrupt change – i.e. *revolution*)? Kuhn defines instances of the latter thus: 'scientific revolutions are here taken to be those *non-cumulative* developmental episodes in which an older paradigm is replaced in whole or in part by an *incompatible* new one' (p. 92, my emphasis). (A 'paradigm' is a set of beliefs and practices shared by members of a scientific community; it partly corresponds to 'myth' as defined in the present chapter.) The key elements here are *non*-cumulative and *in*compatible. And for Kuhn the crucially disruptive and productive ingredient is *anomaly*. What is 'anomalous' is that which 'sticks out', 'doesn't fit', what it is 'difficult to put a name to'. (Appropriately enough, the derivation of the word itself is disputed. It may derive from the Greek for 'without name' or for 'without control'; see *OED* 'anomal-'.) Here is how Kuhn plots the trajectory at a moment of 'scientific revolution' from *old* 'normal' science to *new* 'normal' science via 'anomaly'. It is a process he terms 'paradigm shift':

> Discovery commences with the awareness of anomaly, i.e., with the recognition that nature has somehow violated the paradigm-induced expectations that govern normal science. It then continues with a more or less extended exploration of the area of anomaly. And it closes only when the paradigm theory has been adjusted so that the anomalous has become the expected.
>
> (Kuhn 1970: 52–3)

This is a neatly persuasive model of paradigm-shift. It tells a tidy tale of anomaly discovered, explored and accommodated. In several respects it closely resembles models of the creative process as a series of operations in problem-spotting, problem-posing and problem-solving: Intuitive Awareness of Problem is followed by a period of Incubation and Exploration and leads through Verification to Solution (see above, p. 73). However, the underlying problem with Kuhn's way of modelling 'scientific revolution' (as with 'problem-solving' models of creativity) is precisely that it is *too* neat and *too* apparently complete. The virtual self-sufficiency of the process it so abstractly models makes few allowances for the mess of actuality and multiple determinations (the fact that discoveries may be made by accident and what Gould calls 'contingency' as well as by systematic search – not just the spotting of anomaly). Moreover, given the regular and almost routine transformation of the anomalous into the expected, Kuhn tends to imply a steady passage from the unknown to the known, the lawless to the law-abiding, the new to the old. And so on again till the next time, and the next anomaly to be accommodated, the next paradigm to be shifted.

To be sure, Kuhn acknowledges that scientific revolutions come about through real differences and disputes within scientific communities. His is an expressly Darwinian evolutionary model involving conflict and the survival of the science that is 'fittest': 'the resolution of revolutions is the selection by conflict within the scientific community of the fittest way to practice future science' (p. 172). He also insists that the relation between one paradigm and another is ultimately 'incommensurable': they may not be measured according to the same standard or plotted according to comparable co-ordinates on the same map. (In terms of games theory, the rules of the game change so much that they are playing different games; see above pp. 121–2.) Thus you simply cannot explain a Copernican, sun-centred universe in terms of a Ptolemaic earth-centred one, and neither agree with current models of the universe that see it as expanding from some 'Big Bang' or as an infinitely flexible configuration of many-centred or strictly centre-less multiverses. In this respect, the accounts of creation in Genesis and in Darwin's *The Origin of Species* are radically 'incommensurable'. They belong to two mutually unintelligible 'paradigms' – 'myths', 'orders of truth'. None the less, in Kuhn's *The Structure of Scientific Revolutions* there is still an overarching sense of repeatedly arriving at periods of comparative consensus and relative calm. In the end, with the reassurance of hindsight, it is 'normal' science that always wins out. More-over, the disputes are always *within* the scientific community; there is little sense of interaction with a larger world.

It is precisely these tidy, closed and 'normative' aspects of Kuhn's model of revolu-tionary science that Paul Feyerabend challenges in his controversial *Against Method: Outline of an Anarchistic Theory of Knowledge* (1975). Feyerabend develops a much more openly ongoing, restless, contentious and irreducibly plural view of changes in scien-tific paradigms and communities. In what he terms 'epistemological anarchism' or simply a 'Dadaist' theory of knowledge, Feyerabend argues that there are *always* con-tending theories, world-views and institutions. The concept of 'normal science' is therefore illusory. There is *always* a 'revolution' going on – it's just that we may not be aware of it. Further, Feyerabend maintains that even though science appears to be dedicated to the development of universal and eternal 'laws' (rules, principles), this too is partly illusory. With his characteristic facility for provocative statement and free-booting iconoclasm, he puts it like this:

> [T]here is not a single rule, however, plausible, that is not violated at some time or other. [. . .] [T]here are always circumstances when it is advisable not only to ignore the rule but to adopt its opposite. [. . .] There is only one principle that can be defended under all circumstances and in all stages of human development. It is the principle: *anything goes*.
>
> (Feyerabend 1975: 86)

Unsurprisingly, taken at face value, this outraged the orthodox scientific establishment at the time (though it continues to resonate with many kinds of broadly 'counter-cultural' movement). But an attentive reading of Feyerabend's *Against Method* confirms that his is not an 'anarchistic' approach to science in a *merely* relativist, disorderly or self-indulgent sense (i.e. the common and casual sense of 'anarchy'; see above pp. 123–4). Rather, he is dedicated to opposing those who insist upon the monopoly of a *single* method or model, however persuasive and apparently comprehensive. Instead, he argued for 'theoretical proliferation'. As one of his more sympathetic commentators summarises it, this is an argument that 'scientists should work not with one theory to the exclusion of all rivals, but with a range of incompatible theories, each of which could suggest fruitful ways forward, while all could be sources of empirical criticism' (Belsey in Payne 1996: 195–6). In practice this is precisely what Gould does in his extraordinarily capacious and eclectic *The Structure of Evolutionary Theories* (2002). It is also, for that matter, how Darwin went about putting together the arguments for *The Origin of Species*: 'On my return home it occurred to me [. . .] that something might perhaps be made on this question by patiently accumulating and reflecting on all sorts of facts which could possibly have any bearing on it' (Darwin 1859: 1).

Michel Foucault develops, if anything, an even more radically challenging model of revolutions in science and knowledge than Feyerabend. He also places much greater emphasis upon the *dis*continuous and *dis*parate development of knowledge across society at large. In his *The Order of Things: An Archaeology of the Human Sciences* (*Les Mots et les choses* [1966] 1972), Foucault argues that the various areas of knowledge are chiefly distinguished by the 'epistemes' (structures of linguistic representation, particular ways of seeing and saying) through which images of reality are constructed at a given time. In particular, he insists that it is the 'epistemological breaks', radical discontinuities, that make it historically impossible to evaluate an earlier way of seeing/ saying in terms of a later. This can be compared with Kuhn's principle of 'incommensurability', but Foucault frames the problem and the response to it differently. Thus while it simply does not make sense to compare Newtonian and Einsteinian physics or pre- and post-Darwinian biology (they belong to such different conceptual and material wor(l)ds), it *does* make sense to situate Newton among an array of contemporary seventeenth-century rationalist discourses and Einstein among an array of early twentieth-century relativist discourses. In effect, this means that for Foucault it is virtually impossible to write history diachronically (across periods); but it is possible to conceive culture synchronically (within periods). As a result, he characterises his project not so much as 'historical' but as 'archaeological' or, prompted by Nietzsche, as 'genealogical'. Thus, for Foucault as for Nietzsche, 'Genealogy [. . .] opposes itself to the search for origins' and, in so far as it aspires to write 'history', does so in a deeply sceptical and parodic mode: 'Genealogy is history in the form of a concerted carnival' (Foucault, 'Nietzsche, Genealogy, History' [1971] 1986: 77, 94). This last reference recalls Bakhtin's 'carnivalesque' as well as Nietzsche's 'Dionysiac' notions of culture. Foucault's conception of evolution is therefore complexly ambiguous. His stance is expressly *anti*-evolutionary in so far as evolution is equated with continuous, purposeful and, especially, 'progressive' change: 'Genealogy does not resemble the evolution of a species and does not map the destiny of a people' (p. 81). But his argument is radically *pro*-evolutionary in so far as evolution is equated with the concerted exploration and exploitation of errors, mistakes and contingency:

> to follow the complex course of descent is to maintain passing events in their proper dispersion: it is to identify the accidents, the minute deviations – or conversely, the complete reversals – the errors, the false appraisals, and the faulty calculations that give birth to those things that continue to exist.
>
> (Foucault [1971] 1986: 81)

This emphasis upon 'accidents, minute deviations' might prompt us to align Foucault's views of evolution with, say, Rose and Gould rather than 'reductive determinists' such as Dawkins and Dennett (discussed in Chapter 4). But even more so than Feyerabend's 'epistemological anarchism', Foucault's 'epistemological breaks' point to the radically *dis*continuous development of knowledge. All genuinely revolutionary science is in this respect remarkably 'abnormal': monstrous, unforeseen and strictly non-predictable. Similar gestures, though in very different philosophical idioms and historical moments, are made by Wittgenstein and Lyotard in their characterisation of the sciences as certain kinds of 'language-game' from among the many that are 'played' in culture at large (also discussed in Chapter 4). These, too, are ultra-relativist/culturalist positions with respect – and, some scientists would add, with *dis*-respect – to science. What's more, it is precisely those areas of contemporary science that appear to confirm the sheer *in*determinacy and *dis*continuity of natural and physical 'laws' (in Kuhn's terms the persistent 'anomalies') that are most appealing to Lyotard. Thus it is to theories of chaos, catastrophe, fuzzy logic, quantum mechanics and dynamic information systems that Lyotard has recourse when characterising the contemporary scientific project. He also points to the potential of these interdisciplinary – and radically *in*disciplinary – configurations both to subvert and exceed discrete cultures of knowledge as currently conceived. Thus, as Lyotard puts it in *The Differend: Phrases in Dispute* (1988), contemporary science 'by concerning itself with such things as undecidables, the limits of precise control, conflicts characterised by incomplete information, *'fracta'*, catastrophes, and pragmatic paradoxes, is theorising its own evolution as discontinuous, catastrophic, nonrectifiable, and paradoxical' (quoted by Norris in Payne 1996: 492–3).

For many scientists and some historians and philosophers of science, however, such a vision is far from revolutionary and not at all empowering. It is intellectually feeble, historically underinformed, and ethically and politically ineffectual. What Norris calls 'Critical realists' (writers such as Roy Bhaskar, Nicholas Rescher and Wesley Salomon) put the contemporary Realist-rationalist case for scientific progress in fresh and flexible but still principled and positive (if not quite positivist) ways (see Norris in Payne 1996: 485–96). They insist that science progresses by making closer and closer approximations to 'the Truth' (singular), not just various formulations of 'truths' (plural). And it can do this precisely because it offers finer, more fundamental and more comprehensive analyses of structural properties and processes and can therefore identify ever more subtle and complex kinds of causality. They admit that scientific explanations can never be complete; but they insist that some can be more *powerful* than others and that, by and large, they are getting *more* powerful as knowledge accumulates and technology develops. Thus, they argue, in a real not just illusory or provisional sense, physicists now know far more about the nature and interchanges of matter and energy – including 'fire' – than Heraclitus could possibly have known. Similarly, geneticists and evolutionary biologists now know far more about the nature, structure and development of organic life – including the growth of living things 'from hot water and earth' – than even Anaximander dreamt of. (Presocratic science is discussed in the previous chapter.)

In Bhaskar's view, what modern science offers is an ever more subtle and discriminating grasp of the 'stratified' nature of knowledge and reality: the fact that reality can be explored on ever more levels and in ever more dimensions. This bears comparison both with Gould's multilayered and multidimensional model of theories of evolution and, more especially, with Bohm's concept of 'implicated' and 'explicated' orders – the idea that reality can be apprehended as a ceaseless process of *unfolding* and *enfolding* (as discussed in Chapter 4). Deleuze and Guattari in *A Thousand Plateaus* ([1980] 1988) would probably go along with the 'stratified' image, too. But they would doubtless counter that, as with real geological strata, what we actually encounter are ceaselessly bent, buckled and contorted layers that interrupt as well as overlap one another – and that they are formed by radically different processes (sedimentation, volcanic activity, etc). Bhaskar, however, as the title of his influential *Scientific Realism and Human Emancipation* (1986) confirms, holds resolutely by the humanist enlightenment project of cumulative, if not always continuous, progress. For him, the imperative to grasp knowledge firmly and wield it wisely is inextricably tied up with the emancipation of people from suffering and ignorance and the realisation of personal and social potential. This resonates with Joas's view of 'creative action' that is 'reasonable' and Habermas's model of 'communicative rationality' (Joas 1996 and Habermas 1990).

In a similar vein, Salomon in *Scientific Explanation and the Causal Structure of the World* (1984) and Rescher in *Scientific Realism: A Critical Reappraisal* (1987) both make renewed pleas for the recognition of causality as a central plank in the scientific project. The latter, they maintain, has been needlessly weakened by casual or over-extended senses of relativity and chaos. Indeed, they remind us that the relating of cause to effect is fundamental not only to the scientific project but to any view of historical consequence and human responsibility. That is, if 'cause X' does not in some sense result in (produce, generate, act upon, influence, etc.) 'effect Y' – where X can be anything from an electron discharge to an election vote and Y can be a change in atomic structure or a change in government – there is simply no basis for a coherent world let alone consistent science. Causality also underpins the crucial concepts of *directionality* (e.g. the fact that some processes are irreversible) and of *high probability* (which must be carefully distinguished from absolute predictability). That is, some things are much more likely to happen than others (e.g. the earth continuing to turn rather than stopping) and some things once done cannot be undone (e.g. being born, cutting a flower).

Further, as all these Critical realists recognise (this is what makes them 'critical' *and* 'realistic'), none of this represents 'progress' in an absolute and ideal sense. Particular applications may prove ecologically and socially disastrous – not beneficial. There always remains the double-edged promise/threat that, in Biblical terms, knowledge is 'of good *and* evil', and in Promethean terms may be a *theft* as well as a *gift*. But what cannot be disputed, they maintain, is that knowledge of physical and natural processes has increased in a real sense and that there is a very high probability – even if not an absolute certainty – it will continue to do so.

All this leaves us with a prospect of sciences that are ever 'newer' and in some ways ever more 'powerful'. It may also prompt us to revise fundamentally our understanding of what creativity is and who the really creative people and institutions are. For if the standard definition of creativity is that which is 'new and valuable' or 'original and useful' hold (see above p. 57), then contemporary science and scientists, along with all the associated technologies and technologists, are arguably the most 'creative' sources and resources ever. What's more, they have been becoming so since at least the scientific and technological revolutions of the sixteenth and seventeenth centuries. In fact, in terms of knowledge in the abstract, the 'revolutions' they embody offer a virtually endless vista of 'progress'. This is the ongoing utopian Enlightenment prospect for science as initially sketched by Bacon and tempered by Vico.

HOWEVER (a big one), as both Critical realists and Cultural relativists would agree, albeit in very different terms, it remains not just a moot but a sore point how far this vista *really* extends. Who or what is included or excluded? Who is this power wielded for and with what ends in view? There is also the question of whether *any* science practised by humans can be at all 'pure', and whether it is not always already in some sense 'applied' and therefore 'impure'. Finally as at first, then, there is the matter of how one chooses to see and say all of this: as 'progress' or 'regress' or mere indifferent 'process'? In other words (and there are always other words) we cannot get away from the appeals and perils of language (especially metaphor) and the threats and risks of more or less dominant 'myths' (paradigms, epistemes – call them what you will). Moreover, whatever we call them, the most pressing issue is what we *mean* by and *do* with them: what purposes they express and effects they produce. Those, critically, are the real challenges.

Big Bangs, black holes, bubble baths and soup

> Yes, it altered my picture. [. . .] If I am going to have a model in which there are many creation centres, what we used to call little big bangs, and not just one big bang, I had better make them related to that picture.
>
> (Fred Hoyle, interviewed in Lightman and Brawer 1990: 63)

Fred Hoyle, one of the most eminent cosmologists of the twentieth century, is here talking about the impact upon him of the finding that the universe is in some sense 'flat'. In precisely what sense we shall see shortly. To begin with, however, we shall simply observe that there are many models of the origin and nature of the universe in contemporary cosmology. These are often as striking and exotic as any of those in ancient cosmogony, and some of them also feature 'multiverses' (Hoyle talks of 'many creation centres', notice). The difference with the models offered by contemporary cosmologists (who characteristically include deep-space astronomers and subatomic physicists as well as theoretical mathematicians) is that they are based upon precise combinations of empirical observation and experiment and are proved – and open to disproof – in the various specialised codes of science, chiefly mathematics. None the less, for better and worse, all these models at some point get expressed in 'ordinary' (i.e. naturally occurring, non-specialist) language. This happens between scientific communities no less than in communications with the rest of the world.

Such accounts of the origins of the cosmos typically take the form of a series of 'names' for key theories and events (the four in the heading of this section, for instance), each accompanied by an explanation, analogy and illustration. Inevitably, because they draw on the routine resources of language, all these 'names' are heavily metaphorical; and because the explanatory accounts are invariably framed as kinds of story and/or argument, they draw on the resources of grammar, rhetoric and logic, too. (Though here it should be stressed that this is the logic of 'the word' (*logos*), not that of formal, mathematical logic, which uses its own specialised codes and procedures.) At any rate, the obvious appeal of such accounts for the common reader is that they make otherwise obscure and difficult knowledge accessible and comprehensible. And that, for exactly the same reasons, is the challenge – and potential peril – for the specialist who seeks to communicate with everyone and still make sense to other specialists. In short, we are still engaging with kinds of myth ('truth') and we are still doing it through images and stories. And again, for the moment, I shall leave open the matter of whether these accounts are best described as 'fact' or 'fiction' and 'true' or 'false'. How far you wish to obtrude your own belief or suspend your disbelief is up to you.

Since the mid-twentieth century, the most familiar phrase that popularly encapsulates 'how everything began' is THE BIG BANG. This is still the dominant scientific model, too. However, as already intimated by Hoyle, there turn out to be various kinds of 'big bang': some preceded by a 'big crunch'; some taking the form of a series of 'little bangs'; and some not strictly 'bangs' at all – because the physics of sound (let alone the possibility of something or someone being around to hear it) had not come into being at that point. To get some provisional bearings on a fascinating but also contentious subject, we shall consider two diametrically opposed views of big bang theory. These will be followed by a brief review of the main variants on it and the main scientific alternatives to it. The first, broadly 'pro-big-bang' account is from *Figments of Reality: The Evolution of the Curious Mind* (1997) by Ian Stewart, a professor of mathematics, and Jack Cohen, a professor of biology. The second, 'anti-big-bang' account is from *Grammars of Creation* (2001) by George Steiner, a professor of comparative literature. To be sure, neither account is 'for' nor 'against' in a simple sense. But here it is mainly *how* the authors put their respective cases rather than *what* they claim that most concerns us. Weigh the differences yourself.

Big Bang – a case 'for' . . .

Fifteen thousand million years ago the universe was no bigger than the dot at the end of this sentence.

A tiny, tiny, *tiny* fraction of a second before that – but there was no fraction of a second before that. There was no time before the universe began, and without time, there can be no 'before'. (As well to ask what lies north of the North Pole.) There was no space, no time, and no matter. But when the space that was co-extensive with the universe had grown to the size of a dot, time had already begun to tick. The temperature within the dot was far too high for matter to exist, but there was plenty of what was required to create matter: radiation. The primal dot seethed with radiant energy.

(Stewart and Cohen 1997: 1)

Big Bang – a case 'against' . . .

The new cosmologies regard 'creation' as being ambiguous, mythological and even taboo. To ask what preceded the Big Bang and the primal nanoseconds of the compaction and expansion of our universe is, we are instructed, to talk gibberish. Time has no meaning prior to that singularity. Both elementary logic and common sense should tell us that such a ruling is arrogant bluff. The simple fact that we can phrase the question, that we can engage it with normal thought processes, gives it meaning and legitimacy. The postulate of unquestionable ('not to be questioned') nothingness and intemporality now made dogma by astrophysicists is as arbitrary, is in many regards more of a mystique, than any creation narratives in Genesis and elsewhere.

(Steiner 2001: 279)

Obviously these two accounts are in some respects diametrically opposed. However, for precisely that reason, I suggest, the arguments they present are in large measure reciprocally defining. That is, the position each represents implicitly depends upon the existence of the other to make its case. Each needs at least a shadow or image of the other in order to negate and exceed it. Thus Stewart and Cohen begin by pointing to a precise location in time and space ('the dot at the end of this sentence') only to gesture straightaway before and beyond it to an imagined sphere of non-existence: 'A tiny, tiny, *tiny* fraction of a second before that – but there was no fraction of a second before that. There was no time before the universe began, and without time there can be no "before".' Simply yet crucially, this move depends upon the rhetorical and logical devices of *comparison* ('before') and *negation* ('no . . . no'). The latter is a particularly insistent feature of this passage and essential to the framing of its argument: 'There was no space, no time, and no matter.' In fact, as already argued, 'negation' is essential to the construction of any image of 'nothing' (no-thing): this can only be built out of 'something' (some-thing). The 'thing' must be there in both, even though, paradoxically, it is there as an absence in 'no-thing' and as a presence in 'some-thing'. We encountered an identical device in the last chapter with the Native American creation story of Coyote, when Grandmother was attempting to conjure up a time and place before it all began: 'No mountains then. No rivers then. No forests then.' In fact, we witness similar strategies for establishing states of 'non-being' in all sorts of mystical writings, Eastern and Western, that take the 'way of negation' towards ultimately ineffable enlightenment (see pp. 61, 150). All these texts, simply by virtue of being texts, cannot but make nothing out of something and virtual worlds out of actual words.

Meanwhile, returning to the Stewart and Cohen passage, we may still be wondering about a number of other things. Why the seemingly precise but very large and perhaps quite arbitrary figure of 'Fifteen thousand million years'? Is this rhetorically, if not intrinsically, any more or less convincing than Archbishop Ussher's calculation in his chronology published in 1650 that the creation of the world had taken place in the year 4004 BC on 23 October at noon (see Eco *et al.* 1999: 11)? (Remember we are here talking about rhetorical effects rather than empirical facts.) There also remains the tricky matter of transitions and transformations – metamorphoses, if you like. If not when and where, at least *how* do time and space as we know them come into being? And how do 'radiation' and 'radiant energy' actually 'create matter'? (To be sure, even a non-specialist may invoke Einstein's formula $E = mc^2$ to account for this, but that still does not explain how the former *transforms* into the latter; and the mathematical symbol for this process is > rather than = .) Philosophically speaking, we may still be left asking how *being* as we know it 'comes into being' (i.e. *becomes*). We might try to get round or at least 'fix' the problem with some such ambiguous coinage as 'be(com)ing'. But in its own terms this is likely to be as interesting and irritating as Stewart and Cohen are in theirs. For they, too, are dependent upon the devices of written English. For instance, how would 'the dot at the end of this sentence' translate into *spoken* English. As an airy gesture?

But Steiner's case 'against' the Big Bang is also fraught with problems and possibilities. Though stylistically differently tuned – Steiner develops his argument with considerable rhetorical resource – the lure of language remains much the same. To defend his preferred view of 'creation', he sets up those of his opponents in order to knock them down: 'To ask what preceded the Big Bang . . . is, we are instructed, to talk gibberish. Time has no meaning prior to that singularity'. This, Steiner in turn instructs us, is 'arrogant bluff'. The result is a conveniently reductive version of the Big Bang which can then be easily exposed as inadequate. This can be compared with Stewart and Cohen's strategy of pointing to a 'dot' only to dissolve it, positing 'some-things' so as to turn them into 'no-things'. In short, all these writers are exploiting kinds of *negation*.

Kinds of universe . . .

Big Bang When matter, energy, time and all the forces of physics and nature as we now know them came into existence through the explosion of a super-dense mass (as in Stewart and Cohen above). In some theories this is preceded by a **Big Crunch** in which the conditions for the Big Bang are produced by everything collapsing in on itself. That, in turn, leads to the possibility that it has all happened before, over and over, in a cyclic, recursive or 'oscillating' manner (see 'Kinds of multiverse(s)' opposite). Sticking with a single 'Big Bang', however, there are three main possible 'shapes' envisaged: 'open', 'closed' and 'flat'. The geometry of each depends upon the precise balance between the kinetic energy of the matter being flung outwards and the gravitational energy tending to pull it all back; and that in turn depends upon the initial conditions of the mass density.

- An *'open' universe* has greater (outward) kinetic energy than (inward) gravitational energy and so will expand forever. It has the geometry of an infinitely expanding 'rippling' surface with the same degree of curvature at every point, and it is potentially infinite in size.
- A *'closed' universe* has greater (inward) gravitational energy than (outward) kinetic energy. It has the geometry of a series of surfaces that eventually curve or spiral back on themselves, and it is finite in size.
- A *'flat' universe* has outward and inward, kinetic and gravitational energies that tend to balance out (though never exactly) and thus produce a complex geometry tensed between those of 'open' and closed' universes: rippling outwards and spiralling inwards. The result is an apparently even but highly dynamic 'flatness'; and a size that may be finite or infinite depending upon the *precise* balance of energies over time and the *precise* initial mass density.

Steiner then proceeds to argue his case on the basis of 'elementary logic and common sense', where the 'logic' is most definitely that of language ('The simple fact that we can phrase the question . . . gives it meaning and legitimacy') and the 'common sense' holds for as long as the reader is prepared to go along with it. Further, Steiner proposes that 'The postulate of unquestionable ('not to be questioned') nothingness . . . is in many regards more of a mystique than any creation narratives in Genesis and elsewhere.' He thus weights his argument by means of a loaded comparison, just as Stewart and Cohen gesture to a 'before' only to dismiss it as inadequate. Meanwhile, as this last example confirms, all these writers are highly aware of their own use of language even to the point of highlighting certain terms for especial consideration: 'before' in Stewart and Cohen; 'creation' in Steiner. That is, they use language metalinguistically.

In all these ways, then, for all their manifold differences of sympathy and emphasis, both sets of writers not only use language to talk about a certain version of creation, they also themselves more or less deliberately create wor(l)ds in which that vision can flourish and others will be discouraged. The chief strategies they use for doing this include kinds of negation (and corresponding assertion) along with kinds of comparison, analogy and metaphor. At the same time these writers confirm that they

---

... Kinds of multiverse(s)

These typically take the form of a number of highly discrete yet interconnected universes that exist serially or simultaneously, and may be finite or infinite in number. The main types are:

- **Oscillating** through a series of expansions and contractions, perhaps involving a succession of big bangs and big crunches, and corresponding extreme 'fluctuations' of mass, density and temperature.

- **Many worlds** – sometimes called **parallel universes** – in which, according to a particular interpretation of quantum mechanics, everything exists simultaneously in all of its possible states and is only distinguished as a 'particular' universe at the moment and by virtue of the way in which it is measured. Other moments and methods would realise other possible worlds/universes.

- **Bubble bath, foam** – whereby a vast and potentially infinite variety of space-time and mass-energy continua are generated and exist virtually independent of one another – except for the fact of being linked through some 'singularity' such as a **Black Hole.** (A singularity is an event in which the supposedly 'universal laws of physics' are made up or, alternatively, break down. This happened in a big way with the Big Bang. A Black Hole is a more localised, extremely high density mass with a gravitational force so great that not even light can escape it.) Such singularities may suck one kind of universe in and extrude it as another. They thereby act as 'conduits', 'tunnels' or 'worm-holes' connecting one universe to another and another . . .

---

themselves are both aware and wary of the nature of the verbal medium in which they are working: they actively grasp its strengths and limitations. Moreover, exactly the same challenge extends to us as readers and, by extension, re-writers. For the account we give of their accounts is also part of the process. Interpreting, we too invent. Criticising, we too re-create. It all contributes to the bigger picture, or, if you prefer, to the proliferation of smaller pictures. For that, again, is one of the main points at issue. Is there or is there not, as Lyotard would put it, some single 'grand narrative' (of creation or anything else) or simply a lot of 'small narratives' moving in many directions and dimensions, simultaneously or by turns?

At this point, therefore, we shall take a brief overview – in the above boxes – of the main scientific models. These may be provocatively, if awkwardly, called '*the universe and/or/as multiverse(s)*'. This account draws on various sources: cosmologists talking informally and in interview to one another (Lightman and Brawer 1990) and cosmologists explaining to both students and non-specialists (Kaku 1994, Barrow 1995, 2000, 2001 and Coles 1999, 2001). In the event – and the singularity or generality of events is itself part of the matter at issue – the 'picture' is far more complex and contentious and flexible or fragmented than even the above arguments might lead us to expect. For convenience the above boxes are divided into kinds of 'universe' and kinds of 'multiverse'. But, as usual, the suspension dots *between* are in some sense the most important bits: they signal connections as well as distinctions, and complementary as well as opposed states. They also encourage us to weigh the possibility that the one may turn into the other – and sometimes the many!

But what about the 'soup'?! Readers who have been overawed (or bored) by the sheer (or mere) physics of all of this may be asking where organic 'life' (biology) fits into the picture – these pictures? Doesn't that add another, for us crucial, dimension? And might it not change the proportions and perspectives completely? (After all, we ourselves are organisms as well as mechanisms – and some people would wish to add a dash of 'spirit', too.) With this in mind, here are three snapshots of the origins of life historically conceived. The first is a provocative account of the opening of Richard Dawkins's *The Selfish Gene* (2nd edn 1989) by Kim Sterelny in *Dawkins vs. Gould: Survival of the Fittest* (2001). The second is from *The Fifth Miracle: The Search for the Origin of Life* (1998) by Paul Davies, a physicist who begins by dipping his toes in the 'warm little pond' first mentioned by Darwin in a letter of 1871 as the likely conditions for the formation of life, and who ends by sticking his tongue into the 'primordial soup' from which many scientists now believe life originated. The third is from *The Language of the Genes* (1994) by Steve Jones, which began as the BBC Reith Lectures given in 1991. Together, these accounts offer suggestive and quite different perspectives from within and around evolutionary biology; they also recall some of the debates on genetics introduced in Chapter 4. Here, like all the other accounts in the present chapter, they are presented as kinds of myth made up of certain kinds of metaphor and story.

> *The Selfish Gene* begins with a creation myth. Dawkins asks us to imagine a primitive, pre-biotic world in which physical and biochemical processes make available a soup of chemical and physical resources. In this soup, nothing lives, nothing dies and nothing evolves. But then, Something Happens. A *replicator*, by chance, comes into existence. A replicator is a molecule (or any other structure) that in the right environment acts as a template for its own copying. [. . .] And thus evolution driven by selection begins: *Competition + variation + replication = natural selection + evolution.*
>
> (Sterelny, 2001: 17–18)

> Rather than Darwin's 'warm little pond', Haldane envisages the Earth's entire oceans as the setting. Rain drenching the barren landscape would have washed all manner of chemicals into the sea, there to concentrate until, to use Haldane's evocative phrase, the liquid reached the consistency of 'hot dilute soup'. His words were seized upon, and the description 'the primordial soup' has stuck ever since.
>
> (Davies 1998: 54)

> Because all modern genes are copies of those in earlier generations each can be used as a message from the past. They bring clues from the beginnings of humanity, more than a hundred thousand years ago and from the origins of life three thousand million years before that. [. . .]
>
> The ancestral message from the dawn of life has grown to an instruction manual containing three thousand million letters coded into DNA. Everyone has a unique

edition of the manual which differs in millions of ways from that of their fellows. All this diversity comes from accumulated errors in copying the inherited message.

(Jones 1994: 25, 79)

Futures?

Clearly, none of the 'myths of creation' treated in this part of the book can stand as the last, let alone the first, word on the beginning of things. Indeed, as suggested in 'before the beginning', perhaps it is all 'middle' anyway. And aren't we always left with alternative ways of looking back as well as forwards? I would therefore like to conclude this chapter with an array of texts and topics pointing to very different endings. Each implicitly carries the label 'to be continued'; for they are potential 'futures', too. One ending looks at the persistent 'two cultures' debate between the arts and sciences to see what versions of creators and creations we may set store by in future. It also asks whether the two (three, four and more) cultures we are all currently involved in can possibly add up to a 'common' culture above and beyond those of popular commercial and elite intellectual cultures as presently configured. A second ending picks up the matter of *re . . . creation* introduced in Chapter 3 and puts a perceptibly different spin on it. The third but not so final ending goes out on a playful note. It offers a couple of visions of the future – or is it the past? – from contemporary science fantasy fiction.

Meanwhile, we should remember that 'Futures' is also the name for a kind of high-finance speculation. The 'futures market' is all about plotting, in every sense, what may (should, will . . .) happen in the global economy in the medium to long term. It involves high risks and rewards, and has very real consequences as well as implications for the health and wealth of everyone (and everything) on this planet. So it remains a distinct possibility that the *really* 'creative' people who are *really* 'creating' the future (because they are banking on and thereby tending to ensure it) are neither the artists nor the scientists nor even the technologists – but the stockbrokers and financiers and all those who act on behalf of what used to be called 'capital' but now, with the help of national governments and international trade organisations, tends to be hailed as 'corporate wealth' involved in 'wealth creation'.

But that still begs the question of whether the money markets as such really 'create' anything at all. For by definition many of the earnings of corporate organisations are invisible and, like the value of money itself – whether paper or plastic or pin-numbered – ultimately depend upon the transformation of natural resources and the exchange value of other people's labour. This is an issue tackled at length in Chapter 1 and a reminder is timely here. It may appear to be on the outermost fringes of the creativity debate. In reality – such is the emphasis upon 'creative management' in business and 'creating the right image' in advertising, public relations and government – it is one of its hottest topics. (In addition to the specific references in Chapter 1, see more generally Stiglitz 2002, Monbiot 2003 and Pilger 2003).

Two, three, four . . . cultures

The greatest enterprise of the mind has always been and always will be the attempted linkage of the sciences and humanities.

(Wilson 1998: 6)

> [T]he common goal of human wisdom, achieved through the union of natural
> knowledge and creative art.
>
> (Gould [2003] 2004: 6)

As these epigraphs indicate, we are here expressly concerned with 'the linkages
between the sciences and the humanities' and with 'the union of natural knowledge
and creative art'. These are not, however, the same thing; and, as I hope to show, the
latter is a much more valuable goal than the former. It also, I suggest, holds out a
better prospect for 'creative art' that spans the sciences as well as the humanities. We
begin with a brief review (and summary dismissal) of a couple of much-publicised
controversies that characterise the mythic gaps and gulfs of (mis)understanding of
modern intellectual life: the Snow–Leavis 'two cultures' debate of the mid-twentieth
century and the 'science wars' associated with the 'Sokal affair' of the mid-1990s. This
leads into a critical comparison of two very different, explicitly future-oriented collections of essays from the early twenty-first century, and finally works round to a couple
of frankly fantastic (and unashamedly funny) attempts to grapple with the origin of
life. Or is it the end?

The immediate occasion for the so-called 'two cultures' debate was C. P. Snow's
Reith Lecture of that name in 1959. Snow was a trained physicist and scientific
adviser as well as a successful novelist, and in his lecture he urged more frequent
exchanges and greater mutual understanding between members of the scientific and
artistic establishments. Snow's main complaint was that 'we have lost even the
pretence of a common culture'. (For useful overviews, see Bloom and Day 2000,
Vol. 3: 11–18 and Eaglestone 2002: 12–14.) The literary and cultural critic
F. R. Leavis took exception to all this and, as well as personally abusing Snow as a
novelist, laid into him as a representative of what Leavis saw as 'our technologico-
Benthamite civilisation'. Leavis thereby drew a parallel between what he saw as the
industrial-scientific rationalism ascendant in his own century and the narrowly utilitar-
ian views of Jeremy Bentham in the previous one. In fact, there was not much
substance to the debate on either side (it was mainly grounded in personal animus);
but the academic press and a few opportunist scholars made a meal of it. As a result,
what thereafter became known as 'the two cultures' passed into popular academic
memory as a yawning gulf between sciences and technology on the one side and the
arts and humanities on the other.

A similar storm in a tea-cup was turned into a parting of the academic waters by
media treatment of what was more grandly called 'the science wars' but is now more
familiarly known by the name of its key protagonist. In 1994, Alan Sokal, a professor
of physics at New York University, submitted a superficially plausible but – on closer
inspection – palpably spoof, pseudo-scientific article to the journal *Social Text*. The
problem was that the editors did *not* inspect the article closely, nor apparently get it
properly refereed. It was duly published; Sokal pointed out what he had done – and
the academic press had a field day. The media agenda was simple and, as usual,
adversarial. Depending upon which 'side' you were supposed to be on, it pitted
gullible (or offended) *social* scientists on the one hand against superior (or supercilious)
pure scientists on the other. A full and amusing critical account of all of this can be
found in Stephen Jay Gould's *The Hedgehog, the Fox and the Magister's Pox* ([2003] 2004:
99–105), the subtitle of which is *Mending and Minding the Misconceived Gap between Science*

and the Humanities. This confirms Gould's concerned – and characteristically playful – engagement with the larger implications. But he has no reservation in coming down hard on what he calls 'the nonexistence of these supposed "science wars"' and what he sees as yet another 'false episode of putative conflict between the sciences and humanities' (pp. 101–2; he, too, cites the Snow–Leavis affair as an earlier example of much the same tendency).

But there are serious implications and potentially long-lasting consequences in all of this. So, like Gould, rather than emphasise the persistent *misconceptions* that continue to set the sciences and the humanities at odds, I intend to draw attention to the *missing perceptions* that will enable us to see how these areas of academic and intellectual activity may complement one another without being merely confused. Gould refers to the basis of this preferred relationship as a 'consilience of equal regard' (pp. 189–90). By this he means something very similar to the concept of 'co-operation' offered in the present book (see above, pp. 65–70). 'Consilience' means a 'jumping together', and the crucial thing about the 'equal regard' is that it involves a genuine respect for and appreciation of 'difference' rather than the imposition of a 'sameness' that would privilege the one at the expense of the other. In fact this is precisely Gould's argument with Edward Wilson who, in his controversial book-length study, *Consilience: The Unity of Knowledge* (1998), can only secure that 'unity' by subordinating the materials of the arts and humanities to the methods of the sciences. That is, in the terms of Wilson's epigraph at the head of this section, the 'linkage' he has in mind is fundamentally unequal and hierarchical. Gould will have none of this. Instead, with a couple of metaphors and a grandly utopian flourish that expressly gestures to the best in Enlightenment learning (embracing the arts *and* sciences), he insists that 'the union of the fox and the hedgehog can certainly be accomplished, and would surely yield, as progeny, a many-splendored thing called love and learning, creativity and knowledge' (Gould [2003] 2004: 8).

The fox, it should be explained, is the archetype of the resourceful and wily tactician, the opportunist who always has a tricky way of getting out of – and into – scrapes. The hedgehog, meanwhile, is the archetypal creature with just one strategy but a tried-and-tested one, to curl up into a ball and put out its spikes till the threat has passed. As Gould deploys them, these animals are symbols of what he takes to be the two necessary and complementary aspects of *both* the sciences *and* the arts: the capacity to be a versatile generalist (the fox) *and* a single-minded specialist (the hedgehog). What matters is the task in hand and the purpose in mind – not disciplinary divisions as such. Conversely, and Gould is very particular about this: 'I emphatically *do not claim* that one of the two great ways (either science or the humanities) works like the fox, and the other like the hedgehog' (p. 3, his emphasis). In any event – and arguably in every event fully grasped – what is at stake is neither academic propriety nor intellectual property narrowly conceived, but rather, as Gould insists, 'the common goal of human wisdom, achieved through the union of natural knowledge and creative art' (p. 6).

Having thus resisted and in some measure replaced the dominant myths of the 'two cultures' and 'science wars' debates, it is time to reconfigure the relations between the humanities and sciences in yet other ways. And to do this we look at a couple of relatable yet significantly different books that came out in the same year (Brockman 2002; Wolfreys 2002). These expressly address the matter of where we may be going over the next decades. But each has its own, highly distinctive 'take' on the sciences and technology and/or arts and humanities issue, especially the relations between creativity and criticism.

John Brockman is the author and editor of various books on creativity, innovation and science. He is also the convenor of *Edge*, an on-line symposium of prominent thinkers, the motto of which is 'To arrive at the edge of the world's knowledge' and 'seek out the most complex and sophisticated minds' (www.edge.org). His edited collection *The Next Fifty Years: Science in the First Half of the Twenty-First Century* (2002) features essays by eminent scientists and technologists from most disciplines, including several referred to in the present book (Csikszentmihalyi, Dawkins, Etcoff and Stewart, for instance). *The Next Fifty Years* is fascinating and valuable but also remarkable for its utter exclusion of anyone from the arts and humanities. This is deliberate. In his introduction Brockman insists that 'Science is the big news, and it is scientists who are asking the big questions [. . .] they have become the new public intellectuals, leaders of a new kind of public culture' (p. xi). He then takes a side-swipe at what he terms the 'old-style intellectual culture' and follows this up with the observation that '[w]hat we have lacked until recently is an intellectual culture able to transform its own premises as fast as our technologies are transforming us' (pp. xi, xiii).

Brockman's book, like the *Edge* project as a whole, is both invigorating and irritating. The contributors offer lots of fascinating and more or less plausible visions of the imminent future, many of them directly or obliquely to do with the nature and status of creativity nowadays. But at the same time some essential issues are treated partially or not at all. A characteristic omission is the matter of cultural value and social responsibility: the scientific vistas and technical applications are awesome, but the potentially awful social consequences and political implications are either not thought through or treated cursorily. With a few honourable exceptions (the contributors already mentioned among them) the overall vision is of a 'brave new world' built on familiar and, if anything, still more acutely divisive lines: those who have the knowledge and power (and wealth and health) are highly visible; those who don't aren't.

Similarly post-millenarian but far less bullish and much more circumspect is Julian Wolfreys's collection of essays *Introducing Criticism at the 21st Century* (2002). The contributors to this are drawn *exclusively* from the humanities and social sciences, chiefly English and cultural studies. Again, several of them are referred to in the present book (notably Wolfreys himself, Plotnitsky and Colebrook). In his introduction, Wolfreys describes the overall project of the book as 'if not retrospective exactly [. . .] then *interruptive*': concerned with 'intensities – instants of a provisional gathering of flows and forces' (Wolfreys 2002: 2, his emphasis). The book was unusual when it came out (though I hope will eventually be less so) in that it offers an introduction to critical theory that includes essays on 'Chaos theory, complexity theory and criticism', 'Ecocriticism', 'Spatial criticism' and 'Cybercriticism'; also some freshly configured work on such relatively familiar areas as gender, race and ethnicity. But Wolfreys is careful to caution that 'none of these "orientations" of the act of criticism implies methodologies, approaches, schools of thought'. Instead, he affirms,

> each operates, in a more or less oblique way, by naming certain interests of criticism having emerged in recent years, and which continue to provide different

epistemological foci in the humanities, largely as a result of the increasingly inter-disciplinary nature of critical and cultural studies.

(Wolfreys 2002: 4).

Introducing Criticism at the 21st Century has many and various arguments about the nature, and to some extent the future, of critical cultural studies. Cultural value and social responsibility are high on its agendas. For example, there are contributions on 'Ethical criticism' and 'Trauma, testimony, criticism'; and this last directly addresses the representation of such events as the Holocaust, 'September 11' and acts of international terrorism and war. However, as the steady litany of '-isms', especially 'criticism', confirms, there is an overwhelming emphasis upon *critical* rather than creative processes. To be still more precise, it is the critical process of *reading* in an intelligent, sensitive and informed manner that is made the chief measure of what counts as cultural reflection and, in a purely academic sense, 'practice'. Wolfreys is emphatic on this point in the concluding remarks of his introduction; though in other respects he remains diffident about the precise aims and ends of the whole enterprise: 'In the end, as the chapters in this collection demonstrate, all criticism comes down to reading. But that "in the end" is no ending at all, only the endless demand placed on reading.' Thus he concludes that 'If *Introducing Criticism* can be said to introduce anything at all (and even now, at the end of this introduction, I remain uncertain as to what to think about this), it is to introduce the ends of criticism as the beginning – again – of reading' (Wolfreys 2002: 9). Now, I sympathise with the reflective turn and even the deconstructive twist of this. My own thinking about the crucial importance of beginnings and endings is every bit as picky. But I seriously question whether a project dedicated to 'criticism' and 'reading' alone – however resourcefully and responsibly carried through – is going to be enough, faced with the challenges that we assuredly do face in the current century.

Taking the two books together, then, the overall situation strikes me as decidedly strange and even strained. I also begin to worry whether the 'two cultures' problem is actually alive and – well – ill. On the one hand, Wolfreys and Co. are posing a lot of the most pressingly critical, cultural, social and political questions; but they are arguably light and certainly oblique on answers. Conversely, Brockman and Co. are offering all sorts of exciting prospects and energising solutions; but the vision lacks social and political depth, and the focus is narrowed to questions of how, when and where rather than why and for whom (and equally importantly why not and who else). Either way, the people asking the questions and the people supplying the answers seem to be talking at cross-purposes – even talking different 'languages'. Still more striking (and in terms of 'older', arts-based views of creativity decidedly curious) is the fact that it is precisely the scientists and technologists who are up there claiming to be the really *creative* vanguard in contemporary society, whereas the humanities people are tied – even hung – up with anxiety about the nature and function of *criticism*. It is hard to resist caricature. The scientists are tucking into some new and exciting beginnings, while the cultural critics are still chewing over the odds and ends of old agendas. Alternatively, to flip the caricature and change the metaphor, the scientists are off in hot and excited pursuit of some 'brave new world', while the cultural critics are bringing up the rear pointing out that it may not be all that 'brave' or even 'new', and that there may just perhaps be some alternatives.

But the caricatures have to be resisted and finally replaced. One solution is to seek some kind of 'common ground'; though it is not likely to be Snow's vision of a science-based 'common culture' any more than Leavis's nostalgia for a non-existent 'organic community' or an arts-based 'common pursuit'. Indeed, as we saw in Chapter 1 with Donna Haraway's 'Ironic dream of a common language for women in the integrated circuit' (1985) – itself a comradely yet critical response to Adrienne Rich's 'Dream of a common language' (1979) – the grounds for such a communality are likely to be materially very different from what we currently expect, and in any case not be amenable to a quick fix, either technological or ideological. (Twenty years on, for instance, will the world-wide web still be viewed as the universal panacea for global–local communications, a purveyor of global capital and localised lifestyles, or a curiously archaic irrelevance?) Perhaps the problem therefore needs re-posing. Maybe we need to be more attentive and sensitive to difference: not to dream so much of a 'common language' (in the sense of a unitary and potentially homogeneous culture) but to look for the possibilities of exchangeable and changeable modes of communication and understanding (intensely dynamic and extensively heterogeneous). The aim then would be not so much to 'speak the same language' as to develop facility – and facilities – in 'translating between languages', including varieties of what is nominally 'the same language' ('English' grasped as 'englishes', for example). Theoretically, in terms that spring most readily to mind for me and recur throughout the book, this might be called a Bakhtinian or Deleuzian approach, emphasising 'dialogue' and 'varied-speech', 'translation/transformation', 'multiplicity/heterogenesis'. Gould, more soberly and economically, would perhaps call it 'consilience of equal regard'.

But these are things that each of us needs to say differently as well as in concert: finding our voices through improvisation as well as orchestration, but not necessarily reading from the same score and certainly not being led by a single conductor (compare 'Making musics', pp. 256–7). There are plenty of signs that this can happen – and already is happening – too. Even in the collections of essays by Brockman and Wolfreys there are all sorts of potential crossovers and overlaps: no neat fits but plenty of room for manoeuvre; a sense that people may be playing on the same pitch, even if according to different rules. For example, both collections feature extensive treatments of chaos and complexity, genetics and evolution, intelligence (human, artificial and otherwise), technology and science, and the nature of matter and mind (as does Chapter 4 above). Where the two chiefly differ, as already intimated – and might eventually not just agree to differ but actually learn to learn from one another – is in the fact that one (Brockman's) concentrates on *applications* while the other (Wolfreys's) concentrates on *valuations*. There is no easy way of squaring these circles. But evidently they overlap and intersect. So we ought at least to be able to trace the relations among them – and to grasp how we might reconfigure those relations in future. To be sure, this may sound vague, wide-eyed and even wildly utopian. But I would argue that the future, too, is a 'nowhere' that really does become a 'somewhere'. The trick, with arms and minds as well as ears and eyes open, is to make it the best – not the worst – of all possible worlds. And not just for ourselves narrowly conceived, but for our selves and/as others. Meanwhile, as Oscar Wilde observes in his *Intentions* (Wilde [1891] 1992: 178):

> A map of the world that does not include Utopia is not worth even glancing at, for it leaves out the one country at which Humanity is always landing.

Re . . . creation revisited

What follows is a summary of the findings and makings of this chapter. It draws together what has been shown about myths of creation and, by extension, what has been learnt about models of creativity. It thereby revisits the problems and possibilities posed more theoretically in Chapter 3, within the terms of the overarching proposition that 'Creativity is re . . . creation'. Here such issues are themselves re . . . created through discourses that are overtly mythic, metaphoric and narrative. But again the emphasis falls on the points *between* the 're' and the 'creation' – on the ways in which what is gathered up from the past is cast forward through the present into a perpetually re-made future; how the one transforms and 'translates' into the other – and sometimes the many. That is why you, too, are invited not just to read but also to re-write the propositions that follow. After all, you may not agree that myths of creation are always in some sense myths of re . . . creation because:

1 *Creation is always from something not 'from nothing'* – but always unique and in some sense fresh every time. It is repetition, but with distinct and significant differences.

2 *There is always something (and often someone) 'before the beginning'* and always more than one point in space, time and perception at which to begin. To utter the words 'In the beginning . . .' or 'Once upon a time . . .' (or simply to begin at all) is thus to institute or impose a world – and thereby preclude or exclude others. It is also to anticipate an end to which that beginning tends, even if in the event the ends turn out to be different.

3 *Creation involves interaction and exchange, not just action and change.* This is as true personally (within the person) and socially (between persons) as it is physically and biologically (of machines and organisms). (This may sound de-humanising; but it may be re-humanising.)

4 *Creation may be conceived as imitation or performance:* as the representation or reflection of something that already exists (perhaps as an idea, pattern or model), or as the realisation and embodiment of that which never previously existed and never will again. Indeed, grasped in its full complexity, creation involves some configuration of imitation and/or/as performance.

5 *Metaphors (images, signs) are our most powerful, immediately available tools for projecting possible worlds:* they allow us to project from what is to what may be or may not be. Either way, metaphors are similarity–difference machines (organisms, devices), transforming and translating one experience into another and another . . . They are therefore highly appealing as well as deeply treacherous, and may enslave as well as emancipate.

6 '*. . . people create stories create people create stories . . .*' – *and we never know for sure which comes first or last.* By the same token, stories grow out of and into histories: we can never be absolutely sure where the one shades into the other. So we live by 'narratives' ('grand' or 'small') and they, in turn, live and evolve through us. And so it goes on: '. . . stories create people create stories . . .'

7 *Stories of creation both embody and explore contested power relations,* notably differences of rank, gender, age, ethnicity and knowledge; for creation is always a contentious activity: it often imposes or implies consensus even as it seeks to conceal or resolve conflict.

8 *Every act of creation involves a corresponding act of destruction:* something is 'unbuilt' so that something else can be 'built' in its place. To grasp these two movements simultaneously is to realise the moment of reconstruction deconstructively.

9 *The creation of a 'universe' involves the reduction or suppression of a potential 'multiverse' –* or *two or three . . .* Conversely, notionally plural and potentially infinite multiverses always turn out, on closer inspection and further reflection, to be 'singular' even if not single, peculiarly 'unique' if not particularly complete. (This is the 'w/hole' problem, again, but in a different guise.)

10 *Chaos comes again and again in many forms of formlessness* (the Void or the Plenum/Fullness, for example); it often comes more than once, and sometimes it's there (e.g. here) all the time. Meanwhile, contrary to initial appearances, chaos may turn into or out to be some previously hidden or unrecognised 'order'.

11 *Creation, when sudden, tends to be perceived as a revolution; when gradual, as evolution.* But the latter often prepares the way for the former, and the concepts differ in degree rather than kind. The slashed compound 'r/evolution' is one way of attempting to register this dynamic – but, like 'hi/story', it looks odd and is impossible to say.

12 *The most modern sciences no less than the most ancient religions have their myths that are accounted 'truths'.* Each has its myth of the creation (origin, beginning) of things, as well as its myth of its own development as a set of institutions (practices, disciplines). Some of these myths hold out promises of 'progress' or cumulative regeneration – even eternal life and salvation. Others project a condition of 'regress' and the threat of imminent or gradual degeneration – leading to utter destruction and perhaps damnation. (Utopias and dystopias are often in the picture somewhere.) Yet other myths neither promise nor threaten, caress or cajole. They offer a prospect of sheer (or mere) ongoing 'process': for better and worse, a kind of highly particular or deeply undifferentiated 'becoming' . . .

13 For in the end, as in the beginning – and especially about half-way through – creation may be viewed as a huge joke, a big mistake, an infinite game without determinate rules, *jeux sans frontières*, play within and beyond the system, chaos to order, a happy or unhappy chance . . .

14 Alternatively, it may not.

Back to the future twice

We opened this chapter with a perfectly serious and curiously humorous conclusion from the Hindu *Rig Veda*. We shall close with a couple of seriously funny openings from contemporary comic science fantasy fiction. I must leave it for you to decide whether each of these charts the beginning or the end of some particular universe or, together, they gesture towards a muddle of multiverses perpetually in the middle. In any event, I suggest, they tell us a lot about myths of creation and, in a funny way, the nature of creativity. Here is the creation of the universe according to at least some of the creatures in Douglas Adams's *The Restaurant at the End of the Universe* (1980, the opening):

> The story so far:
>   In the beginning the universe was created.

This has made a lot of people very angry and been widely regarded as a bad move.

Many races believe that it was created by some sort of god, though the Jatravartid people of Viltvodle VI believe that the entire universe was in fact sneezed out of the nose of a being called the Great Green Arkleseizure.

The Jatravartids, who live in perpetual fear of the time they call The Coming of The Great White Handkerchief, are small blue creatures with more than fifty arms each, who are therefore unique in being the only race in history to have invented the aerosol deodorant before the wheel.

However, the Great Green Arkleseizure Theory is not widely accepted outside Viltvodle VI and so, the Universe being the puzzling place it is, other explanations are constantly being sought.

Meanwhile, here is Terry Pratchett setting the whole thing in motion at the beginning of his first Discworld novel, *The Colour of Magic* (1983):

In a distant and second-hand set of dimensions, in an astral plane that was never meant to fly, the curling star-mists waver and part . . .

See . . .

Great A'Tuin the Turtle comes, swimming slowly through the interstellar gulf, hydrogen frost on his ponderous limbs, his huge and ancient shell pocked with meteor craters. Through sea-sized eyes that are crusted with rheum and asteroid dust He stares fixedly at the Destination. [. . .]

There was the theory that A'Tuin had come from nowhere and would continue at a uniform crawl, or steady gait, into nowhere, for all time. This theory was popular among academics.

An alternative, favoured by those of a religious persuasion, was that A'Tuin was crawling from the Birthplace to the Time of Mating, as were all the stars in the sky which were, obviously, also carried by giant turtles. When they arrived they would briefly and passionately mate, for the first and only time, and from that fiery union new turtles would be born to carry a new pattern of worlds. This was known as the Big Bang hypothesis.

Part 4

Creative practices, cultural processes

A critical anthology

The earlier parts of this book offer theoretical, historical and cross-cultural perspectives on creativity. This final part carries through that project by concentrating on specific instances of creative practice: in the area of creative writing and literature in Chapter 7; and across the arts and sciences in Chapter 8. The former is organised historically and by genre or topic; the latter by materials, media and issues. Together, they illustrate – and often demonstrate – what 'being creative' has meant and currently means in a wide range of historical moments and cultural contexts, and by implication may yet mean in others still to come. In this respect, *creative practices* are continuous with and contribute to *cultural processes* – much as a *text* is part and parcel of the *contexts* in which it is conceived and communicated. By the same token, the 'creative' move is what pushes the culture further or in a promising direction; just as, more neutrally, a text affects its context and the relations among texts at large. The materials have been chosen and gathered to help highlight this process.

The anthology is *critical* in two senses. It investigates in practice critical issues that are explored more abstractly in the rest of the book; and it invites readers to critique those ideas in the light of the materials in hand and others they may have in mind. We therefore deal with specific instances of: creativity and constraint; kinds of inspiration; the generative nature of genre; collaboration and co-operation; copying and (re)production; play and game, chaos and order; artificial life/intelligence; in(ter)vention; 'full-fillment'; the 'fe<>male'; and so on. There is also an interrogation, through specific examples, of the myth of 'the Romantic writer/artist'. Each of the examples has been chosen because it is intrinsically interesting and perhaps even inspiring; and they have been gathered in clusters so as to complement or conflict with one another in striking ways. The first part of the anthology, 'Rewriting creativity: the case of "literature"', is more fully framed and annotated. The second part, 'Transforming culture: an open invitation', is precisely that, and presented with a lighter touch. Finally, it should be emphasised that none of these materials had to be chosen; many others could have been. But even then, if what *is* here prompts you to think critically about what *isn't* and creatively about what *might have been*, the anthology will have done its job.

7 Rewriting creativity

The case of 'literature'

But this is not a conventional history of any of these topics. It is rather a project in creative listening. Rather than constructing a standard historical narrative of social and cultural development I have chosen to immerse myself in a sea of stories. [. . .] The archives are full of surprises, stories of stories, and almost any point of entry can be chosen for building a world from a grain of sand.

(Cressy 2001: 1, 8)

This chapter offers a historical case study, through samples, of one mode of creative activity: 'literature'. Its aim is to extend, or even to explode, notions of what it is to write as well as to create, and 'literature' is understood in a capacious sense. The bulk of the chapter is made up of short texts or extracts from longer ones and exemplifies some of the many forms that creativity in writing can take. Most of the texts are drawn from what is traditionally called 'English literature', but would better be called 'literatures in English' since there are many more cultures and traditions in play than one. Some of the texts are in older and newer forms of English quite different from what is currently the standard printed form. Moreover, in their initial modes and moments of circulation (as speech, song or performance, for example) some of these materials are not strictly 'literature' or even 'writing' at all.

The texts featured range from Anglo-Saxon to African-American, and they represent oral and multimedia modes as well as written and printed texts. Even with these last there are huge differences in substance and function: a single copy of a hand-written manuscript on parchment is a different product and involves a different process from a handful of early books printed laboriously on a fixed-letter hand-press, and both of these are materially and socially distinct from the mass-reproduced products that poured from the eighteenth-century hand-presses or the nineteenth-century steam-presses. These are in turn distinct from contemporary modes of computer-assisted photo-reprographics. Further, through the contemporary electronic media, these last can be instantaneously communicated around the world, complete with sound, images and associated web-links. Thus, though all the texts look fairly similar on the page here, this should not disguise their often radical differences of initial form, function and, in the fullest sense, *texture*. Some brief notes on initial modes and moments of re/production are added to help fill out this material and historical context.

The emphasis upon *creativity* presents a revealing kind of challenge, both theoretically and historically, since what counts as specifically *creative* writing is at once absolutely central and curiously incidental to the matter at issue. One reason for this, as observed in Chapter 2, is that the phrase 'creative writing' has only been current since the 1930s and has tended to refer to the teaching and learning of how to write fictional prose, poems and scripts. 'Creative writing' thus has generally modern, Western and specifically educational connotations. Another reason for caution is that what looks the most obvious candidate for a longer-lived counterpart to 'creative writing' – *literature* – is itself a highly variable category and a no less historical concept. Well into the nineteenth century just about any kind of writing felt to be valuable might be termed 'literature', including works of history, philosophy and science. Thus Hazlitt (*c.* 1825) can refer to 'the two greatest names in English Literature, Sir Isaac Newton and Mr Locke'; though Newton was a scientist and Locke a philosopher (see Williams 1983: 183–8; also *OED*, 'literature' sense 3). This flexible sense remains in the modern notion of 'the literature on the subject', where the subject can be of any kind, and even extends to 'advertising literature'. For all these reasons, this chapter is concerned with an exploration of the relations among creativity and literature as intrinsically complex and dynamically interrelated processes. Neither can simply be conflated with the other.

The emphasis upon *rewriting creativity* is also considered. For one thing, this encourages us to conceive writing and reading on a continuum. Writers in effect re-write the world (including other people's words) every time they set pen to paper or fingers to keyboard. Conversely, readers re-write in their own minds what they read every time they set eyes to page or screen. 'Rewriting' thus emphasises the active and interactive aspects of wor(l)d-creation that characterise the open-ended continuum we know as reading-writing . . . writing-reading. Its more general counterpart in the present book is what I term the process of 're . . . creation' (see Chapter 3). 'Re-reading' is also included in so far as it represents the more receptive and responsive aspects of the process. Either way, we are here concerned with 'rewriting/rereading' as processes of change as well as exchange, and one of the concepts that is both challenged and changed over the course of the following writings/readings is that of 'creativity' itself.

Finally, then, as the epigraph to the chapter intimates, this is a 'project in creative listening'. There are traces of many voices here and of course there are many more that are not here – though perhaps they resonate in indirect ways with those that are. If we listen creatively, we may hear them.

Creativity and constraint 1: shapers, makers and patrons

This features the work of two early medieval 'shapers' and a late medieval 'maker' (both terms are Germanic counterparts of the Graeco-Roman 'poet', which also meant 'fashioner' or 'maker'). In each case the work is composed in a highly conventionalised poetic form and a genre that was readily recognised at the time. All three also feature performers/writers who were in some way dependent upon powerful patrons for support and encouragement. Put another way, all of these texts exemplify kinds of creative response to formal and social constraint. It is with such issues in mind – and any others that come to mind – that you are asked to weigh each of these texts.

Further information is supplied in each case, but it is also worth noting that certain basic principles seem to inform the work of all kinds of 'dependent' or 'patronised' writer and artist. To be successful – and sometimes simply to survive – it seems they must (1) recognise and in large measure respect the tastes, expectations and capacities of their patrons; (2) seek to stretch and extend – but not exceed or break – the social and cultural codes in play; (3) appeal to a range of authors, authorities and more or less received opinions so that views, values and arguments can, at need, be passed off as someone else's – and also to show off their knowledge; (4) cultivate a range of structures and strategies so as to appear a relatively unimportant and inconspicuous agent in their own fictions; (5) leave decisions and resolutions artfully open rather than coming down firmly on one side, unless they are sure they are on safe ground.

Perhaps surprisingly, working for a patron requires not just dependence, then, but kinds of interdependence and even independence. For the most part, the writer/artist will work indirectly and discreetly in well recognised conventions. And yet, in order to be genuinely entertaining and interesting, there is also a need for fresh information and insight – and even at times some playful provocation.

(i) 'Sing Creation!': Caedmon, c. 670

[The story of how a shy and illiterate cowherd working for the monastery of Whitby was visited in a dream and instructed to 'Sing Creation'. The song is here given in the Old English and glossed word-for-word in Modern English. Note on Old English pronunciation: the sc was pronounced 'sh'; the g was pronounced 'y', as in 'you'; the ċ was pronounced 'ch' as in 'chair'; and the þ (a thorn) was pronounced 'th'.]

At feasts, whenever it was decided to have a good time by taking turns singing, he [Caedmon] would see the harp getting close to him and would get up in the middle of the meal and go home. Once when he left the feast like this, he went to the cattle shed where he was due to be on guard that night. After he had stretched out and gone to sleep, he dreamed that someone was standing beside him, greeting him and calling out his name: 'Caedmon,' he said, 'sing me something.'

And he replied, 'I don't know how to sing; that's why I left the feast and came here – because I can't sing.'

'All the same,' said the one who was speaking to him, 'you must sing for me.'

'What must I sing?', he said.

'Sing Creation!'

At this, Caedmon straightaway began to sing verses in praise of God the Creator. He had never heard them before and they went like this:

Nu sculon herigean	heofonriċes Weard
Now we must praise	*heaven-kingdom's Guardian*
Meotodes mehte	and his modgeþanc
the Measurer's might	*and his mind-plan*
weorc Wuldor-Fæder	swa he wundra gehwæs
work of the Glory-Father	*as he the wonders of everyone*

e ce Drihten	or onstealde
the eternal Lord	*the beginning established.*
He ærest scop	eorþan bearnum
He first shaped/ created	*for earth's sons*
heofon to hrofe	halig Scyppend
heaven as a roof	*the holy Shaper/ Creator.*
þa middangeard	moncynnes Weard
Then middle-earth	*mankind's Guardian*
e ce Drihten	æfter teode
the eternal Lord	*afterwards made*
firum foldan	Frea ælmihtig
for people the earth	*the Master almighty.*

This is the general sense but not the exact words that he sang in his sleep; for it is impossible to make a literal translation of poetry into another language, no matter how well it is done, without losing some of the beauty and dignity. When he woke up, he remembered everything that he had sung in his sleep, and to this he soon added, in the same poetic measure, more verses praising God.

This is a Modern English translation of the story as told in Latin by the Northumbrian monk, Bede, in his *Ecclesiastical History of the English People* (completed 731). From the first, therefore, we are deeply involved in matters of translation and transformation. The Old English of the 'Song' is a West-Saxon version added to Bede's *History* in later manuscripts. The precise truth of the account and whose words appear in the song are therefore open to debate. It may have all happened exactly as reported, or perhaps someone started composing Christian songs in a traditional verse-form and this story was attached as a suitably miraculous and pious explanation. Alternatively, it is possible that 'Caedmon', like 'Homer' in Greek, may be the conveniently eponymous label for a whole tradition of more or less anonymous oral verse and story-telling, and not the actual name of an individual person at all. Also worth noting are: (1) the claim that Caedmon was instructed in a dream, which is a common motif/motivation in both religious and secular accounts of creative inspiration (cf. Winstanley and Coleridge below, pp. 205, 242 ff.); (2) the fact that the words *scop* and *Scyppend* are here used to refer to the act of divine 'creation' and to the 'Creator' as such, though they were previously used to refer to the processes of 'shaping' in general and to the poet as *scop*/shaper in particular (hence the alternative translations); (3) the use of a traditional Anglo-Saxon poetic measure (alliterative, stressed and organised in half-lines) and the adaptation of a traditional heroic vocabulary ('Lord', 'Master', 'Guardian', for example) to celebrate a Christian subject matter. In fact, whichever way you look at it, this account and the song of creation it contains represent processes of *re . . . creation* on just about every level. (For various – and variant – texts, see Abrams *et al.* 2000, Vol. 1: 23–5 and Hamer 1970: 121–3. The present translations are mine.)

(ii) 'Dear to my lord, "Dear" was my name', before 975

[A shaper/poet who calls himself 'Deor' ('Dear One') complains how he has been passed over for another poet. To console himself, he reviews sad and cruel events from myth, legend and history, concluding each with the refrain 'That passed away – so may this' (þæs ofereode þisses swa mæg).]

We have heard tell of the ceaseless complaint
of Maethhild, the wife of Geat,
that an unhappy love took away all her sleep.
That passed away – so may this.

Theodoric ruled the city of the Mearings
for thirty winters. That was all too well known to many.
That passed away – so may this.

We have also heard about the wolvish mind
of Eormanric, who long ruled the people of the Goths.
Many a man sat bound with sorrows
expecting nothing but grief, and wishing
that the kingdom might be overthrown.
That passed away – so may this.

For one who sits weighed down with grief,
deprived of joys, spirit in turmoil,
the share of sorrows seems endless.
But the thought may then come
that throughout the world the wise Lord
constantly brings change to many a man.
to some he shows mercy and a kind of glory,
to others he deals a portion of woe.
As for myself I shall say just this:
that I once was the shaper [*scop*] of the Heodenings.
Dear to my lord, 'Dear' was my name.
For many years I had a fine position
and a faithful lord – until Heorrenda
a man also skilled in song [leoþcræftig]
has now received the landed rights
that my protecting lord once gave to me.
That passed away – so may this.

This poem, here represented by its latter half, survives in a single manuscript from a monastic collection now called the *Exeter Book*; this dates from the tenth century (hence the reference to 'the wise Lord', i.e. God). But parts of the poem will have been composed much earlier (notably those invoking figures from Norse legend and Germanic history) and at some point it was probably delivered orally, perhaps accompanied by a harp, at a royal or noble court. Unusually for manuscripts of Anglo-Saxon verse, this particular poem is set out in verse paragraphs with each verse headed by a capital letter and the refrain clearly set apart. The form was evidently felt to be distinctive and constitutive of the poem's effects, so there has been an attempt to reproduce this here. In terms of genre, the poem can be variously described as 'elegy' for the passing of people and things, 'consolation' for present suffering, and 'complaint' about unjust treatment. Despite initial appearances and modern expectations, this is almost certainly *not* an autobiographical poem. Heorrenda, the supposed rival and usurper, was a *scop* famous in story and not a historical figure. Deor is therefore probably best understood as the *type* of dispossessed poet who has been 'dear' to his patron but is subsequently passed over in preference for another. As such, 'he' throws a revealing light on the condition of the dependent poet, and the risks as well as rewards of such an office. The poem as a whole also demonstrates the resource with which one who was 'skilled in song' ['leoþcræftig'] could handle traditional allusions and forms in poignant as well as pointed ways. (The present translation is mine. For the Old English text, further commentary and another translation, see Hamer 1970: 87–93.)

(iii) Chaucer's artful apology, c. 1385

[Within a dream, in a magical springtime garden, Chaucer presents himself being defended by Queen Alceste against the charges of the God of Love. The latter has just accused the poet of misrepresenting women in his depiction of the heroine in Troilus and Criseyde *and of translating the satiric part of* The Romance of the Rose. *What follows is the speech of Alceste, the 'Queen of the Daisies', on Chaucer's behalf. Spelling and some of the phrasing have been modernised.]*

> Then spoke this lady, clothed all in green
> And said, 'You must listen if he can reply
> To all that you have brought against him.
> A god should not be so aggrieved
> But in his deity should be stable,
> And also gracious and merciful.
> For if you are a god, that knows all,
> Then might it be as I shall tell:
> This man to you may falsely be accused
> Who as by right ought to be excused
> For in your court is many a flatterer
> And many a tittle-tattling accuser,
> Who drums many a sound in your ears
> Wholly after their own imagining,
> To get your sympathy, and out of sheer spite.
> These are the causes, and I shall not lie.
> Envy always brings out the court's dirty washing. [. . .]
> Also, perhaps, because this man is daft,
> He might do it with no malicious craft,
> For he's always making things up
> Regardless of the material to hand.
> Or perhaps he was told to make those two things
> By some personage, and dared not refuse;

Or maybe he utterly regrets the whole business.
For he hasn't done such a terrible thing
To translate what old scholars have already written.
It's not as though he would maliciously write
To do the dirt on love in his own right!'

(Text based on the F-text, ll. 341–79 in Chaucer 1988: 598–9)

The *Prologue to the Legend of Good Women* exists in two versions, and the present text is based upon the earlier one, ll. 341–79 (*c.* 1385). The overall purpose of the *Prologue* is clear enough: to allow Chaucer to defend himself against charges of impropriety prompted by his versions of *Troilus and Criseyde* (adapted from Boccaccio) and *The Romance of the Rose* (presumably the more satiric continuation of it by Jean de Meun). The strategy in the above passage is clear enough, too: to have a female authority figure, Queen Alceste, bring forward plausible excuses on the accused poet's behalf and thereby intercede for him with the God of Love. Chaucer is eventually let off with a penance: to atone he must write a series of 'Legends – i.e. saints' lives – of Good Women' (these he never completed, and in any case partly turned into satires, too). In all these ways, within and around the *Prologue*, Chaucer skilfully deploys the resources at his disposal as a court poet. The constraints within which he works and the obstacles he overcomes become the very sources of his creativity.

Divine inspiration into political intervention

Here we look at two instances of 'contemplative' writing from late fourteenth-century England and one instance of highly 'active' writing from the mid-seventeenth century. All three help extend and complicate the notions of *inspiration* (introduced in Chapters 1 and 4), even to the point of political *intervention*. The first two writings are usually termed 'mystical' in that they expressly attempt to address the secret, hidden and sometimes ecstatic aspects of religious experience (Latin *mysterium* meant 'hidden'). The third passage shows just how politically engaged and immediately 'this-worldly' a religiously motivated and apparently 'other-worldly' vision can be. All these texts also throw a revealingly variegated light on what may be meant by 'creativity' in a religious context framed in terms of creator–creature, divine–human relations. These relations are far more flexible and vexed than either the orthodox believer or the atheistical disbeliever might expect.

(i) The revelation of Mother Julian of Norwich, c. 1393

[Julian comments upon a revelation she had of 'Christ as mother'. Spelling and phrasing have been modernised.]

We are bought again and redeemed by mercy and grace of our sweet, kind and ever-loving mother Jesus, and of the properties of motherhood; but Jesus is our very mother, not feeding us with milk, but with himself, opening his side to us and challenging all our love. [. . .] This fair lovely word 'mother', it is so sweet and natural of the self that it may not truly be said of anyone but of him, and of her that is the true mother of him and of all people [i.e. Mary]. To the property of motherhood belongs natural love, wisdom and knowing, and it is good; for though it may be that our bodily bringing forth is but little, low and simple in comparison with our spiritual bringing forth, yet it is he who brings it about in the creatures in which it happens. [. . .] Thus he is our mother in nature by the working of grace in the lower part, for love of the higher part. [. . .] And in this I saw that all our debt which we owe, by God's bidding, *by* fatherhood and motherhood – *for* God's fatherhood and motherhood – is fulfilled in true loving of God; which blessed love Christ works in us. And this was shown in all and namely in the high and plenteous words where he says: 'I am it that thou lovest.'

(Text based on Julian of Norwich 1986: 73–4;
also see Larrington 1995: 101–3)

These comments are drawn from the 'Longer Version' of the *Revelations of Divine Love* written by Mother Julian some twenty years after the revelations – what she called 'showings' – that she experienced over three days in May 1373. This particular 'showing' was the fifteenth of sixteen and represents a culmination of her experience. All the revelations were associated with a near-death experience during serious illness. Early in life, Julian tells us, she had prayed for such an illness in order to help cleanse her spiritually. She also tells us that she was 'a simple creature unlettered' at the time, though later in life she became a learned and much sought-after spiritual counsellor for women (Margery Kempe, for example, consulted her in 1413). There are many complex and contentious questions that arise concerning the precise status and significance of the above text in context. How far were Julian's revelations really 'divine': visited upon her by God and/or self-induced? How reliable and revealing – or concealing – is an account revised twenty years after the event? However we answer these questions, at least three things are worth observing about this particular 'showing': (1) It offers a generally religious and specifically mystical model of inspiration that is experienced as revelation and elaborated through reflection. (2) It compounds yet does not confuse 'masculine' and 'feminine' attributes of the godhead, and insists upon a sharing of 'fatherhood' and 'motherhood' within 'true loving of God'. (This resonates interestingly with debates upon the 'fe<>male' dynamic of creativity discussed in Chapter 3.) (3) The female body is thus celebrated as both physical source and symbolic resource in ways which anticipate a wide range of contemporary feminist theorists and woman-centred writers.

(ii) A 'cloud of unknowing' and a 'cloud of forgetting', c. 1375

[The practising contemplative is urged to embrace the 'cloud of unknowing' that comes between God the creator and humanity, and to put a 'cloud of forgetting' between him or herself and the rest of the created world.]

And if you should ever reach this cloud [of unknowing], and dwell and work in it as I am telling you, then, just as this cloud of unknowing is above you, between you and your God, so you will need to put a cloud of forgetting beneath you, between you and everything that was ever created. Perhaps it will seem to you that you are far distant from God because the cloud of unknowing is between you and him, but in fact, rightly understood, you are much further from him when you have no cloud of forgetting between you and everything that was ever created. Whenever I say 'everything that was ever created', I mean not only the created things themselves but all they do and all their attributes. I do not except anything created, whether bodily created or spiritual beings, nor any act or attribute of any such being, whether good or evil; but, in brief, they should all be hidden in this way under the cloud of forgetting. For though it may sometimes be very beneficial to think of particular attributes and acts of specific created beings, it is nevertheless of little or no benefit in this work of contemplation.

(Text from Spearing 2001: 26–7, Chapter 5)

Suspended between a 'cloud of forgetting' and a 'cloud of unknowing', the kind of 'negative' theology projected by *The Cloud of Unknowing* recalls the view of creativity as a dual process of both 'emptying out' and 'full-filling' described in Chapter 3. Thus, notwithstanding the persistent emphasis upon kinds of negation – including annihilation of the sense of a separate self as well as obliteration of all routine sense impressions – the overriding aim of the book is positive: to achieve union with God. As the opening rubric of the book puts it: 'Here begins a book of contemplation called *The Cloud of Unknowing*, in which a soul is made one with God'. Such a union, however, can only be brought about through a process of atonement (i.e. 'at-one-ment', making one, becoming whole). This requires a firm resolve not to be taken in by the attractions and distractions of sense-perception and to mistake the creation for its creator. The more direct 'knowing' of God as Creator therefore demands the 'unknowing' of everything else. A modern editor summarises it thus: the *Cloud* has 'an unwavering focus on God's radical transcendence of human understanding and human language' and operates on 'the assumption that it is impossible to make true affirmative statements about God in human language' (Spearing, cited above, p. ix). Indeed, the only way through to true union with God, the author of the *Cloud* finally insists, is through unconditional love – not reason or knowledge.

(iii) 'Freedom to the Creation!': Gerard Winstanley, 1649

[A seventeenth century political and religious radical dedicated to the reclaiming of the 'common land' bears witness to what inspires his actions.]

Not a full year since, being quiet in my work, my heart was filled with sweet thoughts, and many things were revealed to me which I never read in books, nor heard from the mouth of any flesh, and when I began to speak them, some people could not bear my words, and among these revelations was this one: *That the earth shall be made a common treasury of livelihood to whole mankind, without respect of persons*: and I had a voice within me which bade me declare it abroad, which I did obey, for I declared it by word of mouth wheresoever I came [. . .]

Yet my mind was not at rest, because nothing was acted, and thoughts run in me that words and writings were all nothing and must die, for action is the life of all. If thou dost not act, thou dost nothing. Within a little time I was made obedient to the word in that particular likewise: for I took my spade and went and broke the ground upon George Hill in Surrey, thereby declaring freedom to the

Creation, and that the earth must be set free from entanglements of lords and landlords, and that it shall become a common treasury to all, as it was first made and given to the sons of men.

Gerard Winstanley was one of the most vocal and influential of the radical democratic movement known as the Diggers, active at the beginning of the English Revolution. They were the direct-action or 'true' wing of the Levellers. In 1649, in an attempt to reclaim the 'commons' for 'the common people of England', he and others started a campaign of digging and planting crops on St George's Hill in Surrey. This was towards the beginning of the Commonwealth set up under the 'protection' of Oliver Cromwell, which, despite its name and notwithstanding much preaching about equality and justice, rarely extended beyond the male middle classes. It did not, for example, recognise the rights and interests of peasants and artisans, men and women. It was therefore from among the ranks of the latter that Winstanley, himself the son of a mercer and later a hired labourer, drew support and inspiration – as well as from God's word and divine revelation. One of the other inspirations for the Diggers was the Peasants' Uprising of the late fourteenth century (1381). It, too, took its cue from a radically egalitarian reading of the Genesis story and, and its rallying call, still being chanted by the Diggers, was: 'When Adam delved [dug] and Eve span / Who was then the gentle man?'. In the event, both movements were swiftly and viciously suppressed; so in a narrowly historical sense both actions were short-lived. But in a fuller historical perspective their political as well as religious significance – and their inspiration for other radical popular movements – has been profound and enduring. (The text of Winstanley is from a pamphlet based upon his speech of 26 August 1649, printed as 'A Watch-word to the City of London', as reproduced in Hampton 1984: 231. The full text and context of the song 'When Adam delved' is treated in the same book, pp. 49–82.)

Creativity and constraint 2: sonnets by various hands

Sonnets are reckoned to be among the most exacting of verse forms. They are also commonly assumed to be about little else but love, especially declarations of love by male poets to the female objects of their desire. That these observations are in part true is demonstrated by the sonnets by Philip Sidney and William Shakespeare that follow (though Shakespeare addressed sonnets to young men, too). But sonnets have been written on many other themes: belief and doubt, nature and revolution, for example. And often the matter in hand turns out to be the writing of the sonnet itself. For what sonnet after sonnet shows is that it is the very constraint of composing within highly formalised structures and with apparent limitations of subject matter that constitutes much of the creative challenge and perennial appeal of the genre. But sonnets are also written by women. And though the subject may sometimes be a desired male, it may just as well be another woman or some other topic entirely. In any event, again, there is likely to be an underlying concern with the demands of composition. All these possibilities are in play in the sonnets by Elizabeth Barrett Browning, Edna St Vincent Millay and Adrienne Rich.

Some information on the history and forms of the sonnet will help set the scene. The basic form was already well established in Italy by the time their most famous practitioner, Francis Petrarch (1304–74), came to pen his sequence addressed to Laura. These grew out of a tradition of artful love songs, the *Canzone* and *Canzonetta*. Very quickly, however, the sonnet's intricate verse-form (typically of fourteen lines involving various permutations of quatrains, triplets and couplets) and its tight, often paradoxical argument confirmed it to be a primarily written – not sung – genre. Sonnets did, however, continue to be read out loud in private and to small groups, just as they tended to circulate in single, hand-written copies. The metres, verse-forms and even length of the sonnet can be remarkably various. But the most common form in English is a fourteen-line poem with each line tending towards iambic pentameter (i.e. made of five measures, each with a pattern of 'unstressed + stressed' syllables). An example is the first line of Shakespeare's sonnet 130, with the stressed syllables emboldened: 'My **mist**ress' **eyes** are **noth**ing **like** the **sun**'. In English, a typical Shakespearean sonnet is organised in three distinct four-line verses clinched by a couplet, and has a rhyme-scheme *abab cdcd efef gg* (where each letter signals a distinct rhyme). But precise usage varies within as well as between the work of particular writers. In that respect not all of Shakespeare's sonnets are 'Shakespearean'. Indeed, there are quite a few instances of 'sonnets' of more or less than fourteen lines (Hopkins's, printed below, has ten and a bit); and some have more or less than ten syllables to the line (Sidney's, also below, has twelve). But whatever the precise length, most successful sonnets are characterised by their condensed meaning and tense energy: by a tight argument that pulls against as well as with the formal verse-structures, and by sentences and syntax that contend as well as blend with the line-breaks and rhyme-scheme. William Blake's pithy and paradoxical axiom 'The cistern contains, the fountain overflows' might well stand as a characterisation of the sonnet. For the best ones somehow manage to be and do both.

As with all living genres, it is important to recognise that 'the sonnet' keeps being re-generated. In fact, every fresh instance, in so far as it keeps in touch with some recognisable aspects of form and yet bends them in response to current needs, both re-invigorates and re-invents the genre. As the following instances abundantly attest, the sonnet has long been and still is very much alive and kicking. A particularly lively and wide-ranging anthology is Levin 2001, which includes sonnets (iii), (vi), (vii), (viii), (ix) and (x) (Levin 2001: 46, 110, 124, 164, 213). Sonnets (i), (ii), (v) and (vi) can be found in Abrams et al. 2000, Vol. 1: 917, 1030 and Vol. 2: 1178, 1653. Sonnet (iv) is based on Clare 1990: 311–12.

(i) Philip Sidney, 'Astrophil and Stella', 1591

Loving in truth, and fain* in verse my love to show,	*desiring*
That she (dear she) might take some pleasure of my pain,	
Pleasure might cause her read, reading might make her know,	
Knowledge might pity win, and pity grace obtain,	
I sought fit words to paint the blackest face of woe:	
Studying inventions fine, her wits to entertain,	
Oft turning others' leaves, to see if thence would flow	
Some fresh and fruitful showers upon my sunburned brain.	
But words came halting forth, wanting Invention's stay*;	*prop*

Invention, Nature's child, fled step-dame Study's blows,
And others' feet still seemed but strangers in my way.
Thus great with child to speak, and helpless in my throes,
    Biting my trewand* pen, beating myself for spite   *truant*
    'Fool,' said my Muse to me, 'look in thy heart and write.'

(ii) William Shakespeare, Sonnet 15, 1609

When I consider every thing that grows
Holds in perfection but a little moment;
That this huge stage presenteth naught but shows
Whereon the stars in secret influence comment;
When I perceive that men as plants increase,
Cheered and checked even by the selfsame sky,
Vaunt in their youthful sap, at height decrease,
And wear their brave state out of memory;
Then the conceit* of this inconstant stay   *conception, image*
Sets you most rich in youth before my sight,
Where wasteful time debateth with Decay
To change your day of youth to sullied* night,   *soiled*
    And all in war with Time for love of you,
    As he takes from you, I ingraft* you new.   *pun: graft/ inscribe*

(iii) Mary Wroth, 'In this strange labyrinth how shall I turn', c. 1625

In this strange labyrinth how shall I turne?
wayes are on all sides while the way I miss:
if to the right hand, then, in love I burne;
lett mee goe forward, therein danger is;

If to the left, suspicion hinders bliss,
lett mee turne back, shame cries I ought returne
nor fainte though crosses with my fortunes kiss;
stand still is harder, although sure to mourne;

Thus lett me take the right, or left hand way;
goe forward, or stand still, or back retire;
I must these doubts indure without allay
or help, but travail* find for my best hire;   *labour*
yett that which most my troubled sense doth move
is to leave all, and take the thread of love.

(iv) John Clare, 'I feel I am', c. 1850

I FEEL I am – I only know I am,
And plod upon the earth, as dull and void:
Earth's prison chilled my body with its dram

Of dullness, and my soaring thoughts destroyed,
I fled to solitudes from passions dream,
But strife pursued – I only know I am.
I was a being created in the race
Of men disdaining bounds of place and time –
A spirit that could travel o'er the space
Of earth and heaven – like a thought sublime,
Tracing creation, like my maker, free –
A soul unshackled – like eternity,
Spurning earth's vain and soul debasing thrall
But now I only know I am – that's all.

(v) Elizabeth Barrett Browning, 'To George Sand. A Recognition', 1844

True genius, but true woman! Dost deny
Thy woman's nature with a manly scorn,
And break away the gauds* and armlets worn *trinkets*
By weaker women in captivity?
Ah, vain denial! That revolted cry
Is sobbed in by a woman's voice forlorn –
Thy woman's hair, my sister, all unshorn
Floats back dishevelled strength in agony,
Disproving thy man's name: and while before
The world thou burnest in a poet-fire,
We see thy woman-heart beat evermore
Through thy large flame. Beat purer, heart, and higher,
Till God unsex thee on the heavenly shore
Where unincarnate spirits purely aspire!

(vi) Gerard Manley Hopkins, 'Pied Beauty', 1877

Glory be to God for Dappled things –
    For skies of couple-colour as a brinded* cow *browny-orange*
        For rose-moles all in stipple upon trout that swim;
Fresh-firecoal chestnut-falls, finches' wings;
    Landscape plotted and pieced – fold, fallow and plough;
        And áll trádes, their gear and tackle and trim.

All things counter, original, spare, strange;
    Whatever is fickle, freckled (who knows how?)
        With swift, slów; sweet sóur; adazzle dim;
He fathers-forth whose beauty is past change:
                    Praise him.

(vii) Robert Frost, 'Design', 1936

I found a dimpled spider, fat and white,
On a white heal-all, holding up a moth
Like a white piece of rigid satin cloth –
Assorted characters of death and blight
Mixed ready to begin the morning right,
Like the ingredients of a witches' broth
A snow-drop spider, a flower like a froth,
And dead wings carried like a paper kite.

What had that flower to do with being white,
The wayside blue and innocent heal-all?
What brought the kindred spider to that height,
Then steered the white moth thither in the night?
What but design of darkness to appall? –
If design govern in a thing so small.

(viii) Edna St Vincent Millay, 'I will put Chaos into fourteen lines', 1954

I will put Chaos into fourteen lines
And keep him there; and let him thence escape
If he be lucky; let him twist and ape
Flood, fire, and demon – his adroit designs
Will strain to nothing in the strict confines
Of this sweet Order, where, in pious rape,
I hold his essence and amorphous shape,
Till he with Order mingles and combines.
Past are all the hours, the years, of our duress,
His arrogance, our awful servitude:
I have him. He is nothing more nor less
Than something simple not yet understood;
I shall not even force him to confess;
Or answer. I will only make him good.

(ix) Adrienne Rich, 'Final Notations', 1986

it will not be simple, it will not be long
it will take little time, it will take all your thought
it will take all your heart, it will take all your breath
it will be short, it will not be simple

it will touch through your ribs, it will take all your heart
it will not be long, it will occupy your thought
as a city is occupied, as a bed is occupied
it will take all your flesh, it will not be simple

You are coming into us who cannot withstand you
you are coming into us who never wanted to withstand you
you are taking parts of us into places never planned
you are going far away with pieces of our lives

it will be short, it will take all your breath
it will not be simple, it will become your will

(x) Jason Schneiderman, 'The Disease Collector', c. 1998

Odd word: culture, as though this swab cared
About art and music, loved the opera,
Saw the Ballet Russe when Nijinsky still bared
His chest, could quote the illuminata
In the original Italian. As though this petri dish
Were a center of learning, and parents wished
For their children to go there, like Harvard or Yale,
As though a positive answer would not pale
My cheeks, or force me to wholly rearrange
My life around pills and doctor's visits:
Force me to find old lovers and tricks,
Warn that their bodies may too grow strange;
To play the old game of who gave it to whom,
Gently lowering voices, alone in one's room.

Play world! Real life drama

'All the world's a stage and the men and women merely players' is a truism – but none the less true for all that. Indeed, the very fact that a line from a play (Shakespeare's *As You Like It*, II.7; *c.* 1599) can be circulating in common parlance four hundred years later demonstrates the permeability between the world of drama in the theatre and what we also routinely hail as the 'drama' of everyday life (which also has its tragic and comic moments). Such possibilities are compounded by the rich ambiguity of the word 'play'. '*A* play' (with the article) is what goes on at the theatre or in some imagined theatrical space; but 'play' (without the article) can be any kind of more or less game-like activity As a consequence, as discussed at length in Chapter 4, *both* senses readily extend to everything from 'child's play' (literal or metaphorical) through formal 'role-play' (in education or training) to simply 'playing a role' in life at large (as a mother or daughter, student or patient, for example).

Umberto Eco suggests, 'It is not theatre that is able to imitate life; it is social life that is designed as a continuous performance' ('Semiotics of Theatrical Performance' [1977] in Walder 2004: 120). Conversely, as theatre director Peter Brook points out, 'I can take any empty space and call it a bare stage. A man walks across this empty space while someone else is watching him, and this is all that is needed for an act of theatre to be engaged' (Brook 1968: 11). Either way, it is the close synergy between people 'acting' and 'playing roles', both on and off the stage, that led the playwright Bertolt Brecht to draw on naturally occurring conversations and situations for his model of 'epic theatre'. Brecht is particularly drawn to occasions where speakers demonstrate as well as narrate events: 'For practical experiments I usually picked as my example of completely simple, "natural" epic theatre an incident such as can be seen at any street corner: an eye-witness demonstrating to a collection of people how a traffic accident took place' (Brecht [1949] in Bentley 1968: 85).

It is with the complex interrelations between the 'play world' of the theatre and the ways we 'play' roles in the rest of life firmly in mind, that the following texts have been chosen. The first is an invocation of the audience's power of imagination and a display of the writer's skill in securing it. The second is a dramatic realisation of the problems and possibilities of being an 'original' or a 'copy' in a world of human cloning. The third is an instance of the 'art of common talk' in an informal conversation between female students who share a house. All throw some revealingly oblique lights on the 'games people play' on and off stage, and the verbal and other resources they use to extend as well as bend the rules.

(i) 'on your imaginary forces work': William Shakespeare, Henry V, 1599 (the opening)

[The Chorus figure comes on and verbally 'sets the scene' for the play.]

Enter Chorus as Prologue

CHORUS:
O for a muse of fire, that would ascend
The brightest heaven of invention:
A kingdom for a stage, princes to act,
And monarchs to behold the swelling scene.
Then should the warlike Harry, like himself,
Assume the port* of Mars, and at his heels,   *bearing*
Leashed in like hounds, should famine sword and fire
Crouch for employment. But pardon, gentles all,
The flat unraisèd spirits that hath dared
On this unworthy scaffold to bring forth
So great an object. Can this cock-pit hold
The vasty fields of France? Or may we cram
Within this wooden O* the very casques   *the Globe theatre*
That did affright the air at Agincourt?
O pardon: since a crookèd figure may
Attest in little space a million,
And let us, ciphers to this great account,
On your imaginary forces work.
Suppose within the girdle of these walls
Are now confined two mighty monarchies,
Whose high uprearèd and abutting fronts
The perilous narrow ocean parts asunder.
Piece out our imperfections with your thoughts:
Into a thousand parts divide one man,

And make imaginary puissance*.   *power, forces*
Think, when we talk of horses, that you see them,
Printing their proud hoofs i'th' receiving earth;
For 'tis your thoughts that now must deck our kings
Carry them here and there, jumping o'er times,
Turning the accomplishment of many years
Into an hourglass   for the which supply,
Admit me Chorus to this history,
Who Prologue-like your humble patience pray
Gently to hear, kindly to judge, our play.

Exit

(Text from Shakespeare 1995: Act I: 1–34)

The Chorus figure appears in prologues to the other acts, urging and prompting the audience to use its imagination: 'work, work your thoughts . . . And eke out our performance with your minds' (Act 3); 'But now behold / In the quick forge and working-house of thought' (Act 5). A further practical reason may be that the play was apparently written and produced at high speed, perhaps as a commission, and may have been presented in relatively raw form. For a more poetic, less theatrical, invocation of the 'Muse of invention', compare Sidney's sonnet, (i) in the previous section.

(ii) 'they said that none of us was the original': Caryl Churchill, A Number, 2002 (the opening)

[SALTER, a man in his early sixties, talks with his son BERNARD (B2), who is thirty-five. Bernard/B2 has been cloned – or is a clone – we are not sure which.]

B2:	A number
SALTER:	you mean
B2:	a number of them, of us, a considerable
SALTER:	say
B2:	ten, twenty
SALTER:	didn't you ask?
B2:	I got the impression
SALTER:	why didn't you ask?
B2:	I didn't think of asking.
SALTER:	I can't think why not, it seems to me it would be the first thing you'd want to know, how far has this thing gone, how many of these things are there?
B2:	Good, so if it ever happens to you
SALTER:	no you're right
B2:	no it was stupid, it was shock, I'd known for a week before I went to the hospital but it was still
SALTER:	it is, I am, the shocking thing is that there are these, not how many but at all
B2:	even one

SALTER: exactly, even one, a twin would be a shock
B2:   a twin would be a surprise but a number
SALTER: a number any number is a shock.
B2:   You said things, these things
SALTER: I said?
B2:   You called them things. I think we'll find they're people.
SALTER: Yes of course they are, they are of course.
B2:   Because I'm one.
SALTER: No.
B2:   Yes. Why not? Yes.
SALTER: Because they're copies
B2:   copies? they're not
SALTER: copies of you which some mad scientist has illegally
B2:   how do you know that?
SALTER: I don't but
B2:   what if someone else is the one, the first one, the real one and I'm
SALTER: no because
B2:   not that I'm not real which is why I'm saying they're not things, don't call them
SALTER: just wait, because I'm your father.
B2:   You know that?
SALTER: Of course.
B2:   It was all a normal, everything, birth
SALTER: you think I wouldn't know if I wasn't your father?
B2:   Yes of course I was just for a moment there, but they are still people like twins are all, quins are all
SALTER: yes I'm sorry
B2:   we just happen to have identical be identical identical genetic [. . .] I think I'd like to meet one. It's an adventure isn't it and you're part of science. I wouldn't be frightened to meet any number.
SALTER: I don't know.
B2:   They're all your sons.
SALTER: I don't want a number of sons, thank you, you're plenty, I'm fine.
B2:   Maybe after they've found everything out they'll let us meet. They'll have a party for us, we can
SALTER: I'm not going to drink with those doctors. But maybe you're right you're right, take it in a positive spirit.
B2:   There is a thing
SALTER: what's that?
B2:   I did get the impression and I know I may be wrong because maybe I was in shock but I got the impression there was this batch and we were all in it. I was in it.
SALTER: No because you're my son.
B2:   No but we were all
SALTER: I explained already
B2:   but I wasn't being quite open with you because I'm confused because it's a shock but I want to know what happened

SALTER:	they stole
B2:	no but what happened
SALTER:	I don't
B2:	because they said that none of us was the original.

(Text from Churchill 2002: 3–5, 9–10)

Churchill characteristically develops her plays through workshop collaboration, and has a keen ear for what is naturally dis/continuous in dramatic exchanges. In the present play Salter has three sons – Bernard 1 (B1), Bernard 2 (B2) and Michael Black – all of whom are played by the same actor. Visually as well as verbally, then, Churchill is exploring the nature and status of 'copies' and 'originals' as well as, more specifically, the implications of genetic engineering and cloning. All are issues picked up in the present book, especially in Chapters 3, 4 and 8.

(iii) 'Well we can relate to chocolate': student conversation, c. 1997

[Three female students are having tea at home on a Sunday night. They are the same age (twenty to twenty-one) and share a house in Carmarthen, Wales. Two of the speakers (SI and S3) are from the south-west of England and one (S2) is from South Wales.]

S3:	Does anybody want a chocolate bar or anything?
S1:	Oh. Yeah, Please.
S2:	Oh. Yes please.
(laughter)	
S3:	All right. You can have, you can have either a Mars Bar Kit Kat or erm Cherry Bakewells.
S2:	(laughs)
S1:	Ooh.
S2:	Oh.
S1:	Er er er erm [inaudible]
S2:	Oh it's a toss up between the Cherry Bakewell . . .
S1:	(laughs)
S2:	. . . and the Mars Bar isn't it.
S3:	Well shall I bring them in. And, cos I mean you might want another one. Cos I don't want them all. Cos . . .
S1:	Yeah.
S3:	I'm gonna be
(laughter)	
S2:	Miss paranoid about weight here.
S3:	(from distance) Yeah. But you know.
S2:	You're not fat Sue.
S3:	(from distance) I will be.
(laughter)	
S2:	God.
(laughter)	
S3:	I ate almost a whole jar of Roses this weekend.
S2:	Did you.

(laughter)

S3:	And my mum [inaudible].
S2:	Look at her neck.
S1:	She goes Ooh. Do you [inaudible].
S2:	My God.
S1:	What was that about you you said about your, you and your mum don't get on.

(laughter)

S1:	I'd say you got on all right with that . . .
S3:	Well we can relate to chocolate.
S1:	. . . wadge of food there.

(laughter) [. . .]

S3:	I like Sunday nights for some reason.
S1:	(laughs)
S2:	I don't know why.
S2:	(laughs) Cos you come home
S3:	I come 'ome and . . .
S2:	You come home to us.
S3:	. . . and pig out.
S2:	Yeah.
S3:	(laughs)
S1:	Sunday is a really nice day I think.
S2:	It certainly is.
S1:	It's a really nice relaxing day.
S2:	It's me ear-ring. [. . .]
S3:	Oh. Lovely.
S2:	It's fallen apart a bit. But
S3:	It looks quite nice like that actually. I bet, is that supposed to be straight?
S2:	Yeah.
S3:	I reckon it looks better like that.
S2:	And it was another bit as well, was another dangly bit.
S3:	What . . .
S2:	Separate.
S3:	. . . attached to . . .
S2:	The top bit.
S3:	. . . that one.
S2:	Yeah. So it was even.
S1:	Mobile ear-rings.
S3:	Oh.
S2:	(laughs)
S3:	I like that. It looks better like that.

The transcript of this conversation is based on tape-recordings from the CANCODE corpus reproduced and analysed by Ron Carter in his *Language and Creativity: The Art of Common Talk*, 2004: 6–9, 102–9. At first glance the exchanges are bitty and incoherent. However, on closer acquaintance and after weighing the conversation as a whole, it becomes clear that there is an intricate interdependence built up and that it incorporates playful contributions from individual speakers. 'Such features', says Carter, 'are predominantly interpersonal, relationship-creating and relationship-reinforcing' (p. 107). And the effects are not only textual (in the narrow sense of 'just the words'); they are also gestural and contextual (in that they depend upon actions and much laughter and a communal sense of occasion). The creative co-operation therefore extends all the way through from the sharing of chocolate and family history to the swapping of grammatical structures ('come home/come home'), the coining of fresh words ('dangly') and the offering up of a verbal-visual pun ('mobile'). 'There is a clear sense here', concludes Carter, 'that the term the art of talk is not exaggerated. Indeed it is almost a poetry of talk' (p. 107).

Re-generating genre: new from old in the novel

This section looks at samples of 'the novel'. This is a genre which, as its name suggests, is − or was − ostensibly 'new'. But of course 'new' is a relative term so we cannot grasp what it may mean unless we also have some sense of the 'old' and the 'other-than-novel' from which it derives and is in some sense distinguished. The term came into English from Italian *novella* and Spanish *novela*, and from the sixteenth to the eighteenth centuries was used to refer to all sorts of short prose narratives of a fictional kind. Typically, these were 'about characters and their actions in what was recognisably everyday life and usually in the present, with the emphasis on things being "new" or a "novelty"' (Cuddon 1998: 599). As such, novels were chiefly distinguished from verse romances on chivalric or classical themes, and they were often closer to what we now call 'short stories'. In its modern sense of an *extended* prose narrative, the term 'novel' first became widely current during the nineteenth century. It then tended to be applied retrospectively and fairly indiscriminately to all sorts of things which had previously been referred to very variously as 'histories', 'adventures', 'lives', 'diaries' and 'journals', etc. (see *OED*, 'novel'). As a result, modern understandings of 'novel' are a handy but often anachronistic hold-all for a very mixed bag of materials.

The overall aim of this selection is to show not so much *what* was 'new' about the novel; for many of their materials and strategies were already 'old' in one form or another. Rather, we are concerned with *how* novels changed and developed from existing genres and, eventually, from other novels. As Salman Rushdie put it in his novel *The Satanic Verses* (1988), we are concerned with 'how newness enters the world'. And to do this, as argued in Chapter 4 and as seen with the sonnets earlier in this anthology, we need to recognise that genres and forms are never fixed and finished but are subject to constant transformation. Living *gen*res, by definition, ceaselessly re-*gen*erate. The questions then are: how do existing genres mingle and fuse to generate new mixtures and compounds? and how do old forms of writing and thinking metamorphose under the pressure of new conditions and demands? More specifically, with an eye to an expanding middle class and changes in print technology from the eighteenth century onwards, what were the effects of the increasingly 'mass' readerships, including the growing numbers of literary as well as literate women? And in this respect we need to recognise the rapid rise and steady spread of that other self-consciously 'new' genre, also delivered by print technology to ever wider and more varied readerships: the *news*papers. For it is no accident that both 'novels' and 'news' spring from the same cultural-historical mix; nor that the assumed 'fictionality' of the former should often mimic the supposed 'factuality' of the latter, and vice versa.

The 'rise of the novel' is usually associated with the early eighteenth century, and traditionally with such 'fathers of the novel' as Defoe, Richardson, Fielding, Smollett and Sterne. But, in Dale Spender's phrase, there were also plenty of 'mothers of the novel' such as Behn and Manley and these, along with their male counterparts, can be traced back earlier. For, as already mentioned, very various things called 'novels' had been around in one form or another for a long time. In fact, depending upon one's cultural and historical perspective, there are extended prose fictions (i.e. novel-like narratives) from as long ago as the XIIth dynasty of the Egyptian Middle Kingdom (*The Princess of Backstaw*; *c.* 1200 BCE) and as far away as the most famous of all Japanese stories of love, *The Tale of Genji*, written by a woman under the pseudonym Murasaki Shikibu (*c.* 1000 CE). But even if we restrict ourselves to Western Europe, the supposed homeland of modern prose fiction, we find a variety that from the first offers to exceed any neat critical categories. Robert Burton in his *Anatomy of Melancholy* (1624, IV.ii), for instance, refers to tales 'such as the old women told Psyche in Apuleius, Boccaccio's novels, and the rest', thereby lumping together the second-century North African author of *The Golden Ass* (also called 'Metamorphoses', featured in Chapter 5), the fourteenth-century Italian author of *The Decameron* 'and the rest'. Both wrote extended fictional narratives in prose representing scenes from contemporary life (as well as fantastical events) and therefore qualify for the now-standard definition of 'novel' – even though few critics would be easy about stretching the category that far in time and space.

Thus, as we have seen with all manner of 'beginnings', the beginnings of the novel stretch back in many directions and draw on threads that can be retraced in many genres, ancient and modern. And again, intertextually, it is perhaps better seen as 'all middle'. Indeed, if we care to look for bridges between the ancient and medieval and the Renaissance and modern worlds, we need look no further than the encyclopaedic and carnivalesque prose satire of Rabelais's *Gargantua and Pantagruel* (1534–51) and Cervantes's mock-chivalric romance *Don Quixote* (1605–15). The latter, in particular, is hailed as their inspiration by comic novelists from Fielding and Smollett to Dickens. Though whether it is better described as a 'comic novel' or 'a romance gone mad' is hard to say – and probably beside the point. At any rate, as James Cuddon observes in a particularly capacious account of the novel as a genre, 'No other literary form has proved so pliable and adaptable to a seemingly endless variety of topics and themes' (Cuddon 1998: 599–642, here p. 600). In contemporary theoretical terms, we might add that novels have always tended to be radically *hybrid* in their origins and richly *heteroglossic* in the 'varied voices' that they draw together. Thus, whether drawing on the fundamentally oral tale-telling arts of *The Odyssey* or *The Thousand and One Nights* or the essentially visual and musical modes of the latest Hollywood or Bollywood blockbusters, novels have continued to feed upon and back into the common sources and resources of narrative and drama at large. As a result, the best ones tend to resist attempts to pigeon-hole them as, say, 'fantastic' or 'naturalistic', and 'comic' or 'tragic', Those with most enduring appeal often turn out to be all – and more. Certainly, a novel such as Sterne's *Tristram Shandy* (featured below) makes critical acclaim for the supposed 'newness' of such novelistic forms as 'magical realism' or 'metafiction' faintly obtuse and out of touch. With the novel, as with all living genres, it is better to ask *What's new? What's old?* – and then get on with the business of engaging with the bright particulars and historical specificities of the instance in hand. That is what we do now, albeit necessarily through brief snippets.

(i) 'News of the maker': Thomas Nashe, The Unfortunate Traveller, 1594

[The author introduces himself, his tale and his hero, Jack Wilton, to 'the dapper Monsieur Pages of the Court'. Nashe's style is both highly formal and racily colloquial, lewd and learned by turns. Hence the need for copious annotation. Once grasped, however, it trips – or spits – from the tongue with a sharp relish.]

> Gallant Squires, have amongst you! At Mumchance[1] I mean not, for so I might by chance come to short commons,[2] but at *novus, nova, novum*[3] which is in English, 'news' of the maker. A proper fellow Page of yours called *Jack Wilton* by me commends him unto you, and hath bequeathed waste paper here amongst you certain pages of his misfortunes. In any case keep them preciously as a *privy*[4] token of his good will towards you. If there be some better than others, he craves you would honour them in their death so much as to dry and kindle Tobacco with them. [. . .] Many special grave articles more had I to give you in charge, which your wisdoms waiting together at the bottom of the great chamber stairs, or sitting in a porch (your parliament house) may better consider of than I can deliver: only let this suffice for a taste of the text, and a bit to pull on a good wit with, as a rasher [of bacon] on the coals is to pull [go well with] a cup of wine.
>
> Hey pass, come aloft! Every man of you take
> your places, and hear Jack Wilton
> tell his own Tale

1. A dice game involving 'keeping mum' (silence). 2. Short rations, little reward. 3. Masculine, feminine and neuter forms of Latin for 'new'. 4. Triple pun on 'private', 'privates' (genitals) and 'privy' (toilet).

(The text is from Rhys 1965: 15)

Nashe's induction does indeed give 'a taste of the text' to follow, a picaresque tale of quick wit and grotesque melodrama. His exuberant sporting with the Latin for 'new' and his lewd punning on 'privy' quickly converge on an injunction to use the worst parts of the book either as toilet paper or for drying tobacco. Nashe's precursors in this line are Rabelais and Aretine, his contemporaries are Jonson and Shakespeare, and his successors include Smollett and Joyce. The author's passing reference to himself ('news of the maker') and the claim to be writing a biographical history of his hero (Jack Wilton) become part of the 'factual' stock-in-trade of prose fiction.

(ii) 'A female pen': Aphra Behn, Oroonoko, or The Royal Slave, 1688

[The female narrator is the daughter of the Lieutenant General of British Surinam (later Dutch Guyana). Here she reflects upon the Christian practice of giving slaves European names; the lack of

any official (British) historians in South America then, and upon her own low status as a 'female pen'. All these things are significantly resolved at the end.]

I ought to tell you that the Christians never buy any slaves but they give 'em some name of their own, their native ones being likely very barbarous and hard to pronounce; so that Mr. Trefry gave Oroonoko [a former African chief, now a slave] that of Caesar, which name will live in that country as long as that (scarce more) glorious one of the great Roman for 'tis most evident he wanted [lacked] no part of the personal courage of that Caesar, and acted things as memorable, had they been done in some part of the world replenished with people and historians that might have given him his due. But his misfortune was to fall in an obscure world that afforded only a female pen to celebrate his fame; though I doubt not but it had lived from others' endeavours if the Dutch, who immediately after his time took that country, had not killed, banished and dispersed all those that were capable of giving the world this great man's life, much better than I have done. [Oroonoko and his heroic wife, Imoinda, are subsequently slaughtered while leading a slave uprising.]
[. . .] Thus died this great man, worthy of a better fate, and a more sublime wit than mine to write his praise; yet, I hope, the reputation of my pen is considerable enough to make his glorious name to survive to all ages, with that of the brave, the beautiful, and the constant Imoinda.

(Text from Abrams et al. 2000, Vol. 1: 2193, 2215)

Behn (*c.* 1640–89) was probably the first woman in England to make her living by writing. It is therefore worth observing that her female narrator here is at first apologetic and diffident but finally assertive about her role as writer and historian. Behn was herself probably in Surinam at some time, and there are some biographical and historical as well as perhaps autobiographical aspects to the work. Though broadly fictional, *Oroonoko* was commonly cited over the next hundred and fifty years in the movement to abolish slavery.

(iii) 'Hence sprung Pamela', Samuel Richardson, Pamela, or Virtue Rewarded [1740] 1753

[The author in a letter to a friend tells of the genesis of what became his first novel.]

Two booksellers, my particular friends, entreated me to write for them a little volume of letters, in a common style, on such subjects as might be of use to those country readers who were unable to indite for themselves. Will it be any harm, said I, in a piece you want to be written so low, if we should instruct them how they should think and act in common cases, as well as indite [write]? They were the more urgent with me to begin this little volume, for this hint. I set about it, & in the progress of it, writing two or three letters to instruct handsome girls, who were obliged to go out to service, as we phrase it, how to avoid the snares that might be laid against their virtue, the above story recurred to my thought; and hence sprung Pamela.

(Text in Allott 1959: 134)

Hence, too, following its tremendous success, sprung Richardson's second novel *Pamela, Part II* (1741), and a few year later his *Clarissa, or the History of a Young Lady* (1747–8), now developed into a four-way correspondence. Meanwhile, Henry Fielding, prompted by Richardson's success but sceptical of his pious motives, set to and wrote *his* first novel, *Shamela* (1741). This, the full title of which is *An Apology for the Life of Mrs Shamela Andrews*, uses a bawdy parody of the letter form to poke fun at what Fielding saw as Pamela's 'sham' virtue, hence the title and name of his heroine. Further, following the success of his parody, Fielding went on to write a sequel featuring Shamela's brother, *Joseph Andrews* (1742). Such are the complex knock-on effects of apparently simple, single causes. Richardson also needed the money and Fielding was looking for an alternative to writing for the theatres, which had just been closed down. Also see next item.

(iv) 'Whose assistance shall I invoke to direct my pen?': Henry Fielding, The History of Tom Jones, A Foundling, 1759

[The author invokes, in a mock-heroic manner, all the influences that he would like to inspire his writing.]

First, *Genius*, thou gift of Heaven, without whose aid in vain we struggle against the stream of nature. Thou who dost sow the generous seeds which art nourishes, and brings to perfection. Do thou kindly take me by the hand, and lead me through all the mazes, the winding labyrinths of nature. [. . .] Come, thou that hast inspired thy Aristophanes, thy Lucian, thy Cervantes, thy Rabelais, thy Molière, thy Shakespeare, thy Marivaux, fill my pages with humour; till mankind learn the good-nature to laugh only at the follies of others, and the humility to grieve at their own.

And thou, almost the constant attendant on true genius, *Humanity*, bring all thy tender sensations [. . .]

And thou, O *Learning* (for without thy assistance nothing pure, nothing correct, can genius produce) do thou guide my pen [. . .]

Lastly, come *Experience*, long conversant with the wise, the good, the learned, and the polite. Nor with them only, but with every kind of character, from the minister at his levée, to the bailiff in his sponging house; from the duchess at her drum, to the landlady behind her bar. From thee only can the manners of mankind be known; to which the recluse pedant, however great his parts or extensive his learning may be, hath ever been a stranger.

Come all these, and more, if possible; for arduous is the task I have under-taken; and without all your assistance, will, I find, be too heavy for me to support.

(Text from Fielding [1759] 1994: 583)

Fielding's manner here is genial but less than wholly serious, as is confirmed by the throwaway gesture at the close ('and more, if possible'). Such invocations for assis-tance were usually to the muses or god(s) in Classical and neo-Classical verse, most famously at the openings of the Homer's *Odyssey* and *Iliad* and Milton's *Paradise Lost*. The present piece is a self-conscious display of 'fine writing' stuck part way through the novel (Book XIII, Chapter I), and acts as a preamble to events that are far from solemn.

(v) The art of digression, or beginning in the middle: Laurence Sterne, **The Life and Opinions of Tristram Shandy,** *1759–67*

> Digressions, incontestably, are the sunshine – they are the life, the soul of reading; – take them out of this book for instance, – you might as well take the book along with them [. . .]
>
> For, if he [the 'historian'] is a man of the least spirit he will have fifty deviations from a straight line to make with this or that party as he goes along, which he can no ways avoid [. . .] he will moreover have various
>
> > Accounts to reconcile:
> > Anecdotes to pick up:
> > Inscriptions to make out:
> > Stories to weave in:
> > Traditions to sift:
> > Personages to call upon:
> > Panegyrics to paste up at this door: [. . .]
>
> In short, there is no end of it: for my own part, I declare I have been at it these six weeks, making all the speed I possibly could, – and I am not yet born.
>
> (Text from Sterne [1759–67] 1967: 95)

This note must be digressive, too; for how and where to get hold of it is all part of the challenge with *Tristram Shandy*. The novel *is* its digressions, and in that sense is all middle. For example, the story opens at the moment of Tristram's nearly mis(sed)-conception, and our (anti-)hero is not actually born until Volume 3. Further, even at the end of the novel (Volume 9), one of the first characters introduced is still not at all sure what is going on: 'L—d, said my mother, what is all this story about?' To which the seemingly rude but in the context perfectly proper reply is that, it is all tale of 'A COCK and a BULL – and one of the best of its kind I ever heard.' The above passage is drawn from Vol. 1, Chapters 14 and 22. But the reader should know that I could just as well – or had better – have started with, say: two black pages marking a death; a blank page for the reader to develop the character description she would prefer; a squiggle representing the verbally indescribable flourish of a stick; or a whole barrage of preludes, interludes and postludes, including an off-the-peg all-purpose dedication to a patron of your choice as well as 'a true Virgin-Dedication untried on, upon any soul living' (Vol. 1, Chapters 8 and 9). Failing that, you could have been treated to one of the mock-dissertations on everything from names to noses (e.g. Vol. 4, Chapter 1). Indeed, up until a couple of drafts ago, the text featured above was down in these notes and its place was taken by a passage from near the beginning, and before that from one near the end. Sterne would have understood and perhaps approved. Dr Johnson would probably not, however. He said of the novel that 'Nothing odd will do long. *Tristram Shandy* did not last' (1776). Evidently it has. (For the Johnson quote see p. 8 of the text cited.)

(vi) 'I thought of Mr. Pickwick': Charles Dickens [1836] 1874

[Dickens recalls all the factors that went into the idea for Pickwick Papers.*]*

The idea propounded to me was that the monthly something should be a vehicle for certain plates to be executed by Mr. Seymour; and there was a notion, either on the part of that admirable humorous artist, or of my visitor, that a NIMROD CLUB, the members of which were to go out shooting, fishing, and so forth, and getting themselves into difficulties through their want of dexterity, would be the best means of introducing these. I objected, on consideration, that although born and partly bred in the country I was no great sportsman, except in regard to all kinds of locomotion; that the idea was not novel, and had already been used; that it would be infinitely better for the plates to arise naturally out of the text; and that I would like to take my own way, with a freer range of English scenes and people, and was afraid I should ultimately do so in any case, whatever course I might prescribe to myself at starting. My views being deferred to, I thought of Mr. Pickwick, and wrote the first number; from the proof sheets of which Mr. Seymour made his drawing of the club and his happy portrait of its founder. I connected Mr. Pickwick with a club, because of the original suggestion; and I put in Mr Winkle expressly for the use of Mr. Seymour.

(Text from Forster 1874, Vol. 1, Chapter 5)

The Posthumous Papers of the Pickwick Club, commonly known as *Pickwick Papers,* was serialised in monthly instalments from April 1836 to November 1837.

(vii) 'Dependent on ourselves and each other': the Brontës

[Charlotte Brontë reflects on her childhood circumstances and family influences.]

Resident in a remote district where education had made little progress, and where, consequently, there was no inducement to seek social intercourse beyond our own domestic circle, we were wholly dependent on ourselves and each other, on books and study, for the enjoyment and occupations of life. The highest stimulus, as well as the liveliest pleasure we had known from childhood upwards, lay in attempts at literary composition; formerly we used to show each other what we wrote.

(Text from Brontë [1847] 1985: 30; and see next item)

Charlotte Brontë was here writing under the name of Currer Bell in a 'Biographical Notice of Ellis and Acton Bell' (her sisters, Emily and Anne Brontë) published in 1850. In childhood, along with their brother Branwell, the Brontë sisters wrote much joint work featuring the made-up cities 'Glasstown' and 'Angria' and the world of 'Gondal'. As a commentator observes, 'The fact that the creative activity of writing about an invented world was a joint exercise contributed enormously to the authors' enjoyment. It was a marvellous game, in which each participant eagerly ingested and responded to their sibling's latest instalment. Cooperation and competition were equally in evidence' (Howe 1999: 164).

(viii) 'Hewn in a wild workshop': of Emily Brontë's Wuthering Heights *[1847] 1850*

[Charlotte Brontë reflects on the composition of her sister's novel and its hero.]

Whether it is right or advisable to create things like Heathcliff, I do not know: I scarcely think it is. But this I know; the writer who possesses the creative gift owns something of which he is not always master – something that at times strangely wills and works for itself. He may lay down rules and devise principles, and to rules and principles it will perhaps for years lie in subjection; and then haply without any warning of revolt, there comes a time when it will no longer consent to 'harrow the vallie or be bound with a band in a furrow' – when it 'laughs at the multitude of the city, and regards not the crying of the driver' – when refusing absolutely to make ropes out of sea-sand any longer, it sets to work on statue-hewing [. . .]

Wuthering Heights was hewn in a wild workshop, with simple tools, out of homely materials. The statuary found a granite block on a solitary moor: gazing thereon, he saw how from the crag might be elicited the head, savage, swart, sinister; a form moulded with at least one element of grandeur. With time and labour, the crag took human shape; and there it stands colossal, dark and frowning, half statue, half rock; in the former sense, terrible and goblin-like; in the latter, almost beautiful, for its colouring is of mellow grey, and moorland moss clothes it; and heath, with its blooming bells and balmy fragrance, grows faithfully close to the giant's foot.

(Text from Brontë [1847] 1985: 40–1)

Charlotte Brontë was here writing in the preface to the new edition of *Wuthering Heights* (1850). This is one of the classic statements of a 'Romantic' conception of creativity by one of the (now) most acclaimed nineteenth-century novelists about another. But the passage needs to be weighed carefully: the creator's relation to her materials, methods and models are more complex and vexed than a casual reading may suggest. It should also be observed that all the sisters felt it advisable to write under male or at least non-gender-specific pseudonyms (see previous item), and that the work of all of them was attacked and dismissed as well as praised at the time. It may also be difficult to disentangle the images that the Brontës wished to project of themselves from all the myths surrounding them in popular culture, including films of the novels and Kate Bush's song of 'Wuthering Heights' (1978).

(ix) Object lessons – a scarlet letter, a ring and a book: Nathaniel Hawthorne and Robert Browning

[Two writers weave into their fictions accounts of the things that prompted them to write.]

(a) Hawthorne

But the object that most drew my attention in the mysterious package was a certain affair of fine red cloth, much worn and faded. There were traces about it of gold embroidery, which, however, was greatly frayed and defaced, so that none, or very little, of the glitter was left. It had been wrought, as was easy to perceive, with wonderful skill of needlework; and the stitch (as I am assured by ladies conversant with such mysteries) gives evidence of a now forgotten art, not to be recovered even by the process of picking out the threads. This rag of scarlet cloth – for time and wear and a sacrilegious moth had reduced it to little other than a rag – on careful examination, assumed the shape of a letter. It was the capital letter A. By an accurate measurement, each limb proved to be precisely three inches and a quarter in length. It had been intended, there could be no doubt, as an ornamental article of dress; but how it was to be worn, or what rank, honour, and dignity, in by-past times, were signified by it, was a riddle which (so evanescent are the fashions of the world in these particulars) I saw little hope of solving. And yet it strangely interested me. My eyes fastened themselves upon the old scarlet letter, and would not be turned aside. Certainly, there was some deep meaning in it, most worthy of interpretation, and which, as it were, streamed forth from the mystic symbol, subtly communicating itself to my sensibilities, but evading the analysis of my mind.

(b) Browning

Do you see this Ring?
'Tis Rome-work, made to match
(By Castellani's imitative craft)
Etrurian circlets found, some happy morn,
After a dropping April: found alive
Spark-like 'mid unearthed slope-side figtree-roots
That roof old tombs at Chiusi: soft, you see,
Yet crisp as jewel-cutting. There's one trick,
(craftsmen instruct me) one approved device
And but one, fits such slivers of pure gold
As this was, – such mere oozings from the mine,
Virgin as oval tawny pendent tear
At beehive-edge, when ripened combs o'er flow, –
To bear the file's tooth and the hammer's tap:
Since hammer needs must widen out the round,
And file emboss it fine with lily-flowers,
Ere the stuff grow a ring-thing right to wear.
That trick is the artificer melts up wax
With honey, so to speak; he mingles gold
With gold's alloy, and, duly tempering both,
Effects a manageable mass, then works.
But his work ended, once the thing a ring,
Oh, there's repristination!* Just a spirt   *making fresh/pristine*
O' the proper fiery acid o'er its face,
And forth the alloy unfastened flies in fume:
While self-sufficient now, the shape remains,
The rondure brave, the lilied loveliness,

> Gold as it was, is, shall be evermore:
> Prime nature with an added artistry –
> No carat lost, and you have gained a ring.
> What of it? 'Tis a figure, a symbol, say;
> A thing's sign: now for the thing signified.

> Do you see this square old yellow Book, [. . .]

(a) is from Nathaniel Hawthorne, 'The Custom House', *The Scarlet Letter* (1850) (Baym *et al.* 1994, Vol. 1 1265; (b) is from Robert Browning, *The Ring and the Book*, Book I, ll. 1–33 (Browning [1868] 2001: 3–4). All the objects realised in these fictions were in part prompted by objects that existed in fact and were come across by accident. In both cases the rest of the novel/poem takes the form of an extended meditation on and interpretation of their possible significance and value – for whom, when, where, how and why. Browning's long, involved and intricately crafted poem is commonly referred to as 'a psychological novel in verse'. Both Hawthorne and Browning were fully aware of then-contemporary ideas about 'symbols' and 'signs'. Much of what they say also powerfully anticipates aspects of modern sign theory/semiotics.

(x) 'The house of fiction' and 'the germ of a story': Henry James, Prefaces, 1881, 1897

[Two of the most famous images of the modern novel and of how one came into being.]

> The house of fiction has in short not one window, but a million – a number of possible windows not to be reckoned, rather; every one of which has been pierced, or is still pierceable, in its vast front, by the need of the individual vision and by the pressure of the individual will. These apertures, of dissimilar shape and size, hang so, all together, over the human scene that we might have expected of them a greater sameness of report than we find. [. . .]

> It was years ago, I remember, one Christmas Eve when I was dining with friends: a lady beside me made in the course of talk one of those allusions that I have always found myself recognising on the spot as 'germs'. The germ, wherever gathered, has ever for me been the germ of a 'story', and most of the stories straining to shape under my hand have sprung from a single small seed, a seed as minute and windborne as that casual hint for 'The Spoils of Poynton' dropped unwittingly by my neighbour, a mere floating particle in the stream of talk. What above all comes back to me with this reminiscence is the sense of the inveterate minuteness, on such happy occasions, of the precious particle – reduced, that is, to its mere fruitful essence. Such is the interesting truth about the stray suggestion, the wandering word, the vague echo, at touch of which the novelist's imagination winces as at the prick of some sharp point: its virtue is all in its needle-like quality, the power to penetrate as finely as possible.

From the Prefaces to, respectively, *The Portrait of a Lady* (1881) and *The Spoils of Poynton*

(1897), as first printed in the New York edition of the *Novels and Stories of Henry James* (1907–17), Volumes 3 and 10; also in Allott, 1959: 131–2, 138–9.

(xi) 'Why I wrote The Yellow Wallpaper?': Charlotte Perkins Gilman [1892] 1913

Now the story of the story is this:
    For many years I suffered from a severe and continuous nervous breakdown tending to melancholia – and beyond. During about the third year of this trouble I went, in devout faith and some faint stir of hope, to a noted specialist in nervous diseases, the best known in the country. This wise man put me to bed and applied the rest cure, to which a still-good physique responded so promptly that he concluded there was nothing much the matter with me, and sent me home with solemn advice to 'live as domestic a life as far as possible,' to 'have but two hours intellectual life a day,' and 'never to touch pen, brush, or pencil again' as long as I lived. This was in 1887.
    I went home and obeyed those directions for some three months, and came so near the borderline of utter mental ruin that I could see over.
    Then, using the remnants of intelligence that remained, and helped by a wise friend, I cast the noted specialist's advice to the winds and went to work again – work, the normal life of every human being; work, in which is joy and growth and service, without which one is a pauper and a parasite – ultimately recovering a measure of power. Being naturally moved to rejoicing by this narrow escape, I wrote *The Yellow Wallpaper*. [. . .]
    It was not intended to drive people crazy, but to save people from being driven crazy, and it worked.

'Why I wrote *The Yellow Wallpaper?*' appeared in the October 1913 issue of *The Forerunner*; the story itself was first published in January 1892 in the *New England Magazine*.

(xii) The Moths becomes The Waves: Virginia Woolf, 1929–31

[Woolf talks about 'the same novel' when beginning it and when near the end.]

Tuesday May 28th (1929)

Now about this book, *The Moths* [the initial working title for what became *The Waves*]. How am I begin to it? And what is it to be? I feel no great impulse: no fever; only a great pressure of difficulty. Why write it then? Why write at all? Every morning I write a little sketch to amuse myself. I am not saying, I might say, that these sketches have any relevance. I am not trying to tell a story. Yet perhaps it might be done in that way. A mind thinking. They might be islands of light – islands in the stream that I am trying to convey: life itself going on. The current of the moths flying strongly this way. A lamp and a flower pot in the centre. The flower can always be changing. But there must be more unity between each scene than I can find at present. Autobiography it might be called. How am I to make one lap or act, between the coming of the moths, more intense than another; if there are only scenes? One must get the sense that this is the beginning; this is the middle; that the climax – when she opens the window and the moth comes in. I shall have two different currents – the moths flying along; the flowers upright in the centre; a perpetual crumbling and renewing of the plant, In its leaves she might see things happen. But who is she? [. . .]

Saturday, February 7th (1931)

What interests me in the last stage was the freedom and boldness with which my imagination picked up, used and tossed aside all the images, symbols which I had prepared. I am sure that this is the right way of using them – not in set pieces, as I had tried at first, coherently, but simply as images, never making them work out: only suggest. Thus I hope to have kept the sound of the sea and the birds, dawn and garden subconsciously present, doing their work underground.

> (From Virginia Woolf, *A Writer's Diary* (1953);
> also Allott, 1959: 142–3, 157–8)

(xii) 'from their fragments can come something new': Doris Lessing, *The Golden Notebook [1962] 1973*

The shape of the novel is as follows:
   There is a skeleton, or frame, called *Free Women*, which is a conventional short novel, about 60,000 words long, and which could stand by itself. But it is divided into five sections and separated by stages of the four Notebooks, Black, Red, Yellow and Blue. The notebooks are kept by Anna Wulf, a central character of *Free Women*. She keeps four, and not one because, as she recognises, she has to separate things off from each other, out of fear of chaos, of formlessnes – of breakdown. Pressures, inner and outer, end the Notebooks; a heavy black line is drawn across the page of one after another. But now that they are finished, from their fragments can come something new, *The Golden Notebook*.

> (Lessing [1962] 1973: 7)

(xiii) On the 'experimental novel': Porter and Barth

(a)

> The Creation had
> to find room for the exper-
> imental novel

(b)

That a great many Western artists for a great many years have quarreled with received definitions of artistic media, genres and forms goes without saying: pop art, dramatic and musical 'happenings', the whole range of 'intermedia' or 'mixed means' art, bear recentest witness to the tradition of rebelling against the Tradition. A catalogue I received some time ago in the mail, for example, advertises such items as Robert Filliou's *Ample Food for Stupid Thought*, a box full of postcards on which are inscribed 'apparently meaningless questions', to be mailed to whomever the purchaser judges them suited for; Ray Johnson's *Paper Snake*, a collection of whimsical writings, 'often pointed', once mailed to various friends (what the catalogue describes as The New York Correspondence School of Literature) and Daniel Spoerri's *Anecdoted Typography of Chance*, 'on the surface' a description of all the objects that happen to be on the author's parlour table – in fact, however . . . 'a cosmology of Spoerri's existence'.

'On the surface', at least, the document listing these items is a catalogue of The Something Else Press, a swinging outfit. 'In fact, however', it may be one of their offerings, for all I know. In any case, their wares are lively to read about, and make for interesting conversation in fiction-writing classes, for example, where we discuss Somebody-or-other's unbound, unpaginated, randomly assembled novel-in-a-box and the desirability of printing *Finnegans Wake* on a very long roller-towel. It's easier and sociabler to talk technique than it is to make art, and the area of 'happenings' and their kin is mainly a way of discussing aesthetics, really; illustrating 'dramatically' more or less valid and interesting points about the nature of art and the definition of its terms and genres.

(a) is a 'haiku' by Peter Porter from his *Japaneses Jokes* (1983); (b) is from John Barth's essay 'The literature of exhaustion' (1967), in Bradbury, 1990: 71–2. An example of just such a 'novel-in-a-box' is B. S. Johnson's *The Unfortunates* (1969).

(xiv) 'Chutnification': Salman Rushdie, Midnight's Children, 1981

What is required for chutnification? Raw materials, obviously – fruit, vegetables, fish, vinegar, spices. Daily visits from Koli women with their saris hitched up between their legs. Cucumbers (like his nose, for instance), aubergines, mint. [. . .] and above all a nose capable of discerning the hidden languages of what-must-be-pickled, its humours and messages and emotions. [. . .] I am able to include memories, dream, ideas. [. . .] There is also the matter of the spice bases. The intricacies of turmeric and cumin, the subtlety of fenugreek, when to use large (and when small) cardamoms; their myriad possible effects of garlic, garam masala, stick cinnamon, coriander, ginger . . . not to mention the flavourful contributions of the occasional speck of dirt. (Saleem is no longer obsessed with purity.) In the spice bases, I reconcile myself to the inevitable distortions of the pickling process. [. . .] The art is to change the flavour in degree, but not in kind; and above all (in my thirty jars and a jar) to give it shape and form – that is to say, meaning.

(Text from Rushdie 1981: 460–1)

'Chutnification' is an instance of what Mark Wormald calls 'the intimate and homely preserving work of creativity' in Mengham 1999: 198.

(xv) 'My writing expects, demands participatory reading', Toni Morrison, 1983

The language has to be quiet; it has to engage your participation. I never describe characters very much. My writing expects, demands participatory reading, and that is what I think literature is supposed to do. It's not just about telling the story; it's about involving the reader. The reader supplies the emotions. The reader supplies some of the color, some of the sound. My language has to have holes and spaces so the reader can come into it. He or she can feel something visceral, see something striking. Then we – you, the reader, and I, the author – come together to make this book, to feel this experience.

(From an interview with Toni Morrison in Tate 1985: 125)

(xvi) 'And if the writer and reader . . . have that connection', Amy Tan, 1996

So why do I write?

Because my childhood disturbed me, made me ask foolish questions. And the questions still echo. Why does my mother always talk about killing herself? Why did my father and brother have to die? If I die, can I be reborn into a happy family? Those early obsessions led me to a belief that writing could be my salvation, providing me with the sort of freedom and danger, satisfaction and discomfort, truth and contradiction I can't find in anything else in life.

I write to discover the past for myself. I don't write to change the future for others. [. . .] Writing for me is an act of faith, a hope that I will discover what I mean by 'truth'. I also think of reading as an act of faith, a hope that I will discover something remarkable about ordinary life, about myself. And if the writer and the reader discover the same thing, if they have that connection, the act of faith has resulted in an act of magic. To me, that's the mystery and the wonder of both life and fiction – the connection between the two individuals who discover in the end that they are more the same than different.

And if that doesn't happen, it's nobody's fault. There are still plenty of books on the shelf. Choose what you like.

From Amy Tan's essay 'In the canon for all the wrong reasons' (1996), reproduced in Charters and Charters, 2001: 725. In a later interview, after her mother's death, Tan said: 'I was afraid that when my mother died, I'd lost my muse. But she was more than that. She's a voice within' (Channel 5, UK, 17 April 2001).

Chaoses – some critical moments

Here are four texts, each of which wrestles with 'chaos' of a particular kind at a different moment. Each text is 'critical' in that it offers a critical perspective on as well as a creative enactment of the issues in play; each moment is 'critical' in that it occurs at a time of radical and rapid social change. The first passage is from Milton's *Paradise Lost* (1667) and draws on Classical and Biblical materials to register the republican author's sense of the chaos and confusion following the collapse of the Commonwealth. The second text is a selection of extracts from Pope's poetry, ranging from *An Essay on Criticism* (1711) to *The Dunciad* (1743). These express Pope's essentially neo-Classical and conservative senses of what he considers to be 'chaos' and 'anarchy' – and conversely 'order' and 'reason' – in both poetry and society. The third passage is from Blake's *The Four Zoas* (1797). This projects a phantasmagoric image of Urizen, the paternalistic principle of rationalist law and order, as he strives to keep the world in shape according to his own 'scientific' principles. Blake was writing this at a moment when the French Revolution was perceived to be poised between 'triumph' and 'terror'. The fourth passage is from an essay by the contemporary poet and novelist Michèle Roberts. Hers is a specifically woman-centred vision of the role played by 'chaos' in the process of creation conceived as a kind of birth; and it resonates with the work of Cixous, Kristeva, Ward Jouve and others working in and around a French feminist tradition.

All the writers featured in this section give a creative as well as critical insight into what it means to be working at 'the edge of chaos'. Also relevant are Edna St Vincent Millay's sonnet 'I will put Chaos into fourteen lines' and the various constructions of 'chaosmos' offered by Deleuze and Guattari and Magda Cârneci (see above pp. 5–6, and below p. 269). We approach such issues through contemporary theories of chaos, complexity and emergence in Chapter 4, and they are traced through metaphors and stories of chaos in ancient and modern creation myths in Chapter 5.

(i) 'His dark materials to create more Worlds': John Milton, Paradise Lost, 1667

[Satan, passing through the gates of Hell and heading for the new world created for Mankind, surveys the intervening Chaos.]

> [I]n sudden view appear
> The secrets of the hoary deep, a dark
> Illimitable Ocean without bound,
> Without dimension, where length, breadth, and height,
> And time and place are lost: where eldest Night
> And Chaos, ancestors of Nature, hold
> Eternal Anarchy, amidst the noise
> Of endless wars, and by confusion stand.
> For Hot, Cold, Moist, and Dry, four champions fierce
> Strive here for mastery, and to battle bring
> Their embryon atoms; they around the flag
> Of each his faction, in their several clans,
> Light-armed or heavy, sharp, smooth, swift or slow,
> Swarm populous, unnumbered as the sands
> Of Barca or Cyrene's torrid soil,
> Levied to side with warring winds, and poise
> Their lighter wings. To whom these most adhere,
> He rules a moment; Chaos umpire sits
> And by decision more embroils the fray
> By which he reigns: next his high arbiter
> Chance governs all. Into this wild Abyss,
> The Womb of Nature and perhaps her grave,
> Of neither sea, nor shore, nor air, nor fire,
> But all of these in their pregnant causes mixed
> Confus'dly, and which this must ever fight,

Unless th' Almighty Maker them ordain
His dark materials to create more Worlds,
Into the wild Abyss the wary fiend
Stood on the brink of Hell and looked a while
Pondering his voyage; for no narrow frith*   *channel/firth*
He had to cross.

(From *Paradise Lost*, Book II, ll. 890–920)

In its late seventeenth-century context, Milton's sense of chaos is usually associated with the confusion caused by the collapse of the English Revolution. The poem was composed over the period between the end of the Commonwealth (of which Milton had been an advocate) and the beginning of the Restoration of the monarchy (to which he remained opposed). In terms of literary and philosophical tradition, it draws on such classical materialists as Lucretius and Heraclitus for its vision of 'embryon atoms' (see Chapter 4). From a late twentieth-century perspective, however, as a modern commentator points out, 'Milton's conception of chaos in *Paradise Lost* [. . .] comes arguably closest to [. . .] a radical conception of material' suspended between 'quantum-mechanical' and 'chaos-theoretical' models (Plotnitsky in Wolfreys 2001: 280–2). But even that is by no means the end of the story. Philip Pullman's *His Dark Materials* trilogy (1995–9) expressly recalls the phrase in the above passage, and Lord Azriel, one of his main adult heroes, has much in common with the energetic life-force that William Blake had also intuited Milton's Satan to be (as noted below in iii).

(ii) 'dread Chaos and eternal Night': Alexander Pope, 1711, 1733–4, 1743

['Chaos' vexes and perplexes Pope throughout his poetry. It is something he both censures and mocks; but also, evidently, something he feels he must brace himself against as a measure of his own stan- dards and tastes.]

(a)

Some to conceit* alone their taste confine   *witty images*
And glittering thoughts struck out at every line.
Pleased with a work where nothing's just or fit,
One glaring chaos and wild heap of wit.
Poets, like painters, thus unskilled to trace
The naked nature and the living grace,
With gold and jewels cover every part
And hide with ornaments their want* of art.   *lack*
True wit is nature to advantage dressed,
What oft was thought but ne'er so well expressed.

(b)

Know then thyself, presume not God to scan;
The proper study of Mankind is Man.
Plac'd on this isthmus of a middle state,

A being darkly wise and rudely great: [. . .]
He hangs between; in doubt to act, or rest,
In doubt to deem himself a God, or Beast;
In doubt he mind or body to prefer,
Born but to die, and reasoning but to err;
Alike in ignorance, his reason such,
Whether he thinks too little or too much;
Chaos of thought and passion, all confused;
Still by himself abused or disabused;
Created half to rise, and half to fall;
Great lord of all things, yet a prey to all;
Sole judge of Truth, in endless Error hurled:
The glory, jest and riddle of the world!

(c)

Yet, yet a moment, one dim ray of light
Indulge, dread Chaos and eternal Night!
Of darkness visible so much be lent,
As half to show, half veil, the deep intent,
Ye pow'rs! Whose mysteries restored I sing,
To whom Time bears me on his rapid wing,
Suspend a while your force inertly strong,
Then take at once the poet and the song [. . .]
In vain, in vain – the all-composing Hour
Resistless falls. The Muse obeys the Power.
She* comes! she comes! The sable throne behold   *['Dullness']*
Of Night primeval and of Chaos old!
Before her, Fancy's gilded clouds decay,
And all its varying rainbows die away.
Wit shoots in vain its momentary fires,
The meteor drops, and in a flash expires. [. . .]
Lo! Thy dread Empire, CHAOS! is restored;
Light dies before thy uncreating word;
Thy hand, great Anarch! Lets the curtain fall,
And universal darkness buries all.

(a) is from Pope's *An Essay on Criticism* (1711), ll. 289–98; (b) is from his *An Essay on Man* (1733–4), Epistle II, ll. 1–17; and (c) is from *The Dunciad* (1743), Book IV, ll. 1–8, 627–34, 653–6 (all texts are from Pope 1965). Because of his neatly antithetical cast of mind and verse, as well as his tendency to make a statement and then promptly deflect or redirect it, the precise point of Pope's criticisms is often veiled. None the less, the aesthetic temper of his work is broadly neo-Classical and its politics basically conservative, in that he promotes the virtues of order, discipline, propriety, reason and learning. Conversely, he is unfailingly suspicious and often downright cynical about what he perceives as kinds of vice: disorderly and improper behaviour, unruly emotion and untutored expression. (Stereotypically, these are what came to be positively revalued and identified with 'the Romantics'; but, as the next section shows, *real* Romantic writers were quite different. Byron, for example, greatly admired Pope's verse.)

(iii) 'Creating many a Vortex, fixing many a Science': William Blake, 1795–1804

Oft would he* sit in a dark rift & regulate his books,   [*Urizen*]
Or sleep such sleep as spirits eternal, wearied in his dark
Tearful & sorrowful state; then rise, look out & ponder
His dismal voyage, eyeing the next sphere tho' far remote;
Then darting into the Abyss of night his venturous limbs
Thro' lightnings, thunders, earthquakes & concussions, fires & floods
Stemming his downward fall, labouring up against futurity,
Creating many a Vortex, fixing many a Science in the deep,
And thence throwing his venturous limbs into the vast unknown,
Swift, swift from Chaos to chaos, from void to void, a road immense.
For when he came to where a Vortex ceas'd to operate,
Nor down nor up remain'd, then if he turn'd and look'd back
From whence he came; 'twas upward all; & if he turn'd and view'd
The unpass'd void, upward was still his mighty wand'ring
The midst between, an Equilibrium grey of air serene
Where he might live in peace & where his life might meet repose.
                                        (Text from Blake 1972: 316)

Blake worked on *The Four Zoas*, which was initially called *Vala or The Death and Judgement of the Ancient Man, a Dream of Nine Nights*, for nearly ten years (1795–1804) and never finally prepared it for publication. Along with the Bible and various mystical religious and dissenting political writings, a major influence on Blake was Milton, of whom he said in *The Marriage of Heaven and Hell*, Plates 5 and 6 (1790–3), 'The reason Milton wrote in fetters when he wrote of Angels & God, and at liberty when of Devils & Hell, is because he was a true Poet and of the Devil's party without knowing it.' In fact Blake claimed direct inspiration from Milton in the writing of his *Milton: A Poem in Two Books* (1803–8). Like Milton's, Blake's vision of chaos both recalls ancient materialist science and appears to anticipate some of the insights of modern chaos theory (see the note on Milton above). But Blake gives the whole thing – including the 'Void' – his own particular twist. His theory of 'Vortexes', for example, at once recalls and critiques seventeenth- and eighteenth-century mechanics and mechanistic philosophy.

(iv) 'Out of this chaos of feeling . . . we learn to create something beautiful': Michèle Roberts, 1998

My myth of speaking and writing (a myth, an explanation on the level of poetry, a psychic 'truth') is that we learn to use language as a kind of birth into absence. The mother, the all-giving breast, is not there: out of terrible feelings of physical pain, rage felt in the body, we learn to say 'I want', to try and summon back the life-giving presence which nourishes us and without which we die. [. . .] Out of this chaos of feeling, out of this overwhelming sadness at absence, we learn to create something beautiful: our words, later on our gifts, later still our works of art. We re-create the mother inside ourselves, over and over again.

(From Michèle Roberts's essay 'On inspiration and writing', Roberts 1998: 20–2)

Such a productively 'chaotic' view of creation as birth resonates with the more specifically woman-centred views of procreation and some of the dynamics of 'fe<>male' creativity considered in Chapter 3, especially those of Cixous, Kristeva and Ward Jouve; also compare Mother Julian of Norwich above, pp. 203–4.

Real Romantic writers

Perhaps the greatest obstacles to a genuinely critical and historical understanding of creativity is the persistent stereotype of the 'Romantic writer' and the 'Romantic artist'. For one thing, this is thoroughly inappropriate when applied to more ancient or modern notions of creativity and to other, especially non-European cultures. For another, it is highly inaccurate and deeply misleading as an account of what writers and artists of the Romantic period actually did and how they really saw their work. It also has to be borne in mind that 'romantic' has a range of complex and partly contradictory meanings (see Williams 1983: 274–6 and *OED*). 'Romance' initially referred to all those countries most immediately affected by the *Roman* Empire; hence the Romance languages and cultures of Italy, Spain and France. Thereafter it came to be identified with the medieval tales of chivalric adventure that came from those countries (i.e. 'Romances'), including those concerned with *fin amor* (refined loving, 'courtly love') such as *The Romance of the Rose*. The latter gave the term a twist towards the modern sense of 'romantic' meaning 'amorous' or 'with a love interest'. At the same time, because many of these stories of knightly adventure and courtly love were brought back from the East by the crusaders, the term acquired an exotic and potentially dangerous tinge (hence the notion of 'the Romantic East', enticing but treacherous); and this in turn got mixed up with the perilous appeal of 'Romany gypsies' for good measure (who hailed from Romania, another ex-Roman colony with a Romance language).

The problem with casual notions of the Romantic artist/writer is that all these various senses of Romance tend to get jumbled up and then dumped on something equally confused called 'the Romantic period'. And the latter, notwithstanding the beguiling reassurance of the definite article and the singular noun, quickly turns out to be both historically imprecise and culturally shifty. The 'Romantic movements' in music and painting and literature, for example, are reckoned to start and end at all sorts of different times between the mid-eighteenth and early twentieth centuries. They include everything from German *Sturm und Drang* to French Impressionism, with the grandeur of Tchaikovsky or the clamour of Mahler for good measure (see next chapter). Most historians, meanwhile, tend to avoid the term Romantic completely: they prefer to talk of 'Revolutions' (political, industrial and scientific) or the rise and fall of 'Empires' or 'Nationalism' (which at least recognises some of the things that Romantic artists and writers were involved in, often passionately).

So what is so deeply wrong about common (mis)conceptions of the Romantic artist/writer? And what did those writers we now call Romantic actually do and think and say? First, the stereotype: everyone instantly recognises it, but few realise it comes from a very narrow and remarkably recent phase of cultural history. Stereotypically, the 'romantic artist' lives in a garret, starves for his art and is, by the neat and necessarily contradictory logic of aesthetic elevation and social exclusion, both a great genius and greatly misunderstood. It goes without saying that 'he' is indeed a man – a lone hero and, by extension, a loner and social misfit. In the *super*-romantic scenario, he is also likely to be a drug-addict and/or a drunkard and/or suffering from some terminal, preferably wasting, disease. In any event, he dies young, ideally in poverty and still woefully misunderstood. *But not before he has finished all – or at least most – of his magnum opus.* The latter assures his artistic or literary immortality; while the 'life' – and 'death' – ensure he gets his due share of notoriety and sympathy. End of story: beginning of mythical after-life.

The only thing wrong with this is just about everything. What is more, as already intimated, this view of the great artist as outsider (and therefore above, to one side or simply incidental to everything else) is of very late date. It derives from a much-reduced and crudely simplified version of the late nineteenth-century notion of the 'artist as genius' and 'art for art's sake' (these are discussed at various points in Chapters 1, 2 and 4). In fact, historically, the full-blown concept of 'the Romantic artist' appears at a time well after the main flourishing of Romanticism (however defined) and is, if anything, the merely minor and marginal counterpoint to later aesthetic and social movements chiefly dedicated to kinds of naturalism and realism. Thus even Colin Wilson, the author of *The Outsider*, 'the classic study of alienation, creativity and the mind of modern man' (as it says on the blurb), is obliged to admit: 'The Outsider may be an artist, but the artist is not necessarily an Outsider' (Wilson 1978: 25).

What follows, then, are some preliminary indications of what real – and really major – Romantic writers actually thought and said about what they were doing. In *education*, the emphasis was upon free expression and independence of mind but within a context of thorough information and careful cultivation (Rousseau's 'emotional education' on 'back to nature' principles was much tempered in practice and greatly exaggerated in retrospect). In *politics*, party-political affiliations and (inter)national aims differed widely – sometimes wildly – but the overall tenor was of a committed engagement with the pressing issues of inequality, injustice and violence. *Socially*, therefore, the artist (as artisan) and the poet (as maker) were seen to be thoroughly implicated in, not incidental to, the fundamental processes of social transformation, of ideas and values along with the material conditions of people's lives. In *religion*, meanwhile, the spectrum ranged from atheist to pantheist, and from ecstatic revelation to established church (from Blake and Shelley to Wordsworth and Coleridge, for example, with these last two briefly entertaining some of the former and settling on the last). Meanwhile, even Byron and Percy Shelley, who had earned a reputation for being radicals and rebels – whom the poet laureate Robert Southey dubbed 'the Satanic School' of poets, to which they retorted with the label 'the Lakers' for him, Wordsworth and others with a penchant for Lakeland pastoral – were both relatively well off and, in Lord Byron's case, an aristocrat and heir to a substantial estate. Certainly, neither belonged to the class of artisans (like Blake the engraver and Keats who trained as an apothecary) or rural labourers (like Clare, who promptly got dubbed a 'peasant poet'). To be sure, Shelley and Byron died quite young: Shelley of drowning at twenty-nine and Byron of a fever at thirty-six. But even that needs to be seen in the context of a general mortality in the late forties and of infant mortality under two years of one in three.

In short, as the following texts abundantly attest, **real** *romantic writers* were not **stereotypical** 'romantic writers' at all. They were much more interesting, and much more significant. Also, though they were highly individual and even idiosyncratic, they were far more socially engaged and deeply implicated in one another's lives and works than the cartoon image of the 'lone creator' remotely suggests. For this reason, I have chosen to highlight the interrelations – and in some sense the 'co-operations' – among a specific group of writers: William Godwin and Mary Wollstonecraft as husband and wife; Mary Wollstonecraft Shelley, their daughter, and Percy Shelley, her husband; and George Gordon Byron, their friend and fellow traveller. I have also included John Keats (who was a friend of Shelley) for what he says about his own (and Wordsworth's) writing. Samuel Taylor Coleridge comes in under 'Dreams and drugs' in the next section; and one of John Clare's poems, a sonnet, appears in that section earlier on. Together, all these writers and their writings help throw some very various, direct and oblique lights on the matter of what it is to be a 'creative writer' at any time. They also help us see what it meant and felt like to be a writer in their own.

(i) 'The mind is not, cannot be created by the teacher, though it may be cultivated': Mary Wollstonecraft, 1787

It is an old but very true observation, that the human mind must be employed. A relish for reading, or any of the fine arts, should be cultivated very early in life; and those who reflect can tell, of what importance it is for the mind to have some resource in itself, and not to be entirely dependent upon the senses for employment and amusement. [. . .]

I would have everyone try to form an opinion of an author themselves, though modesty may restrain them from mentioning it. Many are so anxious to have the reputation of taste, that they only praise the authors whose merit is indisputable. I am sick of hearing of the sublimity of Milton, the elegance and harmony of Pope, and the original, untaught genius of Shakespeare. These cursory remarks are made by some who know nothing of nature, and could not enter into the spirit of these authors, or understand them. [. . .]

It may be observed, that I recommend the mind's being put into a proper train, and then left to itself. Fixed rules cannot be given, it must depend upon the nature and strength of the understanding; and those who observe it can best tell what kind of cultivation will improve it. The mind is not, cannot be created by the teacher, though it may be cultivated, and its real powers found out.

From the chapter on 'Reading' in *Thoughts on the Education of Daughters* (1787) (Breen, 1996: 5–6). Mary Wollstonecraft married William Godwin in 1797 and, as the next passage confirms, they had a profound influence on one another's work. She died from complications following the birth of her second daughter, the future Mary Wollstonecraft Shelley (featured in (iv) below).

(ii) 'Study with desire is real activity': William Godwin, 1797

The true object of juvenile education is to provide, against [by] the age of five and twenty, a mind well regulated, active, and prepared to learn. Whatever will inspire habits of industry and observation, will sufficiently answer this purpose. Is it not possible to find something that will fulfil these conditions, the benefit of which a child shall understand, and the acquisition of which he may be taught to desire? Study with desire is real activity: without desire it is but the semblance and mockery of activity. Let us not forget, in the eagerness of our haste to educate, the ends of education. [. . .]

According to the received modes of education, the master goes first, and the pupil follows. According to the method here recommended, it is probable that the pupil should go first and the master follow. The first object of a system of instructing is to give the pupil a motive to learn. [. . .] This plan is calculated entirely to change the face of education. The whole formidable apparatus which has hitherto attended it, is swept away. Strictly speaking, no such characters are left upon the scene as either preceptor or pupil. The boy, like the man, studies because he desires it. He proceeds upon a plan of his own invention, or which, by adopting, he has made his own. Everything bespeaks independence and equality. The man, as well as the boy, would be glad in cases of difficulty to consult a person more informed than himself. That the boy is accustomed almost always to consult the man, and not the man the boy, is to be regarded rather as an accident than anything essential.

(From William Godwin, *The Enquirer* (1797),
as reproduced in Ward 1991: 44–5)

Godwin expressly tells his readers that *The Enquirer* was largely the result of conversation in general, and of conversations with Mary Wollstonecraft in particular: 'The author has always had a passion for colloquial discussion [. . .] there is a vivacity and, if he may be permitted to say it, a richness in the hints struck out in conversation, that are with difficulty attained in any other method' (see Ward, p. 33 and previous item).

(iii) 'I bid my hideous progeny go forth': Mary Shelley, 1831

[By way of an 'Author's Introduction' to her Frankenstein, or The Modern Prometheus, *Mary Shelley tells how she, her husband Percy, Lord Byron and a doctor friend, Polidori, contrived to pass the time during wet days in Switzerland.]*

But it proved a wet, ungenial summer, and incessant rain often confined us for days to the house. Some volumes of ghost stories, translated from the German into French, fell into our hands. [. . .] 'We will each write a ghost story', said Lord Byron, and his proposition was acceded to. There were four of us. The noble author [Byron] began a tale, a fragment of which he printed at the end of his poem *Mazeppa*. Shelley, more apt to embody ideas in the radiance of brilliant imagery, and in the music of the most melodious verse that adorns our language, than to invent the machinery of a story, commenced one founded on the experiences of his early life. Poor Polidori had some terrible idea about a skull-headed lady [. . .]

I busied myself to *think of a story* – a story to rival those which had excited us to this task. One which would speak to the mysterious fears of of our nature and awaken thrilling horror – one to make the reader dread to look round, to curdle the blood, and quicken the beatings of the heart. If I did not accomplish these things, my ghost story would be unworthy of its name. I thought and pondered – vainly. I felt that blank incapability of invention which is the greatest misery of authorship, when dull Nothing replies to our anxious invocation. 'Have you thought of a story?' I was asked each morning, and each morning I was forced to reply with a mortifying negative. [. . .]

Many and long were the conversations between Lord Byron and Shelley, to which I was a devout but nearly silent listener. During one of these, various philosophical doctrines were discussed, and among others the nature of the principle of life, and whether there was any probability of its ever being discovered and communicated. They talked of the experiments of Dr [Erasmus] Darwin (I speak not of what the Doctor really did, or said that he did, but, as more to my purpose, of what was then spoken of as having been done by him), who preserved a piece of vermicelli in a glass case, till by some extraordinary means it began to move with voluntary motion. Not thus, after all, would life be given. Perhaps a corpse would be reanimated: galvanism had given token of such things: perhaps the component parts of a creature might be manufactured, brought together, and endued with vital warmth.

Night waned upon this talk, and even the witching hour had gone by, before we retired to rest. When I placed my head on my pillow, I did not sleep, nor could I be said to think. My imagination, unbidden, possessed and guided me, gifting the successive images that arose in my mind with a vividness far beyond the bounds of usual reverie. I saw – with shut eyes but acute mental vision – I saw the pale student of unhallowed arts kneeling beside the thing he had put together. I saw the hideous phantasm of a man stretched out, and then, on the working of some powerful engine, show signs of life, and stir with an uneasy, half-vital motion. [. . .]

At first I thought but a few pages – of a short tale; but Shelley urged me to develop the idea at greater length. I certainly did not owe the suggestion of one incident, nor scarcely of one train of thought, to my husband, and yet but for his incitement it would never have taken the form in which it was presented to the world. From this declaration I must except the preface [of 1818]. As far as I can recollect, it was entirely written by him.

And now, once again, I bid my hideous progeny go forth and prosper. I have affection for it, for it was the offspring of happy days, when death and grief were but words which found no true echo in my heart. Its several pages speak of many a walk, many a drive, and many a conversation, when I was not alone; and my companion was one who, in this world, I shall never see more. But this is for myself: my readers have nothing to do with these associations.

(Text from M. Shelley [1831] 1993: Appendix A: 192–7)

Mary Shelley's *Frankenstein, or The Modern Prometheus* was worked up for publication during 1816–17 and first published in 1818. As mentioned above, this included a Preface by her husband, Percy. The present 'Author's Introduction' was written by

Mary herself for the 1831 edition. The story of the novel's composition and its first appearance as a story told to a small group of friends and family is interesting in many ways. As well as prompting further reflection on 'creators', 'creation' and 'creatures' (the monster is hardly referred to as such but usually as Frankenstein's 'creature' or 'creation'), it raises other important issues discussed elsewhere in the present book: 'games' of competition and collaboration; the relations between reading and writing and genre; and the process of composition and the nature of conversation. There's even an account of writer's block ('that blank incapability of invention') and some intimations of how to get unblocked (talk to people, wait, rest, do something else for a while).

(iv) 'Poets, . . . in one sense, the creators and, in another, the creations of their age': Percy Shelley, 1820, 1821

(a)

A poet is the combined product of such internal powers as modify the nature of others; and of such external influences as excite and sustain these powers; he is not one, but both. Every man's mind is, in this respect, modified by all the objects of nature and art, by every word and every suggestion which he ever admitted to act upon his consciousness; it is the mirror upon which all forms are reflected, and in which they compose one form. Poets, not otherwise than philosophers, painters, sculptors and musicians, are, in one sense, the creators and, in another, the creations of their age.

(b)

And, although all men observe a similar, they observe not the same order, in the motions of the dance, in the melody of the song, in the combinations of language, in the series of their imitations of natural objects. For there is a certain order or rhythm belonging to each of these classes of mimetic representation, from which the hearer and the spectator receive an intenser and purer pleasure than from any other. [. . .] Those in whom it [a sense of order or rhythm] exists in excess are poets, in the most universal sense of the word; and the pleasure resulting from the manner in which they express the influence of society or nature upon their own minds, communicates itself to others and gathers a sort of reduplication from that community.

(Texts from P. Shelley 1991: 56, 206)

(a) is from Percy Shelley's preface to *Prometheus Unbound* (published 1820), for which see above p. 159; (b) is from his *A Defence of Poetry* (composed 1821, published 1840). In 1816 Percy Shelley married Mary, the daughter of Mary Wollstonecraft and William Godwin (for whom see the earlier items in this section).

(v) 'A Poet . . . the most unpoetical of all God's Creatures': John Keats, 1818

A Poet is the most unpoetical of any thing in existence, because he has no identity – he is continually in for – and filling some other Body – The Sun, the Moon, the Sea, and Men and Women who are creatures of impulse are poetical and have about them an unchangeable attribute – the poet has none; no identity – he is certainly the most unpoetical of all God's creatures. If then he has no self, and if I am a Poet, where is the wonder that I should say I would write no more? [. . .] It is a wretched thing to confess; but it is a very fact that not one word I ever utter can be taken for granted as an opinion growing out of my identical nature – how can it, when I have no nature? When I am in a room with People if ever I am free from speculating on creations of my own brain, then not myself goes home to myself; but the identity of every one in the room begins [so] to press upon me that I am in a very little time annihilated – not only among Men: it would be the same in a Nursery of children.

(From a letter of John Keats to Richard Woodhouse, 27 October 1818, in Abrams *et al.* 2000, Vol. 2: 894–5)

In the same letter Keats insists that his own understanding of poetry should be 'distinguished from the Wordsworthian or egotistical sublime, which is a thing per se and stands alone.' Keats further defines his own position in a letter he wrote to George and Thomas Keats around 12 December 1817: 'several things dovetailed in my mind, & at once it struck me, what quality went to form a Man of Achievement especially in Literature & which Shakespeare possessed so enormously – I mean *Negative Capability*, that is when man is capable of being in uncertainties, Mysteries, doubts, without any irritable reaching after fact & reason –'. The distinctions between the 'Egotistical Sublime' and 'Negative Capability' are sometimes applied to kinds of writer and writing beyond the Romantic period; though even there, of course, they only tell part of the story – Keats's. Wordsworth had a lot of other things to say for and about himself over a much longer life.

(vi) 'This is the patent-age of new inventions': George Gordon, Lord Byron, 1819

[Byron offers a critical review of some of the most celebrated inventions and discoveries of his age. Explanatory notes appear below.]

What opposite discoveries we have seen!
   (Signs of true genius, and of empty pockets)
One makes new noses,[1] one a guillotine,
   One breaks your bones, one sets them in their sockets,
But vaccination certainly has been
   A kind antithesis to Congreve's[2] rockets,
With which the doctor[3] paid off an old pox
By borrowing a new one from an ox.

Bread has been made (indifferent) from potatoes;
   And galvanism[4] has set some corpses grinning,
But has not answered like the apparatus[5]
   Of the Humane Society's beginning,

By which men are unsuffocated gratis:
   What wondrous new machines have late been spinning![6]
I said the small-pox has gone out of late,
Perhaps it may be followed by the great.[7] [. . .]

This is the patent-age of new inventions
   For killing bodies, and for saving souls,
All propagated with the best intentions;
   Sir Humphrey Davy's lantern,[8] by which coals
Are safely mined for in the mode he mentions,
   Timbucto[9] travels, voyages to the Poles,[10]
Are ways to benefit mankind, as true,
Perhaps, as shooting them at Waterloo.[11]

The new noses (1) were early prosthetics designed to replace real ones that got damaged or diseased, often by syphilis; Congreve's rockets (2) were a new kind of artillery. The doctor (3) is William Jenner, who developed the small-pox vaccine using ox tissue. Galvanism (4), a process developed by Galvani to stimulate dead tissue electrically and so produce signs of life. The apparatus (5) was a pneumatic resuscitator. Spinning (6) puns on the new 'spinning jennies' sent 'spinning' by the frame-breaking protests in the textile industry. The great (pox) (7) was syphilis, then incurable. The lantern (8) was the new 'Davy lamp' which allowed miners to work safer (and longer) underground. Timbucto (9) (in deepest Africa) and the North and South Poles (10) were both beginning to be explored and exploited by Western Europeans. Waterloo (11) was fought in 1815.

(Text from Byron [1819] 1986: 410–11)

This passage is from Byron's *Don Juan* (1819), Canto I, verses 129–32. The early nineteenth century was a time of scientific discovery, geographical exploration and technological innovation, all of them taking place in the context of the early industrial revolution, the expansion of empire and war within Europe, and developments in medicine. In many cases, as Byron playfully yet pointedly observes, it remained a moot – and sore – point how far most of these discoveries and inventions really did 'benefit mankind' any more than 'shooting them at Waterloo'.

Dreams and drugs – from Coleridge to 'Coke'

Dreams, whether real or imaginary, have always played an influential role in the inspiration or formation of literature and art. Caedmon's dream of the command to 'Sing Creation!' and Chaucer's dream in which he is forced to apologise for his work to the God of Love are two early examples in English (see above pp. 199, 202). The Aboriginal celebration of 'Dream Time' and 'the Dreaming that never ends' in Billy Marshall-Stoneking's *Passage* is a later, very different one (see Chapter 5). The Australian poet, Les Murray, suggests in his essays *A Working Forest* (1996) that humanity has three 'minds': bodily, rational, and dreaming. All have to be engaged at some point for creation to take place; but the 'dream-mind', he says, is the one without which it is impossible to compose good poetry. Jung, Cixous, Kristeva, Ward Jouve and many others writing on the crucial significance of the unconscious for creation would in very various ways agree (see Chapter 4).

    Here we take a particular and to some extent peculiar view of dreams and related visions as they are induced by drugs. This allows us to tackle a configuration of tricky issues in an oblique and revealing way. It also acts as a convenient follow-through from the previous section dealing with 'real Romantic writers'; for of course many have been left out, and I deliberately left open the matter of what precisely one chooses to mean by 'real'. This is doubly complicated here. Where does the drug end and the dream begin? How does the dreaming make it through to the waking state? And what traces of dreams and/or drugs are we to discern in the fully worked-up compositions of writers and artists who are known to have worked under the influence of both? At a physiological level, this is tantamount to asking where the chemical and electrical processes of the nervous system and brain become the cognitive and perceptual processes of the mind and the psyche. And this last, notice, as 'soul' or 'personality', can be the object of spiritual reflection no less than psychological investigation.

In such areas even the most apparently simple question ('How do I make sense of this text?') quickly becomes involved: 'How do I make sense of the sense that writers and artists made of their senses?' And a single answer becomes all the more unlikely when the particular writer or artist says, perhaps well after the event, that 'something else' – opium, morphine, cocaine, cannabis, LSD, speed, ecstasy, etc., with or without alcohol, tobacco, caffeine, etc. – was in every sense *substantially* driving the whole show. Moreover, if there is 'something else' that is doing the driving (by definition, a *what* rather than a *who*), how are we to name and interpret it: a grotesquely inflated form of Freud's id? a super-charged form of Jung's collective unconscious? or a whole heap of states of altered consciousness? In any event, when creating under the influence of drugs or through drug-induced dreams, the whole matter of agency goes into overdrive and any sense of personal responsibility tends to go out of the window. And that, evidently, is a large part of the initial appeal of the experience – as well as its besetting peril. For, as writer after writer reviewed in Sadie Plant's invaluable *Writing on Drugs* (1999) attests, it is the initial enhancement followed by the rapid deterioration and ultimate destruction of the creative process that characterises the actual experience of 'writing on drugs'. The novelist and theorist of creativity Arthur Koestler put it jocularly like this: '[Magic] Mushrooms whirl you inside, too close to yourself . . . I solved the secret of the universe last night, but this morning I forgot what it was.' But Anaïs Nin, who experimented with almost as many forms of 'artificial' stimulant as 'natural' stimulation, was in no doubt about where she finally stood on this one: striving to create from life at large (including your sex- and dream-lives) is infinitely preferable to and far more pleasurable than depending on drugs to do it for you: 'Those who wrestle their images from experience, from their smoky dreams, to create, are able then to build what they have seen and hungered for. It does not vanish with the effects of the chemical' (see Plant 1999: 122–3).

Most of the issues raised are explored theoretically in Chapter 4: *inspiration* and *influence* as processes of 'breathing' or 'flowing' in, and especially *ecstasy* in the strict sense of 'standing outside' or 'being beside' oneself – 'out of it', 'way out', 'gone'. When dealing with specific texts and authors, however, we have to approach each case as it comes. Invariably this means making our way through a morass of delusion or picking up the threads of a calculating illusion. Either way, it is an intriguing but ultimately impossible task to get at what the writer her or himself may not have known in the first place, or, alternatively, does not care to reveal (or chooses to conceal) in the last. There are few sure guides in the land of dreams, and perhaps none at all in

the muddled landscapes of drugged hallucination. Thinking about the texts and contexts that follow (especially the Coleridge and the De Quincey) will help re-cast some
fundamental questions about creativity in a new light. But the light is oblique and
opaque and does not illuminate all the dark corners. Certainly there is no quick fix.

(i) Kubla Khan: or, A Vision in a Dream. A Fragment, *Samuel Taylor Coleridge, c. 1797, published 1816*

> The following fragment is here published at the request of a poet of great and
> deserved celebrity [Byron] and, as far as the author's own opinions are con-
> cerned, rather as a psychological curiosity, than on the grounds of any supposed
> poetic merits.
>
> In the summer of the year 1797, the author, then in ill health, had retired to a
> lonely farmhouse between Porlock and Linton, on the Exmoor confines of Somer-
> set and Devonshire. In consequence of a slight indisposition, an anodyne had been
> prescribed [later specified as 'two grains of opium'], from the effects of which he
> fell asleep in his chair at the moment he was reading the following sentence, or
> words of the same substance, in Purchas's Pilgrimage: 'Here the Khan Kubla
> commanded a palace to be built, and a stately garden thereunto. And thus ten
> miles of fertile ground were inclosed with a wall.' The author continued for about
> three hours in a profound sleep, at least of the external senses, during which time
> he has the most vivid confidence that he could not have composed less than from
> two to three hundred lines; if that indeed can be called composition in which all
> the images rose up before him as things, with a parallel production of the corre-
> spondent expressions, without any sensation or consciousness of effort. On
> awaking he appeared to himself to have a distinct recollection of the whole, and
> taking his pen, ink, and paper, instantly and eagerly wrote down the lines that are
> here preserved. At this moment he was unfortunately called out by a person on
> business from Porlock, and detained by him above an hour, and on his return to
> his room, found, to his no small surprise and mortification, that though he still
> retained some vague and dim recollection of the general purport of the vision, yet,
> with the exception of some eight or ten scattered lines and images, all the rest had
> passed away like the images on the surface of a stream into which a stone has
> been cast but, alas, without the after restoration of the latter! [. . .]

In Xanadu did Kubla Khan
A stately pleasure dome decree
Where Alph, the sacred river, ran
Through caverns measureless to man
Down to a sunless sea.
So twice five miles of fertile ground
With walls and towers were girdled round:
And there were gardens bright with sinuous rills
Where blossomed many an incense-bearing tree:
And here were forests ancient as the hills,
Enfolding sunny spots of greenery.

But oh! that deep romantic chasm which slanted
Down the green hill athwart a cedarn cover!
A savage place! as holy and enchanted
As e'er beneath a waning moon was haunted
By woman wailing for her demon lover!
And from this chasm, with ceaseless turmoil seething,
As if this earth in fast thick pants were breathing,
A mighty fountain momently was forced:
Amid whose swift half-intermitted burst
Huge fragments vaulted like rebounding hail,
Or chaffy grain beneath the thresher's flail:
And mid these dancing rocks at once and ever
It flung up momently the sacred river.
Five miles meandering with a mazy motion
Through wood and dale the sacred river ran,
Then reached the caverns measureless to man,
And sank in tumult to a lifeless ocean:
And 'mid this tumult Kubla heard from far
Ancestral voices prophesying war!

The shadow of the dome of pleasure
Floated midway on the waves:
Where was heard the mingled measure
From the fountain and the caves.
It was a miracle of rare device,
A sunny pleasure-dome with caves of ice!

A damsel with a dulcimer
In a vision once I saw:
It was an Abyssinian maid,
And on her dulcimer she played,
Singing of Mount Abora.
Could I revive within me
Her symphony and song,
To such a deep delight 'twould win me,
That with music loud and long,
I would build that dome in air,
That sunny dome! those caves of ice!
And all who heard should see them there,
And all should cry, Beware! Beware!
His flashing eyes, his floating hair!
Weave a circle round him thrice,
And close your eyes with holy dread,
For he on honey-dew hath fed,
And drunk the milk of Paradise.

(Texts from Coleridge [1816] 1985 and
Abrams *et al.* 2000, Vol. 2: 439–41)

This is *the* classic 'dream on drugs' poem in English literature. Its critical and historical significance therefore need weighing carefully, even while we remain open to the poem's haunting effects and enduring appeal. Firstly, then, it is *just possible* that the occasion and the events of the poem's composition may be *exactly* as described by Coleridge in the above preface that he added for first publication nearly twenty years later. On the other hand, it is *quite likely* that they may, at least in part, have been fabricated by him after the event in order to help both explain and excuse the text's status as 'a fragment'. We shall probably never know. To be sure, Coleridge was for most of his adult life heavily dependent upon drugs, chiefly morphine, in the then-legal form of laudanum. His poems 'The Pains of Sleep', 'Dejection: An Ode' and parts of 'The Rime of the Ancient Mariner' (1797–1803) evidently all contain traces of bad 'trips'. But then again, Coleridge was an incorrigible and resourceful fabricator of fantasies designed to pass off his incomplete or endlessly delayed work as not only admissible but even admirable. A famous (or infamous) example is Chapter XIII of his *Biographia Literaria* (1817), in which the long-promised disquisition 'On the imagination or esemplastic power' is also cut short, this time at the request of a letter 'from a friend' which is then published instead. This is almost certainly an excuse, whether pitiful or playful; for the letter has all the signs of being bogus and by Coleridge himself.

All that granted, the preface and poem together still offer some fascinating, if ultimately opaque, insights into possible relations between dreams, drugs and the triumphs and tribulations of composition. They also give an invaluable, even if unreliable, insight into the relations between creative and critical processes in general – at least from this particular 'deep romantic chasm'. It remains open to question, however, what precisely one is to make of the whole thing – if indeed it is not simply a series of 'holes' tied to together in a more or less plausible fashion. Is it to be treated as a 'Fragment' and a mere 'psychological curiosity', as Coleridge suggests in the prose preface? Or is it rather, 'at once and ever . . . momently the sacred river' (of inspiration? creation?), as Coleridge images it forth in the body of the poem? Coleridge's many and various and highly influential ruminations on 'Imagination' may help in framing some further questions in all these respects (see above p. 14). But they can hardly be expected to come up with conclusive answers.

(iii) 'the creative state of the eye increased': Thomas De Quincey, Confessions of an English Opium Eater, *1821*

> [A]t night, when I lay awake in bed, vast processions passed along in mournful pomp: friezes of never-ending stories. [. . .] And, at the same time, a corresponding change took place in my dreams: a theatre seemed suddenly opened and lighted up within my brain, which presented nightly spectacles of more than earthly splendour. And the four following facts may be mentioned as noticeable at this time:
>
> 1   That, as the creative state of the eye increased, a sympathy seemed to arise between the waking and the dreaming states of the brain in one point – that whatsoever I happened to call up and to trace by a voluntary act upon the darkness was very apt to transfer itself to my dreams; so that I feared to exercise this faculty; [. . .]
>
> 2   For this, and all other changes in my dreams, were accompanied by deep-

seated anxiety and gloomy melancholy, such as are wholly incommunicable by words. I seemed every night to descend, not metaphorically, but literally to descend, into chasms and sunless abysses, depths below depths from which it seemed hopeless that I could ever reascend. Nor did I, by waking, feel that I *had* re-ascended. [. . .]

3   The sense of space and, in the end, the sense of time were both powerfully affected. Buildings, landscapes, etc. were exhibited in proportions so vast as the bodily eye is not fitted to receive. Space swelled, and was amplified to an extent of unutterable infinity. This, however, did not disturb me so much as the vast expansion of time; I sometimes seemed to have lived for 70 or 100 years in one night; nay, sometimes had feelings representative of a millennium passed in that time, or, however, of a duration far beyond the limits of any human experience.

4   The minutest incidents of childhood, or forgotten scenes of later years, were often revived: I could not be said to recollect them; for if I had been told of them when waking, I should not have been able to acknowledge them as parts of my past experience. But placed as they were before me, in dreams, like intuitions, and clothed in all their evanescent circumstances and accompanying feelings, I *recognised* them instantaneously.

(Text from Thomas De Quincey's 'The pains of opium',
Confessions of an English Opium Eater, 1821)

The *Confessions* is largely based upon the experiences of De Quincey's early life as recalled some years later. But De Quincey (like Coleridge, whose work he knew and appears to recall above) was also a wide reader, especially of travel stories, and he draws upon these for his 'autobiography', too. That said, De Quincey was certainly a long-term 'opium-eater' and wrote the *Confessions* under the influence of as well as about opium. Debt propelled De Quincey into journalism, and he wrote the bulk of his account at speed for publication in the September and October issues of the *London Magazine* (1821). It caused a considerable stir (then as now the 'Confessions of a . . .' formula had a ready popular appeal) and De Quincey published it in book form the following year, and again in a revised and expanded edition in 1856.

(v) 'Things go better with . . .'; 'It's the real thing . . .'

(a)

Thousands proclaim it the most remarkable invigorator that ever sustained a wasting and sinking system . . . a great blessing to the unfortunate who are addicted to the morphine or opium habit.

(b)

Tonic . . . refreshment . . . for a turbulent, inventive, noisy, neurotic new America!

(c)

I get no kick from cocaine (champagne) . . . I get a kick out of you.

(a) is the late-nineteenth-century sales pitch for French Wine Coca, a precursor of Coca-Cola, first developed by Dr John Pemberton using coca leaves, high in natural cocaine. (b) is from an early advert for a soda named Coca-Cola (1886), so called because it contained a combination of coca leaves and kola nuts; the contents but not the name were changed and the Coca-Cola Corporation now insists that the name is 'meaningless but fanciful and alliterative'. (c) is a line from Cole Porter's song 'I get a kick out of you' (1934): 'champagne' replaced 'cocaine' in the recorded and published versions. (For further information on all these texts, see Plant 1999: 67–71, 88.)

(vi) 'burning for the ancient heavenly connection': Allen Ginsberg, 1956

> I saw the best minds of my generation destroyed by madness, starving hysterical
>   naked,
> dragging themselves through the negro streets at dawn looking for an angry fix,
> angelheaded hipsters burning for the ancient heavenly connection to the starry
>   dynamo in the machinery of night,
> who poverty and tatters and hollow-eyed and high sat up smoking in the
>   supernatural darkness of cold-water flats floating across the tops of cities
>   contemplating jazz.

The opening of Allen Ginsberg's *Howl* (published 1956). The night Ginsberg read it out loud at a club in San Francisco was later hailed as 'the birth trauma of the Beat Generation' (see Baym *et al.* 1994, Vol. 2: 2628.)

Literature other-wise

Here, finally, are just a few of the many ways in which 'literature' is currently being constructed 'other-wise': *other* than how it is conventionally supposed to look and sound; and *wise* to verbal resources and cultural concerns that it is commonly expected to ignore. The texts featured illustrate a wide range of strategies and genres:

- 'found' materials that have been shrewdly spotted and craftily 're-made' (every-day documents such as lists of street names, maps, telephone books and time-tables can all be 'defamiliarised' and reactivated like this)
- a list of chemical elements and their properties that, in the event, turn out to mean much more (technical discourses can be highlighted and exposed by being re-formed and re-framed)
- a challenge to think about the performance possibilities of everything from the alphabet to various kinds of silence, here taking a topic and running it out through repetition with variation
- a strikingly 'new' kind of novel that still recalls plenty of previous instances (the persistently 'new/old' dynamic of every live genre)
- science fiction that draws on science fact to engage with the 'creatures' of artificial life and the creation of cyberspace art (another genre constantly in process of transformation)
- a 'jazz' poem as freely 'phonetic' with spelling as freshly swinging with sound and imagery (you just write as you sing and push a big image for all it's worth).

(i) *Glasgow Botanical Walks*

Rose St	G3
Thistle St	G5
Lily St	G40
Myrtle Pl	G42
Daisy St	G42
Moss Rd	G51
Primrose St	G1
Yarrow Gdns	G20
Shamrock St	G4

Distance approx. 12 miles

Chestnut St	G22
Acorn St	G40
Hazel Ave	G44
Mulberry Rd	G43
Walnut Cres	G22

Distance approx. 10 miles

A 'found' poem put together by Gerry Loose. (Text from *The Order of Things: an anthology of Scottish Sound, Pattern and Concrete Poems*, ed. Ken Cockburn with Alec Finlay, Edinburgh: pocketbooks, 2001: 58.)

(ii) *'Chain of Decay', from* Heavy Water, A Poem for Chernobyl, Mario Petrucci, 2004

Lead 207 Stable
via beta and gamma radiation

Thallium 207 – 4.77 minutes
alpha radiation and x-rays

Bismuth 211 – 2.1 minutes
beta and gamma radiation

Lead 211 – 36.1 minutes
alpha radiation

Polonium 215 – 1.78 milliseconds
alpha and gamma radiation

Radon 219 – 3.96 seconds
alpha and gamma radiation

Radium 223 – 11.43 days
alpha and gamma radiation

Thorium 227 – 18.7 days
beta and gamma radiation

Actinium 227 – 21.77 years
alpha and gamma radiation

Protactinium 231 – 32,760 years
beta and gamma radiation

Uranium 235
703.8 million years

(Text from Petrucci 2004: 9)

Petrucci is a nuclear physicist and ecologist as well as a poet. All the elements referred to are radioactive isotopes with a 'half-life' decay rate of the times shown. All were released into the earth and atmosphere – and into the bodies of people, animals and plants – when the nuclear reactor at Chernobyl in the Ukraine melted down in spring 1986. There will continue to be widespread cancers and other fatal diseases associated with the event for (very) many years to come. As the author indicates in his acknowledgements, the collection was initially inspired by reading Svetlana Alexievich's *Voices from Chernobyl*, London: Aurum Press, 1999.

(iii) 'On Performance Writing', Tim Etchells, 1999

here are 26 letters:
a b c d e f g h i j k l m n o p q r s t u v w x y z
now write a text for performance [. . .]
Round midnight he made an end to his listing of texts and tried instead to think about silence. It was silent in the house. He made a list of silences, like the list from *Pleasure* (1998).
The kind of silence you sometimes get in phone calls to a person that you love.
The kind of silence people only dream of.
The kind of silence that is only for waiting in.
The kind of silence as a thief makes away with the gold.
The kind of silence that follows a car crash.
The kind of silence in a crowded house when everyone is asleep.
The kind of silence between waves at the ocean.
The kind of silence which follows a big argument.
The kind of silence that happens when you put your head under the water of the bath.
The kind of silence that only happens at night.
The kind of silence that happens when you close the curtains and climb into bed.
The kind of silence that has everything in it.

(Text from Tim Etchells, *Certain Fragments* (1999)
in Huxley and Witts 2002: 185, 188–9)

Etchells is the director of the UK-based performance company 'Forced Entertainment'.

(iv) 'Mark Z. Danielewski's House of Leaves', 2000

October 31, 1998

Back here again. These pages are a mess. Stuck together with honey from all my tea making. Stuck together with blood. No idea what to make of those last few entries either. What's the difference, especially in difference, what's read what's left in what's left out what's invented what's remembered what's forgotten what's written what's found what's lost what's done?

What's not done?
What's the difference?

October 31, 1998 (Later)

I just completed the intro when I heard them coming for me, a whole chorus, cursing my name, all those footfalls and then the bang of their fists on my door.
I'm sure it's the clerk. I'm sure it's the police. I'm sure there are others. A host of others. Accusing me for what I've done.
The loaded guns lie on my bed.
What will I do?
There are no more guns. There are no more voices.
There is no one at my door.
There's not even a door anymore.
Like a child, I gather up the finished book in my arms and climb out the window.

The full title of this 'novel' – which reads like Sterne and Derrida or Poe and Kafka, simultaneously or by turns – is: 'Mark Z. Danielewski's *House of Leaves* by Zampanò, with introduction and notes by Johnny Truant' (New York: Doubleday, 2000). This extract comes two thirds of the way through (on pp. 515–16) and is a cross between *film noir* crime thriller spoof and self-deconstructing metatextual frolic. But as this particular passage is neither more nor less representative than the other parts (which include concrete poems, collage, blank or near-illegible pages, along with reminiscences of all sorts of other genres), you are urged not to mistake it for the whole.

(v) Diaspora, Greg Egan, 1997

[A computerised artwork programme goes through its paces morphing and spinning one image into another in the year 2975. A 'flesher' is a biological descendant of Homo sapiens; *a 'gleisner' is an artificial descendant. Both are conscious. The observer, Yatima, is a gleisner.)*

One flesher child was turning into a creature of glass, nerves and blood vessels vitrifying into optical fibres. A sudden, startling white-light image showed living, breathing Siamese twins, impossibly transected to expose raw pink and grey muscles working side by side with shape-memory alloys and piezoelectric actuators, flesher and gleisner anatomies interpenetrating. The scene spun and morphed into a lone robot child in a flesher womb; spun again to show a luminous map of a citizen's mind embedded in the same woman's brain; zoomed out to place her, curled, in a cocoon of optical and electronic cables. Then a swarm of nano machines burst through her skin, and everything scattered into a cloud of grey dust [. . .]

The artwork, unbidden, sent Yatima's viewpoint wheeling around the figures.

(Text from Egan 1997: 41)

Greg Egan is one of the foremost writers of contemporary cyberfiction. He alternates between computer programming and full-time writing.

(vi) I Live in Music, *Ntozake Shange, 1978*

i live in music
is this where you live
i live here in music
i live on c$^{\#}$ street
my friend lives on b^{b} avenue
do you live here in music
sound
falls round me like rain on other folks
saxophones wet my face
cold as winter in st. louis
hot like peppers I rub on my lips
thinking they waz lilies
i got 15 trumpets where other women got hips
& a upright bass for both sides of my heart
i walk round in a piano like somebody
else / be walkin on the earth
i live in music
   live in it
      wash in it
i cd even smell it
wear sound on my fingers
sound falls   so fulla music
ya cd make a river where yr arm is &
hold yrself
   hold yrself in a music

(Text from Shange [1978] 1987: 126)

Shange is an African-American poet-performer and playwright as well as a novelist and critic. She took an African name in 1971: Ntozake translates as 'she who comes with her own things', and Shange as 'who walks like a lion'.

8 Transforming culture

An open invitation

What follows is a brief and provocative anthology exploring aspects of creativity across a wide range of cultural practices. The texts are organised by topic and to some extent by mode or medium. They mix passages of practical observation and illustration with those of a more theoretical or speculative nature. Not all the texts agree with one another; many are in open conflict. They also have all the intrinsic limitation of being printed words, whereas most of the practices referred to are in other materials and media and can only be fully realised and experienced as such. That said, there is still some sense in describing and discussing them. With this in mind, each cluster of texts is prefaced by a ***pre-text*** which helps set the scene or bend the agenda, depending how you see it. For the rest, as usual, it is in the gaps *between* the texts and in the reader's attempts to bridge – or fill or widen or get round – those gaps that the most creative moves are likely to be made. The overall aim is to keep on opening up the issue of what 'being creative' has been, is and may yet be.

This is also, therefore, an open invitation to think of other examples that are similar or different, alternative or opposed; as well as whole practices that perhaps relate to those featured here but which are not represented. For again, as in the previous chapter on rewrit*ing* creativity, transform*ing* culture is recognised as an ongoing activity, and one in which we are the agents as well as the objects of change. Grasped like this, 'Culture' is not just a monolithic given entity (singular and with a capital C) but the many and various 'cultures' (lower case and irreducibly plural) through which we ceaselessly re-create ourselves with and with respect to others. Put another way, this is a matter of *human becomings* rather than *human being*. A provisional definition of creativity along these lines was offered 'before the beginning'; and it was the job of Parts 1 and 2 to explore the issues theoretically and historically. It is the aim of this concluding part of the anthology, along with the preceding more specifically 'literary' selection, to confirm that creativity is fundamentally a matter of practice: what we do and how – with whatever materials we have to hand or in mind, and in whatever moments we find or can make time and space for. Obviously, none of the passages that follow is either the first or last word on their subject. They are part of the continuing conversation we call culture, society, history. Nor does this, the last chapter of the book offer to wrap it all up neatly in a single parcel. (That, as I trust will be obvious by now, would defeat the object and misrepresent creativity completely.) For the same reason, 'After the end . . .' there is a series of parting but not conclusive gestures.

Collaboration, installation, confrontation

(i) Pre-text

The artist as collector–exhibitor–classifier–curator–designer has become an increasingly common feature in the making of installations – the type of exhibit that has become one of the most characteristic art forms of the last third of the century. The range of approaches in the assembling and re-working of collections has been remarkably diverse.

> (Martin Kemp and Deborah Schultz, 'Us and them, this and that,
> here and there, now and then: collecting, classifying, creating'
> in Ede 2000: 97)

(ii) Bananas – Exchange Values, Invisible Lives

I have recently completed a project begun twenty years ago entitled *Exchange Values: Images of Invisible Lives*. [. . .] This project has brought together a whole spectrum of people: activists, farmers, economists, ministers of agriculture, ecological campaigners, artists, psychotherapists, writers and consumers. The metaphoric currency is 'sheets of skin' made of dried, blackened bananas. Twenty sheets of skin were made from 20 numbered boxes of bananas. The producer of each box of bananas was then traced. A recording from each farmer plays under each sheet of skin. The consumer stands face to face with the skin whilst listening through headphones to each farmer speaking about their situation and some aspect of our global economy. From the discussion with the farmers as well as the visitors to the installation – who were also all consumers – it would appear that the installation succeeded in creating an imaginative space in which to enter many aspects of the reality of banana growers in particular, of agricultural production, and of our potential power as consumers, to decide what we will consume and why. That, in brief, is one 'social sculpture' project.

'Social sculpture' is a movement initially associated with Joseph Beuys, with whom Shelley Sacks worked in the 1970s. Since 1996, installations of 'Bananas' have been set up in Oxford, London, Brussels, the Windward Isles (where the bananas came from) and elsewhere. For a full account with images, essays and a CD of the voices, see the catalogue for the exhibition at the 2002 World Summit on Sustainable Development in Johannesburg in 2002: *Exchange Values: Images of Individual Lives*. (For the latter, including the above text which first appeared in *Public Art* (1997), see www.exchange-values.org.)

(iii) The Rape of Creativity

For Jake and Dinos Chapman, making art is a collaborative process. Their work is an 'argument' with the viewer, as much as it is with each other. Periodically exploiting the human form to disturbing and often horrific effect, their art is knowingly provocative, challenging the boundaries of taste. [. . .]

In the large upper gallery space, we encounter a life-size sculptural tableau, *The Rape of Creativity* (2003), a scaled-up version of an existing model. There is a narrative here which slowly unravels, and clear visual connection with other works, including the McDonald's trademark 'M'. A silver caravan [with a battered McDonald's M' on its roof] sits rusting on bricks, surrounded by junk, tyres, dog turds and detritus, its door and interior lined with pornography. Its occupant, an artist who has been trying to make a sculpture, but has read all the wrong books, lacks the skill to make something beautiful; the result is ugly and crude. The wooden sculpture of a naked woman resembles the figurehead of a boat, standing proud in the space, but below her all chaos is let loose. The artist, now absent, has severed his hand with an axe, a hybrid dog with a sheep's head runs away with the limb. Long, red, quasi-Nazi banners hang in the windows, the swastikas replaced with smiley faces gazing in at the scene below.

In this tableau, the Chapmans comment on the idea of the artist and making art.

(Emma Dean, programme notes to *The Rape of Creativity* by
Jake and Dinos Chapman, Modern Art, Oxford 2003)

(iv) *Body Worlds* – *'The individual face within'*

Body Worlds – *The Anatomical Exhibition of Real Human Bodies* provides unique insights into the healthy and diseased body. [. . .] All the bodies on display are authentic. They belonged to people who declared during their lives that their bodies should be made available after their deaths for qualification and instruction of medical professionals and non-professionals alike. The specimens are permanently preserved by plastination – an impregnation technique where tissues are completely saturated with plastics in a vacuum. Not only does plastination facilitate the permanent preservation of the specimen, it also allows entirely new forms of anatomical display since the plastics lend a high degree of rigidity to the tissues. Anatomically prepared whole bodies, for instance, can now be displayed in upright, life-like poses. Even isolated anatomical structures can be exhibited in hitherto unseen ways. This is why *Body Worlds* is unique. [. . .]

The authenticity of the specimen on display is essential for such insight. Every human being is unique. Humans reveal their individuality not only through the visible exterior, but also through the interior of their bodies as each one is distinctly different. Position, size, shape and structure of skeleton, muscles, nerves and organs determine our 'face within'. It would be impossible to convey this anatomical individuality with models, for a model is nothing more than an interpretation. All models look alike and are, essentially, simplified versions of the real thing. The authenticity of the specimen, however, is fascinating and enables the observer to experience the marvel of the real human being. The exhibition is thus dedicated to the individual face within.

From the programme notes for *Body Worlds* – *The Anatomical Exhibition of Real Human Bodies* by Professor Gunther von Hagens at the Atlantis Gallery, London, 2002, and previously in Japan, Germany, Switzerland and Belgium. In his review in *The Guardian* (19 March 2002, *G2*, p. 3), Stuart Jeffries chose to introduce and contextualise the London exhibition thus:

Von Hagens' exhibition is opening in a country whose most vaunted recent artistic movement, Britart, is obsessed with the body – be that the pickled sharks and bisected livestock of Damien Hirst, Marc Quinn's frozen-blood head, or Rick Gibson's foetus earrings. Von Hagens' exhibition seems to trump all those – with the possible exception of the earrings – in its capacity to shock and compel attention, and is likely to be as big a cultural draw in London as last year's Hayward Gallery exhibition *Spectacular Bodies*.

Making musics

(i) Pre-text

Some musicians certainly claim a lack of thought and training: but when their output is analysed it often seems to be re-creative rather than creative.

(Roger Dean, *Creative Improvisation*, 1989: 114)

(ii) 'If the soil is ready'

Generally speaking, the germ of a future composition comes suddenly and unexpectedly. If the soil is ready – that is to say, if the disposition for work is there – it takes root with extraordinary force and rapidity, shoots up through the earth, puts forth branches, leaves, and, finally, blossoms. I cannot define the creative process in any other way than by this simile.

(Peter Ilich Tchaikovsky, letter of 17 February 1878
in Vernon 1970: 57)

(iii) Pandemonium or polyphony?

Not only were innumerable barrel-organs blaring out from merry-go-rounds, see-saws, shooting galleries and puppet shows, but a military band and a men's choral society had established themselves there as well. All these groups, in the same forest clearing, were creating an incredible musical pandemonium without paying the slightest attention to each other. Mahler exclaimed: 'You hear? That's polyphony, and that's where I get it from!'

Natalie Bauer Lechner recalls a trip to a country fair with the composer Gustav Mahler, cited by Keith Negus and Michael Pickering, 'Creativity and musical experience' in Hesmondaigh and Negus 2002: 187.

(iv) 'Participants in a common project'

Ask any orchestral player, and he'll tell you: although it may perhaps look to an outsider as if the conductor is totally in charge, in reality he often has a quite minor – even a purely decorative – role. Sure, he can provide a common reference point to assist the players with the timing and punctuation of their playing. And he can certainly influence the overall style and interpretation of a work. But that is not what gets the players to belong together. What truly binds them into one organic unit and creates the flow between them is something much deeper and more magical, namely, the very act of making music: that they are together creating a single work of art.

Doesn't this suggest a criterion for 'belonging' that should be much more widely applicable: that parts come to belong to a whole just in so far as they are *participants in a common project?*

(Nicholas Humphrey, The Mind Made Flesh, 2002: 11–12)

(vi) All what jazz?

Owens (1995) has analyzed the recorded solos of Charlie Parker (1920–1955), who is recognized as the greatest improviser in modern jazz. [. . .] He was also recognized for never repeating himself. Perhaps surprisingly, given Parker's reputation, Owens has reported that Parker can be characterized as a 'formulaic' improviser. Over his career, Parker acquired a large repertoire of formulas – patterns of notes, ranging from two- or three-note clusters to strings encompassing perhaps a dozen notes – which he used in his solos. A significant proportion of even Parker's greatest solos were constructed from the formulas, some of which might be repeated every eight or nine measures.

(T. Owens, Bebop: The Music and its Players (1995) as reported by
Robert Weisberg, 'Creativity and knowledge: a challenge
to theories', in Sternberg 1999: 237)

(vii) Musica practica

There are two musics (at least so I have always thought): the music one listens to; the music one plays. These two musics are totally different arts, each with its own history, its own sociology, its own aesthetics, its own erotic. [. . .] The music one plays comes from an activity that is very little auditory, being above all manual (and thus in a way much more sensual). [. . .] Concurrently, passive, receptive music, sound music, is become *the* music (that of concert, festival, record, radio); playing has ceased to exist; musical activity is no longer manual, muscular, kneadingly physical, but merely liquid, effusive, 'lubrificating', . . .

(Roland Barthes, 'Musica Practica' in Barthes 1977: 149–50)

(viii) Inside 'Eurythmics'

Annie Lennox: We just sit down and play and let the song come gradually. It comes from all sorts of bits and pieces lying around. When we sit down we don't have an agenda.

Dave Stewart: Often it starts with some simple chord shapes, rhythms, ideas, like this. (*plays a few bars*)

Annie Lennox: Then some words come in, more like sounds really. And gradually they build up into a lyric, a situation, or story or something.

Dave Stewart: We lay down the basic music line, sounds, music, words, on an eight-track, put the voices over it, and work over them a few times. Eventually you get something like the finished thing. (*Cut to snatches of finished song and accompanying video: 'I love you like a ball and chain'.*)

(From Inside Eurythmics, BBC 1, 1 January 2000)

Child's play, grown-up art, or just gaming?

(i) Pre-text

> I call this development, in which human play finds its true perfection in being art, 'the transformation into structure'.
>
> (Hans-Georg Gadamer, Truth and Method (2nd edn 1989)
in Kearney and Rasmussen 2001: 325)

(ii)

SASHA (a girl, age eight) sits in front of a kitchen cupboard with stacks of cans, jars and packets on the floor around her:

> I'm making a shop. Can you and mum come and buy something in a minute?

(iii)

IVAN (a boy, age eleven) shows a 'photograph' he has taken and made on a Gameboy camera:

> Look at this, Dad. What do you see? See – it looks like a cottage, doesn't it. But it's actually the back wall, and I've turned it upside down and drawn in some windows.

(iv)

GEORG (a man, age forty-eight) gives a philosophy lecture and prepares it for publication:

> Even a child's first impulse involves this practical alteration of external things; a boy throws stones into the river and now marvels at the circles drawn in the water as an effect in which he gains an intuition of something that is his own doing. [. . .] The universal need for art, that is to say, is man's rational need to lift the inner and outer world into his spiritual consciousness as an object in which he recognises again his own self.
>
> (Georg Hegel, Aesthetics: Lectures on Fine Art (1835) in
Feagin and Maynard 1997: 193–4)

(v)

LUDWIG (another philosopher, at various times between ages forty and fifty-five) talks, takes notes and doesn't quite prepare them for publication:

> Here the term 'language-game' is meant to bring into prominence the fact that *speaking* of language is part of an activity, or of a form of life. Review the multiplicity of language-games in the following examples, and in others:
>
> Giving orders, and obeying them
> Describing the appearance of an object or giving its measurements
> Constructing an object from a description (a drawing)
> Reporting an event

Speculating about an event
Forming and testing a hypothesis
Presenting the results of an experiment in tables and diagrams
Making up a story; and reading it
Play-acting
Singing catches
Guessing riddles
Making a joke; telling it
Solving a problem in practical arithmetic
Translating from one language into another
Asking, thanking, cursing, greeting, praying.
(Ludwig Wittgenstein, *Philosophical Investigations* [1953] 1967: 11–12)

(vi)

DONALD, a psychiatrist and therapist strongly influenced by ANNA and MELANIE, works with children for forty years and prepares this for publication shortly before his death:

Into the play area the child gathers objects or phenomena from external reality and uses these in the service of some sample derived from inner or personal reality. Without hallucinating the child puts out a sample of dream potential and lives with this sample in a chosen setting of fragments from external reality. [. . .] This attitude must include recognition that playing is always liable to become frightening. Games and their organisation must be looked at as part of an attempt to forestall the frightening aspects of play. [. . .] It is in playing and only in playing that the individual child or adult is able to be creative and to use the whole personality, and it is only in being creative that the individual discovers the self. [. . .] There is a direct development from transitional phenomena [e.g. a child's dummy/pacifier, a favourite object] to playing, and from playing to shared playing, and from this to cultural experience.
(Donald Winnicott, *Playing and Reality*, 1971: 58, 60, 63)

Winnicott was much influenced by the work with children and parents of Anna Freud and Melanie Klein.

(vii)

GUNTHER watches his son play and writes it up afterwards as part of a textbook on contemporary literacy:

At times I watch our son and his friends – and it *is* boys usually – playing around and with their Playstation. The skills which they demonstrate – skills of visual analysis, of manual dexterity, of strategic and tactical decision-making at meta-levels – leave me entirely perplexed. It is not clear to me that these children are victims of a general decline in mental abilities. All the games make use of the visual, but they always make use of much more: there is a musical score, there is rudimentary dialogue, and there is writing – usually as in comic strips, in a box above the rest of the visually saturated screen. [. . .] There are astonishing ranges of skill and ability at issue here, which those who make assertions about standards seem not to have taken into cognizance. [. . .]

The question arises for me about what is being demanded and produced here. Certainly, the skills of near instant response are essential; though I am not clear whether there is ever time for reflection, for assessment, for the quiet moment of consideration and review. It is not programmed into the game. What dispositions are imagined here, and prepared for the future, and where can an educational agenda that would wish to encourage other aspects of human-being-in-the-world be developed?

(Gunther Kress, *Literacy in the New Media Age*, 2003: 173–4)

(viii) Abomination 2000

Team-based tactical combat set including 3-D isometric world:

- Explore an entire city, the frozen wastes of Siberia, the jungles of Peru and the 'New World of the Faithful'.
- Multiplay options; LAN; internet; modem and other modes.
- Over 100 realistic contemporary and experimental weapons.
- Unique 'seeded' mission generator with over a million possible game variations.

(Blurb on the box of Eidos, *Abomination 2000*: Interactive Game System)

(ix) 'A fusion of artist, programmer and complexity theorist'

With these new types of games, a new type of game designer has arisen as well. The first generation of video games may have indirectly influenced a generation of artists and a handful were adopted as genuine *objets d'art*, albeit in a distinctly campy fashion. (Tabletop MS. Pac-Man games started to appear at downtown Manhattan clubs in the early nineties, around the time the Museum of the Moving Image created its permanent game collection.) But artists themselves rarely ventured directly into the game-design industry. Games were for kids, after all. [. . .]

But all this has changed in recent years, and a new kind of hybrid has appeared – a fusion of artist, programmer, and complexity theorist – creating interactive projects that challenge the mind and the thumb at the same time.

(Steven Johnson, *Emergence*, 2001: 177)

(x) A new 'arts-and-crafts movement'?

A leading-edge Web-design or games studio is much more like an arts-and-crafts movement pottery or furniture-making workshop than a Henry Ford-style automobile plant. It is not a 'soft' way of working: on the contrary it is intensely disciplined and hard – but it nourishes people's unique intuitive capacities instead of trying to eliminate them, as the Ford regime does.

(Bob Hughes, *Dust or Magic: Secrets of Successful Multimedia Design*, 2000: 246)

Healing: making whole

(i) Pre-text

It is only by putting it into words that I make it whole; this wholeness means that it has lost its power to hurt me; it gives me – perhaps by doing so I take away the pain – a great delight to put the severed parts together.

(Virginia Woolf, 'A sketch of the past' (1928) in Woolf 1985: 85)

(ii) Creative work, mental health

RESTORE provides creative work, rehabilitation and training for people in Oxfordshire who have experienced mental health problems. We offer a supportive and structured environment where people are encouraged to make the most of their abilities, learn new skills, regain confidence and a sense of direction.

One special feature of life at *RESTORE* is the emphasis which is placed upon individual ability and creativity. As one person who recently moved on from *RESTORE* explained, 'Here people are interested in me and not what is the matter with me'. The unique products that are designed and made in our workshops are available through our on-site shop in Manzil Way. Plants and organic vegetables are also grown by us and sold to local customers.

(From a leaflet circulated in Oxfordshire, 2003)

(iii) 'Flow' and the whole person

It is in the field of healthcare that the holistic approach has probably had its greatest impact over the last thirty years. [. . .] The fundamental tenet of the holistic approach is that the human being is not an isolated physical organism, but is part of a complex system which includes the emotions, mind, attitudes and spirit of a total human being a complex organism of many dynamic energies. [. . .] In holistic approaches to healthcare, the major object is to understand and help the patient's whole system come back into a healthy 'flow'. This necessarily requires the active cooperation of the patient and is one of the reasons why holistic healthcare has been so successful. Unlike much Western scientific medicine it empowers individuals to be involved in their own recovery and healing.

(William Bloom (ed.) *Holistic Revolution*, 2000: 149–50)

(iv) Fulfilling life, aesthetic experience

Life itself consists of phases in which the organism falls out of step with the march of surrounding things and then recovers unison with it – either through effort or by some happy chance. And in a growing life the recovery is never mere return to a prior state, for it is enriched by the state of disparity and resistance through which it has successfully passed. [. . .] For only when an organism shares in the ordered relations of its environment does it secure the stability essential to living. And when the participation comes after a phase of disruption and conflict, it bears within itself the germs of a consummation akin to the aesthetic. [. . .]

We have *an* experience [i.e. an experience felt to be aesthetically satisfying as distinct from any old experience] when the material experienced runs its course to fulfillment. Then and only then is it integrated within and demarcated in the general stream of experience from other experiences. A piece of work is finished in a way that is satisfactory; a problem receives its solution; a game is played through; a situation, whether that of eating a meal, playing a game of chess, carrying on a conversation, writing a book, or taking part in a political campaign, is so rounded out that its close is a consummation and not a cessation. Such an experience is a whole and carries with it its own individualizing quality and self-sufficiency. It is *an* experience.

(John Dewey, *Art as Experience* [1934] 1954: 14–15, 35)

Laughter, carnival, revolt

(i) Pre-text

As a writer I know that I must select studiously the nouns, pronouns, verbs, adverbs, etcetera, and by a careful syntactic arrangement make readers laugh, reflect or riot.

(Maya Angelou in conversation, Angelou 1989: 89)

(ii) Slaying 'the Spirit of Gravity'

The creator seeketh companions, not corpses, neither herds nor believers. The
    creator seeketh such as will be creators with him. [. . .]
I would believe only in a god that knew how to dance.
And when I beheld my devil, I found him earnest, thorough, profound, solemn;
    he was the spirit of Gravity – by him all things fall.
One slayeth not by wrath but by laughter. Arise! Let us slay the Spirit of
    Gravity!

(Friedrich Nietzsche. *Thus Spake Zarathustra*, Part 1 [1883] 1933:
sections 14, 33)

(iii) Carnival laughter

Carnival is the people's second life organised on the basis of laughter. [. . .] Carnival celebrated temporary liberation from prevailing truth and from the established order; it marked the suspension of all hierarchical rank, privilege, norms and prohibitions. Carnival was the true feast of time, the feast of becoming, change and renewal. [. . .] This temporary suspension, both ideal and real, of hierarchical rank created during carnival time a special type of communication impossible in everyday life.

(Mikhail Bakhtin, *Rabelais and his World* [1965] 1968: 8–10)

(iv) It's a riot

[A prisoner tells of how a riot/revolt by prisoners in one US jail (Watts) is celebrated by fellow prisoners in another (Folsom).]

Sensing a creative moment in the offing, we all got very quiet, very still, and others passing by joined the circle and did likewise.

'Baby', he said, 'they walking in fours and kicking in doors; dropping Reds [barbiturates] and busting heads; drinking wine and committing crime, shooting and looting, high-siding and low-riding, setting fires and slashing tires; turning over cars and burning down bars. [. . .] My black ass is in Folsom this morning but my black heart is in Watts!' Tears of joy were rolling from his eyes.

It was a cleansing, revolutionary laugh we all shared, something we have not often had occasion for.

(from Eldridge Cleaver, *Soul on Ice* (1968) in
Ricks and Vance 1992: 209–10)

Copying, reproduction, simulation

(i) Pre-text

Technical reproduction can put the copy of the original in situations which would be out of reach for the original itself. [. . .] By making many reproductions it substitutes a plurality of copies for a unique existence. And in permitting the reproduction to meet the beholder or listener in his own particular situation, it reactivates the object produced.

(Walter Benjamin, 'The Work of Art in the Age of Mechanical
Reproduction' (1936) in Benjamin 1979: 221–2)

(ii) 'Replication' or 'reproduction'?

We shall distinguish *replication*, the creation of exact or nominally exact copies, from *reproduction*, the creation of similar copies – in particular, similar enough that they too can reproduce. Normally DNA replicates, but when the occasional inevitable copying error – the technical term is *mutation* – creeps in, then the molecule is better thought of as reproducing.

(Ian Stewart and Jack Cohen, *Figments of Reality*, 1997: 17)

(iii) Simulations 'always already reproduced'?

This [the world of the modern multimedia] is a completely imaginary contact-world of sensorial mimetics and tactile mysticism: it is essentially an entire ecology that is grafted on this universe of operational simulation, multi-stimulation and multi-response. [. . .] The very definition of the real becomes: *that of which it is possible to give an equivalent reproduction*. This is contemporaneous with a science that postulates that a process can be perfectly reproduced in a set of given conditions, and also with the industrial rationality that postulates a universal system of equivalency (classical representation is not equivalence, it is transcription, interpretation, commentary). At the limit of this process of reproducibility, the real is not only what can be reproduced, but *that which is always already reproduced*. The hyperreal. [. . .] Disneyland is a perfect model of all the entangled orders of simulation.

(Jean Baudrillard 'Simulations' (1981) in
Kearney and Rasmussen 2001: 424–7)

(iv) Copyright ©

All rights reserved under International and Pan-American Copyright Conventions, including the right of reproduction in whole or in part in any form.
This collection copyright © 1992 by Christopher Ricks and William L. Vance.
Introduction copyright © 1992 by Christopher Ricks and William L. Vance.
The acknowledgements on pp. 443–446 constitute an extension of this copyright notice.
Christopher Ricks and William L. Vance are hereby identified as the authors of this work in accordance with Section 77 of the Copyright, Designs and Patents Act 1988.

(From preliminary pages of Ricks and Vance, *The Faber Book of America*, 1992)

Artificial–artful–intelligences–lives

(i) Pre-text

Artificial intelligence A branch of computer science whose goal is the design of machines that have attributes associated with human intelligence.
Artificial life A field of study that aims to discover the essential nature and universal features of 'life': not only life as we currently know it, but life as it could be.

(Peter Coveney and Roger Highfield, *Frontiers of Complexity*, 1995: 423)

(ii) A literary automaton

What would be the style of a literary automaton? I believe that its true vocation would be for classicism. The test of a poetic-electronic machine would be its ability to produce traditional works, poems with closed metrical forms, novels that follow all the rules. In this sense the use so far made of machines by the literary avant-garde is still too human. Especially in Italy, the machine used in these experiments is an instrument of chance, of the destructuralization of form, of protest against every habitual logical connection. I would therefore say that it is still an entirely lyrical instrument, serving a typically human need: the production of disorder. The true literature machine will be one that itself feels the need to produce disorder, as a reaction against its preceding production of order: a machine that will produce avant-garde work to free its circuits when they are choked by too long a production of classicism. In fact, given that developments in cybernetics lean towards machines capable of learning, of changing their own programmes, of developing their own sensibilities and their own needs, nothing prevents us from foreseeing a literature machine that at a certain point feels unsatisfied with its own traditionalism and starts to propose new ways of writing, turning its own codes completely upside down.

(From Italo Calvino, 'Cybernetics and ghosts' (1967)
in Bradbury 1990: 230)

(iii) 'So easy to create'?

Be at home with your *creativity*. HP has the perfect choice of digital imaging products for you and your family to enjoy at home, making it so easy to create and edit your own professional quality photos. The net-ready HP Pavilion multimedia home PC with its MD Athlon XP processor together with HP's range of scanners, photOsmart printers and digital cameras are all simple to use, stylish and offer great results at an affordable price.

(Advertisement in *The Guardian*, 'Weekend' supplement,
30 March 2002, p. 72)

(iv) Expressive arts as sciences

It is no surprise that video, film, digitised image-making, performance, live art, superfictions and installations are increasingly used as expressive media. 'The universe is a single, unfolding, self-organising event, something more animal than machine,' states architect and cultural observer Charles Jencks, citing 'the complexity of non-linear architecture' of Frank Gehry's titanium-clad Guggenheim museum in Bilbao, 'something radically interconnected and creative, that jumps suddenly to higher levels of organisation and delights us as it does.' The artists who are now turning to science may be doing so because they are engaged by its new ideas and concepts and, being always drawn to new ways of seeing, are naturally drawn to the changing patterns in living systems.

(Siân Ede, *Strange and Charmed*, 2000: 22; Jencks in interview,
The Times Higher Education Supplement, 6 August 1999, p. 20)

(v) 'Will a computer program ever write beautiful music?'

Speculation: Yes, but not soon. Music is a language of emotions, and until programs have emotions as complex as ours, there is no way a program will write anything beautiful. There can be 'forgeries' – shallow imitations of the syntax of earlier music – but despite what one might think at first, there is much more to musical experience than can be captured in syntactical rules. There will be no new kinds of beauty turned up for a long time by computer music-composing programs.

(Douglas Hofstadter, *Gödel, Escher, Bach*, [1980] 2000: 676)

(vi) Human becomings

Technology has become a challenge – it is the chance we have given ourselves, as a culture, to reinvent ourselves and display some creativity. Technology should assist human evolution. If the question is not 'What are we?', but 'who do we want to become?', then the next step is: how can techno-culture help us achieve this? [. . .] [T]he steps of 'becoming' are neither reproduction nor imitation, but rather empathic proximity and intensive interconnectedness.

(Rosi Braidotti, *Metamorphoses*, 2002: 257, 258)

(vii) '. . . and Dolly was created'

[Ian Wilmut's] colleague Keith Campbell sucked the nucleus out of an egg from a ewe, creating an egg that had no genes at all, an egg that would soon die if it did not get a new nucleus. Then he began the process of adding the nucleus of an udder cell to the bereft egg.

Campbell slipped an udder cell under the outer membrane of the egg. Next he jolted the egg for a few microseconds with a burst of electricity. This opened the pores of the egg and the udder cell so that the contents of the udder cell, including its chromosomes, oozed into the egg and took up residence there. Now the egg had a nucleus – the nucleus of the udder cell. In addition, the electric current tricked the egg into behaving as if it were newly fertilized, jump-starting it into action. After 277 attempts to clone an udder cell, Wilmut's group succeeded and Dolly was created.

(Gina Kolata, Clone: The Road to Dolly and the Path Ahead, 1998
in Bloom and Day 2000: 246–52)

(viii) The answer is '42'. But what's the question?!

[The computer 'Deep Thought' has come up with the answer to 'the meaning of life, the universe and everything'. It is '42'. Deep Thought now tells of who/what will come up with the question . . .]

'I speak of none but the computer that is to come after me,' intoned Deep Thought, his voice regaining its accustomed declamatory tones. 'A computer whose merest operational parameters I am not worthy to calculate – and yet I will design it for you. A computer which will calculate the Question to the Ultimate Answer, a computer of such infinite and subtle complexity that organic life itself shall form part of its operational matrix. And you yourselves shall take on new forms and go down into the computer to navigate its ten-million-year program! Yes! I shall design this computer for you. And I shall name it also unto you. And it shall be called . . . The Earth.'

(Douglas Adams, The Hitch Hiker's Guide to the Galaxy, 1979: 137)

Designs on the future: shaping things to come

(i) Pre-text

Design is prospective, future-oriented: in this environment, with these multiple resources, and out of my interests *now* to act newly I will shape a message.

(Gunther Kress, Literacy in the New Media Age, 2003: 169)

(ii) Design – 'An unregarded art'

I also tell in the introduction of that book [*The Sense of Order*, 1979] how my mother collected peasant embroideries of Slovakia. I was very fond of these, and often wondered as a child why people did not consider them to be art. And so I thought it is a very neglected subject. It was not at all neglected in the nineteenth century. Many people wrote about design and decoration. But in our century this interest has almost totally evaporated. Now it is coming in a little again. [. . .]

Why did this interest in decoration vanish in our century? Why did it become an 'unregarded' art, as you call it in your Introduction?

One of the reasons is, I think, that there was a kind of tension between abstract art and decoration. You often hear people say, looking at a work of abstract art:

'That would look nice as a curtain.' In other words, it looks like decoration. But the abstract painters don't want to produce decoration, they want to produce High Art. For that reason, abstract art has been anxious to distance itself from decoration. So decoration was pushed away from the center of interest. It really is an 'unregarded art'. Many people do not notice the patterns of wallpapers or materials.

(Ernst Gombrich and Didier Erebon, *Looking for Answers*, 1993: 126–7. Gombrich is answering the questions)

(iii) 'Constantly aware of the interrelationships of all things'

Not all engineers dream of designing large aircraft or other highly visible structures, for some engineers find the most elusive dreams in doing less ostensibly dramatic things more effectively, such as providing safe water supplies, disposing of waste, or cleaning up the environment. Because engineering is so inextricably involved with society and its goals, the practice of engineering is a very social endeavor, and this is perhaps nowhere so evident as the case of water supply and disposal. In this field, even where the individual engineer is working alone at a desk, computer terminal, or drawing-board, every part of his or her work must potentially interface with everything else on a technical as well as a non-technical level. In fact, no artifact or system that any engineer designs or analyzes can function independent of a larger social system, and the best designers and analysts are constantly aware of the interrelationship of all things.

(Henry Petroski, *Invention by Design*, 1997: 5–6)

(iv) Cultural morphing

[Morphing is the computer-assisted technique, widely used in film and advertising, of merging one image or figure into another.]

With morphing, technology creates and transforms the world around us. Sublime molten metal metamorphoses to a running person. A Chinese woman blends to a Native American, who in turn with a flick of the hair becomes Mr Middle America. Chameleon like, contemporary culture is full of images of change. From the making of millionaires, to the fall of the famous; images underlie a mutating contemporary experience. There is a constant invitation to re-invent. The make-over invites the mundane to become the magnificent. Shape-shifting, gender-bending, hair-straightening, colour-changing, re-defining is an everyday occurrence.

Technology has radically changed our perceptions of culture. Does this make the legacies of the past, the pain of colonialism, the impact of slavery a redundant image within our transformative present? Does this assign the past to a museum and relegate tradition to the pages of the *National Geographic*? As an artist I am frightened to fall into the trap of a reductionist view of culture. No single idea or image can distil the complexity of our current placing – seen simultaneously by a contemporary artist, cultural ambassador and an Indian in Hyperspace. The internet has brought me closer to friends in Pakistan and cousins in Trinidad. This has meant that my view as to what is understood and perceived as identity has shifted from being a passive response to cultural theory into a proactive self-analysis.

All the work that I make as an artist is informed by this debate about new ways of experimenting with both cultural and artistic morphing. *Moti Roti* produces work that aims to reflect a contemporary tangibility – but does so whilst maintaining a fluidity as to the choice of media.

(Keith Khan in *British Studies Now Anthology*,
ed. Nick Wadham-Smith, 1999: 78–80.)

From an introduction to the work of *Moti Roti* ('Fat Bread'), an international, London-based performance and arts installation company set up and co-directed by Keith Khan (the author) and Ali Zaidi. *Moti Roti* 'relies on a strong visual content and demonstrates a joining of many different art forms including theatre, visual art, dance, music, photography and film-making; site-specific installations and epic carnival engineering'.

(v) 'The shape that will define the coming decades'?

When I imagine the shape that will hover above the first half of the twenty-first century, what comes to mind is not the coiled embrace of the genome, or the etched latticework of the silicon chip. It is instead the pulsing red and green pixels of Mitch Resnick's slime mold simulation [an electronic neural network], moving erratically across the screen at first, then slowly coalescing into larger forms. The shape of those clusters – with their lifelike irregularity, and their absent pacemakers – is the shape that will define the coming decades. I see them on the screen, growing and dividing, and I think: That way lies the future.

(Steven Johnson, *Emergence*, 2001: 23)

after the end . . .

In the end, our society will be defined not only by what we create, but by what we refuse to destroy.

* * * *

In the end
    disorder reaches perfection
language dissolves into the music of wind
    chaos attains pure splendor.

In the end   out of whirlwinds whirlpools evolutions
    the world screeches to a halt   a fixed image
waters   cities the heavens   hand suspended
    the entire universe consummates itself
      in a daring
    and profound photograph

He holds up the print   still wet
    examines it for a long time
      examines himself for as long,
        gulps it down.

* * * *

Almost from the beginning of my sentence on Robben Island, I asked the authorities for permission to start a garden in the courtyard. For years they refused without offering a reason. But eventually they relented, and we were able to cut out a small garden on a narrow patch of earth against the far wall. The soil in the courtyard was dry and rocky. The courtyard had been constructed over a landfill, and in order to start my garden I had to excavate a great many rocks to allow the plants room to grow. [. . .] A garden was one of the few things in prison that one could control. To plant a seed, watch it grow, to tend it and then harvest it offered a simple but enduring satisfaction. The sense of being the custodian of this small patch of earth offered a small taste of freedom.

First passage – John Sawhill, President of the Nature Conservancy, from the epigraph in Wilson 2002.

Poem – Magda Cârneci, *Chaosmos*, translated from Romanian in Sampson 2002: 102.

Third passage – Nelson Mandela, *Long Walk to Freedom*, 1995: 582–3.

Further reading by topic

The further reading is organised by topic and keyed to the bibliography that follows. These topics recur throughout the book and can be followed up through the index, where suggested places to start are highlighted in bold. In every case the rider ' . . . **and Creativity**' should be understood.

Aesthetics

For an extensive selection of classic documents from Plato and Aristotle through Kant and Hegel to Dewey and Heidegger, see Hofstadter and Kuhns (1964) 1976. Briefer extracts that range more widely and are organised by topic can be found in Selden 1988: 245–67, Feagin and Maynard 1997 and Singer and Dunn 2000. Ideological approaches are Eagleton 1990, Willis *et al.* 1990 and Regan 1992. Joughin and Malpas 2003 offers a self-consciously 'new' aesthetics grounded in ethics, poetics and politics. For an early educational aesthetic, see Dewey (1934) 1954; and for a later one, see Abbs 1994. Gender-sensitive and feminist approaches to aesthetics are Battersby 1989, Ward Jouve 1998 and Armstrong 2000; while the body as machine and/or organism bulks large in Haraway 1985 (in Leitch 2001: 2266–99), Haraway 1991, Bordo 1993 (also in Leitch 2001: 2360–77) and Braidotti 2002. Post/modern in emphasis are Cahoone 1996, Cazeaux 2000, and Kearney and Rasmussen 2001. Relevant anthologies on theories of modern and contemporary art are Gaiger and Wood 2003 and Harrison and Wood 2003 (*also see* **Design** and **Performance**).

Business

De Bono 1992 is a popularising overview from the guru of 'lateral thinking' and, latterly, 'thinking hats'. Kirton 1994 distinguishes 'adaptors' and 'innovators' as both social roles and types of person. Rickards 1999 is more theoretical and self-consciously 'postmodern' in management style; while Seltzer and Bentley 1999 push a hi-tech, 'New (Business) Age' mentality. Sutton 2001 draws on advanced models of corporate management, and Hughes 2000 argues for a small-scale and more manageable approach to creative programming. Smith 1998 is a characteristic government programme for corporate-commercial approaches to 'the creative industries'; and Department for Education and Employment 1999 is a corresponding government report with an emphasis on cultural change and diversity (*also see* **Design**).

Chaos, complexity, emergence (including order and pattern)

Fundamental studies are Mandelbrot 1982 and Prirogine 1984, updated by Mandelbrot in Pfenninger and Shubik 2001: 191–212. Influential and accessible overviews are Gleick (1988) 1997, Waldrop 1994, Davies 1995, Coveney and Highfield 1995 and Thuan 2001 (these last two the fullest). There is an emphasis upon various kinds of 'order' in Stewart 1997 (mathematical), Bohm and Peat 2000 (physical and interpersonal), Hofstadter 1980 and 1985 (metaphysical and cognitive) and Boden 2004: 233–55 (cognitive and psychological). 'Emergence' is featured in Grand 2000, Johnson 2001 and Atkins 2003: 1–40, and its relation to personal well-being and public accountability in Brown 1998. An interesting attempt to explore chaos–order relations and complex dynamics in literature and science is Hayles 1991. Collections of essays that include stimulating treatments of chaos, complexity and emergence are Ede 2000 (arts-based), Dixon 1989 and Brockman 2002 (science and technology) and Wolfreys 2002 (humanities). For a compound model of 'chaosmos' (after Joyce and Eco), see Deleuze and Guattari (1991) 1994: 201–18.

Consciousness (including unconscious, cognitive and intelligence)

Consciousness, meaning 'awareness' and 'understanding', was a philosophical term before it was a psychological one, and was used as such by Hegel and Marx; see Lewis (1967) 1990: 181–213; Williams 1983: 320–4 and Joas 1996: 120–30. A broadly philosophical–psychological and specifically pragmatic model of many kinds and degrees of consciousness, including (famously) 'stream of consciousness', is developed by James (1901) 1970 (who effectively does without a model of the unconscious) and in some respects he anticipates both the 'multiple intelligences' notion of Gardner 1993a and 1998 and, in a more neurological vein, the model of a 'dynamic core' of consciousness developed by Edelman and Tononi 2000. Cognitive and gestalt psychologists also tend to work quite happily without a model of the unconscious; they prefer instead to operate simultaneously at various physical, emotional and intellectual levels: see Dennett 1991, 2003, Calvin 1997 and Damasio 2000; also Sternberg 1999: 189–272. For one of the more plausible Western treatments of a spiritual level and 'cosmic consciousness', see Sheldrake *et al.* 2001. The study of 'artificial intelligence', and latterly 'artificial life', is tending both to reinforce and qualify the view of multiple levels of consciousness and parallel and recursive processing: see Gelernter 1994, Grand 2000 and Boden 1996 and 2004. Cognitive models of 'world creation' and 'poetics' are applied to text reception and production by Semeno 1997 and Stockwell 2002. With all this in mind, it is salutary to observe that, even if 'the Unconscious' is allowed to exist, it takes many forms and fulfils many roles: 'individual' in Freud 1986: 135–83; 'collective' in Jung 1976: 301–60; 'linguistic' in Lacan (see Lodge and Wood 2000: 61–87); and 'semiotic' in Kristeva 1984; also see Selden 1988: 222–42. So the Unconscious may not be an 'it' – nor even an 'id' – at all (see Brooke-Rose 1991: 28–44).

Cosmology

For a global review of 'cosmogony' (ancient creation myths of the birth of the universe), see Leeming and Leeming 1994, and for the earliest Greek science, see Barnes

1987. Cosmology proper, the modern scientific study of the cosmos, is reviewed in Coles 1999 and 2001 and in Barrow 1995 and 2000. Barrow 1999 is a lively collection of essays. For other 'Theories of Everything', including 'Theories of (almost) Nothing', see Peat 1992, Gribbin and Gribbin 1998, Barrow 2001 and Atkins 2003: 237–356; and for some revealingly frank interviews with twentieth-century cosmologists, see Lightman and Brawer 1990.

Creativity (including creation)

Early research on creativity is reviewed in Vernon 1970. Koestler (1964) 1989 is an ambitious and still very readable attempt at synthesis, largely on behavioural lines. Ghiselin 1985 gathers assorted reflections on the creative process by earlier twentieth-century artists and scientists. Pfenninger and Shubik 2001 do something similar for the later twentieth century, albeit on a smaller scale; and so does Tusa 2003 through radio interviews but with an emphasis upon the arts. Leeming and Leeming 1994 and Campbell 1968 are the best places to start for creation myths and mythology as a creative resource. Csikszentmihalyi 1996 is an influential case-study-based argument in support of its author's concept of creative 'flow', which is further systematised in his model of the relations among creative 'field, domain and individual'; see Csikszentmihalyi in Sternberg 1999: 313–35 and compare the 'multiple intelligences' model of creativity in Gardner 1993a and 1998. The coming-of-age of creativity as an academic subject, chiefly in and around psychology, can be traced in Sternberg 1988 and Runco and Albert 1990; and its subsequent maturity can be appreciated in Boden 1994 and 2004, Runco and Pritzer 1999 and Sternberg 1999 (all of these are richly stimulating and constantly useful). Bohm 1998, Bohm and Peat 2000 and Peat 2000 offer a philosophically coherent model of creativity based upon a combination of theoretical physics and social interaction. Steiner 2001 is a spirited defence of the concept of (artistic) 'creation' in the face of a perceived threat by the concept of (scientific) 'invention'. Attridge 2004, more positively, revisits and recombines these two concepts in the light of contemporary literary theory. Carter 2004: 15–52 is an invaluable overview of research into creativity with respect to language in general and conversation in particular. For the rest, see the topics above and below.

Design

Through case studies, Petroski 1997 examines innovation in design in everything from paperclips to aeroplanes. Dewulf and Baillie 1999, also through case studies, explore the teaching of creative design in tertiary education in the arts, sciences and technology. Von Stamm 2003 considers the management of design innovation, as does Hughes 2000 for designedly small-scale, team-based computer ventures. Stewart 1995 opens up mathematical orders and patterns in nature. Gombrich and Erebon 1993 talk over Gombrich's earlier work on principles of order and design in the arts; while Ede 2000 takes on board the artistic design potential of kinds of chaotic, complex and emergent behaviour. Sharples 1999 approaches writing of all kinds as a matter of creative design. Design becomes a central organising principle in the theorising of contemporary multimedia practice, and multimodality in general, in Goodman and Graddol 1996, Kress and Van Leeuwen 2001 and Kress 2003.

Education (and learning)

Classic and still valuable studies are Dewey (1934) 1954, with an emphasis upon experiential learning, and Vygotsky 1934, exploring the interplay of 'inner' and 'outer' voices and growth through non-hierarchical 'zones of proximal development'. Abbs 1994 is an argument for creatively integrated and constantly renegotiated teaching and teacher-training; as is Bohm 1996 with respect to dialogue as 'participatory thinking'. *All Our Futures: Creativity, Culture and Education* (Department for Education and Employment 1999) is a valuable policy document relating creativity to multicultural experience and communicative experiment as well as personal expression. Seltzer and Bentley 1999 offer a more overtly corporate/commercial view of 'knowledge and skills for the new economy'. Abbs 2003 offers a powerful critique of both market values and postmodern irony and argues for creative education based upon personally responsive and socially responsible ethics and aesthetics. Centre for Advances in Higher Education 1999 is full of practical advice on creative course and programme design; while Dewulf and Baillie 1999 presents case studies of creative course design in Art, Science and Engineering. Styles of thinking and learning (spatial, kinetic, logical, musical, verbal, etc.) are reviewed by Gardner 1993a, 1998; and Nickerson in Sternberg 1999: 392–430 looks at programmes for enhancing and evaluating creativity. The best of the latter emphasise the building of contexts and conditions that embed and sustain creativity rather than one-off, add-on programmes in 'creative thinking'. So do the case studies in Hart *et al.* 2004, which point, for example, to the need to cultivate trust, confidence, competence and relevance as preconditions for risk-taking and experiment. The latter is rich in policy proposals as well as practical guidance for 'learning without limits' based on principles of 'transformability' rather than 'fixed ability'. More theoretical is Boden 2004: 133–46, which offers a computational 'connectionist' model of classroom interaction that is self-organising, pattern-forming and problem-posing (*also see* **Play**).

Evolution (including genetics)

Ridley 1997 provides an overview of central issues and a sampling of key documents. Arguments over the nature and pace of evolution – determined or contingent, competitive or co-operative, gradual or discontinuous – can be traced in Gould 2002. Though as Gould (1989) 1991 represents one of the positions, this should be compared with Dawkins 1989 and 1998, who represents another (itself gradually modified to the notion of the gene as 'selfish co-operator'). Stereleny 2001 is a handy summary of the debate. Rose 1997, like Gould, insists upon a non-reductive view of interactions across genetic, organismal and environmental levels, and develops a model of dynamic 'lifelines' accordingly. Coen 1999 also emphasises the strictly non-determinist and broadly 'artistic' development of genes within organisms within environments; while Nettle 2001 sees the genetic predisposition to kinds of 'madness' as a distinctly human trait that entails rewards (i.e. 'strong imagination') as well as risks, depending upon the culture in which it is expressed. Stewart and Cohen 1997 develop the notion of 'extelligence' (partly corresponding to Dawkins's notion of 'memes') as the developing cultural repertoire that is passed on from one generation to the next, over and above any innate and genetically transmitted 'intelligence'. Calvin 1997 (neurologically) and Humphrey 2002 (psychologically) explore the evolution of the human mind; as does Greenfield 2004 with an acute awareness of technological in(ter)-vention. Dennett 2003 develops its author's concept of evolving consciousness, Dennett 1991, in the context of the idea of 'freedom' which itself evolves.

Genius

The classic nineteenth-century study is Galton 1869, which relates individual genius to evidence of abilities and disabilities in families; it underwrites a eugenic view of social engineering. Links between kinds of genius and kinds of madness are chronicled in Porter 1991: 490–518, and examined from different points of view in Jamison 1994 (clinical) and Nettle 2001 (anthropological). Eysenck (1995) makes a distinctive case for the adventurously 'over-inclusive' nature of genius, which only turns to pathology when thwarted. Howe 1999 expresses the dominant twentieth-century view by explaining genius as the result of a complex interaction of inherited traits with familial and more broadly cultural factors; he insists that it is continuous with 'ordinary' mental capacities. The tendency to talk of genius in terms of great individual minds persists but is contentious in the research literature (contrast Simonton and Howe in Sternberg 1999: 116–36, 431–48, for example). Bloom 2002 characteristically compounds the issue by on the one hand singling out 'one hundred exemplary creative minds' and on the other conceding that 'genius, however repressed, exists in so many readers' (p. 8). Bloom draws on ancient 'wisdom' traditions, Jewish and Gnostic, for his own inspiration. Further signposts to earlier collective as well as later individualist conceptions of genius are provided by Williams 1983: 143–4 and Preminger and Brogan 1993: 455–6; also see Selden 1988: 150–63. Battersby 1989 exposes the male-based premises of much of the tradition and points to alternatives, as do Gilbert and Gubar (1979) 2000 and Ward Jouve 1998. Koestler (1964) 1989: 674–702, Ochse 1990 and Gardner 1998 establish types of genius (including types of intelligence) characteristic of the arts and sciences and society at large, albeit exemplified through individuals. Geake and Dodson (2004) is a critical review of the education of 'gifted children' – and by extension the potential 'giftedness' of all children – based on a capacious model of 'creative intelligence'.

Imagination (including image)

The classic study of the imagination as a 'mirror' (reflecting) and a 'lamp' (generating) significance is Abrams 1953; the Introduction is in Lodge 1972: 1–27. This may be supplemented by the historical overview in Kearney 1994 and the specifically postmodern image of the 'labyrinth of mirrors' in Kearney 1998; also see the entries in Williams 1983: 158–9 and Preminger and Brogan 1993: 556–75, and the extracts in Selden 1988: 9–39, 125–49. But images of imagination are as theoretically boundless as they are, in any given instance, historically grounded; hence the proliferation of 'images of thought' and pragmatic 'tools/goods for thinking' offered by sign-theory and post/structuralism; e.g. Barthes 1957 and 1977, Hawkes 1977, Brooke-Rose 1991 and Wheeler 1993. Meanwhile, Deleuze and Guattari (1980) 1988 and (1991) 1994 offer the image of the multiply shooting and rooting 'rhizome/tuber' as an alternative model of concept creation to that of the single-trunked and potentially monolithic 'tree'.

Science, too, is replete with images and analogies for what otherwise might remain ineffable and inexpressible outside the specialised codes of mathematics; see Gould (1989) 1991, Gregory 1990, Stewart 1995, Barrow 1999 and Miller 2000. The radically changed nature and status of the art image 'in an age of mechanical reproduction' is recognised early on by Benjamin (*c.* 1935) 1970: 219–53 and carried through in Baudrillard's (1980s) concept of 'the simulacrum' as an image without authenticating reference in the world beyond; both can be found in Kearney and Rasmussen 2001: 166–81, 411–30. *Also see* **Language (including metaphor and dialogue)**.

Inspiration

An excellent historical overview through contemporary theoretical lenses is Clark 1997. This draws on Derrida 1992, among others, and is a project that is carried through in Attridge 2004. Preminger and Brogan 1993: 609–10 provides useful points of reference spanning divine inspiration and human influence. For an eclectic and broadly 'inspirational' view of the creative process drawing on many arts and some sciences, see Ghiselin 1985, also Vernon 1970: 53–88. For literature in particular, these may be supplemented with Allott 1959 (classic novel), Herbert and Hollis 2000 (modern and contemporary poetry) and Monteith *et al.* 2004 (contemporary fiction). Sometimes these talk about 'inspiration' as such; more often they refer, as do Bloom 1973 and Gilbert and Gubar (1979) 2000, to kinds of 'influence' or 'prompt' or 'occasion' – and plenty of *per*spiration.

Language (including metaphor and dialogue)

Language is hailed as a routine yet remarkable creative resource in every linguistic approach featured: generative-transformational (Chomsky 1972, Pinker 1994 and 1999); functional (Halliday 1994); dialogic (Bakhtin 1979 and 1986); psychological (Vygotsky (1934) 1987, Lacan (1957) in Lodge and Wood 2000: 61–87); and cognitive (Semeno 1997, Stockwell 2002). There is a handy overview and selection in Burke *et al.* 2000: 330–72. Metaphor is the most obvious and widely recognised aspect of wor(l)d creation that may refresh and enliven perception; but, as all commentators also observe, much of language consists of 'dead' and over-familiar metaphors that lull or dull the senses and deaden the mind: see Hawkes 1972; Lakoff and Johnson 1980 and 1999; Gregory 1990; Gibbs 1994 and Ricoeur in Kearney 1995. A less obvious but perhaps more pervasive aspect of linguistic creativity is the capacity of speakers to refresh and extend social relations through the 'give and take' of dialogue, notably in conversation: see Tannen 1989, Sawyer 2001 and Carter 2004. This last offers a comprehensive and challenging overview of the subject. Nash 1998 is an engaging series of meditations on the illusions of verbal creation, in and out of literature (*also see* **Literature** and **Play**).

Life

'Life' – like 'creativity' – seems an obvious or imponderable subject till you come to think about it: Joas 1996: 116–25 suggests we do just that. A crucial reference for life *as* 'creative evolution' is Bergson 1911 and, more generally, the collection in Bergson

2002. These writings need to be read carefully and in context to overcome the casual dismissal of Bergson as a mere 'vitalist' obsessed with the 'vital impulse' (*élan vital*). Mullarkey 1999 sets the record straight and also sets Bergson's work in a fresh relation to modern critical theory, especially that of Deleuze 1968 and 1995. For the 'vital', 'viral' and finally 'germinal' tendencies of the latter, see Patton 1996, Marks 1998 and Ansell Pearson 1999. Another key reference is Schrödinger (1944) 1995 which in asking the question 'What is life?' helped prompt the search for a physical–chemical interface for life (subsequently identified as DNA). It also prompted Margulis and Sagan 1995 to re-pose the question half a century later in the light of subsequent discoveries in evolutionary genetics; also see Davies 1998. Meanwhile, Boden 1994, 1996 and 2004 confirm the increasing overlap between contemporary understandings of creativity, artificial intelligence and, latterly, artificial life; this last is also featured in Grand 2000 and Bentley 2001. Very different resonances of these debates can be picked up in Haraway 1991 and Braidotti 2002 (who tend to celebrate the opportunities opened up by our 'cyborg' or 'metallomorphic' selves) and Penrose 1994 and Greenfield 2004 (who view with disbelief or dismay the threats to what they conceive as a distinctly human autonomy and creativity). *Also see* **Evolution**.

Literature and writing (including creative writing)

The temptation to split this entry into two or three separate topics will be resisted. These issues benefit from being grasped in a connected way. The fact that 'literature' used to – and sometimes still can – mean 'anything written' and that it subsequently became narrowed and elevated to its current dominant sense of 'imaginative writing reckoned to be of value' is traced by Williams 1977: 45–54, 145–50 and 1983: 183–8 and Widdowson 1999, and deconstructed by Attridge 1988 and 2004. The range of literature in English featured in the anthology in Part 3 is substantially covered by Baym *et al.* 1994, Thieme 1996, Gates and McKay 1997 and Abrams *et al.* 2000. Carter and McRae 2001 is a relevant history and Walder 2004 a relevant selection of critical and theoretical documents. For the development of courses and programmes in writing (spanning rhetoric and composition, writing across the curriculum and writing within the disciplines, as well as creative writing) alongside or apart from courses in language and literature, see Graff 1987, Berlin 1996 and Scholes 1998 (for US perspectives) and Evans 1993 and Pope 2002 (for UK perspectives). For the phrase 'creative writing', first recorded in American educational contexts in the 1930s, see *OED* 1989 ('creative') and Williams 1983: 82–4. Bennett and Royle 2004: 85–92 and Pope 2002: 9–11, 196–9 introduce issues surrounding the relations between 'creative writing' and (English) 'literature'; Dawson 2004 is a fuller treatment in the context of the 'New Humanities'. Course-books and textbooks that recognise and encourage a wide range of writing and reading practices – critical and creative, expository and experimental – include: Elbow and Belanoff 1995; Scholes *et al.* 1995; Nash and Stacey 1997; Bartholomae and Petrosky 1999; Sharples 1999 and Goatly 2000. More free-standing yet still flexible course-books in creative writing (concentrating on poetry, prose fiction, script-writing and life-writing) include Mills 1995, Bell and Magrs 2001 and Newman *et al.* 2004; also, with an emphasis upon the links with theory, Peach and Burton 1995 and Hunt and Sampson (forthcoming 2005). Meanwhile, there continues to be a steady growth in kinds of creative language and literature practice designed for second-language learners and often adaptable for first-language users. These operate at all levels, from school to university, and extend beyond mere language games and 'fun' activities to full-blown text-production and analysis. Examples are McRae 1991, Bassnett and Grundy 1993, Pope 1995 and 2003, Carter and McRae 1996 and Spiro 2004. Finally, whether we speak of 'literature' *or* 'writing', the challenge is to engage with cultures that are increasingly multimodal (not just verbal) in form and both global and local (not just national) in provenance and destination; for which see Goodman and Graddol 1996, Department for Education and Employment 1999, Kress 1995 and 2003 and Finnegan 2002; also the capacious and challenging volumes on creativity and 'the art of English' edited by Goodman and O'Halloran and by Maybin and Swann (forthcoming).

Performance

Huxley and Witts 2002 is a stimulating sampling of twentieth-century performance theory and practice, and Bentley 1968 a good selection of late nineteenth- and earlier twentieth-century pronouncements on theatre. Hilton 1987 is a useful basic account and Connor 1997: 141–81 an expressly postmodern one. Brook 1968 remains a key reference on the filling of 'the empty space' with various kinds of 'rough', 'holy' and 'dull' theatre; as is Boal 1992 for politically engaged 'theatre games for actors and non-actors', and Lecoq (1997) 2000 for mime and mask work. Improvisation in music is treated by Dean 1989 and Berliner 1994. In concert with Newman and inspired by Vygotsky (1934) 1987, Holzman 1999 articulates a performance-based approach to psychology. For an interventive and performative (post)pedadogy, after Beuys and before Giroux, see Ulmer 1985; and for a further development of Beuys's 'social sculpture', see Sacks 2002. The 'event-full' nature of encounters with texts is emphasised by Derrida 1992, commented upon by Currie in Wolfreys 2001: 152–68 and carried through in Attridge 2004. A good introduction to 'performance criticism' (the exploration of texts through acted interpretation) is Makaryk 1993: 133–9; and Bauman 1986 examines the performance-based nature of oral narrative, as does Vizenour (1989) for Native American narratives in a postmodern context. For 'performatives' and 'speech acts' as aspects of 'pragmatics' in language, see those entries in Wales 2001.

Play and game

A good historical and theoretical overview is Makaryk 1993: 64–9, 145–9. Huizinga (1944) 1970 is the classic study of human culture *as* play. Caillois 1961 offers an influential taxonomy of kinds of game; and Turner 1982 traces 'serious play' in its ritualistic and theatrical aspects. Cook 2000 is an excellent overview with respect to language learning, and Farb 1974 and Crystal 1998 are engaging accounts of language play at large. The psychologically creative aspects of 'child's play', though not only among children, are explored by Winnicott 1971; while Willis *et al.* 1990 examine symbolic work at/as play in contemporary youth culture. Modern philosophies of more or less 'free' and 'infinite' play are explored by Derrida 1966 (in Lodge and Wood 2000: 88–103) and Carse 1987; while 'language games' of one kind and another are played by Wittgenstein (1953) 1967 and Lyotard 1989. Contemporary 'games theory' is articulated in terms of emerging complexity by Coveney and High-field 1995: 222–32 and in terms of evolving freedom by Dennett 2003: 147–50, 196–202.

'Post-'

In so far as the present approach tries to get 'past the post-' of current theories misunderstood as orthodoxies, it seeks to carry through the projects of postmodernism, poststructuralism and postcolonialism in other directions and dimensions. Certainly, this is neither 'pre-' nor 'post-' theory but very much *in theorising*; and in that respect chimes with Eagleton 2003 (also see Pope 2002: 6–7, 127–66). The following are just some of the works that I continue to find both informing and inspiring (not least because they defy such crude if convenient categories):

Postmodernism – Hutcheon 1988, Harvey 1993, Wheale 1995, Connor 1997, Kearney 1998 and Drolet 2004.
Poststructuralism – Young 1981, Derrida 1992, Wheeler 1993 and Spivak 1995 and 1999 (who as a self-styled postcolonial 'practical deconstructionist feminist Marxist' naturally brings us to . . .)
Postcolonialism – Bhabha 1994, Boehmer 1995 (second edition in preparation), Ashcroft *et al.* 1995 and 2000 and Thieme 1996 and 2003; also see Goldberg and Quayson 2002. More generally, I find that Wolfreys 2001 and 2002 point lots of promising ways forwards and around (*also see* **'Re . . .'** next).

'Re . . .'

The present conceptualising of *re . . . creation* draws on various models of repetition with difference (variation with adaptation, evolution through revolution, etc.). Fundamental is the work on 'Difference and Repetition' by Deleuze 1968, also Deleuze and Guattari (1980) 1987: 310–50 and (1991) 1994: 173–90. Crucially, this work is itself being extensively revisited and reworked (in the present terms, re . . . created) by a number of critical philosophers and cultural theorists, notably Ansell Pearson 1997 and 1999, Marks 1998, Colebrook 2002: 103–24 and Williams 2003. Comparison may be made with Derrida's notions of (re)iteration and (re)invention and of deconstruction as a form of reconstruction, especially in so far as he goes beyond his earlier idea of *différance* (difference as deferral) to a more positive notion of difference as provisional preference; see Derrida 1992 and the related re-articulations of difference in Attridge 1988 and 2004. The 'variation on a theme' idea developed in Hofstadter 1980 and 1985 is itself a suggestive variation on a similar idea. More directly relevant are Rich's (1971) concept of feminist 're-vision' (in Bartholomae and Petrosky 1999: 603–20), the concepts of 're-membering' current in both life-writing and postcolonial discourses (e.g. Goldberg and Quayson 2002: 143–73; Kearney 2002; Gates and McKay (1997) 2004) and Gablik's (1991) project for the 'reenchantment' of community art practices. The idea of a fully dialogic 'responsiveness' that may be grasped as a kind of aesthetic and ethical 'responsibility/response-ability' also has a direct bearing on this project: see Bakhtin 1979, 1986 and 1990. Meanwhile, for the idea that prompted the development of suspension dots (. . .) to mark a gap that needs

filling, bridging, or jumping in some particular situation and with a preferred discourse, see Gendlin 1962 and 1997. For the moment at least, such a discourse (duly
're . . . created') is likely to derive in part from one of the available current *'Post-'* positions (for which see the previous topic).

Sciences (and humanities and human sciences)

Especially timely – but sadly his last book – is Gould (2003) 2004 with its express
project of 'mending and minding the misconceived gap between science and the
humanities'. As a critical and creative response to Wilson 1998, this is more respectful
of the differences of culture involved and more positive about the ways in which the
gaps may be bridged or jumped, and not merely filled in or fallen into. In Part Two
of their last book together, Deleuze and Guattari (1991) 1994 grapple more contentiously with the relations among 'philosophy, science, logic and art'; and Critchley
2001: 90–122 provides a broader context for contemporary debates about the nature
of philosophy and science. Thoughtful and thought-provoking general accounts of
science are Gribbin and Gribbin 1998 and Barrow 2000; and generous selections of
classic and contemporary documents are Dixon 1989 and Carey 1995. A particularly
witty and well-informed frolic across the sciences – with fantasy fiction and seriously
funny humour as essential ingredients – is Pratchett *et al.* 2002. Authoritative collections of essays representing dialogues between religion and science are Weber 1988
and Lorimer 1999; while Teilhard de Chardin (1955) 1969 and Capra 1983 offer
stimulating and influential as well as idiosyncratic overviews. All these writers and
writings get well beyond the (British) 'two cultures' debate and the (American) 'science
and culture wars' as conventionally conceived and persistently misrepresented; for
critical accounts of which see Bloom and Day 2000, Vol. 3: 11–21, Eaglestone 2002:
10–12, Newman in Holzman 1999: 133–43 and Gould (2003) 2004: 81–104. An
authoritative general reference for the history of the human sciences is Smith 1997.
For other accounts of the more or less continuous or discontinuous, evolutionary or
revolutionary development of the sciences – pure and applied, human and otherwise
– see Kuhn 1970, Foucault (1966) 1972, Feyerabend 1975, and Feynman 1999.
Various 'Critical realist', as distinct from 'Cultural relativist', positions are argued by
Salomon 1984, Bhaskar 1986 and Rescher 1987, and the debate is provocatively
summarised by Norris in Payne 1996: 485–96. Battle-lines still appear to be being
drawn in the collections of future-oriented essays by Brockman 2002 (sciences and
technology in emphasis) and Wolfreys 2002 (humanities and human sciences in
emphasis). But the substantial overlaps of subject matter, if not of approach, in the
areas of chaos, complexity and emergence as well as artificial life suggest that, at least
potentially, they may be fighting on the same side. (*Also see* **Cosmology**, **Evolution**
and **Genius**.)

Bibliography

Abbs, P. (ed.) (1989) *The Symbolic Order*, London: Hutchinson.
—— (1994) *The Educational Imperative: A Defence of Socratic and Aesthetic Learning*, London and Washington, DC: The Falmer Press.
—— (2003) *Against the Flow: The Arts, Postmodern Culture and Education*, London: Routledge/Falmer.
Abrams. M. H. (1953) *The Mirror and the Lamp: Romantic Theory and the Critical Tradition*, Oxford: Oxford University Press.
Abrams, M. H., Greenblatt, S., *et al.* (eds) (2000) *The Norton Anthology of English Literature*, two vols, 7th edn, New York: Norton.
Adams, D. (1979) *The Hitch Hiker's Guide to the Galaxy*, London: Pan.
Adams, D. (1980) *The Restaurant at the End of the Universe*, London: Pan.
Aeschylus (1961) *Prometheus Bound and other Tragedies*, trans. D. Lee, Harmondsworth: Penguin.
Allott, M. (ed.) (1959) *Novelists on the Novel*, London: Routledge and Kegan Paul.
Angelou, Maya (1989) *Conversations with Maya Angelou*, ed. J. M. Elliott, University Press of Mississippi.
Ansell Pearson, K. (ed.) (1997) *Deleuze and Philosophy: The Difference Engineer*, London: Routledge.
—— (1999) *Germinal Life: The Difference and Repetition of Deleuze*, London: Routledge.
Apuleius (1994) *The Golden Ass*, trans. P. G. Walsh, Oxford: Oxford University Press.
Armstrong, I. (2000) *The Radical Aesthetic*, Oxford: Blackwell.
Ashcroft, B., Griffiths, G. and Tiffin, H. (eds) (1995) *The Postcolonial Studies Reader*, London: Routledge.
—— (2000) *Postcolonial Studies: The Key Concepts*, London: Routledge.
Atkins, P. (2003) *Galileo's Finger: The Ten Great Ideas of Science*, Oxford: Oxford University Press.
Attridge, D. (1988) *Peculiar Language: Literature as Difference from the Renaissance to James Joyce*, London: Methuen, 2nd edn in preparation.
—— (2004) *The Singularity of Literature*, London: Routledge.
Ayto, J. (1990) *The Bloomsbury Dictionary of Word Origins*, London: Bloomsbury.
Badiou, A. (2003) *Infinite Thought*, trans. and ed. Oliver Feltham and Justin Clemens, London and New York: Continuum.
Bakhtin, M. ([1965] 1968) *Rabelais and his World*, trans. H. Iswolsky, Cambridge, MA: MIT Press.
—— (1979) *The Aesthetics of Verbal Creation (Estetika Slovesnogo Tvortchestva)*, Moscow: Iskusstvo.
—— (1981) *The Dialogic Imagination: Four Essays*, ed. Michael Holquist, trans. C. Emerson and M. Holquist, Manchester: Manchester University Press.
—— (1984) *Speech Genres and Other Late Essays*, trans, V. McGee, Austin: University of Texas Press.
—— (1990) *Art and Answerability: Early Philosophical Works*, ed. Michael Holquist and V. Liapunov, Austin: University of Texas Press.

Barnes, J. (ed. and trans.) (1987) *Early Greek Philosophy*, London: Penguin.

Barrow, J. (1995) *The Artful Universe: The Cosmic Source of Human Creativity*, London: Penguin.

—— (1999) *Between Inner Space and Outer Space: Essays on Science, Art and Philosophy*, Oxford: Oxford University Press.

—— (2000) *The Universe that Discovered Itself*, Oxford: Oxford University Press.

—— (2001) *The Book of Nothing*, London: Vintage.

Barthes, R. (1957) *Mythologies*, trans. A. Lavers, New York: Hill and Wang.

—— (1977) *Image–Music–Text*, ed. and trans. S. Heath, London: Fontana.

Bartholomae, D. and Petrosky, A. (eds) (1999) *Ways of Reading: An Anthology for Writers*, 5th edn, Boston: Bedford/New York: St Martin's Press.

Bassnett, S. and Grundy, P. (1993) *Language through Literature: Creative Language Teaching through Literature*, London: Longman.

Battersby, C. (1989) *Gender and Genius. Towards a Feminist Aesthetics*, London: The Women's Press.

Bauman. R. (1986) *Story, Performance and Event: Contextual Studies of Oral Narrative*, Cambridge: Cambridge University Press.

Baym, N. *et al.* (eds) (1994) *The Norton Anthology of American Literature*, two vols, 5th edn, New York: Norton.

Bell, J. and Magrs, P. (eds) (2001) *The Creative Writing Coursebook*, London: Macmillan.

Benjamin, W. (1970) *Illuminations*, ed. H. Arendt, trans. H. Zohn, London: Cape.

Bennett, A. and Royle, N. (2004) *An Introduction to Literature, Criticism and Theory*, 3rd edn, Harlow: Longman.

Bentley, E. (ed.) (1968) *The Theory of the Modern Stage*, Harmondsworth: Penguin.

Bentley, P. (2001) *Digital Biology: the Creation of Life inside Computers*, London: Headline.

Bergson, H. ([1911] 1964) *Creative Evolution*, trans. Arthur Mitchell, London: Macmillan.

—— (2002) *Henri Bergson: Key Writings*, ed. K. Ansell Pearson and J. Mullarkey, New York: Continuum.

Berlin, J. (1996) *Rhetorics, Poetics, Culture: Refiguring College English Studies*, Philadelphia, PA: National Council of Teachers of English.

Berliner, P. (1994) *Thinking in Jazz: The Infinite Art of Improvisation*, Chicago: Chicago University Press.

Bhabha, H. (1994) *The Location of Culture*, London: Routledge.

Blake, W. (1972) *Blake: Complete Writings*, ed. G. Keynes, Oxford: Oxford University Press.

Bloom, C. and Day, G. (eds) (2000) *Literature and Culture in Modern Britain*, Vol. 3, London: Longman.

Bloom, H. ([1973] 1997) *The Anxiety of Influence*, 2nd edn, Oxford: Oxford University Press.

—— (2002) *Genius: A Mosaic of One Hundred Exemplary Creative Minds*, London: Fourth Estate.

Bloom, W. (ed.) (2000) *Holistic Revolution: The Essential New Age Reader*, London: Allen Lane.

Boal, A. (1992) *Games for Actors and Non-actors*, trans. A. Jackson, London: Routledge.

Boden, M. (ed.) (1994) *Dimensions of Creativity*, Cambridge, MA: MIT Press.

—— (ed.) (1996) *The Philosophy of Artificial Life*, Oxford: Oxford University Press.

—— (2004) *The Creative Mind: Myths and Mechanisms*, 2nd edn, London: Routledge.

Boehmer, E. (1995) *Colonial and Postcolonial Literature*, Oxford: Oxford University Press.

Bohm, D. (1996) *On Dialogue*, ed. Lee Nichol, London: Routledge.

—— (1998) *On Creativity*, ed. Lee Nichol, London: Routledge.

Bohm, D. and Peat, F. D. (2000) *Science, Order and Creativity*, London: Routledge.

Bordo. S. ([1993] 2004) *Unbearable Weight: Feminism, Western Culture and the Body*, 2nd edn, Berkeley and Los Angeles: University of California Press.

Bradbury, M. (ed.) (1990) *The Novel Today: Contemporary Writers on Modern Fiction*, London: Fontana.

Braidotti, R. (2002) *Metamorphoses: Towards a Materialist Theory of Becoming*, Oxford: Blackwell.

Breen, J. (ed.) *Women Romantics 1785–1832: Writing in Prose*, London: Everyman.

Brockman, J. (ed.) (2002) *The Next Fifty Years: Science in the First Half of the Twenty-First Century*, London: Weidenfeld and Nicolson.

Brontë, E. ([1847] 1985) *Wuthering Heights*, ed. D. Daiches, Harmondsworth: Penguin.

Brook, P. (1968) *The Empty Space*, Harmondsworth: Penguin.

Brooke-Rose, C. (1991) *Stories, Theories and Things*, Cambridge: Cambridge University Press.

Brown, D. (1998) *Cybertrends: Chaos, Power and Accountability in the Information Age*, Harmondsworth: Penguin.

Browning, R. ([1868–9] 2001) *The Ring and the Book*, ed. R. Altick and T. Collins, Ontario: Broadview.

Burke, E. ([1757] 1990) *A Philosophical Enquiry into our Ideas of the Sublime*, ed. A Phillips, Oxford: Oxford University Press.

Burke, K. (1966) *Language as Symbolic Action*, Berkeley: University of California Press.

Burke, L., Crowley, T. and Girvin A. (eds) (2000) *The Routledge Language and Culture Theory Reader*, London: Routledge.

Byron, G. G. (1986) *Byron*, ed. J. J. McGann, Oxford: Oxford University Press.

Cahoone, L. (ed.) (1996) *From Modernism to Postmodernism: An Anthology*, Oxford: Blackwell.

Caillois, R. (1961) *Man, Play and Games*, trans. M. Barash, New York: Free Press of Glencoe.

Calvin, W. H. (1997) *How Brains Think: Evolving Intelligence, Then and Now*, London: Weidenfeld and Nicolson.

Campbell, J. (1968) *Creative Mythology: The Masks of God*, Harmondsworth: Penguin.

Capra, F. (1983) *The Tao of Physics*, 2nd edition, London: Fontana.

Carey, J. (ed.) (1995) *The Faber Book of Science*, London: Faber and Faber.

Carroll, R. and Prickett, S. (eds) (1997) *The Bible: Authorized King James Version*, Oxford: Oxford University Press.

Carse, J. (1987) *Finite and Infinite Games. A Vision of Life as Play and Possibility*, Harmondsworth: Penguin.

Carter, R. (1997) *Investigating English Discourse: Language, Literacy and Literature*, London: Routledge.

—— (2004) *Language and Creativity: The Art of Common Talk*, London: Routledge.

Carter, R. and McRae, J. (eds) (1996) *Language, Literature and the Learner: Creative Classroom Practice*, London: Longman.

—— (2001) *The Routledge History of Literature in English: Britain and Ireland*, 2nd edn, London: Routledge.

Caws, M. A. and Prendergast, C. (eds) (1994) *The HarperCollins World Reader*, New York: Harper-Collins.

Cazeaux, C. (ed.) (2000) *The Continental Aesthetics Reader*, London: Routledge.

Centre for Advances in Higher Education (1999) *Stimulating Students' Creativity in Higher Education*, Newcastle: University of Northumbria at Newcastle, UK.

Certeau, M. de (1984) *The Practice of Everyday Life*, trans. S. Rendall, Berkeley: University of California Press.

Chan, W.-T. (ed.) (1963) *A Source Book in Chinese Philosophy*, Princeton, NJ: Princeton University Press.

Charters, A. and Charters, S. (eds) (2001) *Literature and its Writers*, 2nd edn, Boston: Bedford/New York: St Martin's Press.

Chatwin, B. ([1987] 1988) *The Songlines*, London: Picador.

Chaucer, G. (1988) *The Riverside Chaucer*, ed. L. Benson, 3rd edn, Oxford: Oxford University Press.

Chinweizu (ed.) (1988) *Voices from Twentieth-century Africa: Griots and Towncriers*, London: Faber and Faber.

Chomsky, N. (1972) *Language and Mind*, New York: Harcourt Brace and World.

Churchill. C. (2002) *A Number*, London: Nick Hern Books.

Clare, J. (1990) *John Clare: Selected Poetry*, ed. G. Summerfield, Harmondsworth: Penguin.

Clark, T. (1997) *The Theory of Inspiration. Composition as a Crisis of Subjectivity in Romantic and Post-Romantic Writing*, Manchester: Manchester University Press.

Coen, E. (1999) *The Art of Genes: How Organisms Make Themselves*, Oxford: Oxford University Press.

Colebrook, C. (2002) *Gilles Deleuze*, London: Routledge.

Coleridge, S. T. (1985) *The Major Works*, Oxford: Oxford University Press.

Coles, P. (ed.) (1999) *The Routledge Critical Dictionary of the New Cosmology*, London: Routledge.

—— (2001) *Cosmology: A Very Short Introduction*, Oxford: Oxford University Press.

Connor, S. (1997) *Postmodernist Culture*, 2nd edn, Oxford: Blackwell.

Cook, G. (2000) *Language Play, Language Learning*, Oxford: Oxford University Press.

Coupe, L. (1997) *Myth*, London: Routledge.

Coveney, P. and Highfield, R. (1995) *Frontiers of Complexity: The Search for Order in a Chaotic World*, London: Faber and Faber.

Cressy, D. (2001) *Agnes Bowker's Cat: Travesties and Transgressions in Tudor and Stuart England*, Oxford: Oxford University Press.

Critchley, S. (2001) *Continental Philosophy: A Very Short Introduction*, Oxford: Oxford University Press.

Crystal, D. (1998) *Language Play*, London: Penguin.

Csikszentmihalyi, M. (1996) *Creativity: Flow and the Psychology of Discovery and Invention*, New York: HarperCollins.

Cuddon, J. (1998) *A Dictionary of Literary Terms and Literary Theory*, 4th edn rev. C. E. Preston, Harmondsworth: Penguin/Oxford: Blackwell,.

Damasio, A. (2000) *The Feeling of What Happens: Body and Emotion in the Making of Consciousness*, New York: HarperCollins.

Danielewski. M. Z. (2000) *House of Leaves*, New York: Doubleday.

Darwin, C. ([1859] 1998) *The Origin of Species*, ed. J. Wallace, Ware: Wordsworth.

Davies, P. (1995) *The Cosmic Blueprint: Order and Complexity at the Edge of Chaos*, London: Penguin.

—— (1998) *The Fifth Miracle: The Search for the Origin of Life*, London: Allen Lane.

Dawkins, R. ([1976] 1989) *The Selfish Gene*, 2nd edn, Oxford: Oxford University Press.

—— (1998) *Unweaving the Rainbow: Science, Delusion and the Appetite for Wonder*, London: Allen Lane.

Dawson, P. (2004) *Creative Writing and the New Humanities*, London: Routledge.

Dean, R. (1989) *Creative Improvisation: Jazz, Contemporary Music and Beyond*, Milton Keynes: Open University Press.

De Bono, E. (1992) *Serious Creativity*, New York: HarperCollins.

Deleuze, G. (1968) *Différence et Répétition*, Paris: Presses Universitaires de France.

—— ([1968] 1994) *Difference and Repetition*, trans. P. Patton, New York: Columbia University Press.

—— ([1988] 1993) *The Fold: Leibniz and the Baroque*, trans. T. Conley, London: Athlone Press.

—— ([1991] 1995) *Negotiations, 1972–1990*, trans. M. Joughin, New York: Columbia University Press.

Deleuze, G. and Guattari, F. ([1972] 1982) *Anti-Oedipus: Capitalism and Schizophrenia*, trans. R. Hurley *et al.*, New York: Viking Press.

—— ([1980] 1988) *A Thousand Plateaus*, trans. B. Massumi, London: Athlone.

—— ([1991] 1994) *What is Philosophy?*, trans. G. Burchell and H. Tomlinson, London and New York: Verso.

Deleuze, G. and Parnet, C. ([1977] 1987) *Dialogues*, trans. H. Tomlinson and B. Habberjam, London: Athlone Press.

Dennett, D. (1991) *Consciousness Explained*, London: Allen Lane.

—— (2003) *Freedom Evolves*, London: Allen Lane.

Department for Education and Employment (1999) *All Our Futures: Creativity, Culture and Education*, Report of the UK National Advisory Committee on Creative and Cultural Education chaired by Ken Robinson, London: The Stationery Office (www.dfes.gov.uk/nacce).

Derrida, J. (1992) *Acts of Literature*, ed. D. Attridge, New York and London: Routledge.

Dewey, J. ([1934] 1954) *Art as Experience*, New York: Capricorn.

Dewulf, S. and Baillie, C. (1999) *Case Studies: How to Foster Creativity. Creativity in Art, Science and Engineering*, London: Department for Education and Employment.

Dixon, B. (ed.) (1989) *From Creation to Chaos: Classic Writings in Science*, Oxford: Blackwell.

Drolet, M. (ed.) (2004) *The Postmodernism Reader: Foundational Texts*, London: Routledge.

Duff, D. (ed.) (2000) *Modern Genre Theory*, London: Longman.

Eaglestone, R. (2002) *Doing English*, 2nd edn, London: Routledge.

Eagleton, T. (1990) *The Ideology of the Aesthetic*, Oxford: Blackwell.

—— (1996) *Literary Theory: An Introduction*, 2nd edn, Oxford: Blackwell.

—— (2003) *After Theory*, London: Allen Lane.

Eco, U., Gould, S. J., Carrière J.-C. and Delumeau, J. (1999) *Conversations about the End of Time*, London: Allen Lane.

Ede, S. (ed.) (2000) *Strange and Charmed: Science and the Contemporary Visual Arts*, London: Calouste Gulbenkian Foundation.

Edelman, G. M. and Tononi, G. (2000) *Consciousness: How Matter Becomes Imagination*, London: Allen Lane.

Elbow, P. and Belanoff, P. (1995) *A Community of Writers: A Workshop Course in Writing*, 2nd edn, New York: McGraw-Hill.

Evans, C. (1993) *English People: The Experience of Teaching and Learning English in British Universities*, Buckingham: Open University Press.

Evans, P. and Deehan, G. (1988) *The Keys to Creativity*, London: Grafton.

Eysenck, H. (1995) *Genius: The Natural History of Creativity*, Cambridge: Cambridge University Press.

Farb, P. (1974) *Word Play: What Happens When People Talk*, New York: Bantam.

Fauconnier, G. and Turner, M. (2002) *The Way We Think: Conceptual Blending and the Mind's Hidden Complexities*, New York: Basic Books.

Feagin, S. and Maynard, P. (eds) (1997) *Aesthetics: A Reader*, Oxford: Oxford University Press.

Feyerabend, P. (1975) *Against Method: Outline of an Anarchistic Theory of Knowledge*, New York: Humanities Press.

Feynman, R. (1999) *The Pleasure of Finding Things Out: The Best Short Works of Richard P. Feynman*, ed. J. Robbins, London: Penguin.

Fielding, H. ([1759] 1994) *The History of Tom Jones, A Foundling*, Harmondsworth: Penguin.

Finke, R. (1990) *Creative Imagery: Discoveries and Inventions in Visualisation*, Hillsdale, NJ: Erlbaum.

Finnegan, R. (2002) *Communicating: The Multiple Modes of Human Interconnection*, London: Routledge.

Forster, J. (1874) *The Life of Charles Dickens*, London.

Foucault. M. ([1966] 1972) *The Order of Things: An Archaeology of the Human Sciences*, trans. A. Sheridan-Smith, London: Tavistock.

—— (1986) *The Foucault Reader*, ed. P. Rabinow, London: Penguin.

Fowler, R. (ed.) ([1987] 1990) *A Dictionary of Modern Critical Terms*, London: Methuen.

Frame. J. (1988) *The Carpathians*, London: Vintage.

Freud, S. (1986) *The Essentials of Psychoanalysis*, ed. A. Freud, trans. J. Strachey, London: Penguin.

Fromm, E. ([1957] 1975), *The Art of Loving*, London: Allen and Unwin.

Gablik, S. (1991) *The Reenchantment of Art*, New York: Thames and Hudson.

Gaiger, J. and Wood, P. (eds) (2003) *Art of the Twentieth Century: A Reader*, 2nd edn, New Haven, CT: Yale University Press/London: Open University Press.

Galton, F. (1869) *Hereditary Genius: An Inquiry into its Laws and Consequences*, London: Macmillan.

Gardner, H. (1993) *Multiple Intelligences: The Theory in Practice*, New York: Basic Books.

—— (1993) *Creating Minds*, New York: Basic Books.

—— (1998) *Extraordinary Minds: Portraits of Exceptional Individuals and an Examination of our Extraordinariness*, London and New York: HarperCollins.

Gates, L. and McKay, N. (eds) [1997] (2004) *The Norton Anthology of African American Literature*, 2nd edn, New York: Norton.

Geake, J. and Dodson, C. (2004) *The Creative Intelligence of Gifted Children*, Oxford: Oxford Brookes University/Sir John Templeton Foundation.

Gelernter, D. (1994) *The Muse and the Machine: Computers and Creative Thought*, London: Fourth Estate.

Gendlin, E. (1962) *Experiencing and the Creation of Meaning*, New York: Free Press.

—— (1997) *Language Beyond Postmodernism*, ed. D. Levin, Evanston, IL: Northwestern University Press.

Ghiselin, B. (ed.) (1985) *The Creative Process: Reflections on Invention in the Arts and Sciences*, Berkeley, CA: University of California Press.

Gibbs, R. W. (1994) *The Poetics of Mind: Figurative Thought, Language and Understanding*, Cambridge: Cambridge University Press.

Gilbert, S. and Gubar, S. ([1979] 2000) *The Madwoman in the Attic; The Woman Writer and the Nineteenth-Century Literary Imagination*, revised 2nd edn, New Haven, CT, and London: Yale University Press.

Ginzburg C. (1990) *Ecstasies: Deciphering the Witches' Sabbath*, London: Hutchinson.

Gleick, J. ([1988] 1994) *Chaos: Making a New Science*, New York and London: Random House.

Glover, J., Reynolds, C. and Ronning, R. (eds) (1989) *Handbook of Creativity*, New York: Plenum.

Goatly, A. (2000) *Critical Reading and Writing: An Introductory Coursebook*, London: Routledge.

Goldberg, D. T. and Quayson, A. (eds) (2002) *Relocating Colonialism*, Oxford: Blackwell.

Gombrich, E. and Erebon, D. (1993) *Looking for Answers: Conversations on Art and Science*, New York: Harry N. Abrams.

Goodman, S. and Graddol, D. (eds) (1996) *Redesigning English: New Texts, New Identities*, London and New York: The Open University and Routledge.

Goodman, S. and O'Halloran, K. (eds) (forthcoming) *The Art of English: Literary Creativity*, Buckingham: The Open University.

Goring, R. (1992) *Chambers Dictionary of Beliefs and Religions*, Edinburgh: Chambers.

Gould, S. J. ([1989] 1991) *Wonderful Life: The Burgess Shale and the Nature of History*, Harmondsworth: Penguin.

—— (2002) *The Structure of Evolutionary Theories*, New Haven, CT: Yale University Press.

—— ([2003] 2004)*The Hedgehog, The Fox and the Magister's Pox: Mending and Minding the Misconceived Gap between Science and the Humanities*, London: Vintage.

Graff, G. (1987) *Professing Literature: An Institutional History*, Chicago: Chicago University Press.

Grand, S. (2000) *Creation: Life and How to Make It*, London: Weidenfeld and Nicolson.

Greenfield, S. (2004) *Tomorrow's People: How 21st-century Technology is Changing the Way We Think*, London: Allen Lane.

Gregory, B. (1990) *Inventing Reality: Physics as Language*, New York: Wiley.

Gribbin, J. with Gribbin, M.(1998) *Almost Everyone's Guide to Science*, London: Weidenfeld and Nicolson.

Habermas, J. (1990) *Moral Consciousness and Communicative Action*, trans. C. Lenhardt and S. Weber Nicholsen, Cambridge: Polity Press.

Halliday, M. A. K. (1994) *An Introduction to Functional Grammar*, 2nd edn, London: Arnold.

Hamer, R. (1970) *A Choice of Anglo-Saxon Verse*, London: Faber and Faber.

Hamilton, S. (2001) *Indian Philosophy: A Very Short Introduction*, Oxford: Oxford University Press.

Hampton, C. (ed.) (1984) *A Radical Reader: The Struggle for Change in England, 1381–1914*, Harmondsworth: Penguin.

Haraway, D. (1991) *Simians, Cyborgs and Women: The Reinvention of Nature*, London: Routledge.

Harrison, C. and Wood, P. (eds) (2003) *Art in Theory, 1900–2000: An Anthology of Changing Ideas*, Oxford: Blackwell.

Hart, S., Dixon, A., Drummond, M. J., McIntyre, D. *et al.* (2004) *Learning without Limits*, Maidenhead: Open University Press.

Harvey, D. (1993) *The Condition of Postmodernity: An Inquiry into the Origin of Cultural Change*, Oxford: Blackwell.

Hawkes, T. (1972) *Metaphor*, London: Methuen.

—— (1977) *Structuralism and Semiotics*, London: Routledge.

Hayles, N. (1991) *Chaos and Order: Complex Dynamics in Literature and Science*, Chicago: University of Chicago Press.

Heidegger, M. (1993) *Basic Writings*, ed. D. Krell, 2nd edn, London: Routledge.

Herbert, W. N. and Hollis, M. (eds) (2000) *Strong Words: Modern Poets on Modern Poetry*, Newcastle: Bloodaxe.

Hesmondaigh, D. and Negus K. (eds) (2002) *Popular Music Studies*, London: Arnold.

Hilton, J. (1987) *Performance*, London: Macmillan.

Hofstadter, A. and Kuhns, R. (eds) ([1964] 1976) *Philosophies of Art and Beauty. Selected Readings in Aesthetics from Plato to Heidegger*, Chicago: University of Chicago Press.

Hofstadter, D. ([1980] 2000) *Gödel, Escher, Bach: An Eternal Golden Braid*, with a new introduction, Harmondsworth: Penguin.

—— (1985) *Metamagical Themas: Questing for the Essence of Mind and Pattern*, Harmondsworth, Penguin.

Holzman, L. (ed.) (1999) *Performing Psychology: A Postmodern Culture of Mind*, New York: Routledge.

Howe, M. (1999) *Genius Explained*, Cambridge: Cambridge University Press.

Hughes, B. (2000) *Dust or Magic: Secrets of Successful Multimedia Design*, London: Addison-Wesley.

Hughes, T. (1997) *Tales from Ovid*, London: Faber and Faber.

Huizinga, J. [1944] (1970) *Homo Ludens: A Study of the Play Element in Culture*, London: Granada.

Humphrey, N. (2002) *The Mind Made Flesh: Frontiers of Psychology and Evolution*, Oxford: Oxford University Press.

Hunt, C. and Sampson, F. (forthcoming 2005) *Creative Writing and the Writer*, London: Palgrave.

Hutcheon, L. (1988) *A Poetics of Postmodernism: History, Theory, Fiction*, London: Routledge.

Huxley, M. and Witts, N. (eds) (2002) *The Twentieth-Century Performance Reader*, 2nd edn, London: Routledge.

James, W. ([1901] 1970) *The Varieties of Religious Experience*, London: Fontana.

Jameson, F. (1981) *The Political Unconscious: Narrative as a Social Symbolic Act*, London: Methuen.

Jamison, K. R. (1993) *Touched with Fire: Manic Depressive Illness and the Artistic Temperament*, New York: Free Press.

Jardine, A. and Smith, P. (eds) (1987) *Men in Feminism*, New York: Methuen.

Jaworski, A. and Coupland, N. (eds) (1999) *The Discourse Reader*, London: Routledge.

Joas, H. (1996) *The Creativity of Action*, trans. J. Gaines and P. Keast, Cambridge: Polity Press.

Johnson, S. (2001) *Emergence: the Connected Lives of Ants, Brains, Cities and Software*, London: Penguin.

Jones, S. (1994) *The Language of the Genes*, London: HarperCollins.

Joughin, J. and Malpas, S. (eds) (2003) *The New Aestheticism*, Manchester: Manchester University Press.

Julian of Norwich (1986) *A Revelation of Love*, ed. M. Glasscoe, Exeter: Exeter University Press.

Jung, C. (1976) *The Portable Jung*, ed. J. Campbell, trans. R. Hull, London and New York: Penguin Viking.

Kaku, M. (1994) *Hyperspace*, New York: Oxford University Press.

Kasulis, T. (1981) *Zen Action, Zen Person*, Honolulu: Hawaii University Press.

Kearney, R. ([1988] 1994) *The Wake of Imagination*, London: Routledge.

—— (ed.) (1995) *States of Mind: Dialogues with Contemporary Thinkers*, Manchester: Manchester University Press.

—— (1998) *Poetics of Imagining: Modern to Post-modern*, 2nd edn, Edinburgh: Edinburgh University Press.

—— (2002) *On Stories*, London: Routledge.

Kearney, R. and Rasmussen, D. (eds) (2001) *Continental Aesthetics, Romanticism to Postmodernism: An Anthology*, Oxford: Blackwell.

Kermode, F. and Hollander, J. (eds) (1973) *The Oxford Anthology of English Literature*, two vols, New York: Oxford University Press.

Kidd, H. (2003) *Ultraviolet Catastrophe*, Salerno: Edizioni Ripostes.

Kirton, M. (ed.) (1994) *Adaptors and Innovators: Styles of Creativity and Problem Solving*, 2nd edn, London: Routledge.

Koestler, Arthur ([1964] 1989) *The Act of Creation*, London: Penguin Arkana.

Kress, G. (1995) *Writing the Future: English and the Making of a Culture of Innovation*, Sheffield: National Association for the Teaching of English.

—— (2003) *Literacy in the New Media Age*, London: Routledge.

Kress, G. and Van Leeuwen, T. (2001) *Multimodal Discourse: The Modes and Media of Contemporary Communication*, London: Arnold.

Kristeva, J. (1984) *Revolution in Poetic Language*, trans. M. Waller, New York: Columbia University Press.

Kuhn, T. ([1962] 1970) *The Structure of Scientific Revolutions*, 2nd edn, Chicago: Chicago University Press.

Lakoff, G. and Johnson, M. (1980) *Metaphors We Live By*, Chicago: Chicago University Press.

—— (1999) *Philosophy in the Flesh: The Embodied Mind and its Challenge to Western Thought*, New York: Basic Books.

Larrington, C. (1995) *Women and Writing in Medieval Europe*, London: Routledge.

Lecoq, J. ([1997] 2000) *The Moving Body: Teaching Creative Theatre*, trans. D. Bradby, London: Methuen.

Leeming, D. and Leeming, M. (1994) *A Dictionary of Creation Myths*, Oxford and New York: Oxford University Press.

Leitch, V. (ed.) (2001) *The Norton Anthology of Theory and Criticism*, New York: Norton.

Lessing, D. ([1962] 1989) *The Golden Notebook*, London: Paladin.

Levin, P. (ed.) (2001) *The Penguin Book of the Sonnet: 500 Years of a Classic Tradition in English*, London: Penguin.

Lewis, C. S. ([1967] 1990) *Studies in Words*, Cambridge: Canto.

Lightman, A. and Brawer, R. (eds) (1990) *Origins: The Lives and Worlds of Modern Cosmologists*, Cambridge, MA: Harvard University Press.

Lodge, D. (ed.) (1972) *20th Century Literary Criticism*, London: Longman.

Lodge, D. and Wood, N. (eds) (2000) *Modern Criticism and Theory*, London: Longman.

Longinus (1965) 'On the sublime', ed. and trans. T. S. Dorsch, *Classical Literary Criticism*, Harmondsworth: Penguin.

Lorimer, D. (ed.) (1999) *The Spirit of Science: From Experiment to Experience*, New York: Continuum.

Lucretius (1951) *On the Nature of the Universe*, trans. R. Latham, Harmondsworth: Penguin.

Lyotard, J.-F. ([1979] 1987) *The Postmodern Condition: A Report on Knowledge*, trans. G. Bennington, Manchester: Manchester University Press.

—— (1989) *The Lyotard Reader*, ed. A. Benjamin, Oxford: Blackwell.

Macherey, P. ([1966] 1978) *A Theory of Literary Production*, trans. G. Wall, London: Routledge and Kegan Paul.

McRae, J. (1991) *Literature with a small 'l'*, London: Macmillan/Prentice Hall.

Makaryk, I. (ed.) (1993) *Encyclopedia of Contemporary Literary Theory*, Toronto: University of Toronto Press.

Mandelbrot, B. (1982) *The Fractal Geometry of Nature*, New York: W. H. Freeman.

Margulis, L. (1998) *The Symbiotic Planet: A New Look at Evolution*, London: Weidenfeld and Nicolson.

Margulis, L. and Sagan, D. (1995) *What is Life?*, London: Weidenfeld and Nicolson.

Marks, J. (1998) *Gilles Deleuze: Vitalism and Multiplicity*, London: Pluto.

Marx, K. (1963) *Selected Writings in Sociology and Social Philosophy*, ed. T. Bottomore and M. Rubel, Harmondsworth: Penguin.

Maybin, J. and Swann, J. (eds) (forthcoming) *The Art of English: Everyday Creativity*, Buckingham: The Open University.

Mengham, R. (ed.) (1999) *An Introduction to Contemporary Fiction*, Cambridge: Polity Press.

Miles, G. (ed.) (1999) *Classical Mythology in English Literature: A Critical Anthology*, London: Routledge.

Miller, A. L. (2000) *Insights of Genius: Imagery and Creativity in Science and Art*, Cambridge, MA: MIT Press.

Mills, P. (1996) *Writing in Action*, London and New York: Routledge.

Moi, T. (1985) *Sexual/Textual Politics: Feminist Literary Theory*, London: Routledge.

Monbiot, G. (2003) *The Age of Consent: A Manifesto for a New World Order*, London and New York: HarperCollins.

Monteith. S., Newman, J. and Wheeler, P. (eds) (2004) *Contemporary British and Irish Fiction*, London: Hodder Arnold.

Morris, P. (ed.) (1994) *The Bakhtin Reader: Selected Writings of Bakhtin, Medvedev, Voloshinov*, London: Arnold.

Mullarkey, J. (ed.) (1999) *The New Bergson*, Manchester: Manchester University Press.

Murray, L. (ed.) (1991) *The New Oxford Book of Australian Verse*, 2nd edn, Melbourne and Oxford: Oxford University Press.

—— (1997) *A Working Forest: Selected Prose*, Sydney: Duffy and Snellgrove.

Nash, W. (1998) *Language and Creative Illusion*, London: Longman.

Nash, W. and Stacey, D. (1997) *Creating Texts: An Introduction to the Study of Composition*, New York and London: Addison, Wesley, Longman.

Nettle, D. (2001) *Strong Imagination: Madness, Creativity and Human Nature*, Oxford: Oxford University Press.

Newman, J., Cusick, E. and La Tourette, E. (eds) (2004) *The Writer's Workbook*, 2nd edn, London: Hodder Arnold.

Nietzsche, F. ([1883] 1933) *Thus Spake Zarathustra*, trans. A. Tille and M. M. Bozman, London and New York: Dent and Dutton.

—— (1977) *A Nietzsche Reader*, ed. and trans, R. Hollingdale, Harmondsworth: Penguin.

—— (2000) *Basic Writings of Nietzsche*, ed. and trans. W. Kaufmann, New York: Random House.

Ochse, R. (1990) *Before the Gates of Excellence: The Determinants of Creative Genius*, Cambridge: Cambridge University Press.

OED (*Oxford English Dictionary*) (1928, 2nd edn 1989) ed. R. Burchfield, J. Simpson, *et al.* Oxford: Oxford University Press.

Ovid (1955) *Metamorphoses*, trans. M. Innes, London: Penguin.

Patton, P. (ed.) (1996) *Deleuze: A Critical Reader*, Oxford: Blackwell.

Payne, M. (ed.) (1996) *A Dictionary of Cultural and Critical Theory*, Oxford: Blackwell.

Peach, L. and Burton, A. (1995) *English as a Creative Art: Literary Concepts Linked to Creative Writing*, London: David Fulton.

Peat, F. D. (1992) *Superstrings and the Search for the Theory of Everything*, London: Abacus.

—— (2000) *The Blackwinged Night: Creativity in Nature and Mind*, Cambridge, MA: Perseus.

Penrose, R. (1994) *Shadows of the Mind*, Oxford: Oxford University Press.

Petroski, H. (1997) *Invention by Design: How Engineers Get from Thought to Thing*, Cambridge, MA: Harvard University Press.

Petrucci, M. (2004) *Heavy Water. A Poem for Chernobyl*, London: Enitharmon Press.

Pfenninger, K. and Shubik, V. (eds) (2001) *The Origins of Creativity*, Oxford: Oxford University Press.

Pilger, J. (2003) *The New Rulers of the World*, London: Verso.

Pinker, S. (1994) *The Language Instinct*, New York: HarperCollins.

—— (1999) *Words and Rules: The Ingredients of Language*, London: Weidenfeld and Nicolson.

Plant, S. (1999) *Writing on Drugs*, London: Faber and Faber.

Plato (1956) *Dialogues*, trans. W. H. D. Rouse, New York: New American Library.

—— (1971) *Timaeus and Critias*, ed. and trans. D. Lee, London: Penguin.

Pope, A. (1965) *The Poems of Alexander Pope*, ed. J. Butt, London: Methuen.

Pope, R. (1995) *Textual Intervention: Critical and Creative Strategies for Literary Studies*, London: Routledge.

—— (2002) *The English Studies Book: An Introduction to Language, Literature and Culture*, 2nd edn, London and New York: Routledge.

—— (2003) 'Re-writing texts, re-constructing the subject: work as play on the critical–creative interface', in T. Agathocleous and A. C. Dean (eds) *Teaching Literature, A Companion*, London: Palgrave Macmillan: pp. 105–24.

Porter, R. (ed.) (1991) *The Faber Book of Madness*, London: Faber and Faber.

Pratchett, T. (1983) *The Colour of Magic* London: Gollancz.

Pratchett, T., Stewart I. and Cohen, J. (2002) *The Science of Discworld*, London: Random House.

Preminger, A. and Brogan, T. (eds) (1993) *The New Princeton Encyclopedia of Poetry and Poetics*, Princeton, NJ: Princeton University Press.

Prirogine, I. with Stengers, I. (1984) *Order out of Chaos*, New York: Bantam.

Regan, S. (ed.) (1992) *The Politics of Pleasure: Aesthetics and Cultural Theory*, Buckingham: Open University Press.

Rescher, N. (1987) *Scientific Realism: A Critical Reappraisal*, Dordrecht: Reidel.

Rhys, E. (ed.) (1965) *Shorter Elizabethan Novels*, London: Dent Dutton.

Rickards, T. (1999) *Creativity and the Management of Change*, Oxford: Blackwell.

Ricks, C. and Vance, W. (eds) (1992) *The Faber Book of America*, London: Faber and Faber.

Ridley, B. K. (1976) *Time, Space and Things*, Harmondsworth: Penguin.

Ridley, M. (ed.) (1997) *Evolution: A Reader*, Oxford: Oxford University Press.

Roberts, M. (1998) *Food, Sex and God: On Inspiration and Writing*, London: Virago.

Rose, G. (1992) *The Broken Middle: Out of Our Ancient Society*, Oxford: Blackwell.

Rose, S. (1997) *Lifelines: Biology, Freedom, Determinism*, London: Penguin.

Rothenberg, A. (1979) *The Emerging Goddess: The Creative Process in Art, Science and Other Fields*, Chicago: University of Chicago Press.

Runco, M. and Albert, R. (eds) (1990) *Theories of Creativity*, Newbury, CA: Sage.

Stewart, I. and Cohen, J. (1997) *Figments of Reality: The Evolution of the Curious Mind*, Cambridge: Cambridge University Press.

Stiglitz, J. (2002) *Globalization and its Discontents*, New York: W. W. Norton.

Stockwell, P. (2002) *Cognitive Poetics: An Introduction*, London: Routledge.

Storr, A. (1972) *The Dynamics of Creation*, London: Secker and Warburg.

Sutton, R. I. (2001) *11½ Ways to Promote, Manage and Sustain Innovation*, New York: Free Press.

Tannen, D. (1989) *Talking Voices: Repetition, Dialogue and Imagery in Conversational Discourse*, Cambridge: Cambridge University Press.

Tate, C. (ed.) (1985) *Black Women Writers at Work*, Harpenden: Oldcastle Books.

Teilhard de Chardin, P. ([1955] 1969) *The Phenomenon of Man*, trans. B. Wall, London: Collins.

Terry, P. (ed.) (2000) *Ovid Metamorphosed*, London: Chatto and Windus.

Thieme, J. (ed.) (1996) *The Arnold Anthology of Post-Colonial Literatures*, London: Arnold.

—— (2003) *Post-Colonial Studies: The Essential Glossary*, London: Hodder Arnold.

Thuan, T. X. (2001) *Chaos and Harmony: Perspectives on Scientific Revolutions of the Twentieth Century*, trans. A. Reisinger, New York: Oxford University Press.

Toynbee, J. (2000) *Making Popular Music: Musicians, Creativity and Institutions*, London: Arnold.

Turner, V. (1982) *From Ritual to Theatre: The Human Seriousness of Play*, New York: PAJ.

Tusa, J. (ed.) (2003) *On Creativity: Interviews Exploring the Process*, London: Methuen.

Ulmer, G. (1985) *Applied Grammatology: Post(e)-Pedagogy from Jacques Derrida to Joseph Beuys*, Baltimore, MD: Johns Hopkins University Press.

Vernon, P. (ed.) (1970) *Creativity*, Harmondsworth: Penguin.

Vico, G. ([1744] 1968) *The New Science*, trans. T. Bergin and M. Fisch, Ithaca, NY: Cornell University Press.

Vizenour, G. (ed.) (1989) *Narrative Chance: Postmodern Discourse on Native American Indian Literatures*, Albuquerque: University of New Mexico Press.

Von Stamm, B. (2003) *Managing Innovation, Design and Creativity*, London: Wiley.

Vygotsky, L. S. ([1934] 1987) *The Collected Works of L. S. Vygotsky*, Vol. 1, New York: Plenum.

Wadham-Smith, N. (ed.) (1999) *British Studies Now Anthology: Issues 6–10*, London: The British Council.

Walder, D. (ed.) (2004) *Literature in the Modern World*, 2nd edn, Oxford: Oxford University Press.

Waldrop, M. (1994) *Complexity: The Emerging Science at the Edge of Order and Chaos*, London: Penguin.

Wales, K. (2001) *A Dictionary of Stylistics*, 2nd edn, London: Longman.

Ward, C. (1991) *Influences: Voices of Creative Dissent*, Bideford: Green Books.

Ward Jouve, N. (1998) *Female Genesis: Creativity, Self and Gender*, Oxford and Cambridge: Polity Press.

Weber. R. (ed.) (1998) *Dialogues with Scientists and Sages: The Search for Unity*, London and New York: Routledge and Kegan Paul.

Weisberg, Robert (1993) *Creativity: Beyond the Myth of Genius*, New York: W. H. Freeman.

Wheale, N. (ed.) (1995) *Postmodern Arts: An Introduction*, London: Routledge.

Wheeler, K. (1993) *Romanticism, Pragmatism and Deconstruction*, Oxford: Blackwell.

Whitehead, A. N. (1926) *Religion in the Making*, New York: Macmillan.

—— (1950) *The Aims of Education and other Essays*, 2nd edn, London: Ernest Benn.

Widdowson, P. (1999) *Literature*, London: Routledge.

Wilde, O. (1992) *The Importance of Being Earnest and Related Writings*, ed. J. Bristow, London: Routledge.

Williams, J. (2003) *Gilles Deleuze's 'Difference and Repetition'*, Edinburgh: Edinburgh University Press.

Williams, R. (1977) *Marxism and Literature*, Oxford: Oxford University Press.

Runco, M. and Pritzer, S. (eds) (1999) *Encyclopedia of Creativity*, San Diego, CA and Lond, Academic Press.

Russell, B. (1946) *A History of Western Philosophy*, London: Allen and Unwin.

Sacks, S. (2002) *Exchange Values: Images of Invisible Lives*, Johannesburg: Johannesburg A Gallery. Available online at www.exchange-values.org.

Salomon, W. (1984) *Scientific Explanation and the Causal Structure of the World*, Princeton, NJ: Prince ton University Press.

Sampson, F. (ed.) (2002) *Orient Express: The Best of Contemporary Writing from Enlargement Europe*, Vols 1 and 2, Oxford: Oxford Brookes University.

Sardar, Z. and Abrams, I. (1999) *Introducing Chaos*, Cambridge: Icon.

Saunders, L. (ed.) (1987) *Glancing Fires: An Investigation into Women's Creativity*, London: The Women's Press.

Sawyer, W. K. (2001) *Creating Conversations: Improvisation in Everyday Discourse*, Cresskill, NJ: Hampton Press.

Scholes, R. (1998) *The Rise and Fall of English Studies*, New Haven, CT: Yale University Press.

Scholes, R., Comley, N. and Ulmer, G. (1995) *Text Book: An Introduction to Literary Language*, 2nd edn, New York: St Martin's Press.

Schrödinger, E. ([1944] 1995) *What is Life?*, Cambridge: Canto.

Selden, R. (ed.) (1988) *The Theory of Criticism*, London: Longman.

Seltzer, K. and Bentley, T. (1999) *The Creative Age: Knowledge and Skills for the New Economy*, Buck-ingham: Demos. Available online at www.creativenet.org.uk.

Semeno, E. (1997) *Language and World Creation in Poems and Other Texts*, London: Longman.

Shakespeare, W. (1995) *King Henry V*, ed. T. Craik, London: Routledge.

Shange, N. ([1978] 1987) *Nappy Edges*, London: Methuen.

Shapcott, J. (2000) *Her Book: Poems 1988–1998*, London: Faber and Faber.

Sharples, M. (1999) *How We Write: Writing as Creative Design*, London: Routledge.

Sheldrake, R., McKenna, T. and Abraham, R. (2001) *Chaos, Creativity and Cosmic Consciousness*, Rochester, VT: Park Street Press.

Shelley, M. ([1818] 1993) *Frankenstein, or The Modern Prometheus*, ed. M. Butler, Oxford: Oxford University Press.

Shelley, P. (1991) *Percy Bysshe Shelley: Selected Poetry and Prose*, ed. A. Macrae, London: Routledge.

—— (2002) *Shelley's Poetry and Prose*, ed. D. Reiman and N. Fraistat, 2nd edn, New York: Norton.

Sinfield, A. (1994) *Cultural Politics: Queer Reading*, London.

Singer, A. and Dunn, A. (eds) (2000) *Literary Aesthetics: A Reader*, Oxford: Blackwell.

Smith, C. (1998) *Creative Britain*, London: Faber and Faber.

Smith, R. (1997) *The Fontana History of the Human Sciences*, London: Fontana.

Spearing, A. C. (ed.) (2001) *The Cloud of Unknowing*, Harmondsworth: Penguin.

Spiro, J. (2004) *Creative Poetry Writing*, Oxford: Oxford University Press.

Spivak, G. C. (1995) *The Spivak Reader*, ed. D. Landry and G. MacLean, Oxford: Blackwell.

—— (1999) *A Critique of Postcolonial Reason*, Cambridge, MA: Harvard University Press.

Steiner, G. (2001) *Grammars of Creation*, London: Faber and Faber.

Sterelny, K. (2001) *Dawkins vs. Gould: Survival of the Fittest*, Cambridge: Icon.

Sternberg, R. (ed.) (1988) *The Nature of Creativity*, Cambridge: Cambridge University Press.

—— (ed.) (1999) *Handbook of Creativity*, Cambridge: Cambridge University Press.

Stewart, I. (1995) *Nature's Numbers: Discovering Order and Pattern in the Universe*, London: Weidenfeld and Nicolson.

—— (1997) *Does God Play Dice? The New Mathematics of Chaos*, 2nd edn, Harmondsworth: Penguin.

—— (1983) *Keywords: A Vocabulary of Culture and Society*, 2nd edn, London: Flamingo.

Willis, P. with Jones, S., Canaan, J. and Hurd, G. (1990) *Common Culture: Symbolic Work at Play in the Everyday Cultures of the Young*, Milton Keynes: Open University Press.

Wilson, C. ([1956] 1978) *The Outsider*, London: Picador.

Wilson, E. O. (1998) *Consilience: The Unity of Knowledge*, London: Little, Brown and Knopf.

—— (2002) *The Future of Life*, London and New York: Little, Brown and Knopf.

Winnicott, D. W. (1971) *Playing and Reality*, Harmondsworth: Penguin.

Wittgenstein, L. ([1953] 1967) *Philosophical Investigations*, ed. and trans. G. Anscombe, 3rd edn, Oxford: Blackwell.

Wolfreys, J. (ed.) (2001) *Introducing Literary Theories: A Guide and Glossary*, Edinburgh: Edinburgh University Press.

—— (ed.) (2002) *Introducing Criticism at the 21st Century*, Edinburgh: Edinburgh University Press.

Woodcock, G. (1986) *Anarchism: A History of Libertarian Ideas and Movements*, 2nd edn, Harmondsworth: Penguin.

Woolf, V. ([1929] 1992) *A Room of One's Own*, ed. M. Shiach, Oxford: Oxford University Press.

—— (1985) *Moments of Being: Unpublished Autobiographical Writings*, ed. J. Schulkind, London: Hogarth Press.

Young, E. ([1759] 1968) 'Conjectures on original composition' in Edmund Jones (ed.) *English Critical Essays: Sixteenth, Seventeenth and Eighteenth Centuries*, Oxford: Oxford University Press.

Young, R. (ed.) (1981) *Untying the Text: A Poststructuralist Reader*, London: Routledge and Kegan Paul.

Journals

Journal of Creative Behaviour (1967–)

Creativity Research Journal (1988–)

New Writing: The International Journal for the Practice and Theory of Creative Writing (2004–)

Index

The index covers topics, names, and titles of anonymous works referred to in the main body of the text, and in the Further Reading where they have already been featured. Pages highlighted in *italic* signal definition or extended discussion; (text) after the page number indicates an extract.